MW00643877

"Both Jesus and Paul warned us about be[...]
cies about the end, and unfortunately many books on the market steer us away
from a biblical understanding of prophecy. Bandy and Merkle have written
a sane and sober (but even more importantly a faithful and biblical) book on
prophecy. Here is a light shining in a dark place for which we can all be grateful."
—*Tom Schreiner, James Buchanan Harrison*
Professor of New Testament Interpretation,
Associate Dean, The Southern Baptist Theological Seminary

"What is prophecy and why should we care? This excellent volume coauthored
by a premillennialist (Bandy) and an amillennialist (Merkle) will answer that
question and countless more. Rooted in a careful treatment of all the relevant
prophetic texts and with a keen awareness to the development of redemptive
history, Bandy and Merkle have given us what may be the standard text on
biblical prophecy for years to come. Highly recommended."
—*Sam Storms, Bridgeway Church, Oklahoma City, OK*

"Merkle and Bandy are diligently, rigorously, and refreshingly honest with
the biblical text, offering valuable insights on an often-contested subject.
They are also fair to various eschatological views with which they disagree—which in some cases the authors do with each other. This is a wel-
come book on a debated topic."
—*Craig Keener, Professor of New Testament, Asbury Theological Seminary*

"Bandy and Merkle accessibly and responsibly introduce prophecy with
a biblical-theological approach rather than a systematic-theological one.
They disagree on two controversial issues regarding the end times: 'all Israel'
in Romans 11:26 and the millennium. However, both Bandy and Merkle
beautifully demonstrate how two academics who disagree on those issues
can agree on so many other issues in light of the Bible's storyline."
—*Andy Naselli, Assistant Professor of New Testament and Biblical Theology,*
Bethlehem College & Seminary

"This is a very fine book on how to understand and interpret biblical prophecy. Very fine. Now, I do not agree with everything in it. After all I am a
progressive dispensationalist who is pretribulational and premillennial. Still,
I found myself far more often in agreement with the authors than in dis-
agreement. Why? Because they are both fair and faithful with the Scriptures.
Further, this comprehensive treatment works through the whole of the Bible.
I am delighted to recommend this book to anyone who wants a better grasp
of the prophetic material in the Bible and who has their eyes heavenward,
looking for the blessed hope and glorious appearing of King Jesus."
—*Daniel L. Akin, President, Southeastern Baptist Theological Seminary*

"Bandy and Merkle's *Understanding Prophecy* brings solid scholarship and an abundance of interpretive wisdom to bear on the difficult topic of biblical prophecy. By locating prophecy in the larger story of Scripture, they help readers grasp its theological significance in God's redemptive plan and—as a result—provide them the framework for understanding and applying prophecy in a reliable fashion. I highly recommend *Understanding Prophecy* as a trustworthy guide to grasping this important portion of Scripture."

—*J. Scott Duvall, Professor of New Testament,*
J. C. and Mae Fuller Chair of Biblical Studies,
Ouachita Baptist University

Understanding Prophecy

Prophecy

A Biblical-Theological Approach

Alan S. Bandy
Benjamin L. Merkle

Kregel
Academic

Published by Kregel Publications, a division of Kregel, Inc., 2450 Oak Industrial Dr. NE, Grand Rapids, MI 49505-6020.

Library of Congress Cataloging-in-Publication Data

Bandy, Alan S.
    Understanding prophecy : a biblical-theological approach / Alan S. Bandy, Benjamin L. Merkle.
        pages cm
    1. Bible—Prophecies. I. Merkle, Benjamin L., 1971- II. Title.
    BS647.3.B36 2015
    220.1'5—dc23

                                                                                    2014048981

ISBN 978-0-8254-4271-1

Printed in the United States of America
15 16 17 18 19 / 5 4 3 2 1

Alan
to my children
|
Alexandra,
Josiah,
Victoria,
Mckenzie,
and Titus

Ben
to my children
|
Brandon,
Mariah,
Jaden,
and Cameron

"The Lord bless you
and keep you;
The Lord make his face shine on you
and be gracious to you;
The Lord turn his face toward you
and give you peace."
—Numbers 6:24–26, NIV

Contents

Preface

The goal of this book is not merely to explain various "prophetic" texts but primarily to give the reader a framework of how to interpret any passage in the context of the Bible. The reason for this framework for reading prophecy is simple: We cannot correctly understand the details of the Bible without also having a grasp of the bigger picture. Evangelicals often dispute interpretations of various prophetic passages so that a consensus view proves elusive. Differences of opinion do not reflect varying levels of intelligence or diligence so much as different presuppositions, which lead to a different understanding of the whole. Unfortunately, many people are not aware of their presuppositions and consequently do not have a firm grasp of how an individual text fits into the larger picture of salvation history. Thus, we want to provide a biblical-theological perspective for interpreting prophecy.

One unique feature of this book is that the two authors hold to different millennial views. Alan is a historic premillennialist and Ben is an amillennialist. That being said, why did we decide to write this book together? There are two primary reasons. First, we discovered that although our millennial views are different, we actually agree with each other most of the time regarding our interpretation of prophetic texts and our way of seeing the big picture of the Bible. Second, we wanted to demonstrate that those who hold to differing millennial views could come together on common ground and focus on where they agree. To be sure, we do disagree with each other at certain points. Nevertheless, we believe that we hold so much in common that our differences are rather minor in comparison. When those differences are noticeable, we have provided the reader with two appendices so that each of us could argue individually for our particular view (these include the meaning of "all Israel" in Romans 11:26 and the meaning of the millennium).

The first section of the book, chapters 1–3, outlines the nature of prophecy and how to approach it from a biblical-theological perspective. Chapter 1 ("Keys to Understanding Prophecy") presents key aspects for why and how we understand predictive prophecy from a biblical-theological and christological perspective. Chapter 2 ("What Is Biblical Prophecy?") provides a basic introduction to the topic of biblical prophecy, including the nature of the ministry and message of the prophets and some of the challenges of interpreting writings in the prophetic genre. Chapter 3 ("Biblical Theology and Prophecy") offers a larger framework for interpreting prophecy, including four vital presuppositions that are affirmed and expanded.

The second section of the book, chapters 4–6, focuses on prophecy in the Old Testament. Chapter 4 covers unconditional prophecies (such as certain covenants), conditional prophecies (such as judgment prophecies), and fulfilled prophecies (such as oracles against various nations). The focus of chapter 5 is Old Testament restoration prophecies regarding the nation of Israel. Here we argue that these prophecies are fulfilled in Christ (primarily in his first coming) and should not be interpreted as being fulfilled in a literalistic manner. Finally, chapter 6 addresses messianic prophecies, especially those that relate to Jesus being the messianic prophet, priest, and king.

The third section of the book, chapters 7–10, explains prophetic texts found in the New Testament. Chapter 7 addresses prophecies connected with the first coming of the Messiah in the Gospels and Acts, including those about (1) the forerunner of the Messiah, John the Baptist; (2) the birth and message of the Messiah; and (3) the coming of the Spirit. Chapters 8–10 address prophecies about the return of the Messiah in the Gospels, the Epistles, and Revelation. Chapter 8 focuses on Jesus' teaching in the Olivet Discourse and also includes a discussion of the "left behind" passages (Matt. 24:40–41 and Luke 17:34–35). Chapter 9 considers prophecies connected with the return of the Messiah from the perspective of the epistles, especially Paul's writings. After examining the New Testament's understanding of the "last days," the following questions are addressed: (1) What do the epistles teach about Jesus' return? (2) Will there be a secret rapture before Jesus' return? (3) Could Jesus return at any moment? (4) What follows Jesus' return? Finally, chapter 10 provides a discussion of Revelation's (1) prophetic genre, (2) symbolism, (3) structure, and (4) content, including an analysis of some of the more prominent (and difficult) passages: (a) the seven seals, trumpets, and bowls, (b) the 144,000, (c) the two witnesses, and (d) the millennium.

This book has been a labor of love born out of our desire to better understand the prophetic texts of Scripture. We are thankful to Oklahoma Baptist University and Southeastern Baptist Theological Seminary, our respective institutions, for providing us the opportunity to pursue our passion for understanding prophecy in the context of teaching and writing. We are deeply appreciative to all those at Kregel who helped to make this book a reality. Alan would also like to thank Jeremy Johnson, an OBU alumnus, for proofreading an earlier draft and offering some feedback from a student's perspective. Ben would like to thank Mrs. Billie Goodenough for her careful reading and double-cshecking of Scripture references. Most of all, we wish to express our deep gratitude to our families who continually support our writing endeavors and especially to our Great King, as we wait "for our blessed hope, the appearing of the glory of our great God and Savior Jesus Christ" (Titus 2:13).

Abbreviations

AB	Anchor Bible
ABD	*Anchor Bible Dictionary.* Edited by D. N. Freedman. 6 vols. New York: Doubleday, 1992.
BDAG	W. Bauer, F. W. Danker, W. F. Arndt, and F. W. Gingrich. *Greek-English Lexicon of the New Testament and Other Early Christian Literature.* 3rd ed. Chicago: University of Chicago Press, 2000.
BECNT	Baker Exegetical Commentary on the New Testament
Bib	*Biblica*
BNTC	Black's New Testament Commentaries
BSac	*Bibliotheca Sacra*
CBQ	*Catholic Biblical Quarterly*
DNTB	*Dictionary of New Testament Background.* Edited by Craig A. Evans and Stanley E. Porter. Downers Grove, IL: InterVarsity Press, 2000.
EBC	Expositor's Bible Commentary
EvQ	*Evangelical Quarterly*
ExpTim	*Expository Times*
HTS	Harvard Theological Studies
ICC	International Critical Commentary
IDB	*The Interpreter's Dictionary of the Bible.* Edited by G. A. Buttrick. 4 vols. Nashville: Abingdon, 1962.
IVPNTC	IVP New Testament Commentary Series
JAOS	*Journal of the American Oriental Society*
JBL	*Journal of Biblical Literature*
JETS	*Journal of the Evangelical Theological Society*
JSNT	*Journal for the Study of the New Testament*
JSOTSup	Journal for the Study of the Old Testament: Supplement Series
LCL	Loeb Classical Library
LNTS	Library of New Testament Studies

MSJ	*The Master's Seminary Journal*
NAC	New American Commentary
NICNT	New International Commentary on the New Testament
NIGTC	New International Greek Testament Commentary
NIVAC	NIV Application Commentary
NovT	*Novum Testamentum*
NovTSup	Supplements to Novum Testamentum
NSBT	New Studies in Biblical Theology
NTL	New Testament Library
NTS	*New Testament Studies*
PNTC	Pillar New Testament Commentary
RTR	*Reformed Theological Review*
SBJT	*Southern Baptist Journal of Theology*
SJT	*Scottish Journal of Theology*
SHS	Scripture and Hermeneutics Series
STI	Studies in Theological Interpretation
TDNT	*Theological Dictionary of the New Testament.* Edited by Gerhard Kittel and Gerhard Friedrich. Translated by Geoffrey W. Bromiley. 10 vols. Grand Rapids: Eerdmans, 1964–1976.
TNTC	Tyndale New Testament Commentaries
TOTC	Tyndale Old Testament Commentaries
TrinJ	*Trinity Journal*
TynBul	*Tyndale Bulletin*
VT	*Vetus Testamentum*
WBC	Word Biblical Commentary
WTJ	*Westminster Theological Journal*
ZECNT	Zondervan Exegetical Commentary of the New Testament

PART 1

INTRODUCING BIBLICAL PROPHECY

Chapter 1

Keys to Understanding Prophecy

"Oh, you are writing a book?" someone asks with genuine interest, "What is it about?" The question is followed by a learned pause in careful consideration, "It is a book about prophecy."

At this point, the conversation usually dissipates as the inquirer's eyes dart quickly in search of an exit, but at other times it evokes more curiosity coupled with some self-assured pontification regarding current events and the rapture. Prophecy is something with which most people are either obsessed ad nauseam or about which they feel so inadequate they avoid it altogether. While these two responses may represent two extreme sides of the reception to prophecy in popular culture, they help to demonstrate the need to understand prophecy from a biblical-theological approach.

Prophecy is in many respects the flesh and bones of biblical revelation. The most basic definition of prophecy is divine communication. The prophets were men and women who, through the Spirit of God, received messages, visions, and instructions to pass along to the people of God and the nations. The prophetic revelation was proclaimed, enacted, written down, and preserved for future generations. Prophecy may be a genre in and of itself, but it is also incorporated by other biblical genres. For instance, historical narratives—Joshua, Judges, Kings, Ezra-Nehemiah—recount the history of God's people from a distinctively prophetic perspective. Prophecy is also found in the form of songs, poetry, and even wisdom literature. Prophecy is the vehicle for divine revelation. God discloses himself, his nature, his will, his requirements, his purposes, and his plan primarily, but not exclusively, through prophecy. Prophecy is not merely a feature of the biblical text; rather, the threads of prophecy crisscross throughout Genesis to Revelation forming the fabric of canonical Scripture. Understanding prophecy is essential for understanding the message of the entire Bible. Prophecy, therefore, is intrinsic to Scripture and its theology.

Many people, when they think about prophecy and theology, naturally associate it with eschatology. Eschatology refers to the theology of last things and it is usually connected to predictive prophecy as foretelling events associated with the last days. While eschatology is related to future events, we want to be careful not to reduce it to a subset of systematic theology pertaining only to last things rather than a consistent characteristic of biblical theology (see chapter 3 for more on biblical theology). One problem is that eschatology is a slippery term used to refer to a wide range of concepts.[1] In his magisterial book on the *Language and Imagery of the Bible*, G. B. Caird rightly suggests the various ways that the term "eschatology" is used:

1. Eschatology^I (Individual) referring to the personal expectation of heaven.

2. Eschatology^H (Historical) that deals with the goal of history in a comprehensive manner from beginning to end.

3. Eschatology^K (Consistent) limits all eschatological references to the end of the world as expected in the near future.

4. Eschatology^R (Realized) views Christ first advent as the *eschaton* that was so complete it leaves no room for a future fulfillment.

5. Eschatology^E (Existential) as defined by Bultmann, who argues that on the one hand eschatology only refers to the transcendent significance of the present, and on the other hand it was the Jewish self-understanding of their corporate involvement through history.

6. Eschatology^N affirms a much more comprehensive meaning for eschatology because it denies that the Greek word for "last" is appropriate for the concept of eschatology.

7. Eschatology^P takes into consideration the Old Testament prophets who believed that God was working out his purpose in history (particularly the history of Israel) and thus it refers to the teleological aspects of historical events.[2]

When scholars speak of eschatology they may be referring to anything from realized eschatology as a current reality, to events associated with the end of the world. To say something is eschatological does not necessarily imply a future event; it may more accurately describe a present reality (e.g.,

---

1. I. Howard Marshall, "Slippery Words, 1: Eschatology," *ExpTim* 89 (January 1978): 264–69.
2. G. B. Caird, *The Language and Imagery of the Bible* (Grand Rapids: Eerdmans, 1997), 243–56.

eternal life in John 3:16 and 11:25). N. T. Wright helpfully develops the categories identified by Caird by suggesting seven senses in which eschatology may be understood, as framed within the context of biblical theology and the story of Israel:[3]

1. Eschatology as the end of the world (i.e., the end of the space-time universe);

2. Eschatology as the climax of Israel's history, involving the end of the space-time universe;

3. Eschatology as the climax of Israel's history, involving events for which end-of-the-world language is the only set of metaphors adequate to express the significance of what will happen, but resulting in a new and quite different phase *within* space-time history;

4. Eschatology as major events, not specifically climatic within a particular story, for which end-of-the-world language functions as metaphor;

5. Eschatology as "horizontal" language (i.e. *apparently* denoting movement forwards in time) whose *actual* referent is the possibility of moving "upwards" spiritually into a new level of existence;

6. Eschatology as critique of the present world order, perhaps with proposals for a new order;

7. Eschatology as a critique of the present socio-political scene, perhaps with proposals for adjustments.

We would therefore contend that eschatology pervades, shapes, and forms all aspects of Christian theology as Wright once remarked:

> Look this word [eschatology] up in the dictionary, and you will probably find something like "the doctrine of death, judgment, heaven and hell." When scholars use the word in relation to first-century Judaism and Christianity, though, they mean something rather different. They use it to denote the Jewish and Christian belief that Israel's history, and thereby world history, was moving towards a great climactic moment in which everything would be sorted out once and for all. . . . "Eschatology" thus refers to the belief that

---

3. N. T. Wright, *Jesus and the Victory of God* (Minneapolis: Fortress, 1996), 208.

history was going to reach, or perhaps that it had just reached, its great climax, its great turning-point.[4]

Christian theology is eschatological since it is rooted in the belief that the one true God is the creator of the world and will redeem and renew his creation at the end of the age, which has been inaugurated and established by Jesus Christ through his death and resurrection.

> *We use eschatology as an all-encompassing term for the cosmic, spiritual, and historical realities fulfilled by the person and work of Jesus the Messiah and which fully expect a future consummation when Jesus will be enthroned on earth in the New Jerusalem/New Creation.*

Eschatology, like prophecy, defies attempts at overly simplistic definitions in some sort of one-size-fits-all approach. The complex, diverse, elastic and all-encompassing nature of both prophecy and eschatology requires an approach to this material that does justice to both smaller passages of Scripture and the sweeping scale of the biblical storyline. In this chapter we will present some guiding principles for understanding predictive prophecy from a biblical-theological and christocentric approach. These principles represent, we believe, a better way to understand prophecy in order to avoid some of the pitfalls that often trap many popular prophecy experts. We are not advocating one particular interpretation of all the prophetic passages or some new eschatological system. What we are advocating is that by reading Scripture within the framework of biblical theology we will have a better avenue to understand prophecy as it relates to the past, present, and future.

Understanding Prophecy within the Story of Scripture and Redemptive History

The Bible is a diverse book filled with individual writings and a plethora of narratives, but the Bible as a whole contains an overarching storyline that spans the expanse of Scripture. Biblical theology emphasizes this unified plan of God by highlighting its main storyline in the midst of diversity.[5] While biblical revelation certainly contains truth propositions about God and the world, it comes to us as a story of God and his relationship to the world. It tells us how God chose to redeem mankind through his Son, Jesus Christ.

---

4. N. T. Wright, *What Saint Paul Really Said: Was Paul of Tarsus the Real Founder of Christianity?* (Grand Rapids: Eerdmans, 1997), 34.

5. Edward W. Klink and Darian R. Lockett, *Understanding Biblical Theology: A Comparison of Theory and Practice* (Grand Rapids: Zondervan, 2012). The view here is best represented in part 2 titled "Biblical Theology as a History of Redemption." See also Craig G. Bartholomew and Michael W. Goheen, *The Drama of Scripture: Finding Our Place in the Biblical Story* (Grand Rapids: Baker, 2004).

Biblical prophecy fits within the grand narrative of this redemptive history.[6] Redemption constitutes one of the major themes permeating the biblical story as it depicts the history of salvation (*Heilsgeschichte*).[7] The story encompasses the creation and fall in Genesis and the ultimate resolution accomplished in the new creation in Revelation—from Eden to the New Jerusalem.[8] When viewed broadly, the biblical sweep is from creation to new creation by way of redemption, which may be seen as the renewing of creation.[9]

The majority of the Old Testament could be classified as prophetic—a category which includes messages of encouragement, calls for repentance, warnings of judgments, historical narratives, poetry, and a variety of oracles intended for various audiences at a specific period in the history of God's people. The Hebrew canon (arrangement of the Old Testament books in the Hebrew Bible) divides into three sections: *Torah* (Law), *Nebi'im* (Prophets), and *Ketubim* (Writings). The section entitled *Nebi'im* (Prophets) is further divided into the *former* and *latter* prophets. The *Nebi'im* represent a massive swath of the Old Testament that richly resounds with texts, themes, and the theology of the *Torah* and *Ketubim*. Prophecy runs like a series of multi-colored threads woven throughout the tapestry of biblical revelation.

The former prophets include Joshua, Judges, Samuel, and Kings. The latter prophets include Jeremiah, Ezekiel, Isaiah, and the Twelve Minor Prophets. The former prophets tell the story of Israel from her entrance into the Promised Land under Joshua to her exile from the land to Babylon. The latter prophets interrupt the storyline of historical narratives in the former prophets and may be categorized as pre-exile, exilic, and post-exilic. The storyline resumes in various books like Daniel and in other books within the Writings. Why this shift from narrative to poetic or prophetic oracles? From a literary and theological perspective the shift in material between 2 Kings and Daniel provides commentary and reflection on the storyline. The latter prophets contain prophetic speeches delivered to Israel during most of the events narrated during the former prophets.

According to the biblical story of salvation, God looks upon his good and glorious creation and says "something is wrong" because of the ruin of sin. Yet, the story does not end there, because God himself will repair, redeem,

---

6. For an overview of the biblical narrative and the contention that the primary purpose for God's redemption in Christ is the restoration, or new creation see, for instance, T. Desmond Alexander, *From Eden to the New Jerusalem: An Introduction to Biblical Theology* (Grand Rapids: Kregel, 2008); G. K. Beale, *A New Testament Biblical Theology: The Unfolding of the Old Testament in the New* (Grand Rapids: Baker, 2011), 29–186 and esp. 129–60; Christopher J. H. Wright, *The Mission of God: Unlocking the Bible's Grand Narrative* (Downers Grove, IL: InterVarsity Press, 2006), 62–65; N. T. Wright, *Paul: In Fresh Perspective* (Minneapolis: Fortress, 2005), 114, 119–22, 130–53.

7. Ronald Youngblood, *The Heart of the Old Testament*, 2nd ed. (Grand Rapids: Baker, 1998), 101.

8. Alexander, *From Eden to the New Jerusalem*. This is an excellent primer on biblical theology and the grand narrative or "meta-story."

9. William J. Dumbrell, *The Search for Order: Biblical Eschatology in Focus* (Grand Rapids: Baker, 1994), 9.

and renew creation from all the disastrous effects of sin and the curse (Rev. 22:1–4). The creation account of Genesis emphasizes the goodness of all the created order with the repeated refrain "it was good" (Gen. 1:10, 12, 18, 21, 25, 31). When Adam and Eve disobeyed God's command regarding the tree of knowledge, it impacted the entire created order and subjected humanity and the Earth to the tyranny of sin (Gen. 3:17–19; Rom. 8:19–22). God, however, promised a seed or offspring from the woman who would crush the head of the serpent (Gen. 3:15). Generations later, God chose Abraham and promised to give him a family (i.e., "seed") because through him all nations would be blessed. Abraham's descendants, the children of Israel, became slaves under the oppression of a cruel master in Egypt. After four hundred years of oppression, God acted in history to redeem and deliver his people from slavery and bring them into a promised inheritance. This redemption from the bondage of slavery accomplished the founding of the nation of Israel that subsequently belonged to her redeemer in a covenantal relationship. God, through Moses, made a covenant with the descendants of Abraham on Mt. Sinai and gave them his Law to obey (Exod. 24). The problem is that Israel failed to keep the Law because their hearts were sinful and needed to be made new (Deut. 29:4; 30:6).

Throughout the history of Israel, the fact that God brought his covenant people out of the land of Egypt formed the basis of all future acts of salvation. David Daube insightfully observes that the "kind of salvation portrayed in the exodus was not, by its nature, an isolated occurrence, giving rise to nebulous hopes for similar good luck in the future: it had its root in, and set the seal on, a permanent institution—hence it was something on which absolute reliance might be placed."[10] Examples of this pattern abound throughout portions of the former and latter prophets as well as in the Writings. The book of Judges depicts a recurring cycle of God's people forsaking him and coming under the subjugation of an outside oppressor as a result. They would cry out to God for deliverance, and his hearing their cries and sending a deliverer to lead them out from under the yoke of their oppressors. The book of Esther tells how God's exiled and oppressed people came under the threat of genocide, and how God placed Esther in such a position that she interceded on her people's behalf to secure their deliverance. Psalms 78, 80, 81, 105, 106, 114, and 135 memorialize and recount how God acted in history to bring his people out of Egypt with the assurance of future acts of salvation. The prophets hark back to how God brought his people "out of Egypt" for the purposes of calling them to repentance and proclaiming their future salvation.[11] For example, Jeremiah declares: "Therefore, behold, the days are coming . . . when it shall no longer be said, 'As

---

10. David Daube, *The Exodus Pattern in the Bible* (London: Faber and Faber, 1963), 14.
11. Cf. Isaiah 11:16; 19:6; Jeremiah 2:6; 7:22, 25; 11:4; 16:14; 31:32; 32:21; 34:13; 37:7; 42:18; 44:28; Ezekiel 20:6–8; 30:15, 25; Daniel 9:15; 11:42; Hosea 11:1; Micah 7:15; Haggai 2:5.

the LORD lives who brought up the people of Israel out of the land of Egypt,' but 'As the LORD lives who brought up the people of Israel out of the north country and out of all the countries where he had driven them.' For I will bring them back to their own land that I gave to their fathers" (Jer. 16:14–15). Another aspect of redemption is seen when God's people spurned their redeemer by reveling in wickedness and therefore needed future redemption.[12]

The New Testament recasts the story of salvation and redemption in light of the ministry and work of Jesus Christ. The New Testament tells of an enslaved people, yet their slavery is not to a political despot but rather to sin. The Gospel of John demonstrates this quite clearly in the very teachings of Jesus in John 8:30–36. Paul also asserted this concept in Romans where he states: "Do you not know that if you present yourselves to anyone as obedient slaves, you are slaves of the one whom you obey, either of sin, which leads to death, or of obedience, which leads to righteousness?" (Rom. 6:16). In a manner similar to the exodus account, God acts in the course of history by sending a deliverer who will be God's instrument of redemption. The apostles recognized that Jesus was a prophet like Moses because, like Moses, he leads his people into salvation (Deut. 18:15, cited in Acts 3:22 and 7:37). Unlike Moses, Christ accomplished their redemption by paying the price with his own blood (Eph. 1:7; Heb. 9:12). As a result, those who are in Christ have been saved and redeemed from the power of sin and now belong to God. As Paul states "you are not your own" because "you were bought with a price" (1 Cor. 6:19–20). In short, the exodus model of "salvation" and "redemption" is completed by the work of Christ.

Jesus Christ inaugurated a new covenant. This new covenant was anticipated in the writings of Jeremiah (Jer. 31:31–34) and Ezekiel (Ezek. 36:24–28) stemming from their reading of Deuteronomy 30:6, which states, "the LORD your God will circumcise your heart and the heart of your offspring, so that you will love the LORD your God with all your heart and with all your soul, that you may live." At his last Passover meal, Jesus said, "This cup that is poured out for you is the new covenant in my blood" (Luke 22:20). The author of Hebrews tells us, "But as it is, Christ has obtained a ministry that is as much more excellent than the old as the covenant he mediates is better, since it is enacted on better promises" (Heb. 8:6). The resurrection of Jesus not only

---

12. Youngblood provides Hosea as an example: "The Israelites usually broke their pledges of loyalty to God almost as soon as they made them.... The prophets warned them that they would once again be enslaved by foreign powers if they did not repent and cry out to God for mercy. The first three chapters of Hosea, for example, compare the spiritual adultery of Israel to the shameless conduct of Hosea's unfaithful wife Gomer. Because of her brazen wickedness she eventually found herself enslaved to another man. In obedience to God's command, however, Hosea redeemed her from her bondage by paying the appropriate price (Hos. 3:1–2). The subsequent verses in Hosea 3 clearly suggest that God, the 'husband' (2:16) of wicked Israel, would in a similar way redeem his people after they had been in exilic bondage for an extended period" (*The Heart of the Old Testament*, 107–8).

secured our salvation, but also inaugurated the new covenant and initiated the first step of the new creation.

The apostle Paul understood the importance of the new covenant and the indwelling Spirit as bringing about the new creation through salvation. In the context of the new covenant and Christ's reconciling work, Paul describes the transformational nature of salvation by stating, "Therefore, if anyone is in Christ, he is a new creation. The old has passed away; behold, the new has come" (2 Cor. 5:17). He also reminds the Galatians, "For neither circumcision counts for anything, nor uncircumcision, but a new creation" (Gal. 6:15). This means that God's redemption of creation begins in the lives of people who are set free from the curse, penalty, and dominion of sin through the work of Christ. The new creation has already begun with believers who are made new by the Holy Spirit and are producing his good fruit in their lives.

While God has already begun his work of new creation through the salvation of individual people, God will completely redeem all of the created order through the consummation of the new creation. Paul tells us that all of creation groans in longing expectation for the time when Christ returns and the people of God are glorified bodily (Rom. 8:19–21). The longing of creation to be liberated from the tyranny of sin will be fully satisfied at the end of the age when Christ "makes all things new" (Rev. 21:5).

The book of Revelation draws upon the exodus model to depict the final and ultimate act of God in human history for the salvation and redemption of his people. The book of Exodus narrates how the tribes of Israel were oppressed under a cruel despot, how God protected and delivered them, and how, after crossing the Red Sea, they sang the song of Moses. In the narrative segments of Revelation a story is told that resembles several aspects of the exodus account, but one segment in particular describes the deliverance of God's people from the evil and tyrannical red dragon. Revelation 7 alludes to the twelve tribes of Israel (symbolic of the Church) who are the object of God's love and protection (coinciding with the woman and her offspring in ch. 12). The dragon seeks to oppress and kill them (12:3–13:18). Chapter 15 depicts these saints gathered by the side of the sea with harps (Rev. 14:2) singing the song of Moses (15:3). At the end of the age God will deliver his redeemed people—the new Israel—from Satan's wrath, and they will dwell with God in the eternal Promised Land.

When we get to the end of the story, the words "something is wrong" will never be uttered again because the creator God has fixed his fallen and broken creation. John the apostle sees the final restoration of creation:

> Then I saw a new heaven and a new earth, for the first heav-
> en and the first earth had passed away, and the sea was no
> more. . . . And I heard a loud voice from the throne saying,
> "Behold, the dwelling place of God is with man. He will

dwell with them, and they will be his people, and God himself will be with them as their God. He will wipe away every tear from their eyes, and death shall be no more, neither shall there be mourning, nor crying, nor pain anymore, for the former things have passed away." (Rev. 21:1, 3–4)

The story of God's plan for the creation and how that plan is consummated is prophetic from start to finish. Individual prophecies may punctuate and flesh out specific details and themes. These specific prophecies and prophetic themes are like tributaries flowing into the mighty river of the Bible's grand narrative. When we read prophecy, we must try to locate it within the larger story. Even if it is a tributary and not part of the main river, we must see how it fits and relates to the story of redemption and God's plan for the world.

Understanding Prophecy as Gospel-Centered and Christocentric

The gospel is at the center of this narrative. Prophecy finds its fulfillment in the ministry, death, and resurrection of Christ. From the gospel all the plans and purposes of God will be fully realized with the consummation of his kingdom on earth as prophesied in Scripture.[13] Graeme Goldsworthy persuasively argues this case as the basis for developing a gospel-centered hermeneutic:

> If Jesus is the one mediator between God and man, then he must mediate the meaning of the whole of God's communication to us. Our understanding of this mediatorial role comes from the unpacking of the New Testament writers of the gospel event and how it works for our salvation. This raises the question of the significance of all the parts of Scripture that are not explicitly expositions of the gospel. We can say that, while not all Scripture is the gospel, all Scripture is related to the gospel that is its centre. . . . In other words, *the gospel is the hermeneutical norm for the whole of reality.*[14]

Christ not only accomplished the means for our redemption, but he also revealed the mystery of God's will and purposes, in the fullness of time, to unite all things in heaven and earth in Christ (Eph. 1:9–10). The gospel is all about Christ—what he has done and what he will do to bring

---

13. See Rob Dalrymple, *Understanding Eschatology: Why It Matters* (Eugene, OR: Wipf & Stock, 2013), 16–26.
14. Graeme Goldsworthy, *Gospel-Centered Hermeneutics: Foundations and Principles of Evangelical Biblical Interpretation* (Downers Grove, IL: InterVarsity Press, 2006), 62–63.

all things to their proper conclusion. All the Scriptures testify to him. About his post-resurrection appearance to the two on the road to Emmaus, Luke says, "And beginning with Moses and all the Prophets, he interpreted to them in all the Scriptures the things concerning himself" (Luke 24:27). In the same way that the Jews of Jesus' day fundamentally misunderstood how Jesus was the Messiah prophesied in Scripture, any reading of Scripture that is not Christ-centered and gospel-centered may not understand prophecy as a whole.

It is odd that Jewish scholars of the first century achieved an almost encyclopedic grasp of the Scriptures and at the same time completely missed how Jesus fulfilled the messianic prophecies. Even Jesus' own disciples faltered clumsily when it came to recognizing, understanding and believing how their messiah was to die on a cross and rise from the dead. The prophecies all pointed to a coming messiah, but misunderstanding and misinterpretation plagued the Jewish people of Jesus' day. It was not until after his resurrection that the disciples had the necessary hermeneutic for interpreting biblical prophecy. After his resurrection Jesus walked along with the two headed to Emmaus and asked them, "Was it not necessary that the Christ should suffer these things and enter into his glory?" This question is followed up with an exhaustive Bible study on the person of the messiah. The text states, "beginning with Moses and all the Prophets, he interpreted to them in all the Scriptures the things concerning himself" (Luke 24:26–27). As such, we see how Jesus gave his disciples an exhaustive lesson in how to understand prophecy christocentrically.

A little later when Jesus appeared to all eleven disciples, he again provided them with the definitive guide to interpreting prophecy:

> Jesus said to them, "These are my words that I spoke to you while I was still with you, that everything written about me in the Law of Moses and the Prophets and the Psalms must be fulfilled." Then he opened their minds to understand the Scriptures, and said to them, "Thus it is written, that the Christ should suffer and on the third day rise from the dead, and that repentance and forgiveness of sins should be proclaimed in his name to all nations, beginning from Jerusalem." (Luke 24:44–47)

Until Jesus opened their minds to understand Scripture they did not fully grasp the meaning of prophecy and the mind-blowing way it all pointed to Christ. One reason why the Jewish leaders and scholars of Jesus' day failed to recognize him as the messiah is because they were operating with a flawed and incomplete hermeneutic that caused them to miss the most significant fulfillment of biblical prophecy that the world has ever witnessed. Jesus, therefore, becomes the hermeneutical key for reading prophecy. He taught his disciples how to interpret the Law and Prophets and they in turn shared that knowledge with us through the writings of the New Testament.

One way to read prophecy from a gospel-centered perspective is established by Christ himself at the start of his public ministry. After Jesus is baptized and withstands the wilderness temptations, Luke 4:14–30 gives us a snapshot of one of his first synagogue sermons in his hometown of Nazareth. During the synagogue service, Jesus stood up to read a portion of Scripture from the scroll of Isaiah. A quiet expectation filled the room as Jesus unrolled this rather large scroll to nearly the end of its length and finding the right spot began to read:

> The Spirit of the Lord is upon me, because he has anointed me to proclaim good news to the poor. He has sent me to proclaim liberty to the captives and recovering of sight to the blind, to set at liberty those who are oppressed, to proclaim the year of the Lord's favor. (Luke 4:18–19)

He rolled the scroll up, sat down, and declared, "Today this Scripture has been fulfilled in your hearing" (Luke 4:21). This statement indicates a moment of eschatological significance as Jesus inaugurates the arrival of the kingdom of God with his ministry.[15] He read primarily from Isaiah 61:1–2a, but the Lukan passage includes a line from Isaiah 58:6d to connect Jesus more directly with the suffering servant.[16] Jesus chooses a passage that not only anticipates a messianic year of jubilee, but also becomes programmatic for his mission. Notice, however, Jesus stopped reading in mid-sentence and omitted the phrase "and [to proclaim] the day of vengeance of our God" (Isa. 61:2b). This omission is most likely an intentional break to say something important about his mission and role. Jesus came to liberate the oppressed and captives through his sacrificial death upon the cross, but it will not be until he returns a second time that he will proclaim the day of God's vengeance. In other words, we may view prophecy as fulfilled either in Christ's life, death, and resurrection or fulfilled in his second coming to execute God's wrath and make all things new.

Christ is the *eschatos* of prophecy who gives meaning to all that has happened or will yet transpire throughout human history.[17] Our approach to prophecy must always be viewed through the gospel and what Christ has

---

15. I. Howard Marshall, *The Gospel of Luke*, NIGTC (Exeter: Paternoster, 1978), 184.

16. Robert H. Stein, *Luke*, NAC 24 (Nashville: B&H, 1992), 156. I. Howard Marshall observes, "In its original context the prophecy may refer to the self-consciousness of the prophet that he is called to make known the good news of God's intervention to help his people, expressed in a variety of metaphors. But since the passage uses a language and style reminiscent of the earlier Servant passages it may have been interpreted in terms of the Servant of Yahweh" (*Gospel of Luke*, 183).

17. Goldsworthy, *Gospel-Centered Hermeneutics*, 65.

already accomplished. Take for example how Christ fulfills the purpose and expectation of the Temple. God's desire to dwell among his people is evident as early as the Garden of Eden where God walked with Adam and Eve in the cool of the day (Gen. 3:8). However, their sin disrupted this fellowship and thus necessitated the need for atonement and reconciliation. Through the tabernacle, God provided a means to once again dwell among his people.[18] This Tabernacle, and the subsequent Temple, became the residence of the glory of God (Exod. 40:34–35; 1 Kings 8:11; 2 Chron. 5:14), although God could not be confined to a limited or man-made location (Isa. 66:1–2). The temple is the place where God dwells. This is evident in the prophecy of Ezekiel 40–48, in which the depiction of the city-temple closes with this statement: "and the name of the city from that time on shall be, 'The LORD is there'" (Ezek. 48:35).[19] Despite the glorious nature of the Tabernacle/Temple the consequences of sin could still disrupt the communion of God and his people. What is more, Ezekiel had a vision of the glory departing from the Temple as a direct result of sin and corruption (Ezek. 10:18; cf. 1 Sam. 4:21; Hos. 10:5). This vision led to a future expectation that God will once again dwell with his people in the prophecy of Isaiah declaring the coming of Emmanuel—"God with us" (Isa. 7:14; 8:10; 9:6–7). The New Testament posits that Jesus is the prophesied Emmanuel (Matt. 1:23).

Simply put, the corpus of the New Testament portrays Jesus as God's presence on earth and as the replacement of the Temple. The Gospel of John describes him as the Logos and as God who "became flesh, and dwelt ["tabernacle"] among us, and we have seen his glory, glory as of the only son from the Father, full of grace and truth" (John 1:14). Commenting on the language of this verse, Beasley-Murray observes that it is "evocative of the revelation of God's glory in the Exodus—by the Red Sea, on Mount Sinai, and at the tent of meeting by Israel's camp" and portrays "Christ as fulfilling the hope of a second Exodus."[20] This theme is developed further in the Gospel of John, when Jesus after cleansing the Temple designates himself as the Temple (John 2:19). In addition, Jesus stated that the true worship is in spirit and truth and thereby negated the earthly Temple as essential for the worship of God (John 4:23–24). Luke's Gospel also establishes a connection between Jesus and the Temple by linking significant events in the life and ministry of Jesus to the Temple (Luke 1:9, 21–23; 2:27, 37, 46; 4:9; 18:10; 19:45, 47; 20:1; 21:5, 37–38; 22:52–53; 23:45;

---

18. This corresponds well with the theme of G. K. Beale's work, *The Temple and the Church's Mission*, NSBT 17 (Downers Grove, IL: InterVarsity, 2004). Beale states, "my thesis is that the Old Testament tabernacle and temples were symbolically designed to point to the cosmic eschatological reality that God's tabernacling presence, formerly limited to the holy of holies, was to be extended throughout the whole earth" (25).
19. Dalrymple, *Understanding Eschatology*, 74–76.
20. George R. Beasley-Murray, *John*, 2nd ed., WBC 36A (Waco, TX: Word, 1999), 14.

24:53). The notion of Jesus as the Temple's replacement finds its ultimate expression in Revelation where John declares: "I saw no temple in it, for the LORD God the Almighty and the Lamb *are its temple*" (Rev. 21:22 NASB; emphasis added). Therefore, God will dwell among his people eternally through Jesus Christ. Between Jesus' ascension and the final consummation spoken of in Revelation, God currently dwells among his people through the indwelling of the Holy Spirit (1 Cor. 3:16–17; 6:19; 2 Cor. 6:16). Thus, the church as a collection of indwelt individuals is the Temple of God in the sense of the indwelling of God's presence.

A gospel-centered hermeneutic filters all prophecy through the lens of the resurrected Christ. This biblical-theological perspective sees Christ as the center of redemptive history, the pinnacle of divine revelation, and the fulfillment of the broad sweep of biblical prophecy. We find that Old Testament persons such as Adam (Rom. 5:14; 1 Cor. 15:22, 45, 47) and Jonah (Matt. 12:40–41; cf. Jonah 1:17), as well as the nation of Israel (Matt. 2:15; cf. Hos. 11:1) typify Christ. He is also prefigured in Old Testament institutions like the Passover (1 Cor. 5:7); the sacrificial system with its atonement for sin (1 Peter 1:18–19; cf. Lev. 17:11), and the temple (John 2:21). Old Testament offices including the prophetic office of Moses (Matt. 5:21; John 1:17, 45; cf. Deut. 18:15); the priestly office of Melchizedek (Heb. 5:6, 10; 6:20; 7:11, 15, 17; cf. Gen. 14:17–20; Ps. 110:4); and the kingly office of David (Matt. 1:1) all typify Christ. Thus, we find that Jesus, in his mission as fully completed through his death, resurrection, and ascension, is the fulfillment of the Old Testament Scriptures. He not only fulfills the Scriptures that predicted the coming redeemer, "but the whole sweep of Old Testament ideas."[21]

> *When it comes to understanding prophecy we must first attempt to flesh out the full implications of what Christ has already fulfilled. Then, and only then, will we see more clearly what prophetic events he has yet to bring to completion in the scope of God's plan.*

Understanding Prophecy as Thematic

Prophecy broadly contributes to the whole of the story of Scripture and the metanarrative of salvation history by developing a number of themes that run throughout the canon. A biblical-theological perspective for understanding prophecy seeks to trace the themes and trajectories running throughout prophecy in an attempt to integrate them into a comprehensive theology of

---

21. R. T. France, *Jesus and the Old Testament: His Application of Old Testament Passages to Himself and His Mission* (Downers Grove, IL: InterVarsity, 1971), 79–80. See, however, the conclusions and summary in 75–80.

the biblical text. Paul Williamson articulates this well with his definition of biblical theology:

> Biblical theology is . . . a holistic enterprise tracing unfold-
> ing theological trajectories throughout Scripture and explor-
> ing no biblical concept, theme or book in isolation from the
> whole. Rather, each concept, theme or book is considered
> ultimately in terms of how it contributes to and advances
> the Bible's meta-narrative, typically understood in terms of
> a salvation history that progresses towards and culminates in
> Jesus Christ.[22]

We must read prophecy first and foremost with contextual sensitivity to the history, literature, and theology of an individual writer, book, and passage. This approach is absolutely essential to the work of exegesis in order to know, as much as possible, what a specific text actually means in and of itself. A biblical-theological approach does not read a specific text in isolation from the entire canon of biblical revelation.[23] The goal is that we would read the historical narratives, prophecy, wisdom literature, gospels, and epistles as holistically presenting a unified biblical theology. We also acknowledge that the entirety of the biblical text is complex and addresses a vast range of themes and topics not always directly related to salvation history.[24] The prophetic messages resound with recurring themes and these themes contribute to our understanding of the biblical revelation as a whole.

While some themes may be independent of the larger theme of salvation history, the majority of the prophetic themes are encompassed within it. Many of these prophetic themes relate to the future restoration and sal-

---

22. Paul R. Williamson, *Sealed with an Oath: Covenant in God's Unfolding Purpose*, NSBT 23 (Downers Grove, IL: InterVarsity, 2007), 17.

23. The use of a canonical approach to biblical theology is one that examines the composition and the final shape of the canon as it has come to us as the means to adjudicate meaning, rather than locating meaning primarily in the original or historical context when it was written. While we would commend much about the canonical approach to biblical theology, we would advocate a moderated form that gives priority to the historical context as more determinative for textual meaning. See Anthony C. Thiselton, "Canon, Community, and Theological Construction: Introduction," in *Canon and Biblical Interpretation*, ed. Craig G. Bartholomew, et al., SHS 7 (Grand Rapids: Zondervan, 2006), 1–30; Brevard S. Childs, *Biblical Theology of the Old and New Testaments* (Minneapolis: Fortress, 1993); James A. Sanders, *From Sacred Story to Sacred Text: Canon as Paradigm* (Philadelphia: Fortress, 1987); Gerald T. Sheppard, "Canonical Criticism," *ABD*, 1:861–66; Christopher R. Seitz, *The Character of Christian Scripture: The Significance of a Two-Testament Bible*, STI (Grand Rapids: Baker, 2011); Klink and Lockett, *Understanding Biblical Theology*, 123–53; Matthew Y. Emerson, *Christ and the New Creation: A Canonical Approach to the Theology of the New Testament* (Eugene, OR: Wipf & Stock, 2013), 1–37.

24. Charles H. H. Scobie, *The Ways of Our God: An Approach to Biblical Theology* (Grand Rapids: Eerdmans, 2003), 90.

vation, which largely comprise the messianic prophecies and the expectation of a new king and kingdom (Isa. 4:2; 9:6–7; 11:1; 63:1–6; Jer. 23:5–6; 33:14–16; Ezek. 37:24; Zech. 3:8; 6:12; Pss. 2; 72; 89; 110; 132), a new covenant (Isa. 54:10; Jer. 31:31–34; Ezek. 37:26–27), and a new creation (Isa. 65:17; 66:22; Dan. 12:1–3; cf. Rev. 21:1–5). The prophetic message contains other themes that resonate and reverberate throughout the prophetic writings. One of the more foundational themes is that God is the sovereign Lord of history and controls the course of people, nations, and events (Isa. 10:5–15; Ezek. 38:3–16; 39:2–3; Hab. 1:5–17). Prophets often proclaim the need to be right with God (Isa. 30:15; Amos 4:6–12) and the need for morality in religion and society (Jer. 7:1–15). Prophets frequently address issues of social justice, confronting the failure of God's people in their treatment of the poor, widows, orphans, and foreigners, or rebuking them for their excessive violence (Isa. 1:17; 5:7; 10:1–2; 61:8; Jer. 5:28; 7:5–6; Ezek. 18:8; 22:29; 45:9; Amos 5:14–15; Mic. 3:9; 6:8). All of these themes intertwine as the prophets announce their messages of judgment and salvation (Isa. 6:13; 28:5; 29:5; 31:5; Amos 9:11–15). There is also a sense in which all biblical themes are eschatological or that eschatology is *a key dimension of every biblical theme.*[25]

> *Every major Old Testament theme has a future aspect to it that finds its fulfillment in the New Testament either in the Christ event or in the final consummation.*

Understanding Prophecy as Progressive Revelation

The history of God's actions, promises, and dealings with his people as recorded in the narratives, propositions, and themes of Scripture indicate a progressive nature for divine revelation. Biblical history is a complex process that collectively contributes to our understanding of who God is, what he is like, what he has done, and what he will do. Progressive revelation recognizes that God's revelation was given in stages to a specific people and that subsequent revelation can add to or modify what was revealed in earlier stages.[26] We would be careful to note, however, that later revelation does not necessarily supplant or abrogate earlier revelation. In other words, further development in the revelation at a later point in history does not automatically replace or do away with what was revealed in prior history. We would contend that the New Testament presents the Christ event as the fulfillment of the Old Testament revelation, so that this fulfillment com-

---

25. Ibid., 93.
26. Ibid., 91.

pletes or *continues* what was prior.[27] Greg Beale expresses the relationship between progressive revelation and how the New Testament provides the fuller meaning of the Old Testament:

> In light of progressive revelation, OT passages do not receive brand-new or contradictory meanings but undergo an organic expansion or development of meaning. . . . This means that OT passages can be understood more deeply in the light of the developing revelation of later parts of the OT and especially of the NT. The OT authors had a true understanding of what they wrote but not an exhaustive understanding. This means that a NT text's contextual understanding of an OT text will involve some essential identity of meaning between the two, but often the meaning is expanded and unfolded, growing out of the earlier meaning.[28]

Therefore, understanding prophecy as progressive revelation enables us to approach the use of the Old Testament in the New.

The New Testament appropriation of Old Testament promises, themes, prophecies, and types cues us as to how to read Scripture as a unified but progressive revelation. Gentry and Wellum write that "the New Testament's interpretation of the Old Testament becomes definitive in helping us interpret the details of the Old Testament, since later revelation brings with it greater clarity and understanding. In other words, we must carefully allow the New Testament to show us how the Old Testament is brought to fulfillment in Christ."[29] The prophecies of the Old Testament were shrouded in mystery so that the precise nature of the fulfillment could not be known until after the fact. While the Scriptures contained numerous prophecies about the coming Messiah, it was not until Jesus stepped onto the stage of human history that the meaning of those prophecies came into sharp focus. This means that the full significance of the revelation given in the Old Testament is not complete until viewed through the Christ event.

The Old Testament contained shadows and copies but the true substance or reality is Christ (Col. 2:17; Heb. 8:5; 10:1).[30] He is the fullest and final

---

27. Ibid.

28. G. K. Beale, *Handbook on the New Testament Use of the Old Testament: Exegesis and Interpretation* (Grand Rapids: Baker, 2012), 27.

29. Peter J. Gentry and Stephen J. Wellum, *Kingdom through Covenant: A Biblical-Theological Understanding of the Covenants* (Wheaton, IL: Crossway, 2012), 85–86.

30. This does not mean that a later text distorts or contravenes the meaning of earlier texts, "but rather develops them in a way which is consistent with the Old Testament author's understanding of the way in which God interacts with this people" (Greg Beale, "Did Jesus and His Followers Preach the Right Doctrine from the Wrong Texts? An Examination of the Presuppositions of Jesus' and the Apostles'

revelation (Heb. 1:1–2). Jesus, in his earthy ministry, perfectly revealed the Father to us (John 1:18; 14:7–11). What is more, Jesus is also the focus of the final revelation. Revelation 1:1 identifies the entire contents of the book as the "revelation of Jesus Christ, which God gave him to show to his servants the things that must soon take place." The book of Revelation may indeed predict future events surrounding the final consummation of God's plan for the world, but it is a book ultimately about Jesus—his glory, his sovereign reign, his judgment, his victory, his return, his kingdom, his accomplishment of final redemption, and his making all things new. As the full and final divine revelation, Jesus is the pinnacle of progressive revelation and he becomes the interpretive key for reading prophecy in the two testaments.

Understanding Prophecy as Historically Conditioned

Another principle for understanding prophecy from a biblical-theological perspective is recognizing that prophecy was always given in particular historical settings. Many popular approaches to prophecy tend to view prophetic passages as almost addressing events thousands of years removed from their original context. These interpreters desire to discover what the prophecy *means* for the contemporary world. While we would affirm that prophecy has meaning in our current context, it is also true that by not giving adequate attention to the original context these interpreters may have inadvertently skipped the first task of discovering what the prophecy *meant*.

The task of biblical theology would certainly aim at a *prescriptive* use of Scripture for the people of God in any culture at any point in time. Yet, biblical theology first aims at a *descriptive* study of biblical thought. Locating prophecy within the historical, sociological, cultural and religious context of its origin is an essential component for proper understanding. Once the prophecy is framed, interpreted, and applied in terms of what it *meant*, then we may explore what it *means* for us today.

Understanding Prophecy as Applicable

A final principle for understanding prophecy from a biblical-theological perspective is that prophecy requires obedience, action, and application to life. The prophets were not navel gazers who sat atop lofty mountains pondering deep philosophical questions as detached spiritual gurus. The prophet spoke the Word of God to afflict the comfortable and comfort the afflicted.[31] They

---

Exegetical Method," in *The Right Doctrine from the Wrong Texts? Essays on the Use of the Old Testament in the New*, ed. G. K. Beale [Grand Rapids: Baker, 1994], 393).

31. Although it has seen many incarnations, this adage derives from a famous line by American journalist Finley Peter Dunne (1867–1936).

called the people to repent of specific sins, to endure faithfully through difficult trials, to act justly toward their neighbors, and to care for the poor and needy. They warned of impending judgment and gave clear instructions for how the recipients should amend their lives. They urged the need for holy behavior as outlined in the Law.

The book of Revelation is a prophecy intended for application for a Christian living in the community of faith and in a world hostile to the sovereign reign of Christ. It is the only book in the Bible that promises a blessing just for reading or hearing it read (Rev. 1:3; 22:7). Notice, however, that the blessing is also tied to keeping or obeying this book of prophecy:[32]

> Blessed is the one who reads aloud the words of this prophecy, and blessed are those who hear, and who *keep what is written in it*, for the time is near. (Rev. 1:3)
>
> And behold, I am coming soon. Blessed is the one who *keeps the words of the prophecy of this book*. (Rev. 22:7)

Prophecy is not a matter of speculation and theorizing, but a matter of practice. Prophecy challenges the way we live our lives and exhorts us to radical faithfulness to the commands of Christ.

If it is just a book about future events, in what way is someone expected to "keep" this prophecy? The notion of *keeping* comes from the Greek verb *tēreō* and mostly occurs throughout Revelation with the sense of obedience:

> The one who conquers and who *keeps my works* until the end, to him I will give authority over the nations... (Rev. 2:26)
>
> Remember, then, what you received and heard. *Keep it, and repent*. (Rev. 3:3)
>
> I know your works.... I know that you have but little power, and yet *you have kept my word and have not denied my name*. (Rev. 3:8)
>
> Because *you have kept my word about patient endurance*, I will keep you from the hour of trial that is coming on the whole world, to try those who dwell on the earth. (Rev. 3:10)
>
> Then the dragon became furious with the woman and went off to make war on the rest of her offspring, *on those who keep*

---

32. Emphasis added to all the following quotations from the book of Revelation.

the commandments of God and hold to the testimony of Jesus. (Rev. 12:17)

Here is a call for the endurance of the saints, *those who keep the commandments of God* and their faith in Jesus. (Rev. 14:12)

Behold, I am coming like a thief! Blessed is the one who stays awake, *keeping his garments* on, that he may not go about naked and be seen exposed! (Rev. 16:15)

Those who obey the divine imperatives of the book are blessed, but a curse is in store for those who disobey (Rev. 22:18–19). Eschatologically, the blessing is that the obedient ones will have clean robes, the right to eat from the tree of life, and unfettered access to the New Jerusalem (Rev. 22:14). Conversely, the curse is that the dogs, sorcerers, sexually immoral, murders, idolaters, and all liars are excluded from the city (Rev. 22:15). The point is that present obedience, faith, and works have future benefits, but present wickedness and rebellion have negative future consequences. Therefore, the prophecy of this book (Rev. 1:3; 22:7) is "primarily a reference not to predictive revelation but to divine disclosure demanding an ethical response, in line with OT 'prophecy,' which primarily addresses present situations and only secondarily foretells."[33]

Conclusion

The church today, on one hand, experiences a kind of *prophecy mania*. It is filled with those who find proof-texts to show current events as some sort of literal fulfillment of a specific prophetic prediction. The mania has flooded popular culture with a mass proliferation of books, best-selling novels, Hollywood productions, television shows, songs, bumper stickers, and has even influenced politics. Yet, on the other hand, the church also suffers from *prophecy apathy*. This apathy manifests when people shy away from prophecy because it is too difficult for them to understand. They automatically plead ignorance and defer to the "prophecy experts." Prophecy, for these people, is seen as irrelevant to their faith and practice in the real world. The polar extremes of prophetic mania or apathy fail to represent an accurate or comprehensive understanding of the entirety of the Bible. We have argued for a biblical-theological and christological approach to prophecy that examines the parts as well as the whole breadth of biblical prophecy.

It is our sincere goal to promote a healthy and robust understanding of prophecy for the benefit of the church. Prophecy represents a significant swath of the biblical revelation. To read, study, grapple with, interpret, and

---

33. G. K. Beale, *The Book of Revelation,* NIGTC (Grand Rapids: Eerdmans, 1999), 184–85.

apply prophecy is an immensely challenging task—but a rewarding one. We do not assume that everyone will share a uniform interpretation of all the prophetic texts because we recognize that genuinely godly believers will disagree when it comes to specific views. The authors of this book even disagree regarding the meaning and interpretation of the millennium, but we believe that a biblical-theological perspective gives a much broader area for agreement. The themes, message, and theology of prophecy find their center in the gospel of Jesus Christ and the gospel unifies us as believers. In the same way we find unity in the diversity of Scripture, we recognize the core of Christian unity even if there is eschatological diversity among faithful believers.

Despite all the challenges, complexities, and controversy we begin this book with a hearty cry —"*maranatha!*"—"*Our Lord Come!*" (1 Cor. 16:22).

Chapter 2

What Is Biblical Prophecy?

The very mention of the word "prophecy" can stir the senses with excitement and expectation as if some mysterious ancient utterance will now reveal a hidden truth about the future.

All too often people read a prophetic text as some sort of cryptic cipher to decode current events. The general assumption is that prophecy is all about making future predictions. The prevailing hermeneutic for many popular books on prophecy is to discover the details of God's plan for the future and how modern events fit with the divine program. In such books, interpreters attempt to sort out how prophecy fits into a systematic scheme that sets forth a comprehensive narrative of the future. It is not surprising then to discover a plethora of "prophecy experts" finding numerous modern fulfillments of prophecy on a daily basis. Remarkably, no one seems to notice when the news reports change or things do not happen as the prophecy expert anticipated.

Contrary to many conceptions in popular culture, prophecy is not exclusively a matter of predicting the future; this becomes clear when prophecy is understood in its historical context. To be sure, there are prophecies pointing well beyond the lifetime of the prophet, but prophecy encompasses so much more than a prediction of future events. To read prophecy as if prophets are primarily predicting events far off in the future actually requires a selective reading that may pull some passages out of context while ignoring others altogether.[1] The prophets addressed their audience with a message that would have been relevant in their own lifetimes. Their messages certainly contained promises and future predictions, but they also called for repentance, social justice, proper

---

1. Joel B. Green, *How to Read Prophecy* (Downers Grove, IL: InterVarsity, 1984), 28; Willem A. VanGemeren, *Interpreting the Prophetic Word: An Introduction to the Prophetic Literature of the Old Testament* (Grand Rapids: Zondervan, 1990), 71; Gordon D. Fee and Douglas Stuart, *How to Read the Bible for All Its Worth: A Guide to Understanding the Bible*, 4th ed. (Grand Rapids: Zondervan, 2014), 188.

theological understanding, comfort, and encouragement. Out of all biblical prophecy only a relatively small percentage actually pertains to events still yet to come in the future.[2] The point is that while the prophets did indeed speak of future events, they were primarily concerned with the situation in Israel, Judah, and neighboring nations at the times in which they were writing.

Because pastors and scholars tend to emphasize one aspect of prophecy to the exclusion of others we are often left with a bipolar schism that can produce a lopsided view of prophecy. Many neglect the literary and historical context of Scripture so as to make prophecy a matter of finding proof-texts to apply to current events. On the other hand, there are those who tend to neglect the su-pernatural and predictive nature of prophecy so as to boil the message down to social reform or nothing more than *vaticinium ex eventu* (a prophecy after the event). A healthy and robust conception of prophecy must carefully navigate the complexity of prophecy as both *forth-telling* and *foretelling*.

Prophecy is primarily *forth-telling* in that the prophet speaks a word from God to address a current situation in the life of his covenant people. The prophet's message, then, is one that is directed to a specific people at a specific point in history. While the majority of prophetic texts may not predict events far into the future, the prophets sometimes delivered messages that anticipat-ed a future fulfillment or *foretelling*. In Deuteronomy 18:18–22, Moses gave criteria for adjudicating true and false prophets, noting that they are only true prophets if (1) they speak for Yahweh and (2) what they say actually comes to pass (cf. Jer. 23). These criteria make the fulfillment of prophecy central to biblical revelation. John Sawyer remarks how the forward-looking criterion casts a shadow across all the prophetic texts:

> The prophet is first and foremost, according to this key pas-sage, one who can successfully predict the future. Moses, the model on which this passage and other Deuteronomic passages on prophecy are based, died before the main bulk of his teaching was fulfilled, his vision of a new world still bright (34:7), and, in that respect, the whole Pentateuch . . . has a forward-looking dimension. . . . But this aspect of prophecy is central to all the other prophetic traditions too. Throughout the whole history of Israel and Judah as recounted in Joshua to Kings, the theme of prophecy and fulfillment runs like a golden thread.[3]

---

2. Fee and Stuart suggest, "Less than 2 percent of Old Testament prophecy is messianic. Less than 5 percent specifically describes the new covenant age. Less than 1 percent concerns events yet to come in our time" (*How to Read the Bible for All Its Worth*, 188). Although it is likely that their statistics may be exaggerated, they nevertheless make a valid point regarding how most prophecy is not predictive in nature.

3. John F. A. Sawyer, *Prophecy and the Biblical Prophets* (Oxford: Oxford University Press, 1993), 17–18.

The criterion of fulfillment indicates that the majority of predictions would be fulfilled in the lifetime of the prophet so as to make a proper and timely assessment regarding the validity of the prophet. The evaluation of prophets based on whether or not their words came to pass suggests a more immediate timeframe for the fulfillment of the prophecy. To be balanced, we must recognize the dual nature of prophecy as addressing situations contemporary to the prophet, but without neglecting the predictive elements.

This chapter will survey a number of aspects related to the nature and scope of prophecy as it relates to God's covenant people. To better understand prophecy we must first consider the ministry and message of the prophets. We must also examine the nature of prophecy as a literary genre and how it communicates theological truth using poetic language. Lastly, we will explore some of the challenges associated with understanding prophecy expressed through the visionary and symbolic texts within the apocalyptic genre. The purpose of this chapter, then, is to introduce the reader to a definition of prophecy and issues related to prophetic literature with a view toward building an appropriate hermeneutic for interpreting prophecy.

Prophecy and the Role of the Prophet

Prophets and Their Ministry

The English word "prophet" comes from the Greek word *prophētēs*, which is the Greek translation (LXX) of the Hebrew word *nābî'*. The word *nābî'* comes from the root *nb'*, which means "to call" and a prophet was regarded as a "called one." The word *prophētēs* is used to describe "one who speaks for a god and interprets his will to man."[4] There are several terms used for prophets. Each of these terms describe one of the different roles that prophets served. These terms include: (1) *seer*: one who sees what is hidden or is given visions (2 Sam. 15:27; 24:11; 1 Chron. 26:28; Amos 7:12); (2) *watchman*: one announcing impending doom or blessings (Ezek. 3:17; Isa. 21:11; Hos. 9:8); (3) *man of God*: a pious man devoted to God (Deut. 33:1; 1 Sam. 9:6; 2 Sam. 9:6; 1 Kings 8:11); (4) *messenger*: God's envoy and representative (Isa. 42:19; Hag. 1:13; Mal. 3:1); and (5) *servant*: one with a mission from God (2 Kings 21:10; 24:2).[5] The prophets originally delivered their messages orally. We may still detect traces of this orality in the written form through the use of impassioned language and other structural clues.[6]

---

4. Henry G. Liddell and Robert Scott, "προφήτης," in *A Greek-English Lexicon* (Oxford: Clarendon, 1996), 1539–40.
5. See David L. Petersen, *The Prophetic Literature: An Introduction* (Louisville: Westminster John Knox, 2002), 5–8.
6. Andreas J. Köstenberger and Richard D. Pattterson, *Invitation to Biblical Interpretation: Exploring the Hermeneutical Triad of History, Literature, and Theology* (Grand Rapids: Kregel, 2011), 320; VanGemeren, *Interpreting the Prophetic Word*, 43.

Therefore, prophecy involves divine communication through a human messenger in both oral and written forms.

The prophets functioned as spokespersons for God, as his ambassador (Heb. 1:1). While they decried the social sins of their contemporaries, their message was particularly focused on the religious apostasy of the nation. Their message and style of delivery frequently varied in content and format. What unifies these diverse characteristics of the prophets is that they all served only one God—Yahweh.

Whenever prophets spoke a specific word from God, they introduced their oracle with the phrase "thus says the LORD" or something like it. This phrase and other attributions of divine origin punctuate the prophetic speeches with the subtlety of a large flashing neon sign. The biblical prophets clearly viewed themselves as those who were called by God to speak for him. The biblical consensus regarding prophecy is that "no prophecy was ever produced by the will of man, but men spoke from God as they were carried along by the Holy Spirit" (2 Peter 1:21). The prophet was one who spoke for God to reveal the will and ways of God so that the people of God could worship and obey the one true God of Israel.

> *Prophecy was rooted in the revelation of God, it was historically conditioned, and the majority of its predictions were fulfilled in relatively close proximity to the time they were uttered.*

While we want to recognize that the majority of prophecy is not necessarily predictive in nature, we also want to emphasize that prophecy is not completely devoid of future predictions. Belief in predictive prophecy stems directly from theological convictions based on the eternality, sovereignty, and providence of God. Any fulfillment of God's Word and decrees should be attributed to his providence. John Calvin argued, "God so attends to the regulation of individual events, and they all so proceed from his set plan, that nothing takes place by chance."[7] This affirmation is echoed by the Westminster Confession of Faith which states, "God from all eternity did, by the most wise and holy counsel of his own will, freely and unchangeably ordain whatsoever comes to pass."[8] Recognizing that providence is the determinative principle of all things, however, does not neglect the realization that during the outworking of his plan God sometimes works through an intermediary and sometimes without an intermediary.[9] While discussing these statements of Calvin and the Westminster Confession of Faith in relation to historical contingencies of predictions, Richard L. Pratt, Jr. states:

---

7. John Calvin, *Institutes of the Christian Religion*, ed. John T. McNeill, trans. Ford Lewis Battles (1559 ed.; reprint, Philadelphia: Westminster, 1967), 1.16.4.

8. *The Westminster Confession of Faith* (1647), 3.1, cited in Philip Schaff, *The Creeds of Christendom*, vol. 3: *The Evangelical Protestant Creeds, with Translations* (New York: Harper & Brothers, 1877), 608.

9. Richard L. Pratt Jr., "Historical Contingencies and Biblical Predictions" in *The Way of Wisdom: Essays in Honor of Bruce K. Waltke*, ed. J. I. Packer and Sven K. Soderlund (Grand Rapids: Zondervan, 2000), 182.

In line with these formulations, we must approach prophetic predictions with full assurance that historical contingencies have never interrupted the immutable decrees of God. No uncertainties ever lay before him; no power can thwart the slightest part of his plan. Yahweh spoke through his prophets with full knowledge and control of what was going to happen in the near and distant future. Any outlook that denies this theological conviction is less than adequate.[10]

Pratt concludes that the prophets "spoke for God within time and space, not before the foundations of the world. . . therefore they did not utter immutable *decrees*, but providential *declarations*."[11]

Biblical prophecy, in written form, finds its origin with Moses who was not only a deliverer and lawgiver but also a prophet. Moses is not always thought of as a prophet, but he actually represents the prototype of all biblical prophets. VanGemeren called Moses the "fountainhead" or "beginning of the stream . . . of the prophetic movement."[12] He goes further to state that every prophet was "like Moses" in many ways: (1) he was an Israelite; (2) he was called by the Lord; (3) was empowered by the Holy Spirit; (4) he was God's spokesman; (5) his authority derived from speaking in the name of the Lord; (6) he was a good shepherd over God's people; and (7) he vindicated the message by signs.[13]

As a prophet Moses was God's mouthpiece as indicated in Exodus 7:1–2 where the basic nature of the prophet as God's spokesman is spelled out very plainly:

> And the LORD said to Moses, "See, I have made you like God to Pharaoh, and your brother Aaron shall be your prophet. You shall speak all that I command you, and your brother Aaron shall tell Pharaoh to let the people of Israel go out of his land."

Moses communicated the will and words of God as an exalted prophet due to the unique relationship he had with God as his messenger. When Aaron and Miriam challenged Moses' authority, God responded with a remarkable affirmation of Moses in Numbers 12:6–8:

> And he said, "Hear my words: If there is a prophet among you, I the LORD make myself known to him in a vision; I

---

10. Ibid.
11. Ibid., 183.
12. VanGemeren, *Interpreting the Prophetic Word*, 28.
13. Ibid., 42–43.

speak with him in a dream. Not so with my servant Moses. He is faithful in all my house. With him I speak mouth to mouth, clearly, and not in riddles, and he beholds the form of the LORD. Why then were you not afraid to speak against my servant Moses?"

This affirmation shows us that Moses held a special prophetic status, but it also gives us a glimpse into the process of prophetic revelation. Moses was unique in that he was given direct access to the presence of God as evidenced by the account of his encounters with God at the burning bush, on Sinai, and in the Tent of Meeting. We also see in this passage that God spoke to his prophets in a variety of ways including visions, dreams, and direct discourse. Although Moses held a special place as God's prophet, he also served as a template for all prophets as those who speak for God (Deut. 18:18–22).[14]

Moses outlined the principles for distinguishing between true and false prophets in Deuteronomy 18. The book of Deuteronomy constitutes a series of sermons to remind the people of God's faithfulness, to explain the covenant, and to warn them of what to expect for future generations. The topic turns to prophets and prophecy in chapter 18:

> I will raise up for them a prophet like you from among their brothers. And I will put my words in his mouth, and he shall speak to them all that I command him. And whoever will not listen to my words that he shall speak in my name, I myself will require it of him. But the prophet who presumes to speak a word in my name that I have not commanded him to speak, or who speaks in the name of other gods, that same prophet shall die. And if you say in your heart, "How may we know the word that the LORD has not spoken?"—when a prophet speaks in the name of the LORD, if the word does not come to pass or come true, that is a word that the LORD has not spoken; the prophet has spoken it presumptuously. You need not be afraid of him. (Deut. 18:18–22)

This important passage spells out the ongoing nature of the prophetic ministry grounded in the will and purposes of God. The office of prophet was established with Moses at Sinai (Deut. 18:16–17). God told Israel that they must not seek out spiritual mediums and listen to them (Deut. 18:9–14), but rather

---

14. The Pentateuch ends with an expectation of a Prophet who is to come (Deut. 34:9–12; cf. Deut. 18:18). This expectation of a prophet like Moses is followed by Joshua 1:1–9 and an exhortation to meditate on the Scripture. See John H. Sailhamer, *The Pentateuch as Narrative: A Biblical-Theological Commentary* (Grand Rapids: Zondervan, 1992), 456.

that they must listen to the prophet like Moses whom God would send them (Deut. 18:15–22). A true prophet would meet certain criteria. First, the prophet would be like Moses (Deut. 18:18). This was ultimately fulfilled in Christ (Acts 3:22–24) but the story of other prophets sometimes parallels the life of Moses (e.g., Samuel or Elijah). Second, the prophet's words would come true (Deut. 18:22). While this would apply to the fulfillment of messianic and other future predictions, the prophet's words would also need to be adjudicated as true or false closer to the time of their utterance. For example, 1 Samuel 3:19–20 and 9:6 state that God would not allow any of Samuel's words to "fall to the ground"; instead, they "all came to pass." The final criterion is that the prophet's words must conform to what God has actually said as revealed in the Law (Deut. 18:18). *Like Moses, the prophets explained, announced, and elaborated the meaning and implications of the covenant and the Law.*

Prophets and Their Message

The prophets were not innovators of a new message, but rather they were more like reformers who reminded the people and interpreted the covenant that bound Yahweh and his people. (Deut. 5:1–3; 6:1–25).[15] A covenant is a legally binding agreement with promises and stipulations required for each party involved. In the Old Testament, a covenant might be a pact of mutuality concerning individuals, but a covenant might also be imposed by a greater power upon a lesser one. The greater power demands loyalty and obligates itself to the protection of the lesser one. The Law was given along with the covenant as a means of outlining the covenant. The covenant for Israel was intended to continue for each successive generation. It is also important to note that some covenants exhibit a conditional quality with the repeated "if . . ., then . . ." refrain. The covenant into which Israel had entered was not simply the legal acquiescence to a detailed contract, but rather "a living relationship that required the loving commitment of both parties."[16] The prophets, then, indicted the people for a breach of covenant stipulations and called them to return to covenant obedience (Isa. 1:11–20; Jer. 7:21–23; Hos. 6:6–7; Amos 5:25; Mic. 6:6–8).

---

15. Osborne expresses this well when he remarks: "The prophets did not develop a new message but rather applied the truths of the past to the nation's current situation. Theirs was a ministry of confrontation rather than of creation. They were not innovative theologians but rather revivalists, seeking to bring the people back to Yahweh and the traditional truths of the Jewish faith. For instance, the prophets did not construct the doctrine of messianic hope; that was already present from Mosaic times (Deut. 18:18). They elaborated it, adding further details, but hardly creating messianism ex nihilo" (Grant R. Osborne, *The Hermeneutical Spiral: A Comprehensive Introduction to Biblical Interpretation* [Downers Grove, IL: InterVarsity, 1991], 208).

16. Tremper Longman and Raymond B. Dillard, *An Introduction to the Old Testament*, 2nd ed. (Grand Rapids: Zondervan, 1994), 114.

Because the covenant defines every aspect of the relationship between God and Israel, the Pentateuch (and particularly Deuteronomy) is foundational to the prophetic message. The book of Deuteronomy is a series of sermons that Moses delivered to the Israelites on the plains of Moab just before he died. The meaning of the title "Deuteronomy" is "second law," and the reason the Septuagint translators used this title is because the book basically repeats the laws of the covenant already given in Exodus, Leviticus, and Numbers. It is, however, more than simply a repetition of the Law; it is a covenant renewal document. Even more than that, it is Moses' commentary or explanation of the covenant and law.[17] As such, the book of Deuteronomy is like a sermon on the Law (i.e., Ten Commandments), training the reader how to love God with all your heart, soul, and strength (Deut. 6:5) and how to love your neighbor as yourself (Lev. 19:18). The book of Deuteronomy transitions from the wilderness generation to the Promised Land generation. The first generation received the covenant and law while encamped at Mt. Sinai. There they agreed to obey all the stipulations of the covenant. The second generation must likewise know exactly what the covenant is and what laws comprise the stipulations they are to obey. Moses reiterates and renews the covenant with the next generation before they enter the Promised Land. The book of Deuteronomy therefore functions, in a sense, as Israel's constitution. It is foundational to the rest of the Old Testament. We also find it quoted over fifty times in the New Testament. During his temptation, Jesus quoted from Deuteronomy 6–8 in all three refutations of Satan's offer. Jesus, as a prophet, quoted more from Deuteronomy than any other Old Testament book.

The themes and message of Deuteronomy reverberate throughout the prophetic writings. Deuteronomy emphasizes obedience to Yahweh, the covenantal God, by reviewing his faithful actions in the past, by promising future faithfulness, and by declaring blessings for obedience and curses for disobedience. The basic message may be summarized as follows:

1. "I am the LORD your God" (Deut. 4:32–39; 6:4–6).

   - "I, your God, will be faithful, loving, forgiving, providing, and will bless you" (Deut. 7:9–13).

2. "You are my chosen people" (Deut. 7:6–9).

   - "You, my people, are to love, obey, and keep my commandments from one generation to the next" (Deut. 4:5–9).

---

17. Sailhamer, *Pentateuch as Narrative*, 423.

3. "I will abundantly bless you if you obey, but I will discipline you sternly if you disobey" (Deut. 11:26–29; 28:1–68).

Deuteronomy focuses on the contrast and choice between obedience and rebellion, blessings and curses, life and death (Deut. 11:26–28). The entirety of Deuteronomy 28 is dedicated to a detailed list of the blessings for obedience to the covenantal stipulations and the curses for disobedience (cf. Lev. 26:1–39; Deut. 4:15–40).

The blessings only occupy fifteen verses whereas it takes fifty-three verses to spell out the curses. An awareness of Israel's failure is implicit in the length, scope, and severity of the curses, which culminates with the curse of exile (Deut. 28:62–68). Although Deuteronomy anticipates Israel's failure to keep covenantal stipulations (Deut. 31:15–21), it also contains a promise of restoration and the new covenant embedded within this prophecy. Moses, in the context of renewing the covenant, cites the reason for Israel's failure to obey: "the LORD has not given you a heart to understand or eyes to see or ears to hear" (Deut. 29:4). In Deuteronomy 30, however, Moses states that if they turn with all their hearts to God when they are in exile that God will restore them. Furthermore, God promises to "circumcise your heart and the heart of your offspring, so that you will love the LORD your God with all your heart and with all your soul, that you may live" (Deut. 30:6). This prophetic promise of the circumcision of the heart becomes the basis for the notion of a new covenant written inwardly as opposed to the external law written on stone. Just prior to the Babylonian exile, Jeremiah prophesied that God would institute a new covenant whereby God's laws would be written internally on their hearts and minds so that all would know him (Jer. 31:31–34). During the exile, Ezekiel echoes this same concept of an inward cleansing associated with the restoration consisting of the forgiveness of sins and the indwelling of the Holy Spirit: "And I will give you a new heart, and a new spirit I will put within you. And I will remove the heart of stone from your flesh and give you a heart of flesh. And I will put my Spirit within you, and cause you to walk in my statutes and be careful to obey my rules" (Ezek. 36:26–27). So we see that even the prophecies regarding the new covenant fulfilled in Christ are rooted in the Pentateuch.

The prophets speak of God's blessings (positive reinforcement; cf. Lev. 26:1–13; Deut. 4:32–40; 28:1–14) and curses or judgment (negative reinforcement; cf. Lev. 26:14–39; Deut. 4:15–28; 28:15–32:42). These blessings and curses may be condensed into six general categories of blessings (life, health, prosperity, agricultural abundance, respect, and safety) and ten types of punishments (death, disease, drought, dearth, danger, destruction, defeat, deportation, destitution, and disgrace).[18] Many of the prophetic messages, then, contain announcements or warnings directly dependent on these cat-

---

18. Fee and Stuart, *How to Read the Bible*, 191.

egories of blessings and curses. Prophecies that promise a blessing or warn of judgment are all rooted in the soil of the Pentateuch. Because all prophecy is so intimately intertwined with the Pentateuch, it is imperative that we always read prophetic literature within the context of the books of Moses.

The prophetic message may also be set against the backdrop of three prominent themes drawn from the Pentateuch: idolatry, religious formalism, and social justice.[19] The worship of any god other than Yahweh is clearly proscribed in the Pentateuch as *idolatry* (Exod. 20:2–5; Lev. 26:1; Deut. 5:7–9; 27:15). God warned them that they were to drive the Canaanites out of the land lest they take on the religious practices of the people (Exod. 34:11–17; Deut. 18:9–10; 31:16–21; Josh. 24:15–24). Israel, however, did not drive them out and, consequently, did take on many of their practices by worshipping other gods (Judg. 2:19; 2 Kings 16:3; 21:2; Ezek. 20:27–30). In addition, the people focused on practicing *religious formalism* whereby they followed the motions of worshipping God as prescribed in the Law while their hearts were far removed from genuine love and obedience to him (Isa. 29:13; Jer. 6:19–20; Hos. 9:4; Amos 4:4–5; cf. Ps. 51:16–17). A final backdrop for the prophetic message concerns the issue of *social justice* and how failure to obey the law results in the mistreatment and exploitation of the poor, widows, orphans, and foreigners. The law carefully spelled out regulations designed to protect the weak and marginal in society (e.g., Exod. 22:22–25; 23:3–6; Lev. 19:10; 23:22; Deut. 10:18; 15:7–14; 24:17–21). The prophets, then, frequently decried all of these transgressions, warned of impending judgments, and pleaded with the people to repent.

At the risk of over-simplification, the message of the prophets may be encapsulated with three basic points:[20]

1. You have broken the covenant, therefore repent!

2. If you refuse to repent, then judgment!

3. Yet, there is hope beyond the judgment for a glorious, future restoration.

The third point, a future restoration, largely comprises the messianic prophecies and the expectation of a new king and kingdom (Pss. 2; 72; 89; 110; 132; Isa. 4:2; 9:6–7; 11:1; 63:1–6; Jer. 23:5–6; 33:14–16; Ezek. 37:24; Zech. 3:8; 6:12), a new covenant (Isa. 54:10; Jer. 31:31–34; Ezek. 37:26–27), and a new creation (Isa. 65:17; 66:22; Dan. 12:1–3; cf. Rev. 21:1–5). This third category is what we may identify as predictive prophecy, which will occupy the focus of the remaining chapters. In addition to these three points,

---

19. J. Scott Duvall and J. Daniel Hays, *Grasping God's Word: A Hands-On Approach to Reading, Interpreting, and Applying the Bible*, 3rd ed. (Grand Rapids: Zondervan, 2012), 401–3.
20. Ibid., 403.

the prophetic message contains other themes that resonate and reverberate throughout their writings. One of the more foundational themes is that God is the Sovereign Lord of history and controls the course of people, nations, and events (Isa. 10:5–15; Ezek. 38:3–16; 39:2–3; Hab. 1:5–17). Prophets often proclaim the need to be right with God (Isa. 30:15; Amos 4:6–12) and the need for morality in religion and society (Jer. 7:1–15). All of these themes intertwine as the prophets announce their messages of judgment and salvation (Isa. 6:13; 28:5; 29:5; 31:5; Amos 9:11–15).

When it comes to the study of the prophetic books, one must think of the message as an oracle or sermon usually conforming to particular patterns or forms. For our purposes, we may group the forms of prophetic oracles under the two broad categories of "announcements of judgment" and "oracles of salvation."[21] The original form of prophetic judgment speech is the "judgment speech to individuals" which consists of an accusation detailing the grounds for judgment and an announcement of future judgment. The formula of a judgment speech coheres with this basic format:[22]

1. The introduction may report the messenger's commissioning or include a summons to hear (Isa. 1:10; Jer. 2:1–2; Amos 4:1–2; Mic. 3:1–2, 9).

2. The accusation may consist of a series of interrogatives or an indictment declaring the guilt of sin (Isa. 7:13; 37:23–29; Jer. 22:15–17; Mic. 2:2).

3. The announcement of judgment often appears simply as a statement of future disaster. The prophet may attach a sign to demonstrate the prophecy's authenticity, since the announced judgment may not occur immediately. The announcement sometimes alludes to the accusation, demonstrating the correspondence of offense and punishment (Isa. 8:7–8; 30:13–14; Jer. 20:4; 28:16; 36:30–31; Amos 4:2–3).

4. Sometimes, but not always, the oracle includes a plea for repentance coupled with stated blessings for obedience (Ezek. 18:30; Joel 2:12–14; Hos. 2:2–3).

This basic structure, however, occurs in a variety of forms such as "woe," "destruction," "dirge," and more commonly as a "covenant lawsuit."

---

21. Claus Westermann, *Basic Forms of Prophetic Speech*, trans. H. C. White (Louisville: Westminster John Knox, 1991); idem, *Prophetic Oracles of Salvation in the Old Testament*, trans. Keith Crim (Louisville: Westminster John Knox, 1991).

22. Ibid., 142–62.

Oracles of salvation function as the positive counterpart to the announcements of judgment by announcing hope for the future. These prophecies announce God's deliverance after a time of experiencing his judgment. What we often see is a pattern of sin, judgment, repentance, and restoration. The major emphasis is on the grace, mercy, and faithfulness of God to his covenant people. The form of the salvation oracles is best recognized as containing one or more of the following elements:[23]

1. A reference to the future. The future time may be near in respect to the life of the individual or nation, or it may be more distant (Isa. 52:4–13; Jer. 30:8; Ezek. 20:32–38; Amos 9:11).

2. A promise of deliverance, salvation, and/or restoration. These promises include deliverance from an oppressing enemy, a return to the land after the exile, and a new creation (Isa. 43:16–21; 48:20–21; 65:17; Jer. 29:10–14).

3. An announcement of blessings. The blessings correspond to the Deuteronomic categories of life, health, prosperity, agricultural abundance, respect, and safety (Isa. 65:9–24; Amos 9:11–15).

Many salvation oracles look to the distant or eschatological future, including those featuring the new exodus motif (e.g., Isa. 51:4–11; Jer. 23:3–8; Ezek. 37:18–20). Such prophecies deal with the establishment of God's kingdom on earth. They not only tell of a future deliverance but contain an announcement of universal judgment. These judgments may deal with the future in such a way that they predict a series of judgments to prepare for the final era of blessing. Many of these oracles were fulfilled with the restoration from exile, others were fulfilled in the finished work of Christ, and yet others still await fulfillment.

The prophetic ministry and prophecy continue in the New Testament.[24] This is evidenced by the ongoing presence of people engaged in prophetic ministry. We see this with Elizabeth (Luke 1:41–45), Zechariah (Luke 1:67–69), Simeon (Luke 2:25–35), and Anna (Luke 2:36–38) in their prophetic utterances surrounding the birth of Christ. During his ministry, John the Baptist was recognized as a prophet by his contemporaries (Matt. 11:9; 14:5) and functioned like a prophet when exhorting his hearers to repent,

---

23. Fee and Stuart, *How to Read the Bible*, 202.
24. See the important contributions of David E. Aune, *Prophecy in Early Christianity and the Ancient Mediterranean World* (Grand Rapids: Eerdmans, 1983); David Hill, *New Testament Prophecy*, New Foundations Theological Library (Atlanta: John Knox, 1979); Wayne Grudem, *The Gift of Prophecy in the New Testament and Today* (Westchester, IL: Crossway, 1988).

warning them of impending judgment (Matt. 3:1–12). Jesus was a prophet whose predictions of the destruction of the temple came to pass when not one stone was left upon another (Matt. 24:2; Mark 13:2; Luke 21:6, 20).[25] We also see that prophecy is a main component of the gift of the Holy Spirit in his descent at Pentecost (Acts 2:17–18; cf. Joel 2:28). The book of Acts makes mention of important prophets in the early church such as Agabus (Acts 11:27–28; 13:1; 21:10), Judas and Silas (Acts 15:32), and the daughters of Philip (Acts 21:9). One may argue that in a sense Paul's whole ministry was prophetic due to the fact he had the gift of prophecy (e.g., 1 Cor. 14:37–38; 2 Cor. 12:9; cf. Gal. 1:18).[26] We also see that in the book of Revelation not only did John draw upon the writings of the prophets as background for the composition of his apocalyptic vision, but he wrote in the same tradition as the prophets. What is more, prophecy was considered an important gift in the early church (cf. 1 Cor. 12:28; Eph. 2:20; 3:5; 4:11). Therefore, it is safe to say that prophecy was alive and well during the formation of the New Testament as well as the Old Testament.

Although prophecy continues in the New Testament, it has several distinctions from prophecy in the Old Testament that will be fleshed out more fully throughout this book. The first is that New Testament prophecy tends to be more universal in nature in light of the new covenant inclusion of Gentiles into the people of God (cf. Matt. 21:43–44; Luke 12:8–10; John 3:14–21; Rom. 11:25–26; Eph. 2:11–22).[27] As a result, there is more of a focus on the nations being the recipients of God's message than there is on the ethnic nation of Israel. Second, the structure of New Testament prophecy is not as clearly defined as it is in the Old Testament.[28] Rather than entire books and sections of prophetic literature, we are more likely to find isolated passages and a smattering of prophetic texts scattered throughout the New Testament. David Aune helpfully suggests three specific criteria for isolating cases of prophetic speech: (1) material that is distinctly attributed to a supernatural being; (2) predictive material that the speaker could not have known by ordinary means; and (3) the presence of some specific formula identifying prophetic speech.[29] Finally, the majority of prophecy is fulfilled in Christ, but we still look to the future consummation of the Kingdom and the end of the age. It is this last point that we believe warrants the need for clarification regarding biblical prophecy and the fulfillment of future predictions.

---

25. On Jesus as a prophet, see especially N. T. Wright, *Jesus and the Victory of God* (Minneapolis: Fortress, 1996), 147–97.

26. Ben Witherington III, *The Paul Quest: The Renewed Search for the Jew of Tarsus* (Downers Grove, IL: InterVarsity, 1998), 130–73.

27. Köstenberger and Patterson, *Invitation to Biblical Interpretation*, 343.

28. Ibid.

29. Aune, *Prophecy in Early Christianity*, 247–48.

Prophecy as Poetry and Prose

The genre of prophetic literature could be thought of as a multifaceted gemstone. When you look closely at a diamond set in a ring, you will observe that the surface of the diamond is covered with several geometrically arranged flat surfaces called facets. Each one of these facets catches and reflects light in a stunning display causing the gemstone to sparkle. A faceted gemstone evinces a complex character that derives from the intricate interplay of multifarious angles, edges, and shapes. Its beauty and complexity may only be fully appreciated when one carefully inspects all the details and subtle nuances of each cut. Prophecy, like a gemstone, is a literary genre faceted with a myriad of types, forms, and subgenres. Individual oracles, narratives, and vision reports exhibit formal features that cast the prophet's message in distinctive lights. Whereas a lapidist (i.e., one who cuts and polishes gemstones) uses angles, lines, and flat surfaces to create specific contours, the prophet uses subgenres, literary conventions, and figurative language. So when one approaches prophecy, its meaning and message will sparkle most clearly when held up to the light of careful attention to the details and subtle nuances through literary analysis. Our understanding of the genre to which a particular text belongs shapes the expectations regarding how the text should be read. We recognize, however, that a great fluidity and overlap exists among all the subgenres of prophecy such that some measure of flexibility is required when it comes to the identification of specific forms of genre.

From a literary perspective, written prophecy alternates between prose and poetry. The sections written in prose contain narrative reports related to the life and ministry of the prophet (e.g., commission, activities, symbolic acts, and vision reports) as well as historical narratives regarding Israel, Judah, or the nations. Narratives most often appear in order to add background details or heighten dramatic tension for theological purposes. In these instances the narrative contains detailed accounts of speeches and dialogues that comprise the scenes or episodes, which make up the full story. As Robert Alter observes, "The biblical writers . . . are often less concerned with actions in themselves than with how [an] individual character responds to actions or produces them; and direct speech is made the chief instrument for revealing the varied and at times nuanced relations of the personages to the actions in which they are implicated."[30] Therefore, the narrative material is not only factual information but also theological and doxological (giving praise to God), didactic (to teach proper faith and conduct), as well as aesthetically constructed (as a pleasing literary work).[31]

---

30. Robert Alter, *The Art of Biblical Narrative* (New York: Basic Books, 1981), 66.
31. Tremper Longman III, *Literary Approaches to Biblical Interpretation* (Grand Rapids: Zondervan, 1987), 68–71.

Prophets did not communicate in the straightforward terminology of the law codes or use the cerebral language of logical discourse; instead, they spoke for God in the most convincing, emotive, and memorable way possible—through poetry. David Freedman states that most of the prophets were poets and "their oracles were delivered and have been preserved in poetic form."[32] They predominately couched their message and oracles in poetry. Concerning the prominence of poetry, Alter has eloquently remarked, "Since poetry is our best model of intricately rich communication, not only solemn, weighty, and forceful but also densely woven with intricate internal connections, meanings, and implications, it makes sense that divine speech should be represented as poetry."[33] This formal awareness has implications for reading prophecy because poetry has certain characteristics and one misunderstand the prophecy if he or she is not aware of certain poetic conventions.[34] Because poetry is less precise and sometimes ambiguous, some interpreters have struggled with how to approach it.[35] Hebrew poetry exhibits features found in all poetry: *terseness, structure,* and *figurative imagery.*[36]

Its *terseness* is evident in that poetry expresses ideas with a minimum of words. The power and impact of poetry does not reside in a quantity of words, but in the quality of how well those few words communicate imagery and meaning. While terseness is part and parcel of the poetic genre, it also helps to accomplish the emotive aspect that impacts the reader. The poet has felt an emotion, observed an event of importance, or considered a worthy idea, and desires that the recipient share the same emotion, excitement, or dread that gripped the writer. We are drawn into his or her experience or perspective and gain wisdom by it. With Moses we rejoice in Yahweh's triumph at the Red Sea (Exod. 15), we celebrate with Hannah at the birth of her son (1 Sam. 2), and we share with David in both victory (2 Sam. 22; Ps. 18) and defeat (Ps. 51). Through Isaiah we recognize the terror of Yahweh's judgment (Isa. 12–24) and the wonder of his salvation by the work of the suffering servant (Isa. 53). With Jeremiah we mourn the loss of Jerusalem (Lamentations) and rejoice at the restoration (Jer. 31:1–22).

All poetry also uses a specific *structure* to communicate its message. It is important to observe that *parallelism* is the chief characteristic of Hebrew

32. David N. Freedman, "Pottery, Poetry and Prophecy: An Essay on Biblical Poetry," in *Pottery, Poetry, and Prophecy,* ed. David Noel Freedman (Winona Lake, IN: Eisenbrauns, 1980), 18.
33. Robert Alter, *The Art of Biblical Poetry* (New York: Basic Books, 1987), 141.
34. For some helpful guides to reading Hebrew poetry, see Adele Berlin, "Introduction to Hebrew Poetry," in *The New Interpreter's Bible,* vol. 4 (Nashville: Abingdon, 1996), 301–15; David Petersen and K. Richards, *Interpreting Hebrew Poetry* (Minneapolis: Fortress, 1992); James Kugel, *The Idea of Biblical Poetry: Parallelism and Its History* (New Haven: Yale University Press, 1981), 40–45.
35. Louis A. Markos, "Poetry-Phobic: Why Evangelicals Should Love Language That Is Slippery," *Christianity Today* (October 1, 2001), 66; W. B. Stanford, *Enemies of Poetry* (London: Routledge & Kegan Paul, 1980). See also D. Brent Sandy, *Plowshares and Pruning Hooks: Rethinking the Language of Biblical Prophecy and Apocalyptic* (Downers Grove, IL: InterVarsity, 2002), 158.
36. Duvall and Hayes, *Grasping God's Word,* 370–71.

poetry rather than the features we usually associate with poetry (rhyme, cadence, plays on words).[37] Parallelism in Hebrew poetry presents a balance of one idea with another idea. Rather than writing in a single sentence, the poet would write a couplet. The relationship of these two "lines" of Hebrew poetry is usually expressed in specific categories. Although more specialized categories exist, these are the most common:

1. *Synonymous*: The second line repeats the thought in other words (e.g., Ps. 114:2; 51:7).

2. *Antithetic*: The second line states a contrary thought or takes up a different or opposing issue, theme, or referent (e.g., Ps. 1:6; 18:18).

3. *Synthetic*: The second line extends the thought of the first line by adding a new idea or nuances a stated idea (e.g., Ps. 9:19; 32:4).

4. *Formal*: The parallelism is one of form only. The verse is simply a single sentence. In the printed Hebrew Bible the sentence is divided into two halves but two ideas are not present (e.g., Ps. 2:6; 110:1).

The prophets used parallelism to their advantage by often saying the same thing more than once, but with different images and different emphases (e.g., Zeph. 2:13–15). Merely observing and identifying parallelism is of little value in and of itself. When applied to interpreting prophetic oracles, it enables us to see the relationship between ideas, concepts and words. The concept of line balance is so pervasive in Semitic poetry that two lines with two statements placed together must be related in some way and are not merely independent thoughts written side by side. The content of one line bears on the interpretation of the other.

Poetry also employs figures of speech or unusual uses of words to communicate concepts through *figurative imagery*. We use these figures of speech on a daily basis in English. One may commonly hear phrases like "cart before the horse," "pave the way," "off the cuff," "between a rock and a hard place," "a smoking gun," or "circle the wagons." Osborne states that "figurative expressions associate a concept with a pictorial or analogous representation of its meaning in order to add richness to the statement."[38] We use these terms and phrases in a non-literal or metaphorical manner to express an idea by comparing it to something else. A figure of speech is a use of language in which there is a comparison, either stated or implied, between two terms. Ian Paul explains

---

37. Bishop Robert Lowth made the first formal presentation of this poetic feature in his *De Sacra Poesi Hebraeorum* (1753).

38. Osborne, *Hermeneutical Spiral*, 105.

that all figures of speech share the same basic feature whereby two terms are brought together that have different, apparently distinct ranges of meaning to express something new.[39] Keep in mind that "literal" and "metaphorical" are terms which describe types of language that have very little to do with the truth or falsity of what we say or the existence or non-existence of the things we refer to.[40] In fact, Leland Ryken goes so far as to state that metaphor and simile are not merely poetic devices, but "a new way of thinking and formulating reality."[41]

To appreciate the complexity of biblical figures of speech, we can turn to E. W. Bullinger's seminal 1898 volume, *Figures of Speech Used in the Bible: Explained and Illustrated.* Bullinger states that there are 200 different types of figures of speech in the Bible.[42] Figures of speech abound in the poetical books and prophetic sections of the Old Testament. In some examples, the figures of speech may be fairly easy to grasp:[43]

"I will sweep it with the broom of destruction" (Isa. 14:23) = Babylon will be utterly destroyed.

"Your neck is an iron sinew and your forehead brass" (Isa. 48:4) = Israel is stubborn.

"These are a smoke in my nostrils, a fire that burns all the day" (Isa. 65:5) = God's people are sinful and obstinate and continue to offer sacrifices, but God is not pleased by them.

At other times, the intended figurative meaning is more challenging to discern:

"Behold, one shall fly swiftly like an eagle and spread his wings against Moab" (Jer. 48:40) = Moab will fall quickly in battle due to God's judgment.

"The sea has come up on Babylon; she is covered with its tumultuous waves" (Jer. 51:42) = This in some way relates to the judgment of Babylon at the end of the exile.

---

39. Ian Paul, "Metaphor," in *Dictionary for Theological Interpretation of the Bible*, ed. Kevin J. Vanhoozer, et al. (Grand Rapids: Baker, 2005), 507.
40. G. B. Caird, *The Language and Imagery of the Bible* (Grand Rapids: Eerdmans, 1980), 131.
41. Leland Ryken, *Words of Delight: A Literary Introduction to the Bible*, 2nd ed. (Grand Rapids: Baker, 1992), 169. See also idem, "'I Have Used Similitudes': The Poetry of the Bible," *BSac* 147 (July 1990): 259–69.
42. E. W. Bullinger, *Figures of Speech Used in the Bible: Explained and Illustrated* (London: Eyre and Spottiswoode, 1898; repr. Grand Rapids: Baker, 1968), xix–xlvi.
43. The following examples are all adapted from Sandy, *Plowshares and Pruning Hooks*, 38–39.

> "I will destroy your mother" (Hos. 4:5) = Here "mother" is a
> metaphor for Israel (cf. Hos. 2:4–5).

Keep in mind, however, that not everything the prophets declared was entirely figurative:

> "I will give all Judah into the hand of the king of Babylon.
> He shall carry them captive to Babylon" (Jer. 20:4) = This
> prophecy was fulfilled literally in 586 bc.

> "A remnant will return" (Isa. 10:21) = This was intended literally, as indeed a smaller group did return to Jerusalem when
> Cyrus released the Jews.

> "Your ancient ruins shall be rebuilt" (Isa. 58:12) = Although
> this figuratively points to their spiritual condition, it was fulfilled literary as depicted in Ezra-Nehemiah.

Together these examples demonstrate the rich, complex, diverse, and figurative nature of prophetic speech.

Prophecy and Apocalyptic Writings

Prophecy covers a broad range of forms and genres spanning a spectrum of methods for communicating divine revelation to mankind. Prophecy was *oral* in that prophets usually proclaimed messages in a straightforward manner that condemned sin and called for repentance. Prophecy was also a *literary* product as prophets composed documents using poetry and prose in which the message was presented through propositions and narratives. Furthermore, prophecy often involved highly *visual* presentations invoking the senses and graphically portraying the intended message. The visual mode of prophecy most frequently corresponds to how the prophet received the message through a dream or vision. Visionary revelations transcend the boundaries of normal experiences by transporting the reader into the realm of supernatural beings, strange creatures, and cryptic images of events and institutions. The nature, language, and content of these visionary revelations distinguish these writings as apocalyptic. When exploring the landscape of biblical prophecy, we find these visionary passages most prominently in Isaiah, Ezekiel, Daniel, and Zechariah in the Old Testament (e.g. Isa. 24–27; Ezek. 38–39; Dan. 7; Joel 2:28–32; 3:9–17; and Zech. 1–6, 12–14) and, in the New Testament, in the book of Revelation.

Prophets sometimes received their message through dreams and visions so that their writings contain strange images and language. The type of prophecy characterized by dreams or visions and filled with highly symbolic images is often called *apocalyptic*. This term denotes a type of revelatory prophecy exhibiting odd images, angelic beings, glimpses of the heavenly world and other such strange content, making it difficult to understand.[44] It is helpful to distinguish between the terms (1) *apocalypse*; (2) *apocalyptic*; and (3) *apocalypticism*. *Apocalypse* normally refers to a genre of literature that is exclusively about a vision or dream and was written between approximately 200 BC and AD 200.[45] The adjective *apocalyptic* is used when describing characteristics of the visionary and prophetic literary genre or worldview. *Apocalypticism*, finally, denotes a worldview, ideology, or theology merging the eschatological aims of particular groups into a cosmic and political arena.

Portions of Isaiah, Ezekiel, Zechariah and Daniel are the earliest occurrences of apocalyptic material in the biblical canon. Apocalyptic literature owes its existence to prophecy and it should be regarded as a prophetic subgenre. Not all prophecy is apocalyptic, but all apocalyptic is prophetic in nature. Due to the intimate relationship between prophecy and apocalyptic we will use the designation prophetic-apocalyptic for canonical writings in this genre. Entire works of the apocalyptic genre, known as apocalypses, did not appear until after the Old Testament era during the intertestamental period. Jewish apocalyptic literature flourished during the Second Temple period, especially between 200 BC and AD 200, and is preserved in a group of collected writings known as the Pseudepigrapha.[46] The Olivet Discourse (Matt. 24:1–31; Mark 13; Luke 21:5–32), often referred to as "the little apocalypse," comprises Jesus' apocalyptic expectations in the Synoptic Gospels. Apocalyptic language and images appear scattered throughout the New Testament letters. The epistle to the Hebrews, for example, exhibits an apocalyptic worldview contrasting the temporary earthly institutions with eternal heavenly realities. 2 Peter 3 also represents eschatological expectations expressed in terms of apocalyptic imagery (i.e., the earth and all the elements consumed by fire). The book of Revelation is the only book in the New Testament that is entirely prophetic-apocalyptic.

The exact identification and the development of a definition for the apocalyptic genre is not an easy task given its subject matter.[47] Early studies sought to identify the genre based on certain *formal features* like pseudonymity, visionary accounts, and historical reviews. They also recognized a particu-

---

44. See Alan Bandy's contribution in Köstenberger and Patterson, *Invitation to Biblical Interpretation*, 22, 517–63.
45. John J. Collins, *The Apocalyptic Imagination*, 2nd ed. (Grand Rapids: Eerdmans, 1998), 21.
46. James Charlesworth, ed., *The Old Testament Pseudepigrapha*, vol. 1: *Apocalyptic Literature and Testaments* (Peabody, MA: Hendrickson, 2010).
47. See the survey by David Mathewson, "Revelation in Recent Genre Criticism: Some Implications for Interpretation," *TrinJ* 13 (1992): 193–213.

lar *doctrinal content* expressing a doctrine of two ages, pessimism and hope, universalism, and imminent expectation of the end. The classic and abiding definition for the apocalyptic genre was written by John J. Collins, in conjunction with a group of scholars, in 1979:

> "Apocalypse" is a genre of revelatory literature with a narrative framework, in which a revelation is mediated by an otherworldly being to a human recipient, disclosing a transcendent reality which is both temporal, insofar as it envisages eschatological salvation, and spatial, insofar as it involves another, supernatural world.[48]

This definition emphasized the *form* as a narrative framework involving an otherworldly mediator and the *content* as containing both temporal (eschatological salvation) and spatial (supernatural world) elements. It was later amended to include a statement regarding the *function* of an apocalypse as "intended to interpret present, earthly circumstances in light of the supernatural world and of the future, and to influence the understanding and behavior of the audience by means of divine authority."[49] While these definitions reflect a broad range of writings from canonical, extra-biblical, rabbinical, and sectarian examples of apocalyptic literature, not all apocalyptic writings contain all of these characteristics all the time.[50]

The apocalyptic genre contains visionary accounts, otherworldly mediators, and symbolic language that expresses a content emphasizing certain heavenly realities in contrast to earthly circumstances as a means to encourage godly behavior and enduring faithfulness even in the midst of suffering or a perceived crisis.

What makes something apocalyptic is that it is a visionary or revelatory means of communication. Apocalyptic literature contains a visual revelation of a spiritual encounter recorded by a seer or prophet. It tends to be written in an autobiographical style and told as a story of the prophet's experiences in the vision. Unlike other forms of prophecy it usually involves the use of spiritual beings and angels who speak, interpret, and guide the prophet through the vision. Although it is a visionary narrative with a high degree of symbolism, it is filled with prophetic instructions for the audience to behave or respond to the vision in a particular manner. The most unmistakable and challenging

---

48. John J. Collins, "Introduction: Towards the Morphology of a Genre," *Sem* 14 (1979): 9.
49. Adela Yarbro Collins, "Introduction: Early Christian Apocalypticism," *Sem* 36 (1986): 7.
50. Collins, *Apocalyptic Imagination*, 5–9. For example, although Revelation is written in a narrative framework recounting an otherworldly journey, it is not pseudonymous, because the author identifies himself as "John" (1:1, 4, 9; 22:8) rather than as a revered historical character such as Enoch.

feature of apocalyptic literature is the ubiquitous use of symbolic, figurative, and metaphorical language. The abundance of symbols, metaphors, and various figures of speech are what gives apocalyptic writing its distinctive flavor. Just about anything can be given a symbolic connotation. Human beings, angelic beings, animals, and descriptions of heavenly bodies all serve as symbolic representations of spiritual truths. These symbolic images may even express historical, contemporary, or future events in ways that resound with cosmic significance. By using symbols and metaphors when describing these cosmic scenarios, apocalyptic writing peers behind the veil concealing the heavenly activity surrounding historical and future events. As such, apocalyptic writings often convey a *dualism* that compares or contrasts earthly and heavenly realities. From an apocalyptic perspective the earthly situations are depicted as temporary and transitory in light of the enduring and eternal realities of the spiritual world. Although some scholars downplay the eschatological nature of the visions, apocalyptic literature provides a provocative and effective vehicle for communicating end-time expectations. Most apocalyptic writings are permeated by the belief that God is sovereign over history and will radically intervene in the near future to consummate his plans for all creation.

Prophecy and the Challenge of Symbolism[51]

How one approaches the interpretation of the symbolic imagery significantly influences the way one reads the prophetic message of a given book. This task is complicated by the fact that not everyone agrees on the nature of apocalyptic language and imagery. This tension results in two major competing hermeneutical approaches: (1) *primarily literal and secondarily symbolic*; or (2) *primarily symbolic and secondarily literal.* We will use the book of Revelation as a test case to highlight the differences between these two approaches.

The first approach advocates interpreting writings like the book of Revelation primarily in a literal manner unless it is impossible to do so. This view is encapsulated in the hermeneutical dictum, "When the plain sense of Scripture makes common sense, seek no other sense."[52] While still recognizing the presence of symbols, this view restricts the identification of a symbol to something that is incomprehensible if understood literally (e.g., Jesus does not have a literal sword protruding from his mouth).[53] One popular proponent of this approach,

---

51. This section is a revision of Alan S. Bandy, "The Hermeneutics of Symbolism: How to Interpret the Symbols of John's Apocalypse," *SBJT* 14, no. 1 (2010): 46–58.
52. David L. Cooper, "An Exposition of the Book of Revelation: The Great Parenthesis," *Biblical Research Monthly* (May 1954): 84.
53. John F. Walvoord, "The Theological Context of Premillennialism," *BSac* 150 (October-December 1993): 390; Roy B. Zuck, *Basic Bible Interpretation: A Practical Guide to Discovering Biblical Truth* (Wheaton, IL: Victor Books, 1991), 146. Zuck offers six guidelines for interpreting figurative language: (1) always take a passage in the literal sense unless there is good reason to do so otherwise; (2) the figurative sense is

Tim LaHaye, maintains that we must "take every word at its primary, ordinary, usual, literal meaning unless the facts of the immediate text, studied in the light of related passages and axiomatic and fundamental truths, clearly indicate otherwise."[54] These interpreters, usually classic or revised dispensationalists,[55] argue that non-literal interpretations result in overly subjective interpretations.[56] Charles Ryrie warned, "If one does not use the plain, normal, or literal method of interpretation, all objectivity is lost."[57]

These interpreters exhibit a tendency to look for the meaning of Revelation's symbols through the lenses of current events as if these symbols were intended to refer to aspects unique only to our modern setting. Literalistic interpretations typically maintain that the figures of speech (i.e., symbols and metaphors) are a result of John's attempt to describe future objects and scenarios from the limited framework of his ancient conceptions and language. It is as if John experienced some sort of spiritual time travel that propelled him into the modern world with its technologically advanced weaponry, banking, and satellite communications. The goal for interpreting the symbols, then, is to identify the one-to-one correspondence between the textual image and a modern parallel (e.g., the locusts are Apache attack helicopters, the mark of the beast is an implanted micro-chip, and the European Union is the revived Roman empire). The merits of this approach are that it takes the text at face value, avoids reducing it to an extended allegory, and often renders a simple straightforward interpretation. While this principle may sufficiently work in narrative and didactic genres, its application to highly figurative genres like apocalyptic literature proves problematic.

The problem with this approach is rooted in the principle that the literary genre establishes the rules for how one interprets a specific text. Meaning is intrinsically bound up in genre. The ensuing implication is that genre provides

intended if the literal would involve an impossibility; (3) the figurative is intended if the literal meaning is an absurdity; (4) take the figurative sense if the literal would demand immoral action; (5) note whether a figurative expression is followed by an explanatory literal statement; and (6) sometimes a figure is marked by a qualifying adjective, as in "Heavenly Father" (Matt. 6:14).

54. Tim LaHaye, *Revelation Unveiled* (Grand Rapids: Zondervan, 1999), 17.
55. Dispensational futurism, associated with dispensational premillennialism, began with the teachings of J. N. Darby that were popularized in America by C. Larkin, D. L. Moody, C. I. Scofield, and L. S. Chafer. The twentieth century witnessed the development of dispensationalism into three distinct expressions: (1) *classic* dispensationalism (Darby, Scofield, Chafer); (2) *revised* dispensationalism (J. Walvoord, C. Ryrie, D. Pentecost, T. LaHaye, and R. Thomas); and (3) *progressive* dispensationalism (D. Bock, C. Blaising, R. Saucy, and M. Pate). The distinguishing difference between classic/revised and progressive dispensationalism is hermeneutical. The hermeneutical hallmark of classic dispensationalism is a consistent and insistent commitment to the literal interpretation of prophetic Scripture. This hermeneutical approach has resulted in a particular theological system that makes a strict and consistent distinction between Israel and the church. The church is merely a parenthesis inserted between God's dealings with Israel, and thus the book of Revelation focuses on the future of ethnic and national Israel.
56. John F. Walvoord, *The Revelation of Jesus Christ* (Chicago: Moody, 1966), 30.
57. Charles C. Ryrie, *Dispensationalism* (Chicago: Moody, 1995), 29.

a context, assigned by the author, to communicate meaning. Since the book of Revelation begins with the word "apocalypse" (*apokalypsis*; 1:1) and, given the use of apocalyptic language and imagery, this word is often understood by some to be an immediate genre classification. Regardless of the extent to which one would classify it as an apocalypse proper, the book of Revelation belongs to the highly symbolic nature of the prophetic-apocalyptic genre. Therefore, it was not intended to be interpreted in a strictly literal manner, but rather as a way of communicating literal truth through symbolism and figurative language.

A rigid literal (literalistic) interpretation or *literalism* may inadvertently obscure the author's intended meaning. Kevin Vanhoozer correctly poses a distinction between the *literal sense* and *literalism*.[58] If the interpreter is concerned with authorial intention, the literal sense must not be reduced merely to letters or words. He argues, "literalistic reading is less than fully 'literal'—that it is insufficiently and only 'thinly' literal—insofar as it ignores the role of authorial intentions and communicative acts."[59] The *literal* sense relates to what the author intended for the meaning of the text, and this is especially true for figurative and symbolic images. In other words, if Revelation is prophetic or apocalyptic, approaching its numbers, proper nouns, and the vast array of other visionary images in a literalistic manner may prevent understanding John's intended meaning—the literal sense, properly understood. A more profitable hermeneutical approach is to reverse the interpretive order by placing the symbolic in the foreground while shifting the literal into the background.

Greg Beale makes the case for giving primacy to the symbolic instead of looking for a straight one-to-one literal correspondence.[60] He argues that the word "signify" (*sēmainō*) in Revelation 1:1 conveys the idea of "communicate by symbols."[61] The basic glosses for *sēmainō* are "to make known," "to report," or "to signify,"[62] but Revelation 1:1 alludes to Daniel 2:28–30, 45 (LXX) where the word translated *signified* denotes a symbolic communication by means of a dream or vision. Nebuchadnezzar's dream of the colossal statue, then, is clearly visual, but it is a picture with symbolic meaning embedded in it. Although *sēmainō* occurs with the general sense of "make known," its normal usage in Scripture typically implies some type of "symbolic communication."[63] In Revelation 1:1, the connotation of "communicate by symbols" is not only confirmed by the allusion to Daniel 2, but also by its use in conjunction with "show" (*deiknymi*) indicating the visual nature of the revelation. Since the book of Revelation communicates symbolically, the literalistic approach for interpreting the "plain sense" of an image may actually distort the intended mean-

---

58. Kevin J. Vanhoozer, *Is There a Meaning in This Text?* (Grand Rapids: Zondervan, 1998), 310.
59. Ibid., 311.
60. G. K. Beale, *The Book of Revelation*, NIGTC (Grand Rapids: Eerdmans, 1999), 50–55.
61. Ibid., 52.
62. BDAG, 920.
63. Beale, *Book of Revelation*, 51.

ing of the text. Beale qualifies his approach by stating, "Of course, some parts are not symbolic, but the essence of the book is figurative. *Where there is lack of clarity about whether something is symbolic, the scales of judgment should be tilted in the direction of a nonliteral analysis.*"[64] We would elevate the primacy of the symbolic imagery, but without reducing symbols to a mere literary reference. As such, we also seek to identify the theological and/or physical realities of the historical and/or future referents behind the symbol.

Conclusion

The correct interpretation of prophecy is not an easy task. The slightest misinterpretation may result in a misunderstanding. Like the biblical interpreters of Jesus' day, we may get much correct and still miss the main point altogether. While we have Jesus, the Holy Spirit, and the teachings of the apostles to guide us in our interpretation of biblical prophecy, there are a number of interpretive challenges that we need to consider for a careful, balanced, and informed understanding of prophetic texts. It seems that the majority of misinterpretations stem from the nature of the prophetic genre and how it communicates truth through figures of speech, metaphors, and symbols. The failure to grasp the way prophecy communicates through figurative language in its literary context is further compounded by a neglect of understanding prophecy within its historical context. Grappling with figurative language is part and parcel of the larger process of biblical interpretation as a whole. We do not suppose that our discussion of interpretive challenges in this chapter resolves all the difficulties and challenges in every prophetic text. We chose to focus on the issues that are most directly responsible for interpretive differences and misunderstanding. Our purpose is to offer a hermeneutically informed understanding with which to approach prophetic and apocalyptic biblical texts.

---

64. Ibid., 52 (emphasis added).

Chapter 3

Biblical Theology and Prophecy

Biblical theology is important to the study of prophecy because we assume that God's purpose of redemption is unified.

Many Christians have been implicitly trained to read the Bible atomistically. That is, they read a passage of Scripture in isolation without the knowledge of how it fits into the larger framework of salvation history. We are accustomed to daily devotionals and topical sermons that rarely pay any attention to the context or to how the passage fits into God's overall plan to redeem humanity through Jesus Christ. Biblical theology gives us the big picture of God's plan, allowing us to fit each text into the grand narrative of redemptive history.

Without the big picture of redemptive history and proper understanding of the nature of biblical prophecy, it is difficult (and sometimes impossible) to comprehend how prophecy will be fulfilled. Oftentimes, a prophecy is vague or expressed in the distinctive language of the original audience. Biblical revelation does not come to us simply as a list of timeless principles (though it contains timeless principles), but as a story. It is a story of how God chose to redeem mankind through his Son, Jesus Christ. It is a story that is full of diversity and variety while at the same time it unfolds the unified plan of God. Biblical theology emphasizes this unified plan of God, not by ignoring its diversity, but by highlighting its main storyline in the midst of diversity. In this chapter we will provide the larger framework for interpreting prophecy. We will accomplish this by first defining "biblical theology" and then discussing the various presuppositions of biblical theology, demonstrating how Jesus is the center of redemptive history and therefore the fulfillment of the most significant prophecies in the Bible.

What is Biblical Theology?

The origin of biblical theology as a distinct discipline in biblical studies is usually traced to J. P. Gabler's inaugural lecture at the University of Altdorf (1787) entitled, "An Oration on the Proper Distinction between Biblical and Dog-

matic Theology and the Specific Objectives of Each." Gabler was committed to
rationalism, rejecting the notion that the Bible is God's inspired and infallible
Word. His goal was to stop the endless debates among systematic theologians
whose focus on confessions and philosophy kept them several steps removed
from the Bible. He argued that a close inductive study of the biblical texts
would bring greater unanimity among scholars. He wanted a strict separation
of this "biblical theology" (as he called it) from dogmatics (systematic theology)
and church tradition. Gabler's admonition helped create this new discipline,
but the end result was the further specialization and isolation of the various
disciplines. Fast-forwarding to the mid-twentieth century, we find a revival of
biblical theology among many scholars who were influenced by neo-orthodoxy
and who embraced higher criticism. Their versions of biblical theology offered
some helpful corrections but were insufficient.[1]

Although there is debate as to the precise meaning and purpose of biblical theology, there are several factors that are found in most definitions. After
offering several definitions below, we will highlight four key presuppositions
which we believe are key to biblical theology.

> Biblical Theology . . . is nothing else than the exhibition of
> the organic progress of supernatural revelation in its historic
> continuity and multiformity.[2]

> Biblical Theology . . . [is] the ordered study of the under-
> standing of the revelation of God contained in the canonical
> scriptures of the Old and New Testaments.[3]

> Biblical theology [is the] discussion of what the Bible teaches
> about God and his dealings with human beings and the rest of
> creation. . . . Biblical theology opens up the unity of the Bible
> by exposing and collecting its major themes. It demonstrates
> the many ways in which diverse books and material are united
> by the character of God the Father, Son, and Holy Spirit.[4]

1. See, e.g., Brevard Childs, *Biblical Theology of the Old and New Testaments: Theological Reflections on the Christian Bible* (Minneapolis: Fortress, 1992).
2. Geerhardus Vos, *Redemptive History and Biblical Interpretation: The Shorter Writings of Geerhardus Vos* (Phillipsburg, NJ: P&R, 1980), 15. See also G. K. Beale, *A New Testament Biblical Theology: The Unfolding of the Old Testament in the New* (Grand Rapids: Baker, 2011), 9.
3. Charles H. H. Scobie, "The Challenge of Biblical Theology," *TynBul* 42, no. 1 (1991): 36. He similarly writes, "Biblical theology . . . [is] the ordered study of what the Bible has to say about God and his relation to the world and humankind" (*The Ways of Our God: An Approach to Biblical Theology* [Grand Rapids: Eerdmans, 2003], 4–5; see also "New Directions in Biblical Theology," *Them* 17, no. 2 [1992]: 4).
4. Paul House, "Theology, Biblical," in *Holman Illustrated Bible Dictionary* (Nashville: Holman Bible Publishers, 2003), 1581, 1586.

> Biblical theology is . . . the study of the unity of the message of the Bible. . . . Biblical theology shows the relationship of all parts of the Old Testament to the person and work of Jesus Christ and, therefore, to the Christian.[5]

> Biblical theology is . . . a holistic enterprise tracing unfolding theological trajectories throughout Scripture and exploring no biblical concept, theme, or book in isolation from the whole. Rather, each concept, theme, or book is considered ultimately in terms of how it contributes to and advances the Bible's meta-narrative, typically understood in terms of a salvation history that progresses towards and culminates in Jesus Christ.[6]

Four presuppositions that emerge from these definitions are:

1. *The Bible is God's Word:* Vos writes that biblical theology is primarily concerned with "supernatural revelation,"[7] and Scobie defines it as "the revelation of God contained in the canonical scriptures of the Old and New Testaments."[8]

2. *God's Word contains a unified message:* House notes, "Biblical theology opens up the unity of the Bible by exposing and collecting its major themes,"[9] and Goldsworthy states, "Biblical theology is . . . the study of the unity of the message of the Bible."[10]

---

5. Graeme Goldsworthy, *According to Plan: The Unfolding Revelation of God in the Bible* (Downers Grove, IL: InterVarsity, 1991), 20–21, 23.

6. Paul R. Williamson, *Sealed with an Oath: Covenant in God's Unfolding Purpose*, NSBT 23 (Downers Grove, IL: InterVarsity, 2007), 17. See also B. S. Rosner who writes, "Biblical theology is principally concerned with the overall theological message of the whole Bible. It seeks to understand the parts in relation to the whole and, to achieve this, it must work with the mutual interaction of the literary, historical, and theological dimensions of the various corpora, and with the interrelationships of these within the whole canon of Scripture" ("Biblical Theology" in *New Dictionary of Biblical Theology*," ed. T. Desmond Alexander et al. [Downers Grove, IL: InterVarsity, 2000], 3; see also Peter Stuhlmacher, *How to Do Biblical Theology* [Allison Park, PA: Pickwick, 1995], 1).

7. Vos, *Redemptive History and Biblical Interpretation*, 15. Elsewhere Vos writes that biblical theology "deals with the process of the self-revelation of God deposited in the Bible" (Geerhardus Vos, *Biblical Theology: Old and New Testaments* [Carlisle, PA: Banner of Truth Trust, 1948], 5).

8. Scobie, "Challenge of Biblical Theology," 36.

9. House, "Theology, Biblical," 1586.

10. Goldsworthy, *According to Plan*, 20. He also makes the following statements: "Biblical theology assumes some kind of unity to the Bible, and that there is . . . one overall message rather than a number of unrelated themes" (ibid., 23); "The great strength of biblical theology is that it uncovers the massive inner coherence of the divine plot in salvation history" (*Preaching the Whole Bible as Christian Scripture* [Grand Rapids: Eerdmans, 2000], 17); "Biblical theology is an exercise in understanding how the diversity relates to the unity of Scripture" (*Gospel-Centered Hermeneutics:*

3. *The unified message of God's Word centers on Jesus:* Goldsworthy explains, "Biblical theology shows the relationship of all parts of the Old Testament to the person and work of Jesus Christ,"[11] and Williamson adds that biblical concepts are considered "in terms of a salvation history that progresses towards and culminates in Jesus Christ."[12]

4. *Jesus' death, resurrection, and ascension are the climax of redemptive history.* Although none of the definitions above specifically touch on this aspect, it is a natural implication that flows from the previous presupposition—that God's Word centers on Jesus. If this is the case, then we must ask precisely what about Jesus receives the most attention. Undoubtedly, the answer must be his death, resurrection, and ascension.

These four elements will form the basis of the rest of the chapter as we seek to demonstrate how biblical theology is crucial to properly understand biblical prophecy.

The Bible Is God's Word

Biblical theology assumes that the Bible is God's inspired and infallible Word. Although not all who practice biblical theology would agree with this presupposition, one wonders how "biblical" such theology can be without it.[13] By affirming that the Bible is God's Word, we are not denying that the Scriptures were written by human authors. Indeed, this view affirms the dual authorship of the Bible. On the one hand, the Bible was written by thinking, feeling human beings who wrote in accordance with their abilities and experience. But at the same time we acknowledge that God so guided or superintended this process that every word written is in accordance with his perfect will and is therefore free from error.

Thus, biblical theology should proceed with the assumption that what is recorded in the Bible is divine revelation. The following verses illustrate how the Bible, although written by human authors, must ultimately be attributed to divine inspiration.

> *"All Scripture is breathed out by God and profitable for teaching, for reproof, for correction, and for training in righteousness" (2 Tim. 3:16).* In this verse Paul clearly records that Scripture is

---

Foundations and Principles of Evangelical Biblical Interpretation [Downers Grover, IL: InterVarsity, 2006], 261).

11. Goldsworthy, *According to Plan*, 23.

12. Williamson, *Sealed with an Oath*, 17.

13. Goldsworthy rightly notes, "A truly biblical theology accepts the biblical view of revelation" (*Preaching the Whole Bible*, 25).

not merely that which is authored by humans, but is in fact "breathed out by God" (*theopneustos*). God is the source of Scripture, which is what makes it so profitable for the believer. Furthermore, he declares that all, and not merely some, Scripture (which in this context refers primarily to the Old Testament), is God-breathed.

"No prophecy of Scripture comes from someone's own interpretation. For no prophecy was ever produced by the will of man, but men spoke from God as they were carried along by the Holy Spirit" (2 Peter 1:20–21). Peter informs us that prophecy is not produced by humans, even though they delivered the prophecy. Instead, the divine revelation was given to those who were "carried along by the Holy Spirit." God spoke through the personality and gifts of these prophets but what they spoke and wrote was indeed God's Word.

"Long ago, at many times and in many ways, God spoke to our fathers by the prophets, but in these last days he has spoken to us by his Son" (Heb. 1:1–2). This passage clearly demonstrates that God is not silent but that he has spoken to his people at various times and through various prophets. God's final and decisive revelation is found in his Son.

To have a truly biblical "biblical theology," we must acknowledge the Bible as God's Word. This means that we interpret the Bible according to its own terms. Because the Bible declares itself to be God's Word, we must receive this revelation as coming from God and therefore containing a unified message.

God's Word Contains a Unified Message

As demonstrated in the definitions above, biblical theology is concerned with both testaments of Scripture. It seeks to understand the overall message of the sixty-six writings that now form one book. Of course, there is much debate about the nature and extent of the Bible's unity. Since the Enlightenment and the advent of historical criticism, scholars have been challenging the unity of the Bible, often claiming that such unity does not exist. As a result, the Bible is sometimes treated as mere history and its disunity is simply assumed. In addition, divine authorship of Scripture is rejected and the Bible is sometimes viewed as a collection of human reflections about God.[14]

---

14. Goldsworthy comments, "The unity of the Bible has been under attack since the Enlightenment in the eighteenth century rejected the notion that God, if such a being existed, had anything to do with the pro-

This approach will simply not suffice for an evangelical Christian. Because the Bible is our highest standard, it cannot be judged by anything. "By definition a final authority cannot be proven as an authority on the basis of some higher authority. The highest authority must be self-attesting. Only God is such an authority."[15] The Bible itself should shape our presuppositions because God has revealed himself in his Word. We must presuppose that the Bible is true and presents a unified story because that is what it claims of itself.[16] If the Bible is in fact divine revelation, then its message will be unified and consistent. "The fact that there is one ultimate author of the whole Bible also means that it is not futile to seek an underlying unity among the sixty-six books."[17] This does not guarantee, however, that we will rightly understand how the entire Bible fits together. But it does mean that even if we cannot arrive at a satisfactory explanation, we should assume the problem is not with the Bible, but with our limited understanding.

This presupposition also means that we should assume the biblical authors do not abuse or misinterpret earlier revelation for their own theological purposes. New Testament authors are often charged with distorting the original meaning of a text in order to apply it to their new context. For example, the author of Hebrews has often been accused of careless exegesis when he quotes 2 Samuel 7:14 in order to demonstrate that Jesus is superior to angels. Hebrews 1:5 reads, "For to which of the angels did God ever say . . . 'I will be to him a father, and he shall be to me a son'?" In the context of 2 Samuel 7, David declares his intent to build a house (temple) for God. But because God is the only sovereign king and in control of everything, he informs David that he will build David a house (dynasty).[18] God then assures David by declaring, "When your days are fulfilled and you lie down with your fathers, I will raise up your offspring after you, who shall come from your body, and I will establish his kingdom. He shall build a house for my name, and I will establish the throne of his kingdom forever. I will be to him a father, and he shall be to me a son" (vv. 12–14a). God is promising David that he will be a father to his son Solomon who will rule over David's throne and build the temple. We know that this promise is referring directly to Solomon and not Christ because the rest of v. 14 reads, "When he commits iniquity, I will discipline him with the rod of men, with the stripes of the son of men." If this text refers to Solomon, and there is no doubt

---

duction of the Bible. It was asserted that the Bible consequently must be treated like any other humanly produced book. Historical criticism has radically changed the way people understand the unity of the Bible. With the One Author out of the way, the unity is dissolved, leaving us with a collection of disparate documents only loosely connected ideologically with one another" (*Preaching the Whole Bible*, 15).

15. Goldsworthy, *According to Plan*, 44.

16. Goldsworthy unashamedly states, "I believe that the Bible gives me a single, accurate, and coherent picture of reality principally because Jesus tells me that it does" (*Preaching the Whole Bible*, 23).

17. Keith A. Mathison, *From Age to Age: The Unfolding of Biblical Eschatology* (Phillipsburg, NJ: P&R, 2009), 4.

18. See Stephen G. Dempster, *Dominion and Dynasty: A Theology of the Hebrew Bible*, NSBT 15 (Downers Grove, IL: InterVarsity, 2003).

that it does, how can the author of Hebrews apply it to Christ? Is the author guilty of distorting the original meaning?

What we must realize is that the author of Hebrews is reading this text canonically. In other words, not only does he know what is written in 2 Samuel 7:14 but he is also familiar with the rest of the Old Testament. He knows that Solomon, although he built a magnificent temple for God, did not establish an everlasting kingdom. Therefore, in the later pages of the Old Testament there is a continued expectation that God would one day bring forth a king who would accomplish what David and Solomon never did. The theme of a messianic king who will reign on David's throne is expanded and developed throughout the Old Testament. A few hundred years after the initial promise to David, Isaiah prophesies, "For to us a child is born, to us a son is given; and the government shall be upon his shoulder, and his name shall be called Wonderful Counselor, Mighty God, Everlasting Father, Prince of Peace" (Isa. 9:6). Ezekiel later writes of one who will shepherd the people of Israel: "And I will set up over them one shepherd, my servant David, and he shall feed them: he shall feed them and be their shepherd. And I, the LORD, will be their God, and my servant David shall be prince among them. I am the LORD; I have spoken" (Ezek. 34:23–24). So, although originally 2 Samuel 7:14 applied to Solomon, it also rightly applies to Christ who accomplished what Solomon did not—he established the kingdom of God and thus fulfills the promise given to David's son because he is the true son of David.

> *If the Bible truly is God's inspired and infallible Word, and not merely the words of humans, it will naturally present a unified message. And if God's Word has a unified message, we must seek to understand the theme that unifies all of Scripture.*

Thus, when studied in light of the entire canon of Scripture, we see that the author of Hebrews is not taking an earlier prophecy out of context, but is instead highlighting the final and fullest fulfillment in Christ. We must do our best to study controversial texts and present reasonable explanations, and must not be afraid to declare our confidence in the unity and coherence of Scripture.

The Unified Message of God's Word Centers on Jesus

A third presupposition of biblical theology properly conceived is that Jesus is the unifying message of the Bible.[19] The Old Testament anticipated the com-

---

19. Kaiser notes, "The culmination of all the specifications (i.e., the individual predicted doctrines that support the one unifying promise-plan) are wrapped up in the one promise doctrine, or promise-plan, which focuses on Jesus Christ" (Walter C. Kaiser, *The Promise-Plan of God: A Biblical Theology of the Old and New Testaments* [Grand Rapids: Zondervan, 2008], 25). Rosner similarly states, "[Biblical theology] reads not only the NT, but also the OT, as a book about Jesus" ("Biblical Theology," 10).

ing of the Messiah from its opening chapters (see Gen. 3:15) and this theme is repeated in various ways through the rest of its pages. From the very beginning, God had a plan to redeem his fallen people through a divinely provided substitute (see Gen. 22:13–14) so that Jesus could say, "Abraham rejoiced that he would see my day. He saw it and was glad" (John 8:56). Later Jesus explained to two disciples on the road to Emmaus how the Scriptures were fulfilled in him (Luke 24:27). Below are New Testament verses that clearly support the notion that Jesus is the center and fulfillment of Scripture:

> *"You search the Scriptures because you think that in them you have eternal life; and it is they that bear witness about me, yet you refuse to come to me that you may have life. . . . For if you believed Moses, you would believe me; for he wrote of me" (John 5:39–40, 46).* Jesus declares that the Old Testament, and specifically the Law of Moses, testifies concerning him.

> *"And he said to them, 'O foolish ones, and slow of heart to believe all that the prophets have spoken! Was it not necessary that the Christ should suffer these things and enter into his glory?' And beginning with Moses and all the Prophets, he interpreted to them in all the Scriptures the things concerning himself. . . . 'These are my words that I spoke to you while I was still with you, that everything written about me in the Law of Moses and the Prophets and the Psalms must be fulfilled.' Then he opened their minds to understand the Scriptures" (Luke 24:25–27, 44–45).* Jesus' disciples should have known about the death and resurrection of the Messiah because the prophets wrote about it. Jesus asserts that everything written about him in Old Testament must be fulfilled. Notice that Jesus references the three main divisions of the Hebrew Bible: (1) the law of Moses (= the Pentateuch); (2) the Prophets (= Joshua–2 Kings, the Major Prophets, and the Minor Prophets); and (3) the Psalms (= Psalm–Chronicles).[20]

> *"When they had appointed a day for him, they came to him at his lodging in greater numbers. From morning till evening he expounded to them, testifying to the kingdom of God and trying to convince them about Jesus both from the Law of Moses and from the Prophets" (Acts 28:23).* Similar to Jesus, Luke informs his readers that Paul used the law of Moses and the Prophets to convince the people about Jesus. There must have been more

---

20. Psalms is referenced because it is the first and longest book of the third section of the Hebrew canon also known as the "Writings."

than just a few verses if he was doing this all day ("from morning till evening").

"Paul, a servant of Christ Jesus, called to be an apostle, set apart for the gospel of God, which he promised beforehand through his prophets in the holy Scriptures, concerning his Son, who was descended from David according to the flesh and was declared to be the Son of God in power according to the Spirit of holiness by his resurrection from the dead, Jesus Christ our Lord" (Rom. 1:1–4). Paul indicates that the gospel of Jesus Christ was promised in the Old Testament through God's prophets.

Although all of Scripture in some way anticipates the coming Messiah, this revelation was given progressively.[21] That is, God's plan of redemption was not revealed all at once but was progressively revealed in stages, with each stage providing more light than the previous stage. Consequently, although Abraham could rejoice at the coming of the Messiah, Moses had a clearer or fuller understanding of who the Messiah was and what he would accomplish—and that revelation was surpassed by the Old Testament prophets who were given even more insight concerning the coming Messiah. But only in the New Testament is the full revelation of the Messiah given. The Old Testament saints had promises concerning Jesus but in the New Testament the fulfillment of those promises is revealed. Therefore, we cannot understand the full implications of the Old Testament without knowledge of the New Testament. Gentry and Wellum write that "the New Testament's interpretation of the Old Testament becomes definitive in helping us interpret the details of the Old Testament, since later revelation brings with it greater clarity and understanding. In other words, we must carefully allow the New Testament to show us how the Old Testament is brought to fulfillment in Christ."[22] The Old Testament contained shadows and copies but the true substance or reality is Christ (Col. 2:17; Heb. 8:5; 10:1).[23] He is the fullest and final revelation (Heb. 1:1–2). This means that the sum of the revelation given in the Old Testament does not constitute what is found in the New Testament. In other words, by progressive revela-

---

21. See Peter J. Gentry and Stephen J. Wellum, *Kingdom through Covenant: A Biblical Theological Understanding of the Covenants* (Wheaton, IL: Crossway, 2012), 33, 85–86, 602–6.
22. Ibid., 85–86.
23. This does not mean that the later texts distort or contravene the meaning of the earlier text, "but rather develops them in a way which is consistent with the Old Testament author's understanding of the way in which God interacts with his people" (Greg Beale, "Did Jesus and His Followers Preach the Right Doctrine from the Wrong Texts? An Examination of the Presuppositions of Jesus' and the Apostles' Exegetical Method," in *The Right Doctrine from the Wrong Texts? Essays on the Use of the Old Testament in the New*, ed. G. K. Beale [Grand Rapids: Baker, 1994], 393).

tion, we do not simply mean that over time more and more revelation was given until the Messiah was finally revealed.[24] The prophecies of the Old Testament were often given in veiled language and the precise nature of the fulfillment could not be known until after the fact.[25]

In his book, *According to Plan*, Goldsworthy identifies three different ways to view revelation.[26]

- *Literalism:* The fulfillment must correspond exactly to the form of the promise.

- *Allegory:* A supposed hidden meaning is read out of something that on the surface is historical but which in fact has no value as history.

- *Typology:* There is a relationship between what precedes and what follows but the form in which it is given undergoes a certain development or expansion until the fulfillment is reached.

The first perspective, literalism, is insufficient because it assumes that revelation in the Old Testament must be interpreted literalistically (i.e., in a woodenly literal fashion that ignores progress in revelation).[27] But if this were the case, the Jewish people would not have missed Jesus as the fulfillment of the Old Testament because the prophecy would have been abundantly clear. A prophecy, however, is often unclear as to the precise nature in which it will be fulfilled.[28] The prophecies are truth-

> *Literalism assumes that the form in which the prophecy was given is equal to form of the fulfillment of that prophecy.*

---

24. Beale explains: "In light of progressive revelation, OT passages do not receive brand-new or contradictory meanings but undergo an organic expansion or development of meaning. . . . This means that OT passages can be understood more deeply in the light of the developing revelation of later parts of the OT and especially of the NT. The OT authors had a true understanding of what they wrote but not an exhaustive understanding. This means that a NT text's contextual understanding of an OT text will involve some essential identity of meaning between the two, but often the meaning is expanded and unfolded, growing out of the earlier meaning." (G. K. Beale, *Handbook on the New Testament Use of the Old Testament: Exegesis and Interpretation* [Grand Rapids: Baker, 2012], 27).
25. Numbers 12:6–8 indicates the enigmatic feature of prophecy when God tells Moses his unique position as a prophet. God will speak to Moses not like with other prophets who God communicates with through visions, dreams, and riddles.
26. Goldsworthy, *According to Plan*, 67.
27. As noted above, we are differentiating between "literal" and "literalistic." "Literal" typically refers to interpreting a text according to the intention of the author, allowing for figurative or symbolic language. By "literalistic" we are referring to interpreting prophecy in such a way that what is predicted must correspond exactly to the fulfillment, without allowing for development or expansion.
28. For example, the Jewish people knew where the Messiah was to be born (Mic. 5:2; cf. Matt. 2:5–6) but still missed that Jesus fulfilled this prophecy (John 7:42, 52).

ful in all that they proclaim but that does not mean they proclaim the entire truth.[29] Some things remain hidden to the hearer or reader. Because Jesus is the fullest and final revelation, the way in which he fulfills the promises of God often surpasses the description given in the Old Testament.[30] Osborne remarks,

> Later prophecies often add details to earlier ones, and the fulfillment is greater than the sum total of the preceding promises. Messianic prophecies in particular demonstrate this. Even with all the details predicted by successive prophets, the Jews were not ready for Jesus (note the constant misunderstanding of the disciples) and the reality far exceeded the expectations. The fact is that God gave the prophets only limited glimpses and never the entire picture.[31]

The Jewish people of Jesus' day seem to have embraced a certain type of literalism. They were looking for a Messiah who would physically overthrow the Roman government but Jesus stated, "My kingdom is not of this world" (John 18:36). They were waiting for the physical appearance of Elijah but Jesus informs them that "Elijah has already come, and they did not recognize him" (Matt. 17:12). They wondered how Jesus could build the physical temple in three days but Jesus "was speaking about the temple of his body" (John 2:21). They could not fathom how an old person can be born again but Jesus replies that "unless one is born of water and the Spirit, he cannot enter the kingdom of God" (John 3:5). They longed for physical water but Jesus offered them living water (John 4:10). They longed for physical bread but Jesus offered them the bread of life (John 6:35). They claimed to be the physical children of Abraham but Jesus informed them that their father was the devil (John 8:44). They were focused on one's physical family but Jesus announced "whoever does the will of God, he is my brother and sister and mother" (Mark 3:35). At almost every turn

---

29. Osborne notes, "Both Old Testament and New Testament prophecy are ambiguous, and while pointing to actual historical events, they do not reveal them in their entirety" (Grant R. Osborne, *The Hermeneutical Spiral: A Comprehensive Introduction to Biblical Interpretation*, rev. and exp. [Downers Grove, IL: InterVarsity, 2006], 266).

30. Goldsworthy agrees, "Jesus does not simply fulfill the promises. Rather, he is the final and the fullest revelation of what the promises are really about. This means that the form and the content of the fulfillment exceed by far the form and the content of the promises themselves" (*According to Plan*, 65).

31. Osborne, *Hermeneutical Spiral*, 266. Mickelsen similarly writes that "prophecy never gives as complete a picture of an event as does an historian's account.... Prophecy cannot be history written beforehand because God does not disclose major and minor elements that are essential for even an incomplete historical picture.... As history moves on, the full-orbed picture emerges.... Later revelation often discloses elements omitted from earlier revelation. Even so the sum total of what God discloses does not comprise a complete picture. The progressive character of prophecy gives us more materials" (A. Berkeley Mickelsen, *Interpreting the Bible* [Grand Rapids: Eerdmans, 1963], 289, 292). See also Willem A. VanGemeren, *Interpreting the Prophetic Word* (Grand Rapids: Zondervan, 1990), 94–95.

the Jewish people misunderstood the true nature of prophecy and the meaning of Jesus' teaching due to their literalistic hermeneutic.

A literalistic interpretation does not allow for progression or expansion in prophecy. An example of this is found in the descriptions of heaven in the Old Testament. The depiction given in Isaiah 11:6–9 is written in language that the Old Testament reader would understand and is therefore insufficient to describe the reality of the renewed earth:

> The wolf shall dwell with the lamb, and the leopard shall lie down with the young goat, and the calf and the lion and the fattened calf together; and a little child shall lead them. The cow and the bear shall graze; their young shall lie down together; and the lion shall eat straw like the ox. The nursing child shall play over the hole of the cobra, and the weaned child shall put his hand on the adder's den. They shall not hurt or destroy in all my holy mountain; for the earth shall be full of the knowledge of the LORD as the waters cover the sea.

Those who interpret the Bible literalistically will insist that this passage refers to a future millennial state—life described in Isaiah 11 is better than it is now but not quite as good as it will be when sin is eradiated on the renewed earth. But such a reading of the text does injustice both to the language, as well as the nature, of biblical prophecy. Isaiah is describing the consummated kingdom of God or the new heavens and the new earth in words and concepts that his original audience could grasp. But this does not mean that Isaiah is providing us with the fullest description of the renewed earth—for what words could adequately describe the magnificence and glory of the presence of God? We must allow for the actual fulfillment of such passages to develop and expand beyond the original prophecy.

The second method, allegory, is also insufficient because it downplays or ignores history. To discard history in the search for some deeper, spiritual meaning is to misunderstand biblical revelation. God is Lord over history and all history is accomplishing his purposes. For this reason, much of the Old Testament is given to us in the form of historical narrative. To eliminate history from God's revelation is to distort and misrepresent that revelation.

Furthermore, the allegorical method opens wide the door of speculation. Although this method has been used by many in the history of the Church, and although many who embrace a "theological interpretation of Scripture" now affirm this method, it should not be used as the normal way of interpreting the Bible.[32] Some insist that allegorization is legitimate, not only because the

---

32. Of course, much of the debate depends on the definition of "allegory" and "allegorization." Davidson defines allegory as the "arbitrary assigning of externally imposed meaning to the words of Scripture,

Church has embraced it over the centuries, but because Jesus himself employed it. Jesus supposedly used the allegorical method in two of his parables (the parable of the sower and the parable of the wheat and the tares) and therefore it is argued that Jesus is giving us a model of how to interpret all the parables. Two responses can be given to this argument: (1) because a parable by definition involves a comparison,[33] it is incorrect to call a parable that has multiple points of comparison "allegorical." Giving meaning to the details of the parable does not necessarily constitute allegorization. (2) It is likely that the reason Jesus gave interpretations for only some of his parables is precisely because the comparisons in the parable were more complex and may not have been self-evident. For other parables, however, no interpretation was given because none was needed. In fact, the meanings of Jesus' parables were often understood by the crowds without being given any interpretation (see the parable of the wicked tenants, Mark 12:12).

Others claim that Paul used allegory in Galatians 4:21–30. In this text, Paul references the births of Ishmael and Isaac and their respective mothers, Hagar and Sarah. He further states that Hagar represents Mount Sinai (which in turn represents bondage or slavery) and Sarah represents Mount Zion (which in turn represents freedom). Because Paul states in v. 24 that this Old Testament story "may be interpreted allegorically [*allēgoroumena*]," many assume that Paul is using and thus endorsing the allegorical method. But Paul is not giving the meaning of the Old Testament texts. He is not saying that the real meaning of Hagar is a physical mountain in the Middle East. Rather, he is simply making an analogy or comparison.[34] Hagar and Mount Sinai have something in common and so Paul employs this analogy to make his point—which is different than saying that Paul is giving the deeper or spiritual meaning of the text. Paul is not denying the historical value of the Old Testament text and finding some secret meaning but is using the text to demonstrate a spiritual truth. Bruce comments, "[Paul] is not thinking of allegory in the Philonic sense . . . ; he has in mind that form of allegory which

---

which meaning is foreign to the ideas conveyed by the words, and often disregards the historical sense of the passage" (Richard M. Davidson, *Typology in Scripture: A Study of Hermeneutical τύπος Structures* [Berrien Springs, MI: Andrews University Press, 1981], 101n. 1). The type of allegorization we oppose involves finding a hidden or spiritual meaning of which (1) the author and/or original audience was unaware and/or (2) is anachronistic.

33. See Robert H. Stein, *An Introduction to the Parables of Jesus* (Philadelphia: Westminster, 1981), 22. He defines parable as "a figure of speech in which there is a brief or extended comparison."

34. Foulkes insists, "When St. Paul used the word *allēgoreō* . . . he meant something different from what we commonly mean by allegorizing. . . . This can rightly be classed as typological interpretation" (Francis Foulkes, "The Acts of God: A Study of the Basis of Typology in the Old Testament," in *The Right Doctrine from the Wrong Texts? Essays on the Use of the Old Testament in the New*, ed. G. K. Beale [Grand Rapids: Baker, 1994], 367–68). See also A. B. Caneday, "Covenant Lineage Allegorically Prefigured: 'What Things Are Written Allegorically' (Galatians 4:21–31)," *SBJT* 14, no. 3 (2010): 50–77. Caneday argues that the Genesis text itself presents the characters as symbolic or representative and thus the allegory was not created by Paul but already existed in the historical narrative.

is commonly called typology: a narrative from OT history is interpreted in terms of the new covenant."[35]

Because the allegorical method is prone to speculation, it is more susceptible to multiple and varied interpretations. For example, throughout the history of the church, in the parable of the good Samaritan, the innkeeper has been identified as (1) an angel (Origen), (2) the apostle Paul (Augustine), and (3) the preacher of the Word of God (Luther). Because the meaning is secret or hidden and devoid of the original context, each interpreter is free to choose the meaning that best fits his theology. Other uses of allegory have been even more extreme. For example, while it is true that Jesus describes his body as the temple (John 2:21), it is going too far to state that the wood of the temple represents Jesus' humanity, while the gold represents his divinity.[36] Other allegorical interpretations include:

- The tent pegs of the tabernacle not only anticipate the cross of Jesus but also indicate his death and resurrection because they were buried in the ground and were later taken out of the ground when the tabernacle was moved.

- While it is true that Jesus is compared to the bronze serpent in the wilderness (John 3:14; cf. Num. 21:8–9), it is going too far to state that bronze (a metal inferior to gold or silver) represents the fact that Jesus' outward appearance was rather plain.

- Rahab's scarlet cord represents the blood or death of Christ.

- The axe Elisha brought up from the bottom of the river is a foreshadowing of the cross of Christ.[37]

- The pomegranates on priests' robes are types of the fruits of the Spirit, or that the circular hole for the cut out for the priest's head is a representation of Christ's eternal nature.

- The stone cut out of the mountain without hands in Daniel 2:45 is a reference to Jesus' virgin birth.[38]

---

35. F. F. Bruce, *The Epistle to the Galatians*, NIGTC (Grand Rapids: Eerdmans, 1982), 217. Longenecker argues that Paul's use of the Hagar-Sarah story was done for polemical purposes in order to counter the Judaizers' message that charged Paul with an Ishmaelian form of truth. Paul, then, is simply turning their argument on its head by claiming that their message leads to bondage but his leads to freedom (Richard N. Longenecker, *Galatians*, WBC 41 [Dallas: Word, 1990], 200, 210).

36. C. I. Scofield, *Scofield Reference Bible* (New York: Oxford University Press, 1917), 101.

37. Justin Martyr, *Dialogue with Trypho*, 86.

38. Ibid., 70, 76.

- Herod's killing of the infants in Bethlehem who were two years and under signifies that Binitarians and Unitarians will perish, whereas Trinitarians will be saved.[39]

The typological model is to be preferred to the previous two options because it allows for development or expansion to the prophecy until it is fulfilled. A *type* can be defined as "a biblical event, person or institution which serves as an example or pattern for other events, persons or institutions"[40] and *typology* is "the study of analogical correspondences among revealed truths about persons, events, institutions, and other things

> *The key element with typology is to correctly identify the point(s) of comparison.*

within the historical framework of God's special revelation, which, from a retrospective view, are of a prophetic nature and are escalated in their meaning."[41] In other words, an initial event (or person or institution) foreshadows a corresponding event (or person or institution) which occurs at a later time in salvation history. The earlier divine intervention is called the "type" and the corresponding figure is called the "antitype."[42] Typology is often viewed as a type of prophecy that lacks an overt verbal prediction.[43] In other words, there is no predictive element to typology because it is only after the pattern or example is repeated that a correspondence can be made.[44] For example, Moses was commanded to make a bronze serpent and place it on a pole so that when the Israelites were bitten by the serpents, they might live. There is nothing predicted in this passage about

---

39. Cited in G. W. H. Lampe and K. J. Woollcombe, *Essays on Typology* (Naperville, IL: Allenson, 1957), 31–32.

40. David L. Baker, *Two Testaments, One Bible: A Study of the Theological Relationship Between the Old and New Testaments*, rev. ed. (Downers Grove, IL: InterVarsity, 1991), 195. The chapter in which this material is found ("Typology") was originally published as "Typology and the Christian Use of the Old Testament," *SJT* 29 (1976), 137–57 and under the same title is also found in *The Right Doctrine from the Wrong Texts? Essays on the Use of the Old Testament in the New*, ed. G. K. Beale (Grand Rapids: Baker, 1994), 313–30. See also Mickelsen, *Interpreting the Bible*, 336–64; Davidson, *Typology in Scripture*; Leonhard Goppelt, *Typos: The Typological Interpretation of the Old Testament in the New*, trans. Donald H. Madvig (Grand Rapids: Eerdmans, 1982).

41. Beale, *Handbook*, 14. Based on this definition, Beale lists five essential characteristics of a type: (1) analogical correspondence; (2) historicity; (3) a pointing-forwardness; (4) escalation; and (5) retrospection.

42. Six texts explicitly use the term "type" in the New Testament (Rom. 5:14 [*typos*]; 1 Cor. 10:6 [*typoi*], 11 [*typikōs*]; Heb. 8:5 [*typon*]; 9:24 [*antitypa*]; 1 Peter 3:21 [*antitypon*]).

43. Foulkes notes that a New Testament author's affirmation of a type "does not necessarily mean that "the [Old Testament] writer was conscious of presenting a type or foreshadowing of the Christ, although we have seen that there was sometimes in the Old Testament the consciousness that the acts of God in the past pointed forward to similar but much more glorious acts in the future" ("Acts of God," 370).

44. This is not to say that an antitype cannot be predicted because Jesus predicted that he would be lifted up like the bronze serpent. The point is, until Jesus made the comparison, we were not expecting the comparison to be made because Moses never predicted that a future savior would be lifted up in like manner.

the coming of the Messiah who will hang on a cross. And yet, Jesus looked to this Old Testament story and saw a parallel or a type. So Jesus says, "As Moses lifted up the serpent in the wilderness, so must the Son of Man be lifted up, that whoever believes in him may have eternal life" (John 3:14–15). In this case, the comparison involves: (1) both the serpent and Jesus are lifted up; and (2) those who look to the object lifted up receive life.

Typology embraces history because it assumes that God is controlling history and that there is a pattern to the way God works in salvation history.[45] Snodgrass explains:

> The presupposition is that the way God worked in the past is mirrored in the way he works in the present and future. There is a correspondence between what happened to God's people in the past and what happens now or in the future. Climactic events in Israel's history become the paradigms by which new events are explained. For example, the exodus was the climactic event by which God saved his people. Later writers use exodus terminology to describe God's saving his people from Assyria (Isa. 11:6) or salvation generally. The suffering of a righteous person (Ps. 22) finds correspondence in the crucifixion of Jesus (Matt. 22:39–46).[46]

We must also be sure to distinguish types from symbols and allegory. Symbols serve as signs of something they represent without necessarily being similar in any respect. For example, the bread is symbolic of Jesus' body (1 Cor. 11:24) and a golden lampstand is symbolic for a church (Rev. 1:20). In addition, types point forward in time, whereas symbols may not.

Typology is also different from allegory. As we mentioned earlier, typology is based on salvation history. Allegory tends to downplay or ignore history whereas typology is firmly rooted in God's acts in history. Beale comments, "Most scholars today agree that typology is not allegory because it is based on the actual historical events of the Old Testament passage being dealt with and because it essentially consists of a real, historical correspondence between the Old Testament and the New Testament event."[47] Finally, allegory searches for a

---

45. See Foulkes, "The Acts of God," 342–71; Baker, *Two Testaments*, 188, 195; Mickelsen, *Interpreting the Bible*, 237; Beale, *Handbook*, 98.

46. Klyne Snodgrass, "The Use of the Old Testament in the New," in *The Right Doctrine from the Wrong Texts? Essays on the Use of the Old Testament in the New*, ed. G. K. Beale (Grand Rapids: Baker, 1994), 38. This essay was originally published with the same title in *New Testament Criticism & Interpretation*, ed. David Alan Black and David S. Dockery (Grand Rapids: Zondervan, 1991), 407–34.

47. Beale, "Did Jesus and His Followers Preach the Right Doctrine from the Wrong Texts?" 395. See also Ellis who notes, "Unlike allegorical exposition, the typology of the NT writers represents the OT not as a book of metaphors hiding a deeper meaning but as an account of historical events and

hidden meaning that invites speculation but typology is based on a correlation rooted in the biblical testimony itself. In determining whether something is a type or antitype in the Bible, there are several qualities that should be evident. For example, John Currid lists four characteristics found in typology:

1. It must be grounded in history; both type and antitype must be actual historical events, persons, or institutions.

2. There must be a historical and theological correspondence between type and antitype.

3. There must be an intensification of the antitype from the type.

4. Some evidence that the type is ordained by God to foreshadow the antitype must be present.[48]

Biblical theology sees Christ as the center of redemptive history and therefore the focus of typology is seeing how Christ fits the pattern of these Old Testament types.[49] Old Testament persons are types of Christ: Adam (Rom. 5:14; 1 Cor. 15:22, 45, 47), Jonah (Matt. 12:40–41; cf. Jonah 1:17), and the nation of Israel (Matt. 2:15; cf. Hos. 11:1). Old Testament institutions are types of Christ: the Passover (1 Cor. 5:7); atonement through the sacrificial system (1 Peter 1:18–19; cf. Lev. 17:11), and the temple (John 2:21). Old Testament offices are types of Christ: Moses in his prophetic office (Matt. 5:21; John 1:17, 45; cf. Deut. 18:15); Melchizedek in his priestly office (Heb. 5:6, 10; 6:20; 7:11, 15, 17; cf. Gen. 14:17–20; Ps. 110:4); David in his kingly office (Matt. 1:1). R. T. France summarizes,

> [Jesus] uses *persons* in the Old Testament as types of himself (David, Solomon, Elijah, Elisha, Isaiah, Jonah) or of John the Baptist (Elijah); he refers to Old Testament *institutions* as types of himself and his work (the priesthood and the covenant); he sees in the *experiences* of Israel foreshadowing of his own; he finds the *hopes* of Israel fulfilled in himself and his disciples; and sees his disciples as assuming the *status* of Israel; in Israel's *deliverance* by God he sees a type of the

---

teachings from which the meaning of the text arises. Unlike a Judaizing hermeneutic, typology views the relationship of OT events to those in the new dispensation not as a 'one-to-one' equation or correspondence, in which the old is repeated or continued, but rather in terms of two principles, historical correspondence and escalation" ("Foreword," in Goppelt, *Typos*, x).

48. John Currid, "Recognition and Use of Typology in Preaching," *RTR* 53, no. 3 (1994): 121.

49. For a chart showing the macro-typology of the Bible (how Christ fulfills the OT), see Goldsworthy, *Gospel-Centered Hermeneutics*, 253–56.

gathering of men into his church, while the *disasters* of Israel are foreshadowings of the imminent punishment of those who reject him, whose *unbelief* is prefigured in that of the wicked in Israel and even, in two instances, in the arrogance of the Gentile nations.

In all these aspects of the Old Testament people of God Jesus sees foreshadowing of himself and his work, with its results in the opposition and consequent rejection of the majority of the Jews, while the true Israel is now to be found in the new Christian community. Thus in his coming the history of Israel has reached its decisive point. The whole of the Old Testament is gathered up in him. He himself embodies in his own person the status and destiny of Israel, and in the community of those who belong to him that status and destiny are to be fulfilled, no longer in the nation as such.[50]

The way in which an Old Testament prophecy is "fulfilled" in the New Testament is not restricted to a future prediction. There are several possible ways the terms "fulfill" or "fulfillment" can be used in the Bible:[51]

- *Drawing out the full implications of something.* For example, Jesus said, "Do not think that I have come to abolish the Law or the Prophets; I have not come to abolish them but to fulfill them" (Matt. 5:17). He then goes on to give the true meaning or full implications of the law by saying in a somewhat formulaic fashion, "You have heard that it was said to those of old. . . . But I say to you . . . ." (Matt. 5:21–22). Thus, Jesus is not contradicting or in any way repudiating what is found in the Old Testament. Rather, he is providing the true or full implications of the text.

- *Completion of a fixed time.* Jesus came preaching, "The time is fulfilled, and the kingdom of God is at hand; repent and believe in the gospel" (Mark 1:15; see also Luke 21:24).

- *Conforming to or obeying a requirement.* Paul states, "For the whole law is fulfilled in one word: 'You shall love your neighbor as yourself'" (Gal. 5:14; see also Matt. 3:15).

---

50. R. T. France, *Jesus and the Old Testament: His Application of Old Testament Passages to Himself and His Mission* (Downers Grove, IL: InterVarsity, 1971), 75–76.
51. See Henry A. Virkler, *Hermeneutics: Principles and Processes of Biblical Interpretation* (Grand Rapids: Baker, 1981), 204–5.

- *Correspondence of phrases, illustrations, or events between one historical period and another.* In the following examples, the Old Testament text that is quoted as being fulfilled was not given as a prediction in the Old Testament. Rather, the New Testament authors see Jesus as fulfilling a correspondence with what was written in the Old Testament (= typology).[52]

  – And [Jesus] remained [in Egypt] until the death of Herod. This was to fulfill what the Lord had spoken by the prophet, "Out of Egypt I called my son." (Matt. 2:15; cf. Hos. 11:1)

  – Then was fulfilled what was spoken by the prophet Jeremiah: "A voice was heard in Ramah, weeping and loud lamentation, Rachel weeping for her children; she refused to be comforted, because they are no more." (Matt. 2:17–18; cf. Jer. 31:15)

  – And he went and lived in a city called Nazareth, that what was spoken by the prophets might be fulfilled: "He shall be called a Nazarene." (Matt. 2:23; cf. Isa. 11:1; 53:3; Num. 6:2)

In each of these examples, Matthew cites the Old Testament passage as being "fulfilled." But upon closer examination of the original context, we find that there is no prediction given. In the first example, Matthew quotes from Hosea 11:1 in order to show why it was important for Jesus to have gone down to Egypt. But the context of Hosea 11 clearly demonstrates that verse 11 was not a prophecy. The full verse reads, "When Israel was a child, I loved him, and out of Egypt I called my son." It is clear that the "son" refers to the nation of Israel and "out of Egypt" refers to the exodus event under the leadership of Moses. Therefore, in its original context, "Hosea 11:1 is a reference to the exodus, pure and simple."[53] Thus, Hosea was not predicting a future event about the coming Messiah but was recalling the past event of the exodus from Egypt.[54] Jesus "fulfills" Hosea 11:1 not by means of a prediction and subsequent fulfillment but

---

52. Virkler offers two other categories: (1) satisfying a request or desire (Esther 5:8; Ps. 145:19; Prov. 13:19) and (2) carrying out what is promised (Lev. 22:21). These two categories were not included above because they are based on the English words "fulfill" and "fulfillment." In the four categories above, the same Greek word (πληρόω) is used (ibid.).

53. Craig L. Blomberg, "Matthew," in *Commentary on the New Testament Use of the Old Testament*, ed. G. K. Beale and D. A. Carson (Grand Rapids: Baker, 2007), 7.

54. Fee and Stuart state, "Good exegesis of Hosea indicates that there is no reason to think that Hosea was referring to the coming Messiah" (*How to Read the Bible*, 210). Goldsworthy notes, "In fact the Hosea passage was not predicting anything but was recalling the historic event of the exodus from Egypt under Moses" (*Preaching the Whole Bible*, 78). France writes, "It is a statement about the past, not a prediction of the future" (R. T. France, *The Gospel of Matthew*, NICNT [Grand Rapids: Eerdmans, 2007], 80). Beale maintains, "The specific verse in Hosea is clearly an allusion to Israel's exodus from Egypt and not a prophecy" (*Handbook*, 17; see also his *New Testament Biblical Theology*, 406–11).

through typology. Matthew clearly sees Israel as a typifying Christ. Blomberg maintains that "Matthew's actual use of Hosea 11:1 [is] a classic example of pure typology."[55] He explains: "The original event need not have been intentionally viewed as forward-looking by the OT author; for believing Jews, merely to discern striking parallels between God's actions and history, especially in decisive moments of revelation and redemption, could convince them of divinely intended 'coincidence.'"[56] Jesus then accomplishes a new exodus as the son who will complete the mission that Israel was called to accomplish, but failed.[57]

Another example of typology is found just a few verses later in Matthew 2:17–18 where Matthew quotes from Jeremiah 31:15 in which the prophet recounts the suffering of the people of Israel being taken into exile, with "Rachel" being used somewhat figuratively as the mother of the nation. Furthermore, Rachel had been buried in Bethlehem (Gen. 35:19). Although this text is not a prediction, Matthew sees a correspondence between the killing and exile of the people of Israel and the killing of the babies in Bethlehem. Blomberg notes, "The text in Jeremiah is not a prediction, nor does it even use the future tense."[58] Just as the nation suffered and "Rachel" wept, so also the people of Bethlehem (the very place Rachel wept so long before) suffered and wept because of their grief and personal loss.

In the final example, Matthew explains that Jesus grew up in Nazareth so that he could fulfill that which was spoken by the prophets, "He shall be called a Nazarene." The problem here is that there is no Old Testament verse that contains the words that Matthew quotes. That Matthew was not attempting to give a direct quotation is evident from the fact that he states that this was spoken not just by one prophet but by the "prophets." The closest parallels to Matthew's quotation include Isaiah 11:1 where Isaiah refers to a "shoot" or "branch" (Hebrew, *nēzer*) and Numbers 6:2 which mentions a "Nazarite" (Hebrew, *nazir*). It could be that Matthew finds a correspondence to these words and the home of Jesus. Another possibility is that Matthew is drawing a conclusion about Christ from the general thrust of Old Testament prophecy that the Messiah would be one who was "despised and rejected by men" (Isa. 53:3).[59] Because Nazareth was somewhat of an obscure town, the title "Nazarene" would have been viewed as

---

55. Blomberg, "Matthew," 7.

56. Ibid., 8.

57. Beale argues that Matthew's use of Hosea 11:1 is not purely retrospective. He comments that "this was not a perspective understood by Matthew *only after* the events of Jesus's coming. Rather, there are substantial indications *already in Hosea itself and its immediate context* that Israel's past exodus out of Egypt was an event that would be recapitulated typologically in the eschatological future" (*Handbook*, 64; see also G. K. Beale, "The Use of Hosea 11:1 in Matthew 2:15: One More Time," *JETS* 55, no. 4 [2012]: 697–715).

58. Blomberg, "Matthew," 10.

59. So France, *Gospel of Matthew*, 91. He comments that "what Matthew is here providing is not a quotation of a specific passage but rather a theme of prophecy" (ibid.). He continues, "Whatever Matthew is doing with this 'quotation,' it is not going to be at the level of simple prediction and fulfillment" (ibid., 94).

somewhat of an insult (cf. John 1:46; Acts 24:5).[60] Although Luke indicates that Jesus' family was originally from Nazareth, perhaps Matthew is providing a biblical rationale for why Jesus would have settled there (instead of Bethlehem which was a royal city carrying messianic overtones).[61]

There is no doubt the New Testament authors saw Jesus as embodying the fulfillment of the Old Testament. Once they were convinced that Jesus was the Christ, they began to see how his life, death, and resurrection fit the pattern of so many elements contained in the Old Testament. They did not so much look at the Old Testament and then see Christ as the fulfillment of all that was predicted and foreshadowed. Rather, they saw Christ and then saw that he was indeed the fulfillment of all the Old Testament expectations.

> The early church applied such texts to Jesus because of their conviction about his identity. The conviction about his identity did *not* derive from the Old Testament. They did not find texts and then find Jesus. They found Jesus and then saw how the Scriptures fit with him. They were not *proving* his identity in the technical sense so much as they were demonstrating how the Scriptures fit with him.[62]

Properly understood Biblical theology acknowledges that the Bible contains a unified message and that Christ is the center of that message. The revelation about Christ was made progressively clearer throughout the Old Testament but has been fully revealed only in the New Testament. Because the Old Testament contains concealed revelation, we must allow for development or expansion of revelation. Thus, typology is an important method of interpreting biblical prophecy.

Jesus' Death, Resurrection, and Ascension Are the Climax of Redemptive History

Not only is Jesus the center of God's redemptive plan, but specifically Jesus' death, resurrection, and ascension are the pinnacle of that plan.[63] As Gold-

---

60. So Leon Morris, *The Gospel According to Matthew* (Grand Rapids: Eerdmans; Leicester: InterVarsity, 1992), 49.

61. So Craig S. Keener, *The Gospel of Matthew: A Socio-Rhetorical Commentary* (Grand Rapids: Eerdmans, 2009), 113.

62. Snodgrass, "Use of the Old Testament in the New," 39–40. Similarly, Ladd notes, "Jesus, and the apostles after him, reinterpreted the Old Testament prophecies in light of Jesus' person and mission" (George Eldon Ladd, *The Last Things: An Eschatology for Laymen* [Grand Rapids: Eerdmans, 1978], 17).

63. The resurrection of Jesus is often referenced in the early church. For uses of *anastasis*, see Acts 4:2, 33; 17:18, 32; Romans 1:4; 6:5; 1 Corinthians 15:12, 13, 21, 42; Philippians 3:10; 1 Peter 1:3; 3:21. For uses of *egeirō*, see Acts 3:15; 4:10; 5:30; 10:40; 13:30, 37; Romans 4:24–25; 6:4, 9; 7:4; 8:11, 34;

sworthy writes, "The resurrection is the ultimate demonstration of Christology and of God's hermeneutical reference point."[64] This claim is evidenced by the fact that the preaching of the early church centered on the death and resurrection of Jesus. On the day of Pentecost, Peter proclaimed, "This Jesus . . . you crucified and killed by the hands of lawless men. God raised him up, loosing the pangs of death, because it was not possible for him to be held by it" (Acts 2:23–24). While in Athens, Luke records that Paul "was preaching Jesus and the resurrection" (Acts 17:18). Later, Paul explains to the Corinthian church the tradition he received concerning the gospel: "For I delivered to you as of first importance what I also received: that Christ died for our sins in accordance with the Scriptures, that he was buried, that he was raised on the third day in accordance with the Scriptures" (1 Cor. 15:3–4).

Jesus ushered in the kingdom of God during his earthly ministry (Mark 1:15). He perfectly obeyed his heavenly Father so that he could become a perfect substitute for the sins of his people (2 Cor. 5:21). He was crucified on the cross, becoming a curse on behalf of those who trust in him by absorbing the wrath of God (Gal. 3:13; Rom. 3:25; Heb. 2:17; 1 John 2:2; 4:10). By his resurrection he demonstrated that all his claims were valid, securing new life for his people (Rom. 1:4; 1 Peter 1:3). After his resurrection, he ascended to his Father and now rules over his creation (Acts 1:9; Eph. 1:20–22; 2:6; Col. 3:1; Heb. 1:3; 10:12; 12:2). Paul understood the centrality of Christ's death and resurrection which is why he could say, "For I decided to know nothing among you except Jesus Christ and him crucified" (1 Cor. 2:2).

All of God's promises given in the Old Testament are primarily fulfilled in Jesus' first coming. Many who read the Old Testament tend to read certain prophecies (especially Old Testament promises concerning the restoration of ethnic Israel) as being fulfilled not in the first coming of Christ, but only in his second coming. It is our contention that this is a flawed way of reading such prophecies (see chapter 4). Goldsworthy writes,

> I want to assert categorically that ALL prophecy was fulfilled in the gospel event at the first coming of Jesus. . . . There

---

10:9; 1 Corinthians 6:14; 15:4, 12–52 (x18); 2 Corinthians 4:14; 5:15; Galatians 1:1; Ephesians 1:20; Colossians 2:12; 1 Thessalonians 1:10; 2 Timothy 2:8; 1 Peter 1:21. For uses of *anistēmi*, see Acts 2:24, 32; 10:41; 13:33–34; 17:3, 31; 1 Thessalonians 4:14.

64. Goldsworthy, *Gospel-Centered Hermeneutics*, 64. Elsewhere he states that "the meaning of all the Scriptures is unlocked by the death and resurrection of Jesus" (*Preaching the Whole Bible*, 54). Likewise, Silva comments, "Indeed, it is clear that Paul saw the coming of Christ—in particular, his resurrection and exaltation—as the most important turning point in the history of redemption" (Moisés Silva, "How to Read a Letter," in *An Introduction to Biblical Hermeneutics*, by Walter C. Kaiser and Moisés Silva [Grand Rapids: Zondervan, 1994], 135). See also Richard B. Gaffin, *The Centrality of the Resurrection: A Study in Paul's Soteriology* (Grand Rapids: Baker, 1978); Beale, *New Testament Biblical Theology*, 19–24, 249–354.

is a tendency to try to differentiate Old Testament prophecies of the end into two groups, those applying to the first
coming and those applying to the second coming. . . . This is
a mistake. A more biblical perspective is one that recognizes
that the distinction between the first and second coming is
not in what happens but in how it happens. Nothing will
happen at the return of Christ that has not already happened
in him at his first coming. [65]

Although the second coming of Christ is important and often emphasized in the New Testament, it is not the climax of redemptive history. Emphasizing the fulfillment of Old Testament prophecies as taking place only
in the second coming, minimizes the greatest work of God—the death and
resurrection of his Son, Jesus Christ.

Summary

The focus of this chapter has been to demonstrate the importance of biblical
theology in gaining a proper interpretation of prophecy. Biblical theology
gives us the big picture of redemptive history so that we understand the grand
narrative of Scripture, allowing us to see how each prophecy fits into God's
unified plan. Four of the most important assumptions or presuppositions of
biblical theology are: (1) the Bible is God's Word—which means that the
Bible is divinely inspired and therefore reliable; (2) God's Word contains a
unified message—which means that although there is much diversity in the
Bible, there is one overarching message; (3) the unified message of God's
Word centers on Jesus—which means that even the Old Testament should
be read christologically; and (4) Jesus' death and resurrection are the climax
of redemptive history—which means that the fulfillment of God's promises
is focused on Christ's first coming.

65. Goldsworthy, *Preaching the Whole Bible*, 93. Elsewhere he states, "Everything was fulfilled in [Jesus]
representatively at his first coming, and everything will be fulfilled in a universal consummation at
his return" (Graeme Goldsworthy, *Christ-Centered Biblical Theology: Hermeneutical Foundations and
Principles* [Downers Grove, IL: InterVarsity, 2012], 185).

Part 2

Old Testament Prophecies

Chapter 4

Unconditional, Conditional, and Fulfilled Prophecies

*"OT prophecy presents a veritable
snake pit of interpretive problems."[1]*

This is because Old Testament prophecy often includes obscure or symbolic language, strange images, and partial fulfillments. But we do not need to give up and despair. If we follow the principles laid out in the previous chapters we can arrive at a proper understanding of the text.

The next three chapters will discuss prophecy in the Old Testament. These chapters will not provide a comprehensive analysis discussing every prophecy. Rather, we will discuss the material under topical categories using key representative texts. In this chapter we will consider unconditional and conditional prophecies, as well as Old Testament prophecies that have already been fulfilled (either in the Old Testament or in the New Testament).[2]

Just how much of the Old Testament is considered predictive in nature? We must admit that this is a very difficult question to answer. J. Barton Payne calculates that there are 8,352 verses containing predictive material out of the 31,124 verses in the Bible (about 27 percent).[3] 6,641 of these verses come from the Old Testament (about 28.6 percent) and 1,711 come from the New Testament (about 21.6 percent). The only books in the Bible that contain no predictive prophecy are Ruth and the Song of Songs in the Old Testament, and Philemon and 3 John in the New Testament. The Old Testament books with the highest amount of predictive prophecy are Isaiah (754 verses or 59 percent), Jeremiah (812 verses or 60 percent), and Ezekiel

---

1. William W. Klein, Craig L. Blomberg, and Robert L. Hubbard, *Introduction to Biblical Interpretation* (Dallas: Word, 1993), 302.
2. We should note that some texts will apply to more than one category.
3. These and the following statistics are found in J. Barton Payne, *Encyclopedia of Biblical Prophecy: The Complete Guide to Scriptural Predictions and Their Fulfillment* (New York: Harper & Row, 1973), 674–75, 681.

(821 verses or 65 percent).[4] Payne maintains that of the 23,210 verses in the Old Testament, 535 verses are related to Christ's second coming, 614 to the millennium, 269 to the final judgment, and 128 to the New Jerusalem. Fee and Stuart offer the following summary: "Less than 2 percent of Old Testament prophecy is messianic. Less than 5 percent specifically describes the new covenant age. Less than 1 percent concerns events yet to come in our time."[5] They continue, "The prophets *did* indeed announce the future. But it was usually the more immediate future of Israel, Judah, and other nations surrounding them that they announced rather than *our* future."[6]

Part of the difficulty in knowing how much of the Old Testament contains prophecy is due to the different types of fulfillment. For example, not everything that is placed under the banner of prophecy is strictly predictive in nature. Many assume that when a New Testament writer quotes an Old Testament text as being "fulfilled," that the text must have been a direct prediction. But this is simply not the case. Osborne goes as far to say that "few if any of the fulfillment passages were intended originally as messianic prophecies."[7] As we discussed in the previous chapter, much of what is fulfilled in the New Testament is fulfilled through typology, which does not contain a specific prediction but rather a correspondence in history. Therefore, we must understand that the Old Testament can be fulfilled in more ways than simply a direct prediction.

Another area of debate and confusion concerns whether or not a text can have a double or deeper meaning (sometimes called *sensus plenior*). Brown defines *sensus plenior* as "*that additional, deeper meaning, intended by God but not clearly intended by the human author, which is seen to exist in the words of a biblical text (or group of texts, or even a whole book) when they are studied in the light of further revelation or development in the understanding of revelation.*"[8] Although many evangelical scholars affirm the possibility of a text having a *sensus plenior*, most are quick to note that the additional meaning must be (1) a development of the original or literal meaning and

---

4. Some of the Minor Prophets, due primarily to their length, actually have a higher percentage. These books include Zephaniah (89 percent), Obadiah (81 percent), Nahum (74 percent), Micah (70 percent), Zechariah (69 percent), and Joel (68 percent). In the New Testament, the books with the highest amount of predictive prophecy are Matthew (278 verses or 26 percent), Revelation (256 verses or 63 percent), and Luke (250 verses or 22 percent). Other New Testament books with a high percentage include Hebrews (45 percent), 2 Peter (41 percent), and Jude (40 percent). See Payne, *Encyclopedia of Biblical Prophecy*, 674–75, 681. These statistics are given as examples and may not reflect the authors' position.

5. Gordon D. Fee and Douglas Stuart, *How to Read the Bible for All Its Worth: A Guide to Understanding the Bible*, 4th ed. (Grand Rapids: Zondervan, 2014), 188.

6. Ibid.

7. Grand R. Osborne, *The Hermeneutical Spiral: A Comprehensive Introduction to Biblical Interpretation*, rev. and exp. ed. (Downers Grove, IL: InterVarsity, 2006), 333.

8. Raymond Brown, *The* Sensus Plenior *of Sacred Scripture* (Baltimore: St. Mary's University Press, 1955), 92 (emphasis original).

(2) must be identified as such in the New Testament. Bock notes that the concept of *sensus plenior* "is not a bad one, provided what the human author said and whatever more God says through him have a relationship in sense to what the human author originally said."[9] And yet, not everyone agrees on the definition and application of this term. In fact, because this term sometimes used to justify fanciful or illegitimate interpretations, many scholars prefer terms such as "multiple fulfillment,"[10] "progressive prediction" (or "development fulfillment"),[11] "progressive fulfillment,"[12] "analogous (or typological) fulfillment"[13] or simply "implication."[14] All of these terms demonstrate an attempt to allow for a type of "fulfillment" that does not require a direct prediction.

Unconditional Prophecies

As is clear from reading the Old Testament, some prophecies come in the form of promises. God declares that he will do something based on his covenant faithfulness which is certain to happen. In other words, some prophecies are unconditional in the sense that God commits himself to bring about a particular result.[15] Kaiser notes, "The actual list of unconditional prophecies is not long, but they occupy the most pivotal spots in the history of redemption."[16] These prophecies are usually given in the form of a covenant. These covenants have been described as "unilateral" or "royal grant" cove-

---

9. Darrell L. Bock, "Single Meaning, Multiple Contexts and Referents," in *Three Views on the New Testament Use of the Old Testament*, ed. Kenneth Berding and Jonathan Lunde (Grand Rapids: Zondervan, 2008), 113.

10. A. Berkeley Mickelsen, *Interpreting the Bible* (Grand Rapids: Eerdmans, 1963), 300; Kaiser and Silva, *Introduction to Biblical Hermeneutics: The Search for Meaning* (Grand Rapids: Zondervan, 1994), 158. Kaiser writes, "Therefore, while we deny the presence of 'multiple sense,' 'double sense,' . . . we affirm that there is 'multiple fulfillment'" (ibid.).

11. Payne, *Encyclopedia of Biblical Prophecy*, 129–40.

12. Willem A. VanGemeren, *Interpreting the Prophetic Word* (Grand Rapids: Zondervan, 1990), 82–83.

13. Osborne, *Hermeneutical Spiral*, 266. He argues, "The terms *double* or *multiplex* are unnecessary, for the New Testament writers would see analogous situations in salvation history and link them prophetically."

14. Robert H. Stein, *A Basic Guide to Interpreting the Bible: Playing by the Rules*, 2nd ed. (Grand Rapids: Baker, 2011), 147–49.

15. We understand Gentry and Wellum's concern for refraining from labeling certain covenants as unconditional or conditional. They argue that "the Old Testament covenants blend both aspects and in an unfolding way tell a story of God's incredible promises, his unilateral action to save, and the demand for a covenant mediator who, unlike his Old Testament counterparts, obeys perfectly, even unto death on a cross, and thus accomplishes our redemption" (Peter J. Gentry and Stephen J. Wellum, *Kingdom through Covenant: A Biblical Theological Understanding of the Covenants* [Wheaton, IL: Crossway, 2012], 120 [see also 608–11]). Thus, in using the label "unconditional" we are not denying the need for conditions to be met (either by Christ or the believer) but that because God has promised something, it is certain to happen because God will ensure that the conditions will be met.

16. Kaiser and Silva, *Introduction to Biblical Hermeneutics*, 148. See also Walter C. Kaiser, *Toward Rediscovering the Old Testament* (Grand Rapids: Zondervan, 1987), 149–55.

nants.[17] Scott Hahn succinctly explains the differences between the various types of covenants:[18]

1. *The Kinship/Parity Covenant.* The obligations of the covenant are more or less equally distributed between two parties. In such a covenant the parties are usually—but not always—of equal status.

2. *The (Vassal) Treaty Covenant.* The obligations of the covenant are imposed on the inferior party by the superior.

3. *The (Royal) Grant Covenant.* The obligations of the covenant rest predominantly with the superior party, who freely accepts responsibility toward the inferior, usually in response to the inferior's faithfulness or other meritorious qualities. The initiative in establishing a covenant of this form also rests with the superior; it is generally *granted* as a reward to a faithful vassal or servant.

It should be noted that royal grant covenants often involve man's response (cf. Gen. 12:1; 17:1, 9–14; 22:16, 18) but "the suzerain [in this case God] is bound unconditionally to fulfill his 'grant'."[19] For example, the covenant God made with Abraham is arguably the most important promise that God made in the Old Testament as it forms the basis on which other covenants are made. God declared several promises to Abraham, including the following:

> And I will make of you a great nation, and I will bless you and make your name great, so that you will be a blessing. I will bless those who bless you, and him who dishonors you I will curse, and in you all the families of the earth shall be blessed. (Gen. 12:2–3)

> And he brought him outside and said, "Look toward heaven, and number the stars, if you are able to number them." Then he said to him, "So shall your offspring be." (Gen. 15:5)

> On that day the LORD made a covenant with Abram, saying, "To your offspring I give this land, from the river of Egypt to the great river, the river Euphrates." (Gen. 15:18)[20]

17. See Moshe Weinfeld, "The Covenant of Grant in the Old Testament and in the Ancient Near East," *JAOS* 90 (1970): 184–203.
18. Scott W. Hahn, *Kinship by Covenant: A Canonical Approach to the Fulfillment of God's Saving Promises* (New Haven, CT: Yale University Press, 2009), 29.
19. Ibid., 93.
20. See also Genesis 17:4–8: "Behold, my covenant is with you, and you shall be the father of a multitude

In order to confirm these promises, God made a covenant with Abraham, telling him to take several animals (a three-year-old heifer, a three-year-old female goat, a three-year-old ram, a turtledove, and a young pigeon) and cut the larger animals in half. He was then to lay the carcasses over against each other, forming an aisle down the middle (Gen. 15:9–11). In such ceremonies those involved in making the covenant would walk between the carcasses. This action was symbolic and in essence communicated that if one who walked between the carcasses failed to keep his end of the covenant, he deserved to be killed like the animals who were slaughtered. With the covenant God made with Abraham, however, only God passed through the dead animals (Gen. 15:17). At the time, God put Abraham into a deep sleep and so Abraham did not pass through (Gen. 15:12). This covenant is therefore a unilateral or royal grant covenant in which God declares that he will keep his promises and will ensure that his promises are fulfilled. In this sense, then, the Abrahamic covenant is an unconditional covenant.

A second crucial promise that God made in the Old Testament that is considered unconditional is the covenant to establish a kingdom and dynasty for David and his descendants.

> And I will make for you a great name, like the name of the great ones of the earth. And I will appoint a place for my people Israel and will plant them, so that they may dwell in their own place and be disturbed no more. . . . And I will give you rest from all your enemies. Moreover, the LORD declares to you that the LORD will make you a house. When your days are fulfilled and you lie down with your fathers, I will raise up your offspring after you, who shall come from your body, and I will establish his kingdom. He shall build a house for my name, and I will establish the throne of his kingdom forever. I will be to him a father, and he shall be to me a son. . . . my steadfast love will not depart from him, as I took it from Saul, whom I put away from before you. And your

---

of nations. No longer shall your name be called Abram, but your name shall be Abraham, for I have made you the father of a multitude of nations. I will make you exceedingly fruitful, and I will make you into nations, and kings shall come from you. And I will establish my covenant between me and you and your offspring after you throughout their generations for an everlasting covenant, to be God to you and to your offspring after you. And I will give to you and to your offspring after you the land of your sojournings, all the land of Canaan, for an everlasting possession, and I will be their God," and Genesis 22:15–18: "And the angel of the LORD called to Abraham a second time from heaven and said, 'By myself I have sworn, declares the LORD, because you have done this and have not withheld your son, your only son, I will surely bless you, and I will surely multiply your offspring as the stars of heaven and as the sand that is on the seashore. And your offspring shall possess the gate of his enemies, and in your offspring shall all the nations of the earth be blessed, because you have obeyed my voice.'"

> house and your kingdom shall be made sure forever before
> me. Your throne shall be established forever. (2 Sam. 7:9–16;
> cf. 1 Chron. 17:11–14)[21]

This is a covenant that God promises ("I will . . .") because of his love and faithfulness. Jeremiah later records this promise: "For thus says the LORD: David shall never lack a man to sit on the throne of the house of Israel" (Jer. 33:17). In order to confirm the unconditional nature of the covenant, God assures Jeremiah saying, "Thus says the LORD: If you can break my covenant with the day and my covenant with the night, so that day and night will not come at their appointed time, then also my covenant with David my servant may be broken, so that he shall not have a son to reign on his throne. . . . As the host of heaven cannot be numbered and the sands of the sea cannot be measured, so I will multiply the offspring of David my servant" (Jer. 33:19–22; see also Ezek. 37:24–25).

The difficulty with this promise is twofold. First, it can be argued that David's throne was not established forever since his kingdom essentially ended with the Babylonian destruction of Jerusalem. Second, there are other texts that seem to indicate that the Davidic covenant was indeed conditional.[22] For example, on his deathbed David exhorts his son Solomon to walk according to God's commandments "that the LORD may establish his word that he spoke concerning me, saying, 'If your sons pay close attention to their way, to walk before me in faithfulness with all their heart and with all their soul, you shall not lack a man on the throne of Israel'" (1 Kings 2:4; see also Ps. 89:29–32; 132:12; 1 Kings 8:25; 9:4–5). In this verse David seems to suggest that the promise God gave him concerning an everlasting dynasty is contingent on ("if") his son's obedience to the law of God. Therefore, God made an unconditional covenant with David and his descendants that contained conditional elements. This probably means that in general terms the Davidic covenant would not fail, although specific individuals might fail to obtain certain benefits.[23] As Kaiser notes, "The 'breaking' or conditionality can only refer to *individual* and *personal* invalidations of the benefits of the covenant, but it cannot affect the certainty of God's oath. . . . The covenant is to be continued in force in each case even though the *individual* participa-

---

21. See also Psalm 89:3–4: "You have said, 'I have made a covenant with my chosen one; I have sworn to David my servant: I will establish your offspring forever, and build your throne for all generations.'"

22. For a review of the debate as to whether the Davidic covenant is unconditional or conditional, see S. L. McKenzie, "The Typology of the Davidic Covenant," in *The Land That I Will Show You: Essays on the History and Archeology of the Ancient Near East in Honor of J. Maxwell Miller*, ed. J. A Dearman and M. P. Graham, JSOTSup 343 (Sheffield: Sheffield Academic Press, 2001), 154–78.

23. Again we are in virtual agreement with Gentry and Wellum who warn against labeling the Davidic covenant as unconditional or a royal grant covenant since that could be misunderstood to mean that there are no conditions involved in this covenant (*Kingdom through Covenant*, 397).

tion may be delayed or even forfeited. . . . This is precisely the situation of the Davidic blessing. [Although some may be unfaithful,] the blessing may never be revoked for the family."[24]

Another unconditional promise is the new covenant mentioned in Jeremiah and Ezekiel:

> Behold, the days are coming, declares the LORD, when I will make a new covenant with the house of Israel and the house of Judah, not like the covenant that I made with their fathers on the day when I took them by the hand to bring them out of the land of Egypt, my covenant that they broke, though I was their husband, declares the LORD. But this is the covenant that I will make with the house of Israel after those days, declares the LORD: I will put my law within them, and I will write it on their hearts. And I will be their God, and they shall be my people. And no longer shall each one teach his neighbor and each his brother, saying, "Know the LORD," for they shall all know me, from the least of them to the greatest, declares the LORD. For I will forgive their iniquity, and I will remember their sin no more. (Jer. 31:31–34)

> I will sprinkle clean water on you, and you shall be clean from all your uncleannesses, and from all your idols I will cleanse you. And I will give you a new heart, and a new spirit I will put within you. And I will remove the heart of stone from your flesh and give you a heart of flesh. And I will put my Spirit within you, and cause you to walk in my statutes and be careful to obey my rules. (Ezek. 36:25–27; see also Ezek. 11:19–20; 39:29)

According to Jeremiah, the newness of the "new covenant" is first and foremost that it is an unbreakable covenant—it is not like the Mosaic covenant. It must be stressed that this new covenant is not contrasted with the (unconditional) Abrahamic covenant, but with the (conditional) Mosaic covenant. God declares that the new covenant will not be like the covenant he made

---

24. Walter C. Kaiser, "The Blessings of David: The Charter for Humanity," in *The Law and the Prophets*, ed. J. Skillen (Nutley, NJ: P&R, 1974), 307–8. Elsewhere Kaiser summarizes, "Thus, there was an obligation to *transmit* the unconditional promise to each Davidic generation, even though that was not in itself a guarantee that each transmitter was also automatically a *participant* in the benefits of that promise" (*Rediscovering*, 154). W. J. Dumbrell comments, "In physical terms, the virtual failure of the Davidic line occurred in 586 BC but in spiritual terms we cannot but read 2 Samuel 7:13 finally in terms of New Testament Christology" (*Covenant and Creation: A Theology of the Old Testament Covenants* [Carlisle: Paternoster, 1984], 150).

with them at Sinai ("not like the covenant that I made with their fathers," Jer. 31:32). The reason the old covenant was a failure was because the people of Israel failed to keep their end of the covenant (cf. Heb. 8:8). But the people will not fail to keep the new covenant because God will take it upon himself to see that they are fit to be called his people. This time he will write his laws on their minds and hearts.[25] Ezekiel adds that the new covenant will include a new heart and a new Spirit that will enable the people to keep God's commands. In both of these texts the point to be stressed is that it is God who will do these things. His new covenant will be fulfilled because he unconditionally promises to accomplish all that the covenant requires. Although there are other unconditional promises in the Bible,[26] the three mentioned above are perhaps the most important.

Conditional Prophecies

But not all of the prophecies given in the Old Testament are unconditional promises. The conditional nature of prophecies is based on many of the conditional promises recorded in Leviticus 26, Deuteronomy 4, and Deuteronomy 28–32 related to the Mosaic covenant. If the people were obedient, God would bless them but if they were disobedient, he would curse them.

> If you walk in my statutes and observe my commandments and do them, then I will give you your rains in their season, and the land shall yield its increase, and the trees of the field shall yield their fruit. Your threshing shall last to the time of the grape harvest, and the grape harvest shall last to the time for sowing. And you shall eat your bread to the full and dwell in your land securely. (Lev. 26:3–5)

Some prophecies are conditional. That is, the outcome of the prophecy is largely determined by the response of the person or persons to whom the prophecy is directed.

> But if you will not listen to me and will not do all these commandments, if you spurn my statutes, and if your soul abhors my rules, so that you will not do all my commandments, but

---

25. It should be noted that there are conditions in the new covenant, but the difference is that God will ensure that his people will remain obedient by writing his law on their hearts and minds. "The new covenant does not mean a change in God's standards of righteousness, of right and wrong, of what is appropriate in a covenant relationship. No, what is new about the new covenant is the ability of both partners to keep the covenant" (Gentry and Wellum, *Kingdom though Covenant*, 506).
26. E.g., the covenant God made with the seasons (Gen. 8:21–22) and the God's promise of a new heavens and a new earth (Isa. 65:17–19; 66:22–24).

> break my covenant, then I will do this to you: I will visit
> you with panic, with wasting disease and fever that consume
> the eyes and make the heart ache. And you shall sow your
> seed in vain, for your enemies shall eat it. I will set my face
> against you, and you shall be struck down before your en-
> emies. Those who hate you shall rule over you, and you shall
> flee when none pursues you. (Lev. 26:14–17)

The prophets often refer back to these covenantal stipulations warning the
people to repent of their sins. Unlike the Abrahamic covenant, the Mosaic covenant was a conditional covenant (cf. Heb. 8:6–8). In the Old Testament, many
of the conditional prophecies come in the form of judgment prophecies.[27]

An example of a conditional prophecy is found in the ministry of the
prophet Jonah. When Jonah finally arrived in Nineveh he announced the
prophecy that the Lord had given to him, "Yet forty days, and Nineveh shall
be overthrown!" (Jonah 3:4). But when the people of Nineveh heard this message, they repented (v. 5). We then read, "When God saw what they did, how
they turned from their evil way, God relented of the disaster that he had said
he would do to them, and he did not do it" (v. 10). Does this make Jonah a false
prophet? He first predicted that God would destroy Nineveh but in the end "he
did not do it." The answer to this question is found in Jeremiah 18:7–10:

> If at any time I declare concerning a nation or a kingdom,
> that I will pluck up and break down and destroy it, and if that
> nation, concerning which I have spoken, turns from its evil,
> I will relent of the disaster that I intended to do to it. And if
> at any time I declare concerning a nation or a kingdom that
> I will build and plant it, and if it does evil in my sight, not
> listening to my voice, then I will relent of the good that I had
> intended to do to it.

In this text, Jeremiah gives us an important principle: If the hearers repent, the judgment will not take place. So, although there is no explicit mention of this principle in Jonah, it was simply assumed. What then is the purpose of the prophecy if it is conditional?

The answer to this question is found in Ezekiel 3:18–19:

> If I say to the wicked, "You shall surely die," and you give him
> no warning, nor speak to warn the wicked from his wicked
> way, in order to save his life, that wicked person shall die for

---

27. Some refer to such judgment prophecies as "prophecies of disaster" (see Klein, Blomberg, and Hubbard, *Introduction to Biblical Interpretation*, 292).

> his iniquity, but his blood I will require at your hand. But if you warn the wicked, and he does not turn from his wickedness, or from his wicked way, he shall die for his iniquity, but you will have delivered your soul.

The reason God warned the wicked was so that they might repent of their sins and stay God's judgment. It is based on God's character—that he is "merciful and gracious, slow to anger and abounding in steadfast love" (Ps. 103:8). Thus, a judgment prophecy assumes something—whether stated or not. It assumes that if people heed the warning and repent, the judgment will not take place. Jonah knew this, and this is why he did not want to go to Nineveh. After he proclaimed the coming judgment and the people of Nineveh repented, Jonah became angry. He prayed, "O Lord, is not this what I said when I was yet in my country? That is why I made haste to flee to Tarshish; for I knew that you are a gracious God and merciful, slow to anger and abounding in steadfast love, and relenting from disaster" (Jonah 4:1–2). Jonah did not run away because he was shy or because he was afraid of the Ninevites. Rather, he did not want the Ninevites to repent and experience God's mercy. In his view, they were a godless people who deserved God's unfettered judgment. There was no reason to preach about the impending judgment if there was never any possibility of repentance. If this had been a judgment with no opportunity of repentance, Jonah would have happily gone to Nineveh to preach such a message. He knew that if he went and prophesied the upcoming judgment, the Ninevites just might heed his message, repent of their sins, and receive God's mercy. Thus, the prophecy was conditioned on the response of the hearers.

Conditional prophecies are often found in the Old Testament. For example, Micah prophesied that Jerusalem would be destroyed during the reign of Hezekiah: "Therefore because of you Zion shall be plowed as a field; Jerusalem shall become a heap of ruins, and the mountain of the house a wooded height" (Mic. 3:12). Later, Jeremiah quotes how this prophecy was avoided:

> Micah of Moresheth prophesied in the days of Hezekiah king of Judah, and said to all the people of Judah: "Thus says the Lord of hosts, 'Zion shall be plowed as a field; Jerusalem shall become a heap of ruins, and the mountain of the house a wooded height.' Did Hezekiah king of Judah and all Judah put him to death? Did he not fear the Lord and entreat the favor of the Lord, and did not the Lord relent of the disaster that he had pronounced against them? But we are about to bring great disaster upon ourselves." (Jer. 26:18–19)

Jeremiah uses the earlier prophecy of Micah as an encouragement to the people of his day. Just as Hezekiah feared the Lord, seeking his favor, so too the people of Jeremiah's day should follow Hezekiah's example—and perhaps they also will avoid God's judgment.

Another example of conditional prophecy relates to the life of King Hezekiah. Isaiah prophesied that Hezekiah would not recover from his illness but would die: "In those days Hezekiah became sick and was at the point of death. And Isaiah the prophet the son of Amoz came to him and said to him, 'Thus says the LORD 'Set your house in order, for you shall die; you shall not recover'"" (2 Kings 20:1). But Hezekiah did not hear this prophecy and then resign himself to his fate. He knew that God was gracious and the very fact that Isaiah was sent to proclaim this prophecy was a merciful act. Although he knew he did not deserve God's grace, he knew that God delights in being compassionate.

> Then Hezekiah turned his face to the wall and prayed to the LORD, saying, "Now, O LORD, please remember how I have walked before you in faithfulness and with a whole heart, and have done what is good in your sight." And Hezekiah wept bitterly. And before Isaiah had gone out of the middle court, the word of the LORD came to him: "Turn back, and say to Hezekiah the leader of my people, Thus says the LORD, the God of David your father: I have heard your prayer; I have seen your tears. Behold, I will heal you. On the third day you shall go up to the house of the LORD." (2 Kings 20:2–5)[28]

A final conditional prophecy we will consider was given to Ahab by Elijah.

> Ahab said to Elijah, "Have you found me, O my enemy?" He answered, "I have found you, because you have sold yourself to do what is evil in the sight of the LORD. Behold, I will bring disaster upon you. I will utterly burn you up, and will cut off from Ahab every male, bond or free, in Israel." . . . And when Ahab heard those words, he tore his clothes and put sackcloth on his flesh and fasted and lay in sackcloth and went about dejectedly. And the word of the LORD came to Elijah the Tishbite, saying, 'Have you seen how Ahab has humbled himself before me? Because he has humbled himself before me, I will not bring the disaster in his days; but

---

28. See also how Jeremiah brought the message of judgment to the people (Jer. 4:6–7, 11–18; 6:1–7) while still exhorting them to repent of their sins so that they might be saved from the judgment (Jer. 4:1–2, 14; 6:8; 7:1–7). See Francis Foulkes, "The Acts of God: A Study of the Basis of Typology in the Old Testament," in *The Right Doctrine from the Wrong Texts? Essays on the Use of the Old Testament in the New*, ed. G. K. Beale (Grand Rapids: Baker, 1994), 349n. 51.

in his son's days I will bring the disaster upon his house.'"
(1 Kings 21:20–21, 27–29)

Because Ahab repented of his sins and humbled himself, God delayed the impending judgment so that the prophecy would only come to pass during the days of Ahab's sons.

Fulfilled Prophecies

The third category we will discuss includes those prophecies that are already fulfilled—either during the period of the Old Testament or the New Testament. As was already mentioned, the vast majority of Old Testament prophecies were fulfilled within the Old Testament period. For example, in Genesis 15 God made a promise to Abraham: "And he brought him outside and said, 'Look toward heaven, and number the stars, if you are able to number them.' Then he said to him, 'So shall your offspring be'" (Gen. 15:5). Some might immediately object by declaring that this prophecy is not yet fulfilled because Abraham's descendants are not as numerous as the stars of heaven. But we must remember that the Bible contains figures of speech or metaphorical language. God was not declaring to Abraham that he will actually have more children than the stars in the sky. Rather, this was a common way of saying that he will have more descendants than he could possibly imagine. We know this is the meaning of the promise that God gave to Abraham because Moses later informed the people of Israel that this promise was indeed fulfilled. He declared to them, "Your fathers went down to Egypt seventy persons, and now the LORD your God has made you as numerous as the stars of heaven" (Deut. 10:22; see also Deut. 26:3–5; Josh. 21:43–45; Neh. 9:7–8). According to this text, this promise was already fulfilled in the days of Moses—not literalistically, but according to the intended meaning of the words. The fulfillment of this promise was later confirmed in the New Testament: "Therefore from one man, and him as good as dead, were born descendants as many as the stars of heaven and as many as the innumerable grains of sand by the seashore" (Heb. 11:12).

Another example is found in 1 Kings 13:1–3 which narrates the account of an unnamed "man of God" who travels to Bethel to denounce Jeroboam's idolatrous altar. The prophet declares, "Behold, a son shall be born to the house of David, Josiah by name, and he shall sacrifice on you the priests of the high places who make offerings on you, and human bones shall be burned on you" and the sign of the prophecy is that "the altar shall be torn down, and the ashes that are on it shall be poured out." Not surprisingly, we find every detail of this prophecy fulfilled in 2 Kings 23:15–16 when King Josiah burns the bones of the priests upon the altar just after he destroyed it.

There are many examples of fulfilled prophecies proclaimed by the prophets concerning God's coming judgment on the nations. Among others, there are prophetic judgments or woe oracles proclaimed against the nations of Babylon (Isa. 13; 14:3–22; 21; 47; Jer. 50–51; Daniel), Assyria (Isa. 10:5–19; 14:24–27), Philistia (Isa. 14:28–32; Jer. 47; Ezek. 25:15–17), Moab (Isa. 15–16; Jer. 48; Ezek. 25:8–11; Amos 2:1–3), Damascus (Isa. 17; Jer. 49:23–27; Amos 1:2–5), Ethiopia (Isa. 18, 20), Egypt (Isa. 19, 20; Jer. 46; Ezek. 29–32), Tyre (Isa. 23; Ezek. 26–28; Amos 1:9–10), Ammon (Jer. 49:1–6; Ezek. 25:1–7; Amos 1:13–15), Nineveh (Jonah; Nahum; Zeph. 2), Edom (Jer. 49:7–22; Ezek. 25:12–14; Amos 1:11–12; Obadiah), and Samaria (Hosea; Amos; Micah). Concerning these prophecies, Fee and Stuart write, "It is important to see that God refers to the fate of those nations, and that the fulfillment came *within decades* of the time the prophecies were delivered, that is, mostly during the sixth century BC."[29]

Isaiah 13 records a judgment prophecy against Babylon. We know this oracle is a prophecy against Babylon because the first verse of the chapter reads, "The oracle concerning Babylon which Isaiah the son of Amoz saw" (Isa. 13:1). In verse 19 we again read that this judgment prophecy relates to the nation of Babylon: "And Babylon, the glory of kingdoms, the splendor and pomp of the Chaldeans, will be like Sodom and Gomorrah when God overthrew them." And yet, many who read this text assume that this prophecy was only partially fulfilled because of the cosmic language found in the oracle.

> Behold, the day of the LORD comes, cruel, with wrath and fierce anger, to make the land a desolation and to destroy its sinners from it. For the stars of the heavens and their constellations will not give their light; the sun will be dark at its rising, and the moon will not shed its light. . . . Therefore I will make the heavens tremble, and the earth will be shaken out of its place at the wrath of the LORD of hosts in the day of his fierce anger. (Isa. 13:9–10, 13; cf. Isa. 34:3–4)

Because of the imagery used, many assume that this prophecy must pertain to the day of the great judgment of God at the end of history (the last judgment). But it was common for the prophets to use figurative, cosmic language to describe God's intervention in history and his sovereign rule of all nations. Based on the context, however, this prophecy refers to the Babylonian empire of the sixth century BC which was going to be punished for destroying Jerusalem and sending God's people into exile. Robert Stein explains:

> Such imagery was not meant to be interpreted literalistically. The sun was not actually going to be darkened; the moon would not stop giving its light; the stars would not stop

---

29. Fee and Stuart, *How to Read the Bible*, 207.

showing their light. What the author willed to communicate by this imagery, that God was going to bring judgment
upon Babylon, was to be understood literally but not literalistically. And that willed meaning, God's judgment upon
Babylon, did take place. . . . Babylon had been judged just as
the prophecy proclaimed, and the cosmic imagery indicates
that this was God's doing. The imagery itself, however, was
understood by the prophet and his audience as part of the
stock terminology used in this kind of literature to describe
God's intervention into history.[30]

Although the phrase "day of the Lord" and cosmic terminology can be
used to describe the end of time in the Bible, we should not assume that these
texts must refer to that event. Rather, we should let the context determine
the meaning of the passage in question. In this case, Isaiah is using cosmic
imagery to describe God's intervention into history so that when it occurred,
the people knew that it was God who caused the events to transpire—even
though it was the Persians who judged and conquered them. The imagery was
not meant to be interpreted literalistically.[31]

Similar language is found in Ezekiel 32 where the prophet describes the
judgment of God against the king of Egypt, Pharaoh Neco:

> Son of man, raise a lamentation over Pharaoh king of Egypt
> and say to him. . . . "When I blot you out, I will cover the
> heavens and make their stars dark; I will cover the sun with
> a cloud, and the moon shall not give its light. All the bright
> lights of heaven will I make dark over you, and put darkness
> on your land, declares the Lord GOD." (Ezek. 32:2, 7–8)

Ezekiel proclaims this lamentation about the king of Egypt because of the evil
his kingdom had done. Again, cosmic terminology is used to communicate that
God is sovereign and will judge the king. The figurative language meaningfully
communicates that God is going to bring a great judgment against the land of
Egypt.[32] But Ezekiel also declares that God is going to use the Babylonians and

---

30. Stein, *Basic Guide to Interpreting the Bible*, 141. Wright maintains that the meaning is "Babylon will
 fall—an earth shattering event!" (N. T. Wright, *Jesus and the Victory of God* [Minneapolis: Fortress,
 1996], 354).

31. For the interpretation that the events describe both local and universal judgment, see Edward Adams,
 The Stars Will Fall from Heaven: "Cosmic Catastrophe" in the New Testament and Its World, LNTS 347
 (London: T&T Clark, 2007), esp. 42–44.

32. Wright comments, "The cosmic language (32:7–10) signifies the cataclysmic effects of the destruction
 of this great power among the rest of the nations" (Christopher J. H. Wright, *The Message of Ezekiel*
 [Leicester: InterVarsity, 2001], 253).

other nations to deliver his judgment: "The sword of the king of Babylon shall come upon you. I will cause your multitude to fall by the swords of mighty ones, all of them most ruthless of nations. They shall bring to ruin the pride of Egypt, and all its multitude shall perish" (Ezek. 32:11–12). This prophecy was fulfilled when the Egyptians were conquered by the Babylonians.

Not only does the Old Testament contain prophecies concerning the judgment of other nations but the prophets also predict the upcoming judgment on Israel and Judah. Because of the sin of Jeroboam, the prophets warned that Samaria, Israel's capital during the divided kingdom, would fall to Assyria (Isa. 8:4; Hos. 10:5–6; Mic. 1:1–6). This occurred as predicted in 722 BC (2 Kings 17:21–24). Likewise, the fall of Jerusalem is predicted several times in the prophetic literature.

> I will encamp against you all around, and will besiege you with towers and I will raise siegeworks against you. And you will be brought low .... (Isa. 29:3–4; see also Isa. 3, 22).

> Thus says the LORD, the God of Israel.... "I myself will fight against you with outstretched hand and strong arm, in anger and in fury and in great wrath. And I will strike down the inhabitants of this city, both man and beast. They shall die of a great pestilence. Afterward, declares the LORD, I will give Zedekiah king of Judah and his servants and the people in this city who survive the pestilence, sword, and famine into the hand of Nebuchadnezzar king of Babylon and into the hand of their enemies, into the hand of those who seek their lives. He shall strike them down with the edge of the sword. He shall not pity them or spare them or have compassion." (Jer. 21:4–7; see also Jer. 6:6, 19; 25:8–9; 34:1)

> Thus says the Lord GOD: This is Jerusalem.... Because you are more turbulent than the nations that are all around you, and have not walked in my statutes or obeyed my rules, and have not even acted according to the rules of the nations that are all around you, therefore thus says the Lord GOD: Behold, I, even I, am against you. And I will execute judgments in your midst in the sight of the nations. (Ezek. 5:5, 7–8; see also Ezek. 12, 24, 33)

> "I will utterly sweep away everything from the face of the earth," declares the LORD. "I will sweep away man and beast; I will sweep away the birds of the heavens and the fish of the sea, and the rubble with the wicked. I will cut off mankind

from the face of the earth," declares the LORD. "I will stretch out my hand against Judah and against all the inhabitants of Jerusalem." (Zeph. 1:2–4)

All of these prophecies were fulfilled when God raised up Nebuchadnezzar and the nation of Babylon to destroy Jerusalem and the temple in 586 BC. After being besieged by the Babylonians for several months, the city was finally overthrown. Its inhabitants were either killed by the sword or taken into captivity (Jer. 52:12–34; 2 Kings 25:1–11). As a matter of fact, some of the prophets like Jeremiah warned the people not to fight against the Babylonians but to surrender because it was God's judgment they were carrying out (e.g., see Jer. 21:8–10).

But the Lord not only promised to judge Judah and the inhabitants of Jerusalem by sending them into captivity, he also promised that he would restore them to the land after seventy years:

This whole land shall become a ruin and a waste, and these nations shall serve the king of Babylon seventy years. . . . When seventy years are completed for Babylon, I will visit you, and I will fulfill to you my promise and bring you back to this place. (Jer. 25:11; 29:10)

Other Old Testament prophets look to God's promise of restoration mentioned in Jeremiah as a message of comfort and hope. Daniel writes, "In the first year of [Darius's] reign, I, Daniel, perceived in the books the number of years that, according to the word of the LORD to Jeremiah the prophet, must pass before the end of the desolations of Jerusalem, namely, seventy years" (Dan. 9:2). Based on this promise, Daniel pleads with God to remember his covenant and return the people to their land (see also Zech. 1:12). God was indeed faithful to his promises and fulfilled the prediction given by Jeremiah. This promise was also noted by the chronicler as being fulfilled:

He took into exile in Babylon those who had escaped from the sword, and they became servants to him and to his sons until the establishment of the kingdom of Persia, to fulfill the word of the LORD by the mouth of Jeremiah, until the land had enjoyed its Sabbaths. All the days that it lay desolate it kept Sabbath, to fulfill seventy years. Now in the first year of Cyrus king of Persia, that the word of the LORD by the mouth of Jeremiah might be fulfilled, the LORD stirred up the spirit of Cyrus king of Persia, so that he made a proclamation throughout all his kingdom and also put it in writing: "Thus says Cyrus king of Persia, 'The LORD the God of heaven, has given me all the kingdoms of the earth, and he has charged me to build him a house at Jerusalem, which is in Judah. Whoever is among you of all his people, may the LORD his God be with him. Let him go up.'" (2 Chron. 36:20–23; see also Isa. 44:24–45:3; Ezra 1:1–5)

Another example of a prophecy that was fulfilled in the Old Testament and Intertestamental period is the dream given to King Nebuchadnezzar that was interpreted by Daniel concerning the rise and fall of various nations. In his dream King Nebuchadnezzar saw a statue with a head of gold, chest and arms of silver, middle and thighs of bronze, legs of iron, and feet partly iron and partly clay (Dan. 2:32–33). Daniel interprets this image as a picture of four nations that will rule the world in consecutive order. The gold head represented the Babylonian Empire (625–539 BC), the silver chest and arms represented the Medo-Persian Empire (539–331 BC; cf. Dan. 8:20), the middle and thighs of bronze represented the Greek Empire (331–63 BC; cf. Dan. 8:21), and the legs of iron and feet of iron and clay represented the Roman Empire (63 BC–AD 476). References to these kingdoms are probably also seen in Daniel's vision of the four beasts (Dan. 7) and his vision of the ram and the goat (Dan. 8). These visions represented predictions of future events that have now already come to pass.

Although there are many other examples of prophecies that have already been fulfilled during the Old Testament period, we will now turn our attention to consider a prophecy that was fulfilled in the New Testament.[33] On the day of Pentecost, Peter explained to those in Jerusalem that the events taking place were a fulfillment of an Old Testament prophecy:

But this is what was uttered through the prophet Joel: "And in the last days it shall be, God declares, that I will pour out my Spirit on all flesh, and your sons and your daughters shall prophesy, and your young men shall see visions, and your old men shall dream dreams; even on my male servants and female servants in those days I will pour out my Spirit, and they shall prophesy. And I will show wonders in the heavens above and signs on the earth below, blood, and fire, and vapor of smoke; the sun shall be turned to darkness and the moon to blood, before the day of the Lord comes, the great and magnificent day. And it shall come to pass that everyone who calls upon the name of the Lord shall be saved." (Acts 2:16–21)

After the Spirit came at Pentecost, Jewish pilgrims from all over the world began to hear the disciples of Jesus speak their languages. Many were amazed

33. Specifically messianic prophecies will be covered in chapter 6.

at this phenomenon, but others mocked and said those speaking were merely drunk with wine. At this point, Peter stood up and declared to the large crowd that these people were not drunk but rather what was taking place was spoken through the prophet Joel: "And in the last days it shall be, God declares, that I will pour out my Spirit on all flesh" (Acts 2:17). Peter quoted from Joel 2 because he believed that with the coming of the Spirit, this text was being fulfilled. Furthermore, he applied Joel's vision not to the nation of Israel, but to the church.

This prophecy also includes cosmic language similar to other Old Testament apocalyptic prophecies. In Acts 2:19–20 Peter, quoting from Joel 2:30–31, states, "And I will show wonders in the heavens above and signs on the earth below, blood, and fire, and vapor of smoke; the sun shall be turned to darkness and the moon to blood, before the day of the Lord comes, the great and magnificent day." Some might respond by claiming that this prophecy has not yet been completely fulfilled.[34] The sun has not turned to darkness and the moon has not turned to blood. But we must be careful not to force the text to mean something it was never intended to mean. John Stott offers a powerful warning:

> It is the unanimous conviction of the New Testament authors that Jesus inaugurated the last days or Messianic age, and that the final proof of this was the outpouring of the Spirit, since this was the Old Testament promise of promises for the end-time. This being so, we must be careful not to re-quote Joel's prophecy as if we are still awaiting its fulfilment, or even as if its fulfilment has been only partial, and we await some future and complete fulfilment. For this is not how Peter understood and applied the text.[35]

Peter (and Luke) had no difficulty in affirming that the prophecy given by Joel was fulfilled in the coming of the Spirit. Peter specifically states that the Spirit's coming at Pentecost "is what was spoken of through the prophet Joel" (Acts 2:16 NASB). Peter could have omitted the references to the sun and moon by ending his quotation from Joel earlier. But he specifically includes them as what has been fulfilled. Peter knew that such cosmic language should not be interpreted literalistically. Rather, he knew that such language meant that God would sovereignly intervene in history and do something miraculous. He knew that this marked a key event in the history of redemption. It was a sign that they were living in the end times. As Stein rightly comments, "These cosmic signs did not literally take place at Pentecost, even though what the author

---

34. E.g., Kaiser contends that Joel 2:30–31 still "awaits a full and final realization at the second coming of Christ" (Kaiser and Silva, *An Introduction to Biblical Hermeneutics*, 144).
35. Stott, *Message of Acts* (reprint, Downers Grove, IL: InterVarsity, 1994), 73.

willed to convey by those signs did. . . . The conventional cosmic imagery used in this prophecy of Joel was understood by both Peter and Luke as being fulfilled in the events of Pentecost."[36] If we interpret this passage literalistically, we are forced to say this text (and many other texts) has not yet been fulfilled. The text pointed to a literal reality (that God would miraculously intervene in history), but that reality was described using figurative language.

Conclusion

The most important prophecies given in the Old Testament are unconditional promises. These promises (covenants) are unilateral in that they are based on God's graciousness and his purpose to accomplish his sovereign will. These include the Abrahamic, Davidic, and new covenants. The majority of prophecies—especially judgment prophecies—are conditional. The very reason these prophecies were given was to provide the hearers with the opportunity to humble themselves and repent in order to avoid the coming judgment. Most of the prophecies given in the Old Testament have already been fulfilled. Particular judgments against various nations, the promise of return from exile, and the prophetic interpretation given by Daniel concerning Nebuchadnezzar's dream about the rise and fall of four empires, among many others, have already been fulfilled. Furthermore, many Old Testament prophecies are fulfilled in the New Testament, such as Joel's prophecy concerning the coming of the Spirit. In the next chapter, we will consider Old Testament restoration prophecies regarding ethnic Israel and whether such prophecies should be interpreted literally or symbolically.

---

36. Stein, *Basic Guide to Interpreting the Bible*, 143. Goldsworthy similarly states, "Peter . . . has no qualms about using a passage [Acts 2:16–21 quoting Joel 2] that describes not only prophesying and visions, but also the apocalyptic signs of the end such as the darkened sun and bloodlike moon. He regards this coming of the Spirit as an end-time event. . . . The apostles seemed to find no difficulty in proclaiming the end as having already come" (*Preaching the Whole Bible*, 57, 91).

Chapter 5

Restoration Prophecies

We must acknowledge that many Old Testament prophecies
remained unfulfilled until the coming of the Messiah.

In the previous chapter we established that the Old Testament contains both conditional and unconditional prophecies. We also demonstrated that most of the prophecies in the Old Testament were already fulfilled before the beginning of the New Testament era. In this chapter we will consider what are called restoration prophecies given to the nation of Israel. In the following chapter we will discuss messianic prophecies. Although we will consider these two categories separately, these two categories overlap in that the restoration prophecies given to Israel are ultimately fulfilled in the Messiah.

In the Old Testament there are many passages where God promises to restore the nation of Israel.[1] This restoration includes (1) return from exile, (2) rebuilt cities, (3) continual harvest of good crops, (4) long life, (5) peace from all enemies, and (6) a restored temple. The difficulty in interpreting these texts is in knowing the precise nature of the fulfillment. Are some or all of these texts already fulfilled? Should the descriptions in these texts be taken literally? Do these texts apply to ethnic Israel or do they apply to the church?

Perhaps the greatest difficulty in answering these questions is knowing when an author is referring to the return from Babylonian exile and the subsequent inhabiting of the land, and when he is describing a future existence in the consummated kingdom of God. As was briefly discussed in the previous chapter, the promise that God would return his people to their land has already been fulfilled. And yet, some of the descriptions given by the prophets seem to be talking about an existence that surpasses anything experienced by the exiles who returned from captivity. An additional difficulty is that references to the new covenant are sometimes couched in passages that seemingly describe the

---

1. Most of the material in Chapter 5 was previously published in Benjamin L. Merkle, "Old Testament Restoration Promises Regarding the Nation of Israel: Literal or Symbolic?" *SBJT* 14 (2010): 14–25, and was used by permission.

return from Babylonian captivity. The vision the prophets were given of the future was one that did not clearly distinguish between the immediate return from exile and the new covenant with the fullness of its blessings.

At this point, it will be helpful to identify some of the Old Testament restoration prophecies concerning Israel that do not seem to refer to the return from Babylonian captivity.

> *Isaiah 60:1–22:* This text describes a time when the wealth of the nations will come to Israel. There will be no more violence (v. 18), there will be no more sun because the Lord will be Israel's light (vv. 19–20), and the people of Israel "shall possess the land forever" (v. 21).

> *Isaiah 65:17–25:* This passage begins with God declaring that he will "create new heavens and a new earth" (v. 17; cf. Isa. 66:22). Interestingly, the existence of life in the new heavens and new earth is still centered on Jerusalem (vv. 18, 19). Infants will not die and old men will live to be a hundred (v. 20). The houses they build will be inhabited by them and the crops they plant will be enjoyed by them (v. 22). They will have children (v. 23) and wild animals will be domesticated (v. 25; cf. Isa. 11:6–9).

> *Jeremiah 31:38–40:* After God describes the new covenant (Jer. 31:31–34), he then indicates that Jerusalem will be rebuilt (v. 38) and will "not be uprooted or overthrown anymore forever" (v. 40).

> *Ezekiel 34:25–31:* In this text, God declares that he will make a covenant of peace with Israel (v. 25). This covenant includes banishing wild beasts from the land (vv. 25, 28; cf. Isa. 35:8–10), along with providing rain in season with good crops (vv. 26–27, 29), security for the inhabitants of the land (vv. 25, 27–28), and freedom from enemies (vv. 27–28). Later, in Ezekiel 37:26–28, a covenant of peace is again mentioned. This covenant is described as an "everlasting" covenant that includes Israel being established in their land (v. 26). God states that he "will set [his] sanctuary in their midst" (v. 26) and this sanctuary will be "in their midst forevermore" (v. 28; cf. Ezek. 40–48).

> *Ezekiel 36:29–37:* After God declares that he will remove Israel's heart of stone and give them a new heart and a new Spirit, causing them to obey his commands (Ezek. 36:26–27), he continues by promising them that they will dwell and prosper

in the Promised Land (vv. 28, 33). The crops will be continually abundant and famine will never occur (vv. 29–30).

Joel 3:17–20: The promised restorations recorded by Joel include the reestablishment of Jerusalem (v. 17), the absence
of strangers (v. 17), and an abundance of food and rain (v.
18). This prophecy also states that Judah shall be inhabited
forever, and Jerusalem to all generations (v. 20).

Should these Old Testament prophecies regarding God's promise to restore the nation of Israel be taken literally? Must our eschatology allow for
an age in the future in which these prophecies are fulfilled? One of the major
reasons why some insist on a future millennium when Jesus will reign as king
over the nation of Israel is that many Old Testament prophecies seem to remain unfulfilled.[2] In other words, a future reign of Jesus over the people of
Israel (in fulfillment of Old Testament prophecies) is one of the main reasons a
millennial kingdom is needed.[3] For without such a kingdom, dispensationalists
believe that God would have failed to deliver the promises given in his word.
To spiritualize these promises, it is sometimes argued, does not do justice to
the specific nature of these promises. For example, Wayne Grudem explains
that a characteristic of pretribulational (or dispensational) premillennialism "is
its insistence on interpreting biblical prophecies 'literally where possible.' This
especially applies to prophecies in the Old Testament concerning Israel."[4]

As a representative text, we will consider the meaning of Amos 9:11–15:

"In that day I will raise up the booth of David that is fallen
and repair its breaches, and raise up its ruins and rebuild it
as in the days of old, that they may possess the remnant of

---

2. This is especially true for dispensational premillennialists. For example, Walvoord admits, "The issue
of literal versus figurative or allegorical interpretation is a major issue because on it hangs the question as to whether the Bible teaches a future millennial kingdom following the Second Advent, or
whether it does not" (John F. Walvoord, *The Prophecy Knowledge Handbook* [Wheaton, IL: Victor
Books, 1990], 15). Grenz explains one of the major tenets of dispensationalism: "The millennium is
the occasion for God to fulfill the Old Testament prophecies to bless the nation" (Stanley J. Grenz,
The Millennial Maze: Sorting Out Evangelical Options [Downers Grove, IL: InterVarsity, 1992], 99).

3. Ryrie states, "The literal interpretation of Scripture leads naturally to . . . the literal fulfillment of Old
Testament prophecies. If the yet unfulfilled prophecies of the Old Testament made in the Abrahamic,
Davidic, and new covenants are to be literally fulfilled, there must be a future period, the Millennium,
in which they can be fulfilled, for the church is not now fulfilling them. In other words, the literal
picture of Old Testament prophecies demands either a future fulfillment or a nonliteral fulfillment.
If they are to be fulfilled in the future, then the only time left for that fulfillment is the Millennium"
(Charles C. Ryrie, *Dispensationalism*, rev. and exp. [Chicago: Moody, 1995], 147).

4. Wayne Grudem, *Systematic Theology: An Introduction to Biblical Doctrine* (Grand Rapids: Zondervan,
1994), 1113–14.

Edom and all the nations who are called by my name," declares the LORD who does this. "Behold, the days are coming," declares the LORD, "when the plowman shall overtake the reaper and the treader of grapes him who sows the seed; the mountains shall drip sweet wine, and all the hills shall flow with it. I will restore the fortunes of my people Israel, and they shall rebuild the ruined cities and inhabit them; they shall plant vineyards and drink their wine, and they shall make gardens and eat their fruit. I will plant them on their land, and they shall never again be uprooted out of the land that I have given them," says the LORD your God.

Does this prophecy refer to a time in the future when God will restore the nation of Israel and grant them unprecedented peace and prosperity? A time when their cities are restored, their enemies are defeated, and their land yields abundant crops? Or, should this prophecy be interpreted symbolically referring to a time when God will bless his covenant people in ways that words cannot really describe. In this section we will demonstrate that certain prophecies, especially Old Testament restoration prophecies regarding the nation of Israel, should be interpreted symbolically.[5] The reasons for a symbolic interpretation include (1) the true nature of biblical religion, (2) the unique genre of biblical prophecy, (3) the symbolic manner in which the New Testament interprets Old Testament prophecies, and (4) the central role of Jesus' death and resurrection in salvation history.

The True Nature of Biblical Religion

The Christian faith is a religion of the heart. It is not primarily external but internal.

True Circumcision

Circumcision was a significant part of both the Abrahamic and Mosaic covenants. It was the outward sign that separated God's chosen people from the other nations. And yet, according to the Old Testament, true circumcision was not the outward, physical act but the inward circumcision of the heart.

> *Mere outward external religion is never the goal of our faith. God is primarily interested in the deeper inner faith of his people. This is true not only for the New Testament but also for the Old Testament.*

---

5. By a "symbolic" interpretation we simply mean not according to a literalistic reading of the text. In other words, we believe that the text will be literally fulfilled but not necessarily according to the precise wording of the prophecy.

> Circumcise therefore the foreskin of your heart, and be no longer stubborn. (Deut. 10:16)

> And the LORD your God will circumcise your heart and the heart of your offspring, so that you will love the LORD your God with all your heart and with all your soul, that you may live. (Deut. 30:6)

> Circumcise yourselves to the LORD; remove the foreskin of your hearts, O men of Judah and inhabitants of Jerusalem. (Jer. 4:4a)

This emphasis on the inner circumcision of the heart is continued in the New Testament (Rom. 2:25–29; 1 Cor. 7:19; Gal. 5:6; 6:15; Phil. 3:2–3; Col. 2:11).

True Sacrifice

In the Old Testament God required daily sacrifices from his people. These sacrifices usually required the shedding of an animal's blood. But we know that such sacrifices were merely an outward sign that signified God's perfect standard and the need for atonement. God was always more interested in heart-felt obedience than he was in the mere shedding of an animal's blood.

> Behold, to obey is better than sacrifice, and to listen than the fat of rams. (1 Sam. 15:22b)

> In sacrifice and offering you have not delighted, but you have given me an open ear. Burnt offering and sin offering you have not required. (Ps. 40:6)

> The sacrifices of God are a broken spirit; a broken and contrite heart, O God, you will not despise. (Ps. 51:17)

> For I desire steadfast love and not sacrifice, the knowledge of God rather than burnt offerings. (Hos. 6:6)

True Fasting

The act of denying the body food or drink often signifies devotion to God. It demonstrates that God and his Word are more important than satisfying the desires of the body. It is an outward act that reflects the inward commitment. But if the inward attitude does not accompany the external act, fasting becomes a mockery to God.

Behold, in the day of your fast you seek your own pleasure, and oppress your workers. . . . Is such the fast that I choose, a day for a person to humble himself? Is it to bow down his head like a reed, and to spread sackcloth and ashes under him? Will you call this a fast, and a day acceptable to the LORD? Is not this the fast that I choose: to loose the bonds of wickedness, to undo the straps of the yoke, to let the oppressed go free, and to break every yoke? Is it not to share your bread with the hungry and bring the homeless poor into your house; when you see the naked, to cover him, and not to hide yourself from your own flesh? (Isa. 58:3b, 5–7)

Though they fast, I will not hear their cry, and though they offer burnt offering and grain offering, I will not accept them. (Jer. 14:12a)

Even with all of its external rituals and requirements, the old covenant was essentially about the heart. In the new covenant, this inward focus becomes more evident as many of the outward elements are stripped away.

The above comments and Scripture references do not prove that certain Old Testament prophecies concerning the nation of Israel must be taken symbolically. God is certainly interested in the physical aspect—even in heaven. For instance, the Bible clearly teaches that believers will be given a physical, resurrected body. Our point is simply this: If the new covenant, with its focus on the spiritual, is the fulfillment of God's plan, why should we go back to the shadows and images? (Col. 2:17; Heb. 8:5; 10:1).[6] The Jews of Jesus' day were expecting the Messiah to establish a tangible, earthly kingdom based on their (mis)understanding of the Old Testament. Thus, the messianic kingdom became primarily the political rule of Israel over all the nations—a time when there would be an abundance of

> *By returning to shadows and images, we are guilty of reversing God's plan of redemptive history.*

---

6. Ladd writes, "The law with its temple and sacrificial system was only a shadow of the blessings—the reality—which has come to us in Christ. The shadow has fulfilled its purpose. . . . It is inconceivable that God's redemptive plan will revert to the age of shadows" (George Eldon Ladd, *The Last Things: An Eschatology for Laymen* [Grand Rapids: Eerdmans, 1978], 25). Likewise, Mickelsen comments, "Because of what God did in Christ, there will be no return to the shadows, but rather there will be the worship of God on a transcendently higher level" (A. Berkeley Mickelsen, *Interpreting the Bible* [Grand Rapids: Eerdmans, 1963], 297). Gentry and Wellum also note, "The flow of redemptive-history as traced through the biblical covenants reaches its *telos* in Christ. What our Lord has inaugurated does *not* go back to the types and patterns of old; it transforms and fulfills them" (Peter J. Gentry and Stephen J. Wellum, *Kingdom through Covenant: A Biblical Theological Understanding of the Covenants* [Wheaton, IL: Crossway, 2012], 714n. 146).

wealth and prosperity. But they were mistaken. Could it be that we are guilty of the same? Could it be that we have mistaken the shell for the core?[7] Is it really God's intention for the nation of Israel to restore its cities, for them to defeat their enemies, or for their land to yield abundant crops (Amos 9:11–15)? Or do these promises have an even greater significance? Could it be that the prophets used metaphorical language to describe the nature in which God would fulfill his promises?

The Unique Genre of Biblical Prophecy

How do we know if a prophecy should be taken literally or symbolically? Certainly not all prophecy is symbolic or figurative. For example, the prophet Micah informs us that the Messiah would be born in Bethlehem (Mic. 5:2). Such prophecies were fulfilled literally—why not the rest?[8] The answer to this question depends (1) on the nature of the prophecy and (2) the language used in the prophecy. Prophecy concerning the end of time or the coming of God's kingdom is often written using metaphorical language. The prophets often employed earthly imagery to describe a heavenly reality. The messianic kingdom was often pictured as a return from exile and frequently included a rebuilt temple (built on mount Zion which will become the highest mountain), resumed temple sacrifices, and wild animals dwelling together peacefully. The reason for this was simple. The prophets spoke and wrote in terms that both they and their audience would understand. They described the messianic kingdom in terms of concepts and imagery that was meaningful to the people of that day.[9] Amos describes the future in terms that communicate the highest blessings of God. Their cities would be rebuilt, their enemies would be conquered, their land would produce more than seemed possible, and they would dwell in the land forever.

---

7. This terminology is from Herman Bavinck, *The Last Things: Hope for This World and the Next*, ed. by John Bolt, trans. by John Vriend (Grand Rapids: Baker, 1996), 90. He writes, "In Jesus' day Israel expected a tangible, earthly, messianic kingdom whose conditions were depicted in the forms and images of the Old Testament prophecy. But now these forms and images were taken literally. The shell was mistaken for the core, the image of it for the thing itself, and the form for the essence. The messianic kingdom became the political rule of Israel over the nations—a period of external prosperity and growth."

8. Ryrie, for example, argues that a literal interpretation should always be used because "the prophecies in the Old Testament concerning the first coming of Christ—His birth, His rearing, His ministry, His death, His resurrection—were all fulfilled literally" (*Dispensationalism*, 81).

9. Mickelsen notes, "The language of the prophet is colored by all of his present and past surroundings. He speaks to his people in their language, in their patterns. He makes use of the customs which they know" (*Interpreting the Bible*, 295). See also Gordon D. Fee and Douglas Stuart, *How to Read the Bible for All Its Worth: A Guide to Understanding the Bible*, 4th ed. (Grand Rapids: Zondervan, 2014), 191. Unlike those who interpret prophecy in a literalistic manner, we are not arguing that the prophets were accommodating their language to merely describe futuristic, literal realities (e.g., cities, walls, crops), but were symbolically conveying future blessings in words his audience could understand.

The prophets often employed figurative or cosmic language to describe the great works of God in history (see Isa. 13:9–10, 13). While much of the Bible can be read and interpreted literally, certain parts of the Bible (especially poetry, prophecy, and apocalyptic literature) are not meant to be interpreted literally.[10] The prophets often communicated a divine message using earthly language. That is, the prophets used earthly language to describe a more profound heavenly reality—a reality that finds its fulfillment in Christ. Graeme Goldsworthy correctly insists that we should not interpret prophecies literally "if by literal is meant that fulfilment must be in the precise terms of the promise, and that the reality is only a future repetition of the foreshadowing."[11] He continues:

> The New Testament knows nothing of this kind of literalism. It repeatedly maintains that Christ is the fulfilment of these terms, images, promises and foreshadowings in the Old Testament which were presented in a way that is different from the fulfilment. For the New Testament the interpretation of the Old Testament is not "literal" but "Christological". That is to say that the coming of the Christ transforms all the Kingdom terms of the Old Testament into gospel reality.[12]

Restoration prophecies regularly use figurative or symbolic language which find often find their ultimate fulfilment in Christ.

The Symbolic Manner in Which the New Testament Interprets Old Testament Prophecies

One of the principles of sound hermeneutics is that we should let Scripture interpret Scripture. We might be inclined to interpret a passage one way but we must give precedence to the wisdom of God. How, then, do the New Testament writers interpret Old Testament prophecies and promises to the nation of Israel?

In Acts 15 Luke recounts the proceedings of the so-called Jerusalem Council. In seeking to refute the notion that Gentiles had to be circumcised in order to be saved (Acts 15:1), Peter declared his conviction that God makes no distinction between Jews and Gentiles. Paul and Barnabas also related all

---

10. For example, all must admit that Amos 9:11–15 uses nonliteral language when the prophet says, "the mountains shall drip sweet wine, and all the hills shall flow with it" (v. 13). Figurative language is used to communicate a reality: God will abundantly bless his people by supplying all their needs. The issue, then, is whether the physical blessing is a metaphor for the greater spiritual blessings we receive in Christ and his kingdom.
11. Graeme Goldsworthy, *Gospel and Kingdom: A Christian Interpretation of the Old Testament* (Carlisle: Paternoster, 1994), 88. See also his more recent work *Gospel-Centered Hermeneutics: Foundations and Principles of Evangelical Biblical Interpretation* (Downers Grove, IL: InterVarsity, 2006), 169–71.
12. Goldsworthy, *Gospel and Kingdom*, 88.

that God had done among them with the Gentiles. Finally, James stood up and quoted Amos 9:11–12 as proof that God had made the Gentiles his own people, just as was foretold by the prophets.

> After this I will return, and I will rebuild the tent of David that has fallen; I will rebuild its ruins, and I will restore it, that the remnant of mankind may seek the Lord, and all the Gentiles who are called by my name, says the Lord, who makes these things known from of old. (Acts 15:16–17)

James does not apply this text to some future millennial kingdom when the people of Israel regain their independence and rebuild the city of Jerusalem. Instead, it is used as justification for accepting the Gentiles into the people of God without needing to be circumcised. "James is saying that the wonderful thing which is now happening, namely, that the Gentiles are now coming into the fellowship of God's people, is a fulfillment of the words of the prophet Amos about the building up again of the fallen tabernacle of David."[13] Some might respond by arguing that James is not claiming this text is fulfilled but is merely drawing attention to the fact that Amos mentions the Gentiles (or nations) seeking the Lord. But James could have simply quoted verse 12 and left out verse 11. The reason James includes verse 11 is that he sees the salvation of Gentiles as part of the restoration process of Israel. The house of David is being rebuilt—not just out of physical Jews but also out of spiritual Jews. John Polhill rightly comments:

> In the Gentiles, God was choosing a people for himself, a new *restored* people of God, Jew and Gentile in Christ, the true Israel. In the total message of Acts it is clear that the rebuilt house of David occurred in the Messiah. Christ was the scion of David who fulfilled the covenant of David and established a kingdom that would last forever (2 Sam 7:12f., cf. Acts 13:32–34). From the beginning the Jewish Christians had realized that the promises to David were fulfilled in Christ. What they were now beginning to see, and what James saw foretold in Amos, was that these promises included the Gentiles.[14]

---

13. Anthony A. Hoekema, "An Amillennial Response," in *The Meaning of the Millennium: Four Views*, ed. Robert G. Clouse (Downers Grove, IL: InterVarsity, 1977), 110. He continues, "In other words, the fallen tabernacle of David is being built up not in a material way (by means of a restored earthly kingdom) but in a spiritual way (as Gentiles are coming into the kingdom of God)." Grenz likewise comments, "The prophet anticipated an eschatological re-emergence of Israel as a dominant nation under the reign of David's greater son, the Messiah. But the leader of the Jerusalem church claimed that the fulfillment of this text was the coming of the Gentiles to faith in Jesus" (*Millennial Maze*, 109).

14. John B. Polhill, *Acts*, NAC 26 (Nashville: Broadman, 1992), 330. I. Howard Marshall suggests that "the rebuilding of the tabernacle is to be understood as a reference to the raising up of the church as

Could this text also have a literal fulfillment? Klein, Blomberg, and Hubbard give two reasons for denying a literal fulfillment: "First we contend that the NT assumes that such prophecies have already achieved their fulfillment through Christ and the Church. It leaves no reason to anticipate a second, later fulfillment. Second, to expect the latter implies that God has two separate peoples, Israel and the Church, each serving a different historical purpose and each having separate dealings with God."[15] They conclude, "We see no persuasive biblical reason to expect a future literal fulfillment of what the NT says has already occurred."[16]

Based on the interpretation given by James and recorded by Luke, we have a clear example of the New Testament interpreting an Old Testament restoration passage in a nonliteral or symbolic (or christological) manner. But there are still other examples in the New Testament. In seeking to demonstrate that the new covenant is superior to the old covenant, the author of Hebrews quotes several verses from Jeremiah 31. Through the prophet Jeremiah, God promises, "I will establish a new covenant with the house of Israel and with the house of Judah" (Heb. 8:8). The point to be made here is that this covenant is said to be with the people of Israel and Judah. Does this covenant include Gentile Christians? Or is this a special covenant made only with the Jewish people? Although it is true that this particular letter was written to a primarily (or perhaps even exclusively) Jewish audience, there is no New Testament evidence that God makes one covenant with the Jews and then a separate covenant with the Gentiles.[17] Rather, the mentioning of Israel and Judah indicates that God's people will again be reunited. "The promise of the reunion of Israel and Judah was symbolic of the healing of every human breach and the reconciliation of all nations and persons in Christ, the seed of Abraham in whom all the peoples of the earth are blessed and united."[18] For, as we are taught in the New Testament,

---

the new place of divine worship which replaced the temple" (*Acts*, TNTC, vol. 5 [Leicester: InterVarsity; Grand Rapids: Eerdmans, 1980], 252). John Stott maintains that Christians see this passage "as a prophecy of the resurrection and exaltation of Christ, the seed of David, and the establishment of his people" (*The Message of Acts* [Leicester: InterVarsity, 1990], 247). This is also the position of Klein, Blomberg and Hubbard who state that in Acts 15:16–17, "James says the fulfillment of Amos 9 is the admission of non-Jewish believers to the company of Jesus' followers. He does so by interpreting Amos' prediction of David's future political rule as representing Christ's spiritual rule over non-Jewish Christians" (William W. Klein, Craig L. Blomberg, and Robert L. Hubbard, *Introduction to Biblical Interpretation* [Dallas: Word, 1993], 308).

15. Klein, Blomberg, and Hubbard, *Biblical Interpretation*, 308.

16. Ibid.

17. Ladd rightly notes, "It is difficult to see how anyone can deny that the new covenant of Jeremiah 31 is the new covenant made by Christ with his church" (*The Last Things*, 27).

18. Philip Edgcumbe Hughes, *A Commentary on the Epistle to the Hebrews* (Grand Rapids: Eerdmans, 1977), 300. Similarly, Kistemaker suggests that "because the ten tribes of Israel failed to return after the exile, the phrases ought to be understood in a more universalistic sense to include both Jews and Gentiles" (Simon J. Kistemaker, *Exposition of the Epistle to the Hebrews* [Grand Rapids: Baker, 1984], 225). See also Klein, Blomberg, and Hubbard, *Biblical Interpretation*, 308.

what makes someone a real Jew is not physical birth, but spiritual birth. Paul boldly declares, "For no one is a Jew who is merely one outwardly, nor is circumcision outward and physical. But a Jew is one inwardly, and circumcision is a matter of the heart, by the Spirit, not by the letter. His praise is not from man but from God" (Rom. 2:28–29). Abraham is the father of all believers, not just those from the physical people of Israel. He is also the father of those Gentiles who believe in the Messiah and, consequently, are grafted into the covenant that God made with Abraham (Rom. 4:11; 11:17). In Galatians Paul affirms that "it is those of faith who are the sons of Abraham" (Gal. 3:7). Similarly, he later adds, "And if you are Christ's, then you are Abraham's offspring, heirs according to promise" (Gal. 3:29). He labels the churches in Galatia (which consisted of both Jews and Gentiles) "the Israel of God" (Gal. 6:16).

The new covenant is not a covenant that merely applies to those who are physical descendants of Abraham. It is offered to all those who place their trust and hope in the Messiah, who was a physical descendant of Abraham. To claim that the promises of Jeremiah 31:31–34 (or Ezek. 11:19–20; 36:26–27) do not apply to the church seems to ignore how the New Testament writers themselves applied such promises.[19]

Peter offers us another example for how we should interpret Old Testament language regarding Israel. In his first epistle, Peter writes to the elect exiles scattered throughout Pontus, Galatia, Cappadocia, Asia, and Bithynia:

> But you are a chosen race, a royal priesthood, a holy nation, a people for his own possession, that you may proclaim the excellencies of him who called you out of darkness into his marvelous light. Once you were not a people, but now you are God's people; once you had not received mercy, but now you have received mercy. (1 Peter 2:9–10)

These verses echo several Old Testament references describing the nation of Israel. Peter claims that Christians are a "chosen race" (Isa. 43:20), a "royal priesthood" and a "holy nation" (Exod. 19:6; cf. 23:22, LXX), "a people for his own possession" (Exod. 19:5; Isa. 43:21; Mal. 3:17), and once they were "not a people" who had "not received mercy" but now they are "God's people" who have "received mercy" (Exod. 6:7; Jer. 7:23; 11:4; 30:22; Ezek. 37:23; Hos. 1:6, 9; 2:1, 23). Originally, these verses signified God's covenant with the people of Israel. And yet, Peter applies these verses to the church. "Peter saw

---

19. Interestingly, the promises of the new covenant often include restoration promises for Israel. For example, after Jeremiah describes the blessings of the new covenant (Jer. 31:31–34), he states, "Behold, the days are coming, declares the Lord, when the city shall be rebuilt for the Lord from the tower of Hananel to the Corner Gate" (Jer. 31:38; see also Ezek. 36:26–38). If the new covenant is given to the church, then the restoration promises to Israel should also be seen as being fulfilled in the church.

these promises as fulfilled in Jesus Christ, and God's elect nation is no longer coterminous with Israel but embraces the church of Jesus Christ, which is composed of both Jews and Gentiles."[20]

Some may argue that Peter was writing only to Jewish Christians so that these verses cannot be used as evidence. After all, it is thought, Peter was the apostle to the Jews. There is, however, ample evidence to suggest that Peter's audience consisted primarily of Gentile Christians. In the first chapter Peter states, "As obedient children, do not be conformed to the passions of your former ignorance" (v. 14). Later in the same chapter he adds, "knowing that you were ransomed from the futile ways inherited from your forefathers" (v. 18). They formerly carried out the desires of the Gentiles (1 Peter 4:3–4) but now have been "called out of darkness" (1 Peter 2:9). These verses indicate that at least a strong majority of Peter's audience was Gentile.

What is crucial for our argument, then, is that Peter unashamedly applies the well-known Old Testament covenant terminology to the church. Gentile believers are "being built up as a spiritual house"; they are God's "holy" or "royal priesthood"; they are a "chosen race"; they are a "holy nation"; they are "God's people" who have received mercy (1 Peter 2:5, 9–10). God has bestowed on the church the blessings promised to Israel in the Old Testament.[21] Just as Abraham did not merely look to the physical land of Canaan but to "a better country, that is, a heavenly one" (Heb. 11:16), so too we should not expect God's promises to be fulfilled in regards to merely a physical people, a physical place, or a physical blessing.

The New Testament writers do not seem to expect all the Old Testament prophecies about the nation of Israel to be fulfilled literally. Some might object and claim that in Romans 11 Paul expects Israel as a nation to someday turn to Christ in faith. Although there is doubt as to whether Paul teaches a future mass conversion of the nation of Israel in Romans 11:26 (see Appendix 1), Bavinck rightly notes that "even if Paul expected a national conversion of Israel at the end, he does not say a word about the return of the Jews to Palestine, about a rebuilding of the city and a temple, about a visible rule of Christ: in his picture of the future there simply is no room for all this."[22] A

---

20. Thomas R. Schreiner, *1, 2 Peter, Jude*, NAC 37 (Nashville: B&H, 2003), 114. Similarly, Klein, Blomberg, and Hubbard state, "1 Pet 2:9–10 assumes that the Church in this messianic era now constitutes *the people of God*" (*Introduction to Biblical Interpretation*, 308).

21. Klein, Blomberg, and Hubbard comment, "NT writers believed that Jesus Christ and the Christian Church represent the fulfillment of Israel's God-given mission in history" (*Biblical Interpretation*, 309).

22. Bavinck, *Last Things*, 107. Similarly, Berkhof comments, "It is remarkable that the New Testament, which is the fulfillment of the Old, contains no indication whatsoever of the re-establishment of the Old Testament theocracy by Jesus, nor a single undisputed positive prediction of its restoration, while it does contain abundant indications of the spiritual fulfilment of the promises given to Israel" (Louis Berkhof, *Systematic Theology* [Grand Rapids: Eerdmans, 1941], 713). Along the same lines, Goldsworthy notes, "Many people in effect regard the second coming of Christ as involving a whole new work of God. This conclusion is forced upon them because they do not accept that all promise is fulfilled

literal fulfillment was not expected but rather New Testament writers correctly saw fulfillment in Christ and in the gospel. They correctly understood John the Baptist to be Elijah (Mal. 4:5–6; Matt. 17:11–13). They correctly understood the promise to David—that his son would someday establish an eternal kingdom—was fulfilled in the resurrection of Jesus (2 Sam. 7:12–16; Acts 2:29–36; see also Acts 13:29–32). There was no hesitation to say Christians have already come to "Mount Zion," which is also called "the heavenly Jerusalem" and "the city of the living God" (Heb. 12:22). As we see how the New Testament writers approached the Old Testament, we will see that the Old Testament prophecies concerning the nation of Israel are fulfilled in Christ and in the gospel.

> We should not impose an overly literalistic hermeneutic on the texts. Rather, we must learn from how the New Testament writers themselves interpreted the Old Testament.

The Central Role of Jesus' Death and Resurrection in Salvation History

One of the problems with interpreting Old Testament prophecies regarding the nation of Israel in a literal manner is that doing so tends to minimize the work of Christ, especially his suffering, death, and resurrection (see chapter 3). How is this so? The New Testament teaches that the death and resurrection of Christ are the climax of God's work in redemptive history. But if we interpret the many Old Testament restoration prophecies regarding the nation of Israel literalisticallly, then we are forced to say that such prophecies do not find their fulfillment in God's greatest work. Instead, the first coming of Christ becomes ignored and all attention shifts to Christ's second coming and the millennial kingdom.[23]

Another problem with a literal interpretation is that the Old Testament consistently pictures a messianic kingdom that includes the restoration of the temple, the priesthood, and the temple sacrifices. Bavinck explains, "All the prophets, with equal vigor and force, announce not only the conversion of Israel and the nations but also the return to Palestine, the rebuilding of Jerusalem, and the restoration of the temple, the priesthood,

---

in the gospel. Thus, despite the scriptural evidence ... to the contrary, they see the return of Israel, the rebuilding of the Temple, the restoration of Davidic kingship as unrelated to the gospel and requiring separate fulfilment on some future occasion" (*Gospel and Kingdom*, 95). He later writes, "The New Testament seems to be completely indifferent to the restoration referred to [in the Old Testament]" (*Gospel-Centered Hermeneutics*, 170).

23. Bavinck affirms that a literal interpretation "attributes a temporary, passing value to Christianity, the historical person of Christ, and his suffering and death, and only first expects real salvation from Christ's second coming, his appearance in glory" (*Last Things*, 98).

and sacrificial worship."[24] Some of these features seem to be purposefully ignored. Hoyt, for example, while insisting on a literal kingdom seems to intentionally ignore the prophetic references of restoration of the priesthood and the temple sacrifices:

> The actual place of its central location will be Jerusalem and vicinity (Obad. 12–21). A real King will sit on a material throne (Is. 33:17). Nations of mankind will participate in its ministry of welfare and deliverance (Is. 52:10). The wicked kingdoms of this world will be brought to a sudden and catastrophic end at the coming of Christ, and his kingdom will supplant them (Dan. 2:31–45). This kingdom will be a revival and continuation of the historical Davidic kingdom (Amos 9:11; see Acts 15:16–18). A faithful and regenerated remnant of Israel will be restored and made the nucleus of this kingdom, and thus the covenant with David will be fulfilled (Mic. 4:7–8; Jer. 33:15–22; Ps. 89:3–4, 34–37). Jerusalem will become the capital city of the great King, from which he will govern the world (Is. 2:3; 24:23).[25]

But if we maintain that the prophet's picture of the future must be literal, then we must take all the aspects literally.[26] In other words, if we insist that the nation of Israel will someday return to the Promised Land, rebuild the cities of Israel, and have Christ rule as their King, then we are also forced to include the notion that the Jews will again have a priesthood and offer sacrifices in the temple.

Listen to how the prophet Isaiah describes the restoration of Israel.

> And the foreigners who join themselves to the LORD, to minister to him, to love the name of the LORD, and to be his servants ... these I will bring to my holy mountain, and make them joyful in my house of prayer; their burnt offerings and their sacrifices will be accepted on my altar; for my house shall be called a house of prayer for all peoples. (Isa. 56:6–7)

---

24. Ibid., 94.
25. Herman A. Hoyt, "Dispensational Premillennialism" in *The Meaning of the Millennium: Four Views*, ed. Robert G. Clouse (Downers Grove, IL: InterVarsity, 1977), 78–79. Some maintain that the temple sacrifices will resume but not for purpose of atonement. Rather, they will serve as a reminder of Christ's sacrifice. But are such sacrifices appropriate? Has not God already given his people a memorial in the Lord's Supper?
26. In Bavinck's words, "It is nothing but caprice to take one feature of this picture literally and another 'spiritually'" (*Last Things*, 94).

All the flocks of Kedar shall be gathered to you; the rams of Nebaioth shall minister to you; they shall come up with acceptance on my altar, and I will beautify my beautiful house. (Isa. 60:7)

And they shall bring all your brothers from all the nations as an offering to the LORD, on horses and in chariots and in litters and on mules and on dromedaries, to my holy mountain Jerusalem, says the LORD, just as the Israelites bring their grain offering in a clean vessel to the house of the LORD. And some of them also I will take for priests and for Levites, says the LORD. For as the new heavens and the new earth that I make shall remain before me, says the LORD, so shall your offspring and your name remain. (Isa. 66:20–22)

A similar picture is given by Jeremiah (3:16–17; 30:18; 31:21, 38), Ezekiel (36:28–38; 37:21–28; 39:25–29), Joel (3:17–20), Amos (9:11–15), Obadiah (17, 21), Micah (4:1–2; 7:11), Haggai (2:6–10), and Zechariah (1:17; 2:1–5; 6:9–15; 8:3–23).

While in exile Ezekiel was given a vision of the land of Israel and specifically the temple (Ezek. 40–48). The prophet was given a virtual tour of the temple which included a precise floor plan with measurements. Was this vision a prophecy concerning the temple that will be built by the people of Israel at a future time? This does not appear to be the case. First, when the Second Temple was built, they did not follow the plan nor the scale envisaged by Ezekiel (cf. *Tobit* 14:5). Second, there is not sufficient information to build a temple from his design. Third, Ezekiel was told to convey to the exiles all that he had seen, but nowhere was he told to build such a temple (cf. the Mosaic tabernacle). Instead, Ezekiel's vision communicates the restoration of the true worship of God.[27] Christopher Wright insists, "[T]he purpose of Ezekiel's vision was not to provide guidance as to *how* the temple was to be rebuilt, but to provide reassurance of the hope *that* it would be rebuilt, and to point beyond the physical temple to the restored relationship between God in his holiness and his humble and obedient people."[28] In other words, this prophecy was given in response to the promise God gave to Ezekiel: "I will make a covenant of peace with them. It shall be an everlasting covenant with them. And I

---

27. See J. B. Taylor, "The Temple in Ezekiel," in *Heaven and Earth: The Temple in Biblical Theology*, ed. T. D. Alexander and S. Gathercole (Carlisle: Paternoster, 2004), 67–69; T. Desmond Alexander, *From Eden to the New Jerusalem: An Introduction to Biblical Theology* (Grand Rapids: Kregel, 2008), 57.
28. Christopher J. H. Wright, *The Message of Ezekiel* (Leicester: InterVarsity, 2001), 338.

will set them in their land and multiply them, and will set my sanctuary in their midst forevermore. My dwelling place shall be with them, and I will be their God, and they shall be my people" (Ezek. 37:26–27). The main thrust of the vision is not to be found in the details "but in the restoration of the dwelling place of God in the midst of his people" (see Ezek. 48:35).[29]

To suppose that this temple will literally be built in the millennium (since it has not yet been built) is to fail to see the progress of redemptive history and is to return to copies and shadows. As Mickelsen aptly remarks, "[T]here seems to be no reason why Ezekiel's description may not depict the worship of God by his people in the time of the consummation. Because of what God did in Christ, there will be no return to the shadows, but rather there will be the worship of God on a transcendently higher level. . . . *Hence the worship of God in the future will not return to the shadow but will exalt the reality.*"[30]

Couched in the midst of prophecies concerning the return to the land, rebuilding of the temple, and the continuation of the temple practices is also the expectation that what awaits Israel will be something that far exceeds any earthly fulfillment. There will be no need for the ark of the covenant because "Jerusalem shall be called the throne of the LORD" (Jer. 3:17). There will be no sin, sickness, or death: "He will swallow up death forever; and the Lord GOD will wipe away tears from all faces, and the reproach of his people he will take away from all the earth" (Isa. 25:8). There will be a new heaven and a new earth (Isa. 65:17; 66:22) which have no need for the sun or the moon because the Lord himself will be the everlasting light (Isa. 60:19–20). Thus, "although it is true that Old Testament prophecy cannot conceive the future kingdom of God without a temple and sacrifice, over and over it *transcends* all national and earthly conditions."[31]

If we insist on an overly literal interpretation we end up with Jewish believers who return to Jerusalem and reinstate the Old Testament sacrificial system as Christ reigns over them. Instead, we must see the prophets as using earthly language to describe a greater reality. At times, the prophets are forced

---

29. Ibid., 329. See also G. K. Beale, *The Temple and the Church's Mission: A Biblical Theology of the Dwelling Place of God*, NSBT 17 (Downers Grove, IL: InterVarsity Press, 2004), 335–64. Beale argues that Ezekiel's temple is fulfilled in Revelation 21–22 and thus "is not to be established in a temporary 'millennial' period, but in the eternal new heavens and earth" (351–52).

30. Mickelsen, *Interpreting the Bible,* 297–298. He continues, "To suppose that the ancient ritual will be restored should be abhorrent to everyone who takes seriously the message of the book of Hebrews" (ibid., 298). See also Charles H. H. Scobie, *The Ways of Our God: An Approach to Biblical Theology* (Grand Rapids: Eerdmans, 2003), 587. He writes, "Just as Ezekiel's vision of the restored Land is ideal and apocalyptic rather than practical and historical, so it is with his vision of the future temple." Surprisingly, *The New Scofield Reverence Bible* (New York: Oxford University Press, 1967) posits that the references in Ezekiel's vision of a restored temple "is not to be taken literally . . . but is rather to be regarded as a presentation of the worship of the redeemed in Israel . . . using terms with which the Jews were familiar in Ezekiel's day" (888n. 1).

31. Bavinck, *Last Things*, 95.

to picture the future kingdom in terms that transcend the earthly or physical. Therefore, we must not interpret their earthly, physical descriptions in a literal manner. To do so minimizes the work of Christ. Christ is the one great prophet, priest, and king. His sacrifice was alone able to make atonement for the sins of the world. He is the fulfillment of all that the Old Testament predicted.[32] To still be looking for the fulfillment of those Old Testament prophecies is to minimize the significance of the Messiah. All the benefits of our salvation that were promised and foreshadowed in the Old Testament have become a reality in Christ. Or, as Paul put it, all the promises of God are "yes" and "amen" in Christ (2 Cor. 1:20).

Conclusion

The Old Testament presents a vivid and detailed picture of Israel's future restoration. We have seen, however, that these descriptions are not meant to be taken literalistically. Although it is true that these predictions and promises have a real meaning, the meaning is not expressed *in* the actual language, but *through* the actual language of the prophecies. By insisting on a literalistic interpretation, we are in danger of forcing the text to mean something that God did not intend. The new covenant is characterized by the inner transformation of a person. This core was found in the old covenant but it was wrapped in an external shell. Now that the external shell has been shed, is it really God's plan to reinstitute it? In addition, a literalistic interpretation does not do justice to the genre of biblical prophecy. There is no virtue in claiming to apply a literalistic interpretation consistently to texts that were not designed to be interpreted literally. The Old Testament prophets used metaphorical language to describe truths in terms with which the audience could relate. Furthermore, the New Testament itself teaches us that we should not insist on a literalistic interpretation. There are abundant examples where New Testament authors offer a symbolic interpretation of Old Testament prophecies concerning the nation of Israel. Finally, affirming that the restored people of Israel will rebuild the temple, reinstate the priesthood, and restore animal sacrifices, seems to minimize the complete and perfect work of Christ. His death and resurrection is the focal point of God's great work in redemptive history. To go back to the shadows and images of the Old Testament is to neglect the centrality of Christ's finished work on the cross.

---

32. Strimple rightly notes, "With regard to any type—whether it be sacrifice, feast, temple, or land—when the reality is introduced, the shadow passes away. And it does not pass away in order to be at some future restored; it passes away because in Jesus Christ it has been fulfilled!" (Robert B. Strimple, "Amillennialism" in *The Millennium and Beyond*, ed. Paul E. Engle and Steve B. Cowan [Grand Rapids: Zondervan, 1999], 86).

Chapter 6

Messianic Prophecies

There is much debate as to what
constitutes a passage as being "messianic."

Various rabbinic writings have identified at least 456 separate Old Testament passages that refer to the Messiah.[1] J. Barton Payne lists 113 prophecies with personal reference to Christ.[2] Most modern critical scholars, however, maintain that the concept of a Messiah is post-exilic, arising from the demise of the Davidic kingdom. It will be argued in this chapter that the concept of a Messiah—a future deliverer or savior—is found throughout the Old Testament, including the earliest accounts in the book of Genesis.[3] From the outset, we must clarify that many passages considered "messianic" are not predictive in nature. The New Testament writers considered passages to be messianic that were both predictive (explicitly messianic) but also typological (implicitly messianic).[4] In this chapter, after first discussing some of the more general messianic texts found in Genesis, we will discuss messianic texts that relate to Jesus as (1) prophet, (2) priest, and (3) king.

Genesis 3:15 comprises what many believe to be the first messianic text. Before the fall of Adam and Eve, there was no need for a Messiah and thus

---

1. See Alfred Edersheim, *The Life and Times of Jesus the Messiah*, 2 vols. (Grand Rapids: Eerdmans, 1953), 2:710–41. Of the 456 passages, 75 are found in the Law, 243 are found in the Prophets, and 138 in the Writings. It must be noted that many of these so-called messianic references are not legitimate but are based on illegitimate spiritualizing or allegorizing the text.
2. J. Barton Payne, *Encyclopedia of Biblical Prophecy: The Complete Guide to Scriptural Predictions and Their Fulfillment* (New York: Harper & Row, 1973), 665–68. These prophecies do not include typological references.
3. T. Desmond Alexander declares that "messianic ideology permeates the book of Genesis" ("Messianic Ideology in the Book of Genesis" in *The Lord's Anointed: Interpretation of Old Testament Messianic Texts* [Carlisle: Paternoster; Grand Rapids: Baker, 1995], 20).
4. Kaiser identifies three types of prophecies: (1) direct prophecies (e.g., Mic. 3:1; 5:2; Zech. 9:9), (2) typical prophecies (e.g., Exod. 25:8–9), and (3) applications (e.g., Isa. 11:1; cf. Matt. 2:23) (Walter C. Kaiser, *The Messiah in the Old Testament* [Grand Rapids: Zondervan, 1995], 34–35).

no need to record the promise of a future deliverer. After the Fall, however, everything changed. Adam and Eve went from a state of sinless perfection to being cursed by God and banished from the garden. But God not only punished the man and the woman, he also cursed the serpent and Satan, who deceptively used the serpent to accomplish his purposes. God himself declared, "I will put enmity between you and the woman, and between your offspring and her offspring; he shall bruise your head, and you shall bruise his heel." This verse is often called the *protoevangelium* because it records the first words of the gospel: the serpent (that is, Satan)[5] will bruise the heel of the woman's offspring (or seed), but that offspring of the woman will bruise the serpent's head.[6] Because "seed" can be a collective singular, there is no consensus as to whether this prophecy refers to the whole human race or to a specific individual. The imagery (and the grammar) of the text, however, suggests that there will be a representative who will do the actual stepping on the serpent's head ("*he* shall bruise your head, and you shall bruise *his* heel").[7]

Thus, this verse is a prophecy regarding a future victory of the seed of the woman over Satan.[8] Just as Satan used the woman to bring the defeat of the human race, so God will use the woman to bring their victory. Through his death, resurrection, and ascension, Jesus fulfills this prophecy. The author of Hebrews writes that Jesus was incarnated and made able to die so that "through death he might destroy the one who has the power of death, that is, the devil" (Heb. 2:14). Thus, "Christ is the seed of the woman, who tramples Satan under his feet, not as an individual, but as the head both of the posterity of the woman

---

5. That the serpent represents Satan, see Romans 16:20; 2 Corinthians 11:3, 14; Revelation 12:9.

6. Although some translations such as the NIV and the Jerusalem Bible use two different verbs (e.g., "crush" and "strike"), the Hebrew term is the same (*šûp*).

7. The masculine singular personal pronouns suggest a specific individual. This interpretation is supported by the Septuagint translation of Genesis 3:15 which uses the masculine personal pronoun *autos* even though the antecedent (*sperma*) is neuter. This suggests that the translators of the Septuagint understood this verse to point to the Messiah (see Ralph A. Martin, "The Earliest Messianic Interpretation of Genesis 3:15," *JBL* 84 [1965]: 425–27; Jack Collins, "A Syntactical Note [Genesis 3:15]: Is the Woman's Seed Singular or Plural?" *TynBul* 48, no. 1 [1997]: 139–48; Walter C. Kaiser, *Messiah in the Old Testament* [Grand Rapids: Zondervan, 1995], 39–40; T. Desmond Alexander, "Further Observations on the Term 'Seed' in Genesis," *TynBul* 48 [1997]: 363–67; idem, *From Eden to the New Jerusalem: An Introduction to Biblical Theology* [Grand Rapids: Kregel, 2008], 105–6; James Hamilton, "The Skull Crushing Seed of the Woman: Inner-Biblical Interpretation of Genesis 3:15," *SBJT* 10, no. 2 [2006]: 30–54; idem, "The Seed of the Woman and the Blessing of Abraham," *TynBul* 58, no. 2 [2007]: 253–73).

8. Alexander comments, "If the 'seed of the woman' does not have the ultimate victory over the serpent, as some writers think, then the divine curse upon the serpent is also a punishment inflicted by God upon humanity. Consequently, the man and the woman are punished twice over. Yet, given the serpent's role as instigator of the rebellion against God, it is surely unlikely that it received a lesser punishment than that imposed upon the human couple. Although the man and the woman are held responsible for disobeying God, and punished accordingly (3:16–19), it is surely fitting that the 'seed of the woman' should be instrumental in punishing the one who tempted the woman to sin" ("Messianic Ideology in Genesis," 30).

which kept the promise and maintained the conflict with the old serpent before his advent, and also of all those who are gathered out of all nations, are united to him by faith, and formed into one body of which he is the head."[9] Throughout history this "seed" has been narrowed down: through Seth and not Cain or Abel; through Shem, not Ham or Japheth; through Abraham and his son Isaac, not Ishmael; through Jacob, not Esau; through David, not Saul or David's brothers. In Galatians 3:16, Paul clearly affirms that Christ is the promised seed: "Now the promises were made to Abraham and to his offspring. It does not say, 'And to offsprings,' referring to many, but referring to one, 'And to your offspring,' who is Christ." Based on later revelation, we understand that Jesus is the one who reigns until he has put all his enemies under his feet, including Satan (1 Cor. 15:25; Heb. 1:13; cf. Rom. 16:20).

Because of his mercy and grace, God chose Abraham and made a covenant with him. In Genesis 12:2–3 God promises Abraham, "I will make of you a great nation, and I will bless you and make your name great, so that you will be a blessing. I will bless those who bless you, and him who dishonors you I will curse, and in you all the families of the earth shall be blessed." Later, when God made the covenant with Abraham, he tells Abraham, "Look toward heaven, and number the stars, if you are able to number them. . . . So shall your offspring [seed] be. . . . To your offspring [seed] I give this land, from the river of Egypt to the great river, the river Euphrates" (Gen. 15:5, 18; see also Gen. 17:2–8; 18:18). In sum, God made three main promises to Abraham: (1) to make his descendants into a great nation; (2) to give him the land of Canaan; and (3) to bless all the nations through him.[10] It is clear that God intends to reverse what happened in Genesis 11 with the tower of Babel. God divided and scattered the nations because of their wickedness and pride but through Abraham he will unite and bless them.[11]

Regarding the promises God made to Abraham, Christopher Wright calls the third promise ("in you all the families of the earth shall be blessed") "the climax of God's promise to Abraham."[12] He notes that this promise is so prominent in Genesis that it occurs five times in various forms (Gen. 12:3; 18:18; 22:18; 26:4–5; 28:14). Consequently, Wright confidently asserts that

9. C. F. Keil and F. Delitzsch, *The Pentateuch*, trans. James Martin (repr., Grand Rapids: Eerdmans 1991), 1:102.
10. See Paul R. Williamson, *Sealed with an Oath: Covenants in God's Unfolding Purpose*, NSBT 23 (Downers Grove, IL: InterVarsity, 2007), 77–91; Stephen G. Dempster, *Dominion and Dynasty: A Theology of the Hebrew Bible*, NSBT 15 (Downers Grove, IL: InterVarsity, 2003), 77–85.
11. The comparison with the tower of Babel is further seen when the builders wanted to make a name for themselves (Gen. 11:4), whereas God promises to make Abraham's name great (Gen. 12:2). Moreover, five times the Babel account mentions all the earth (Gen. 11:1, 4, 8, 9 [x2]) and in Genesis 12:3 God promises to bless "all the families of the earth" through Abraham.
12. Christopher J. H. Wright, *The Mission of God: Unlocking the Bible's Grand Narrative* (Downers Grove, IL: InterVarsity, 2006), 194.

this promise is no mere afterthought but "*is the bottom line . . . of God's promise to Abraham.*"[13] This is precisely how Paul interpreted this promise when he states, "And the Scripture, foreseeing that God would justify the Gentiles by faith, preached the gospel beforehand to Abraham, saying, 'In you shall all the nations be blessed.' So then, those who are of faith are blessed along with Abraham, the man of faith" (Gal. 3:8–9).[14] Now, through faith in Christ, Gentiles are included as the people of God and as children of Abraham (Gal. 3:7, 29). The gospel was preached to Abraham in the words of the promise that he would be a blessing to the nations.[15] Ultimately, this promise was fulfilled in Christ through his death and resurrection.

The promises to Abraham were later passed on to Isaac, Jacob, and to Jacob's sons. Before his death, Jacob blessed his sons. In his blessing to Judah, Jacob states, "The scepter will not depart from Judah, nor the ruler's staff from between his feet, until he comes to whom it belongs and the obedience of the nations is his" (Gen. 49:10 NIV[84]).[16] In this blessing we see that the messianic line would continue through Jacob's fourth son, Judah. Kaiser suggests the following meaning: "The scepter [an insignia of dominion] shall not depart from Judah, nor the ruler's staff from between his feet [i.e., 'from him'], until he [i.e., 'the Messiah'] comes to whom it [i.e., the rule, reign, and/or dominion] belongs."[17] This verse suggests that Judah will rule until the coming of the Messiah. And when the Messiah comes he rules not only over Israel but also over all the nations of the world. Verses 11–12 indicate that the reign of this descendant from Judah will include a time of abundant crops. Some maintain that this passage is not messianic but instead is limited to the monarchy under David and Solomon where many nations were conquered

13. Ibid. (emphasis original).
14. Genesis 12:3 is also quoted in Acts 3:25–26 ("You are the sons of the prophets and of the covenant that God made with your fathers, saying to Abraham, 'And in your offspring shall all the families of the earth be blessed.' God, having raised up his servant, sent him to you first, to bless you by turning every one of you from your wickedness").
15. Jesus states, "Your father Abraham rejoiced that he would see my day. He saw it and was glad" (John 8:56). Precisely how did Abraham foresee the coming of the Messiah? Most likely Jesus is referring to the promises given to Abraham found in Genesis 12:1–3 and act of offering his son Isaac on Mount Moriah (see Gen. 22:8, 13–14).
16. There is debate as to the meaning of the Hebrew *šîlōh*. This noun probably does not refer to the city of Shiloh but is a reference to a person. The Qumran community viewed this text as messianic. In 4Q Patriarchal Blessings the somewhat mysterious *šîloh* is glossed as "the Messiah of Righteousness" (see R. T. France, *Jesus and the Old Testament: His Application of Old Testament Passages to Himself and His Mission* [Downers Grove, IL: InterVarsity, 1971], 175–76; see also Dempster, *Dominion and Dynasty*, 117–18).
17. Kaiser, *Messiah in the Old Testament*, 53. Keil and Delitzsch likewise conclude, "We regard *Shiloh*, therefore, as a title of the Messiah, in common with the entire Jewish synagogue and the whole Christian Church, in which . . . there is perfect agreement as to the fact that the patriarch is here proclaiming the coming of the Messiah" (*Pentateuch*, 1:397). See also Dempster, *Dominion and Dynasty*, 90–92.

and the land enjoyed a time of peace and prosperity.[18] While such a link is certainly possible, it also seems clear that these verses point to a time beyond David and Solomon to a more glorious age.[19] This promise also harkens back to the promise that the seed of the woman will overcome the serpent (Gen. 3:15) and that the seed of Abraham will overcome his enemies (Gen. 22:17). A similar prophecy is found in Numbers 24:17 where Balaam, who was hired by Balak to curse Israel, pronounces a blessing upon them: "I see him, but not now; I behold him, but not near: a star shall come out of Jacob, and a scepter shall rise out of Israel; it shall crush the forehead of Moab and break down all the sons of Sheth." Similar to Genesis 49:10, this passage was interpreted by the targums (the Aramaic translations of the Old Testament) as messianic, which, although not authoritative, indicates that some early Jewish interpreters understood the passage as messianic. For example, where the Hebrew text reads, "a star shall come out of Jacob, and a scepter shall rise out of Israel," the Aramaic states, "a king shall arise out of Jacob and be anointed the Messiah out of Israel" (*Tg. Onq.*).[20]

Throughout Genesis (and the Pentateuch) there is the expectation that a descendant of Adam, Abraham, and Judah will conquer his enemies and rule as the king over all the nations. Alexander rightly summarizes:

> [There] is the expectation of a divinely appointed king who will play a vital role in mediating God's blessing throughout the earth. Significantly, in Genesis this future king is linked to a royal dynasty descended from the tribe of Judah.[21] Furthermore, the activity of this king is associated with the restoration of the harmonious state which initially existed between God, humanity and nature in the Garden of Eden. In spite of the disobedience of Adam and Eve and their expulsion from Eden, the book of Genesis envisages a time when the consequences of humanity's rebellion against God will be reversed through the mediation of a future monarch.[22]

---

18. E.g., Claus Westermann, *Genesis 37–50*, trans. John J. Scullion (Minneapolis: Augsburg, 1986), 230.
19. E. Jenni comments that the promise in Genesis 49:10–12 "clearly goes beyond the condition attained under David ('until . . . comes') and must refer to a new messianic ruler in a new era of paradisiacal fruitfulness" ("Messiah, Jewish," in *IDB*, 3:362; see also Alexander, "Messianic Ideology," 35–36). This interpretation is unanimously affirmed by the Targums (see C. A. Evans, "Messianism," in *DNTB*, 99).
20. See Evans, "Messianism," 699.
21. Genesis anticipates a royal lineage (Dempster, *Dominion and Dynasty*, 115–17). God says to Abraham, "I will make you into nations, and kings shall come from you" (Gen. 17:6; cf. 17:16). Later God promises Jacob, "A nation and a company of nations shall come from you, and kings shall come from your own body" (Gen. 35:11). Furthermore, although never designated as "kings," the patriarchs were often portrayed as possessing royal status (see Gen. 14:1–24; 21:22–34; 26:26–31; 37:8–11; 41:39–43).
22. Alexander, "Messianic Ideology," 21. Keil and Delitzsch write, "The expectation of a personal Saviour did not arise for the first time with Moses, Joshua, and David, or first obtain its definite form after

Messianic Prophecies of a Prophet

Scripture reveals that Jesus fulfills the Old Testament office of prophet. Abraham is the first person in the Bible referred to as a prophet. God says to Abimelech in a dream, "Now then, return the man's [i.e., Abraham's] wife, for he is a prophet, so that he will pray for you, and you shall live. But if you do not return her, know that you shall surely die, you and all who are yours" (Gen. 20:7). Aaron, the brother of Moses, is also called a prophet: "And the LORD said to Moses, 'See, I have made you like God to Pharaoh, and your brother Aaron shall be your prophet'" (Exod. 7:1). We also read about Eldad and Medad who were prophesying in the camp (Num. 11:26). When Moses is informed, instead of being jealous he laments, "Would that all the LORD's people were prophets, that the LORD would put his Spirit on them!" (Num. 11:29). Later, in Deuteronomy 13, Moses warns of false prophets.

It is clear, however, that Moses possessed a unique position among those who are referred to as prophets in the Old Testament. This uniqueness became evident when Miriam and Aaron rose up against Moses and questioned, "Has the LORD indeed spoken only through Moses? Has he not spoken through us also?" (Num. 12:2). The Lord then responded, "If there is a prophet among you, I the LORD make myself known to him in a vision; I speak with him in a dream. Not so with my servant Moses. He is faithful in all my house. With him I speak mouth to mouth, clearly, and not in riddles, and he beholds the form of the LORD. Why then were you not afraid to speak against my servant Moses?" (Num. 12:6–8). Of all the prophets in the Old Testament, Moses stood out in a class by himself.

Moses himself prophesies: "The LORD your God will raise up for you a prophet like me from among you, from your brothers—it is to him you shall listen" (Deut. 18:15). Moses declares that in the future, God will again raise up a prophet like himself, a prophet who receives his words directly from God.[23] No other Old Testament prophet was equal to Moses: "And there has not arisen a

---

one man had risen up as the deliverer and redeemer, the leader and ruler of the whole nation, but was contained in the germ in the promise of the seed of the woman, and in the blessing of Noah upon Shem. It was then still further expanded in the promise of God to the patriarchs . . . by which Abraham, Isaac, and Jacob . . . were chosen as the personal bearers of that salvation, which was to be conveyed by them through their seed to all nations" (*Pentateuch*, 1:397–98).

23. Some maintain that Deuteronomy 18:15 refers to the prophets in general and not to only one future prophet (i.e., the Messiah). See Duane L. Christensen, *Deuteronomy 1:1–21:9*, WBC 6A, rev. ed. (Nashville: Nelson, 2001), 409. For example, Keil and Delitzsch write that "the promise neither relates to one particular prophet, nor directly and exclusively to the Messiah, but treats the sending of prophets generally" (*Pentateuch*, 1:394). They suggest that the phrase "like me" should be understood to mean "that he would act as a mediator between Jehovah and the people, and make known the words or the will of the Lord" (ibid.). At the same time, however, while they do not believe that this text has direct and exclusive reference to the Messiah, they do not deny that the words are fulfilled in Jesus (ibid., 1:395–96).

prophet since in Israel like Moses, whom the LORD knew face to face" (Deut. 34:10). Moses was the prophet of all prophets. He brought the law of God to the people, establishing the covenant that would continue for 1,500 years.

The expectation of a prophet like Moses is clearly seen in the New Testament. There was an anticipation that God would fulfill his promise and send a unique prophet who would speak the words of God unlike anyone before him. The last of the Old Testament prophets writes about the return of the prophet Elijah: "Behold, I will send you Elijah the prophet before the great and awesome day of the LORD comes" (Mal. 4:5). Although there is debate as to whether this text indicates the actual return of Elijah or someone who comes in the spirit of Elijah, it is clear that the contemporaries of John the Baptist understood the text in the latter sense. For when John the Baptist came dressed like Elijah and preached a message of repentance like Elijah, the priests and Levites question him, "Are you Elijah?" (John 1:21). After John denied that he was Elijah they pressed him further, "Are you the Prophet?" (John 1:21). At this point John did not need clarification as to which prophet they were referring. He knew they were referring to the long-awaited prophet like Moses (Deut. 18:15). John likewise responded that he was not "the" prophet that they were anticipating.

When Philip believed that he had found the Messiah, he said to Nathanael, "We have found him of whom Moses in the Law and also the prophets wrote, Jesus of Nazareth, the son of Joseph" (John 1:45). After Jesus performed the miracle of feeding the five thousand (similar to Moses feeding the people with manna from heaven), John informs his readers, "When the people saw the sign that he had done, they said, 'This is indeed the Prophet who is to come into the world!'" (John 6:14). On the last day of the Festival of Tabernacles, Jesus stood up and cried out that those who are thirsty should come to him and drink (similar to Moses providing water for the people in the wilderness, Exod. 17:6; Num. 20:11). What was the crowd's response? "When they heard these words, some of the people said, 'This really is the Prophet'" (John 7:40). Peter also expressly relates the person of Jesus to Deuteronomy 18:15. After healing the lame man he announced, "Moses said, 'The Lord God will raise up for you a prophet like me from your brothers. You shall listen to him in whatever he tells you'" (Acts 3:22). In Stephen's last sermon he alluded to Deuteronomy 18:15 declaring that Moses said, "God will raise up for you a prophet like me from your brothers" (Acts 7:37). Philip, Peter, and Stephen saw the fulfillment of this prophecy in Jesus Christ.

In other New Testament passages, Jesus is identified as a prophet (or potential prophet) without specifically connecting his prophetic status to Deuteronomy 18:15. The crowds often considered Jesus to be one of the prophets (Matt. 21:46; Mark 6:14–15; 8:28). After Jesus raised the widow's son the crowd said, "A great prophet has arisen among us!" (Luke 7:16). Interestingly, the Samaritan woman perceived Jesus to be a prophet (John 4:19). When questioned by the Pharisees regarding who Jesus was, the blind man responded, "He is a prophet" (John 9:17). Most of the Pharisees refused to believe that Jesus was a prophet because they knew that "no prophet arises from Galilee" (John 7:52). The two men on the road to Emmaus declare that Jesus "was a prophet, powerful in word and deed before God and all the people" (Luke 24:19).

Not only did others see Jesus as a prophet but he viewed himself as a prophet, specifically a prophet in the likeness of Moses. Speaking to the Jewish leaders who were hostile to him, Jesus commented, "Do not think that I will accuse you to the Father. There is one who accuses you: Moses, on whom you have set your hope. For if you believed Moses, you would believe me; for he wrote of me. But if you do not believe his writings, how will you believe my words?" (John 5:45–47). Although Jesus does not specifically mention or allude to a particular passage from Moses, if there is one particular Scripture in mind, it must be Deuteronomy 18:15 (see also John 12:48–50).[24] Elsewhere Jesus states, "A prophet is not without honor, except in his hometown and among his relatives and in his own household" (Mark 6:4; cf. Luke 4:24; John 4:44). Although this statement was a well-known proverb, Jesus' use of this statement suggests that he sees himself as a prophet. When some of the Pharisees warn Jesus of Herod's plan to kill him, he responds, "Nevertheless, I must go on my way today and tomorrow and the day following, for it cannot be that a prophet should perish away from Jerusalem" (Luke 13:33).

Many have noted the parallel between the statement, "you shall listen to him" (*autou akousesthe*, Deut. 18:15, LXX) with the voice of the Father on the Mount of Transfiguration, "This is my beloved Son, with whom I am well pleased; listen to him" (*akouete autou*, Matt. 17:5). Just as Moses went upon the cloud-enveloped mountain to meet with God and then declare his words, so Jesus went upon the mountain overshadowed with a cloud to meet with God and declare his words. France rightly notes, "The added command to listen to him . . . is probably to be understood as an echo of Deuteronomy 18:15, 19, the promise of a future prophet like Moses to whom the people are to listen. The presence of Moses on the mountain underlies this echo."[25]

Other New Testament texts support the idea that Jesus is the fulfillment of the prophet who was to come, a prophet like Moses. For example, this is seen in his authority as a teacher of the law. The law was given by Moses and was revered by the Jewish people. And although Jesus stated that he did not

---

24. While Carson acknowledges that Deuteronomy 18:15 is the most likely passage in view, he suggests that "it is perhaps more likely that this verse is referring to a certain *way* of reading the books of Moses . . . than to a specific passage" (D. A. Carson, *The Gospel According to John*, PNTC [Grand Rapids: Eerdmans, 1991], 266).

25. R. T. France, *The Gospel of Matthew*, NICNT (Grand Rapids: Eerdmans, 2007), 650. Cf. Stein who maintains that the phrase "listen to him" is a rebuke of Peter for his misunderstanding of Jesus' messianic role (Robert H. Stein, *Jesus the Messiah: A Survey of the Life of Christ* [Downers Grove, IL: InterVarsity, 1996], 173).

come to destroy the law but rather to uphold the eternal validity of the law (Matt. 5:17–19), Jesus speaks as the true interpreter of the law ("You have heard that it was said to those of old . . . but I say to you," Matt. 5:21–22) and even rescinds certain aspects of the law (see Mark 7:14–23). Only a prophet who was greater than Moses could make such claims.

There are other Old Testament texts that emphasize the prophetic office of the Messiah (often closely associated with the office of king). For example, Isaiah 61 states,

> The Spirit of the Lord God is upon me, because the Lord has anointed me to bring good news to the poor; he has sent me to bind up the brokenhearted, to proclaim liberty to the captives, and the opening of the prison to those who are bound; to proclaim the year of the Lord's favor. (vv. 1–2; cf. Isa. 11:2; 42:1)

Here the prophet-king is described as possessing the Spirit of the Lord who has been anointed for the purpose of preaching. He is to proclaim good news to the poor, proclaim liberty to the captives, and proclaim the year of the Lord's favor.[26] Again, there is debate as to whether this text refers to Isaiah or to the Messiah—or both. Leupold firmly maintains that this passage is messianic because (1) the achievements the speaker assigns to himself are too grand and wonderful for any human to accomplish, and (2) the second half of the book of Isaiah frequently references this "Suffering Servant."[27] He also notes, "Here, since most of the activities described have to do with the *word*, it is the *prophetic* office for which the spirit is given."[28] Similarly, Kaiser writes, "He will be endowed with the Spirit of the Lord so that he can carry out his role as a prophet."[29]

According to Luke's Gospel, Jesus, as the Prophet-Messiah, fulfills this passage.[30] In chapter 4, Luke emphasizes the role of the Spirit in the life of

---

26. Cf. 1 Kings 19:16 where Elijah was commanded to anoint his successor, Elisha: "And Jehu the son of Nimshi you shall anoint to be king over Israel, and Elisha the son of Shaphat of Abel-meholah you shall anoint to be prophet in your place."

27. H. C. Leupold, *Exposition of Isaiah* (Grand Rapids: Baker, 1971), 2:318–19. Although France has some hesitancy identifying Isaiah 61 as a Servant Song, he suggests that the "similarity to the 'Servant Songs' is, however, sufficient to render improbable the suggestion that the speaker is the prophet himself; the passage bears a much greater resemblance to passages about the servant than to any place where the prophet speaks of himself, both in the wording, and in the figure described" (*Jesus and the Old Testament*, 133).

28. Ibid., 320.

29. Kaiser, *Messiah in the Old Testament*, 183.

30. See also Matthew 11:4–5 where Jesus responds to John's question as to whether Jesus really was the "one who is to come" (Matt. 11:3) by alluding to Isaiah 61: "Go and tell John what you hear and see: the blind receive their sight and the lame walk, lepers are cleansed and the deaf hear, and the dead are raised up, and the poor have good news preached to them."

Jesus. Jesus was "full of the Holy Spirit" when he returned from the Jordan and was led into the wilderness "by the Spirit" (v. 1). After his temptation by the devil in the wilderness, he returned to Galilee "in the power of the Spirit" (v. 14). Then, when he went to the synagogue in Nazareth on the Sabbath day, he stood up and read from Isaiah 61:1–2 which begins, "The Spirit of the Lord is upon me" (v. 18). After reading this passage he sat down and announced, "Today this Scripture has been fulfilled in your hearing" (v. 21).

Thus, Jesus was the long awaited prophet who was to come in the likeness of Moses. The Jewish people were anticipating the fulfillment of Deuteronomy 18:15 and when Jesus came performing miracles and teaching the people unlike the scribes (see Matt. 7:29), they immediately began to ask themselves whether Jesus was "the" prophet. But not only is Jesus a prophet, he is also a priest.

Messianic Prophecies of a Priest

A central function of Old Testament priests was to represent the people to God. This was because the people were sinful and therefore did not have direct access to God. The Levites were set apart for the service of the sanctuary, the descendants of Aaron were set apart to serve as priests, and one of the priests was selected to serve as the high priest. Although not many, there are a few passages that associate the coming Messiah with the office of priest. One such text is found in Psalm 110:4: "The LORD has sworn and will not change his mind, "You are a priest forever after the order of Melchizedek." Again, we should note that in the context this priest is also a king. Verses 1–2 of the psalm read, "The LORD says to my Lord: 'Sit at my right hand, until I make your enemies your footstool.' The LORD sends forth from Zion your mighty scepter. Rule in the midst of your enemies!" This priest is one who will sit on his throne, ruling his people with a mighty scepter. This priest is not a descendant of Aaron or even from the tribe of Levi. He comes from a different order. He is from the order of Melchizedek. Who precisely was Melchizedek?

The story of Melchizedek is found in Genesis 14. God chose Abraham, giving him great promises and sending him to Canaan. When Lot (Abraham's nephew) and Abraham parted ways, Lot chose the best land for himself and eventually ended up in Sodom. Lot was later captured when the kings of Sodom and Gomorrah were defeated by four kings from the East. Abraham, however, defeated the four kings and rescued Lot. After Melchizedek, king of Salem (i.e., Jerusalem) and priest of the Most High God, met Abraham, he blessed Abraham who then gave him a tithe of the spoils (see Gen. 14:18–20). Just as Melchizedek held the unique position of a priest ("priest of God Most High") and a king ("king of Salem"), so the Psalmist, King David, envisioned a Messiah who was also a king-priest.

Although some have attempted to apply this psalm to David under the category of a royal psalm, the evidence will not allow for such an interpretation. First, the title of the psalm includes the superscription "A Psalm of David" (David presumably did not write this about himself). Second, David was never considered a priest.[31] Third, because the psalm "contains no specifically royal terminology," it should not even be considered a royal psalm.[32] Finally, it would be inappropriate to apply the language of this psalm to David or any of the kings who followed him. France summarizes, "If then Psalm 110:4 were applied to any historical king, it would be more than extravagant language of a Royal Psalm; it would be either nonsense, or verging on blasphemy. It is best seen as referring to the Messiah."[33]

In fact, Psalm 110 is quoted more than any other psalm in the New Testament.[34] In every one of these quotations or allusions a messianic reference is not argued, but is assumed, which implies that a messianic interpretation was the accepted understanding of the text.[35] Verse 4 is specifically quoted at least three times (Heb. 5:6; 7:17, 21) and alluded to another four times (Heb. 5:10; 6:20; 7:11, 15). In these texts the author of Hebrews is arguing that Jesus is superior to the Old Testament Aaronic priesthood because he is from a superior priesthood. The author proves this in two ways. The first has to do with Abraham's encounter with Melchizedek. Genesis 14 states that two things happened when they met: (1) Melchizedek blessed Abraham and (2) Abraham paid a tithe to Melchizedek. Both of these actions demonstrate that Melchizedek is greater than Abraham because (1) the greater blesses the lesser and (2) the lesser pays tithes to the greater. Thus, if Melchizedek is greater than Abraham, then he is certainly greater than Levi (and Aaron) since Abraham, the Patriarch, was greater than Levi (his great-grandson). It could even be said that Levi, through Abraham, paid tithes to Melchizedek (Heb. 7:9–10). In this way, the Levites therefore paid tithes to a superior priesthood.

The second argument that the author uses to demonstrate the superiority of Jesus over the Aaronic priesthood has to do with the nature of the priesthood itself. That is, the priesthood of Melchizedek is a universal, royal, righteous, and eternal priesthood. First, Melchizedek's priesthood is universal. Melchizedek was not Jewish since Abraham was the father of the Jews. Rather, Melchizedek was "without father or mother or genealogy" (Heb. 7:3) which probably means that there is no Old Testament record of his ancestry. Second, his priesthood is royal. He was the king of Jerusalem. The Levitical

31. Sometimes kings performed priestly tasks (e.g., David eating the showbread in 1 Sam. 21:1–9; cf. Luke 6:3–4).
32. France, *Jesus and the Old Testament*, 166.
33. Ibid.
34. Matthew 22:44; 26:64; Mark 12:36; 14:62; 16:19; Luke 20:42–44; 22:69; Acts 2:34–35; Romans 8:34; 1 Corinthians 15:25; Ephesians 1:20; Colossians 3:1; Hebrews 1:3, 13; 5:6; 7:17, 21; 8:1; 10:12–13; 12:2.
35. France, *Jesus and the Old Testament*, 164–65. France notes that non-messianic interpretations later emerged in the second and early third centuries due to conflict between the synagogue and the church. He concludes, however, "that in the time of Jesus Psalm 110 was agreed to refer to the Messiah" (165).

priests never served as kings. But Melchizedek was both a priest and a king. Third, his priesthood is righteous. He is called the "king of righteousness" and the "king of peace" (Heb. 7:2). The Aaronic priests did not always display righteous behavior. Finally, his priesthood is eternal. Psalm 110:4 prophesies that this messianic priest will be "a priest forever." Just as it is nowhere recorded that Melchizedek died ("having neither beginning of days nor end of life," Heb. 7:3), so also Christ will remain a priest forever. This does not mean that Melchizedek lived forever, but that his priesthood remains since there is no record of an earthly successor to Melchizedek.

Another key text that identifies the coming Messiah as a priest is found in Zechariah 6:12–13:

> Thus says the LORD of hosts, "Behold, the man whose name is the Branch: for he shall branch out from his place, and he shall build the temple of the LORD. It is he who shall build the temple of the LORD and shall bear royal honor, and shall sit and rule on his throne. And there shall be a priest on his throne, and the counsel of peace shall be between them both."[36]

Does this text refer to someone during the time of Zechariah or to the Messiah? Those who opt for the former interpretation usually maintain that Zerubbabel is the kingly figure (since he was of Davidic lineage) while Joshua is the priestly figure (since he was a high priest) or that the entire passage refers exclusively to either Zerubbabel or Joshua. While such interpretations are possible, it is necessary to see this text as pointing beyond a symbolic representative (Zerubbabel or Joshua) to the Messiah who would reign as king and priest.[37] McComiskey insists that we must look "beyond Joshua to one who yet stands outside these events" and that the "use of the high priest in the prophetic symbolism of this passage . . . makes Zerubbabel an unlikely Messiah, since the point of the symbolism is that the offices of priest and king will peacefully coalesce in the Branch."[38] He therefore concludes, "It is more likely that the prophet's symbolic act expresses a hope that extends beyond the

---

36. See also Jeremiah 33:14–26 and Ezekiel 46:1–8 which see the coming Messiah as possessing the traits of both royal and priestly dignity.

37. So Martin J. Selman, "Messianic Mysteries," in *The Lord's Anointed: Interpretation of Old Testament Messianic Texts* (Carlisle: Paternoster; Grand Rapids: Baker, 1995), 295–96; France, *Jesus and the Old Testament*, 100. The Qumran community believed that two messiahs would reign: one as king and one as priest.

38. Thomas Edward McComiskey, "Zechariah," in *The Minor Prophets: An Exegetical and Expository Commentary* (Zephaniah, Haggai, Zechariah, and Malachi), ed. Thomas Edward McComiskey (Grand Rapids: Baker, 1998), 1113. Barker likewise notes, "Thus restored Israel is seen in the future under the glorious reign of the messianic King-Priest. . . . Joshua serves as a type of the Messiah, but at certain points the language transcends the experience of the type and becomes more directly prophetic of the antitype" (Kenneth L. Barker, *Zechariah*, in EBC [Daniel–Malachi], rev. ed. [Grand Rapids: Zondervan, 2008], 770).

moment to a figure who more closely fits the symbol."[39] This interpretation is supported by the fact that the Aramaic Targum Jonathan, the Jerusalem Talmud, and the Midrash all interpret these verses as messianic.[40]

This coming Messiah is identified as the "Branch." This is not the first time Zechariah has mentioned the "Branch." Earlier he writes, "Hear now, O Joshua the high priest, you and your friends who sit before you, for they are men who are a sign: behold, I will bring my servant the Branch. For behold, on the stone that I have set before Joshua, on a single stone with seven eyes, I will engrave its inscription, declares the LORD of hosts, and I will remove the iniquity of this land in a single day" (Zech. 3:8–9). Some have suggested that the "stone" mentioned in the text is possibly related to some precious jewel placed in the turban of the high priest.[41] If this is the case, then we again have the two offices of king and priest being brought together. The "Branch" was associated with the coming of a Davidic king,[42] whereas the stone was associated with the coming of a great high priest.[43] Another option is to view the stone as the symbol of the rebuilding of the temple which again points to a priestly function (cf. Zech. 6:12–13). The stone then represents the foundation-stone for the new temple (or the Messiah himself).[44] This interpretation would then tie into the concept of removing "the iniquity of the land in a single day." The king-priest would be able to make an offering in the temple that would cleanse the land (people) in one day.

Thus, the Branch or Messiah will come as the king-priest and will rebuild the temple (Zech. 6:13). But since the temple had already begun under Zerubbabel, the author envisions the temple of the messianic age (cf. Isa. 2:2–4; Ezek. 40–43; Hag. 2:6–9). In the New Testament, Jesus claimed that his body was the temple (John 2:21; cf. Mark 14:58). Jesus also became a stumbling block and rock of offense for those who rejected him as the Messiah (Ps. 118:22–23; Isa. 8:13–15; Matt. 21:42; 1 Peter 2:7–8; Eph. 2:19–22) but is the chief cornerstone for the church (Eph. 2:19–20). The author of Hebrews identifies Jesus as the great High Priest who offered a once-for-all sacrifice to make propitiation

---

39. McComiskey, "Zechariah," 1114. See also Baldwin who comments, "The symbolic coronation and the enigmatic term 'Branch' referred to a future leader, who would fulfil to perfection the offices of priest and king, and build the future Temple with all appropriate spendour (Hag. 2:6–9). In this way the priestly and royal offices will be united. The old interpretation that Messiah is meant has not been displaced. Nowhere else in the OT is it made so plain that the coming Davidic king will also be a priest" (Joyce G. Baldwin, *Haggai, Zechariah, Malachi*, TOTC [Downers Grove, IL: InterVarsity, 1972], 136–37).

40. Barker, *Zechariah*, 771.

41. See discussion in McComiskey, "Zechariah," 1078–79.

42. See Isaiah 4:2; 11:1; Jeremiah 23:5–6; 33:14–17; Ezekiel 17:22.

43. Smith, for example, notes, "It seems by using the two metaphors of 'branch' and 'stone' to refer to the coming Messiah, Zechariah . . . saw him as both king and priest" (Ralph L. Smith, *Micah–Malachi*, WBC 32 [Word: Waco, 1984], 201).

44. See McComiskey, "Zechariah," 1079; Eugene H. Merrill, *An Exegetical Commentary: Haggai, Zechariah, Malachi* (Chicago: Moody, 1994), 142.

for the sins of his people (2:17; 4:14–16; 9:11–28; 10:5–18). He did not offer the blood of bulls and goats because they could never take away sins (Heb. 9:9–14; 10:1–4, 11). Rather, he offered himself as a lamb without blemish to atone for the sins of all who trust in him. Isaiah writes,

> But he was pierced for our transgressions; he was crushed for our iniquities; upon him was the chastisement that brought us peace, and with his wounds we are healed. All we like sheep have gone astray; we have turned—every one—to his own way; and the LORD has laid on him the iniquity of us all. He was oppressed, and he was afflicted, yet he opened not his mouth; like a lamb that is led to the slaughter, and like a sheep that before its shearers is silent, so he opened not his mouth. (Isa. 53:5–7)

Jesus was not only the long awaited prophet and the perfect priest, but he was also the son of David who would be the eternal king.

Messianic Prophecies of a King

In the Old Testament the Messiah is most closely linked to the office of king. He is one who will come from the lineage of David and rule his people with a rod of iron. He will redeem his people by defeating his enemies and establishing peace in the land. He is the anointed one who is filled with God's Spirit and his kingdom will have no end. Thus, the Messiah is first and foremost the perfect king.

David was a great king and was a man after God's own heart (1 Sam. 13:14). But David was not perfect. He had Uriah killed and committed adultery with Bathsheba. And because David was also a man of war, he was not to build the temple for God. Although David wanted to build God a house (temple), God declares to him that he will build David a house (dynasty).[45] God does not need anything and is the one who makes the plans and sets the agenda. "David does not have to perform a service for God to secure God's blessing; rather it is God who will perform the service for David."[46] God then makes a promise to David:

> I will raise up your offspring after you, who shall come from your body, and I will establish his kingdom. He shall build

---

45. See Williamson, *Sealed with an Oath*, 125–31.
46. Philip E. Satterthwaite, "David in the Books of Samuel: A Messianic Expectation?" in *The Lord's Anointed: Interpretation of Old Testament Messianic Texts*, ed. Philip E. Satterthwaite, Richard S. Hess, and Gordon J. Wenham (Carlisle: Paternoster; Grand Rapids: Baker, 1995), 54.

> a house for my name, and I will establish the throne of his
> kingdom forever. I will be to him a father, and he shall be
> to me a son.... And your house and your kingdom shall be
> made sure forever before me. Your throne shall be established
> forever. (2 Sam. 7:12–16; cf. 1 Chron. 17:11–14)

This verse obviously relates to Solomon, David's son. God is saying that he will be with Solomon who will build him a house/temple and that he will establish his kingdom forever. This verse is not messianic in the narrow sense of only referring to the Messiah and not to Solomon. We know that the initial promise refers directly to Solomon because part of the passage that was omitted above reads, "When he commits iniquity, I will discipline him with the rod of men, with the stripes of the son of men" (2 Sam. 7:14b). Here, God is promising David that he will not abandon Solomon as he did Saul. Instead, when Solomon sins, out of his love God will discipline him as a son. The Messiah, however, was to be one who was righteous and without iniquity (Isa. 11:5; 53:11). And yet, the New Testament interprets Jesus as the fulfillment of this text. For example, the author of Hebrews quotes the first half of 2 Samuel 7:14 ("I will be to him a father, and he shall be to me a son") as referring to Jesus (Heb. 1:5) and applies it to Jesus since he is reading this verse through the perspective of the whole Old Testament. As such, we see the theology of this verse expanded and developed throughout the Old Testament. That is, subsequent Old Testament writers understood that (1) the covenant God made with David was eternal and (2) Solomon was not the Messiah who would bring about the fullness of God's kingdom. Therefore, throughout the latter parts of the Old Testament there is the continued expectation of a coming son:[47] a son who will accomplish what David and Solomon failed to do; a son who will reign on the throne of David as the perfect king. The prophet Isaiah speaks of this coming son:

> For to us a child is born, to us a son is given; and the govern-
> ment shall be upon his shoulder, and his name shall be called
> Wonderful Counselor, Mighty God, Everlasting Father,
> Prince of Peace. Of the increase of his government and of
> peace there will be no end, on the throne of David and over
> his kingdom, to establish it and to uphold it with justice and
> with righteousness from this time forth and forevermore.
> The zeal of the LORD of hosts will do this. (Isa. 9:6–7)

---

47. Leupold writes that "by the time Isaiah appeared on the scene the great promise to David about the continuance of his line was very well known and accepted in Israel" (*Isaiah*, 1:187). He continues, "It goes without saying that this is one of the clearest and most meaningful Messianic prophecies in the whole Old Testament" (ibid.).

In this text, the royal titles of sonship are applied to the coming Messiah. Childs notes, "The description of his reign makes it absolutely clear that his role is messianic."[48] Gary Smith maintains that the pledge that this person will reign on the throne of David "certifies beyond the shadow of a doubt that the text refers to the ultimate fulfillment of the Davidic covenant through a 'messianic' figure."[49]

Later, Isaiah records God's continued love for David and his covenant to him: "Incline your ear, and come to me; hear, that your soul may live; and I will make with you an everlasting covenant, my steadfast, sure love for David" (Isa. 55:3; see also Isa. 32:1; Hos. 3:4–5). This commitment to David is continued during the ministry of Ezekiel. God reminds his people, "And I will set up over them one shepherd, my servant David, and he shall feed them: he shall feed them and be their shepherd. And I, the LORD, will be their God, and my servant David shall be prince among them. I am the LORD; I have spoken" (Ezek. 34:23–24). This text does not necessarily mean that David himself would come back to rule over Israel, but rather someone from David's lineage.

Thus, there was the ongoing expectation that the promise God made to David in 2 Samuel 7 was not limited to Solomon. Even the promise that God would "establish the throne of his kingdom forever" (2 Sam. 7:13; see also Ps. 89:3–4, 28–29) gives this prophecy eschatological or messianic overtones.[50] Solomon failed to accomplish all that God had asked of him. He was not the righteous son who established the throne of David forever. To some extent, his kingdom ceased to exist immediately after his death. But in the future there would be a son who would himself be called "mighty God" (cf. Isa. 10:21) who would rule on the throne of David. This Messiah would accomplish what David and Solomon did not do. He would establish the kingdom of God. In this way, Christ fulfills the promise given to David's son. Thus, when Christ was born the angel Gabriel said to Mary, "He will be great and will be called the Son of the Most High. And the Lord God will give to him the throne of his father David, and he will reign over the house of Jacob forever, and of his kingdom there will be no end" (Luke 1:32–33; cf. Matt. 1:1). Jesus himself implicitly claimed to be the fulfillment of the prophecy to David. He claimed he would build a temple (cf. Matt. 26:61; 27:40; Mark 14:58; 15:29; John 2:19–22), and possess an eternal throne (cf. Matt. 19:28–29), and an imperishable kingdom (cf. Luke 22:29–30; John 18:36).[51] The New

---

48. Brevard Childs, *Isaiah* (Louisville: Westminster John Knox, 2001), 81. If Isaiah 9:6–7 is such a clear messianic passage, why is it never quoted in the New Testament? This is probably due to the fact that the Septuagint omits these titles and simply reads, "His name will be called messenger of great counsel" (see Fredrick C. Holmgren, *The Old Testament and the Significance of Jesus: Embracing Change—Maintaining Christian Identity* [Grand Rapids: Eerdmans, 1999], 53).

49. Gary V. Smith, *Isaiah 1–39*, NAC 15A (Nashville: B&H, 2007), 242.

50. See Robert D. Bergen, *1, 2 Samuel*, NAC 7 (Nashville: B&H, 1996), 340.

51. Ibid.

Testament writers clearly understood Jesus to be the Son of God (Mark 1:1; John 20:31; Acts 9:20). Jesus is the son of David who fulfills all that the Old Testament had predicted.

Another key messianic Old Testament text is found in Psalm 2. This psalm is usually considered a coronation psalm (a subset of the royal psalms) that reflects the crowning of the king of Israel but was also interpreted in a messianic way in the later Old Testament and New Testament periods. The psalm speaks of the kings of the earth who plot against the Lord's "anointed" (v. 2). But the Lord simply laughs at their efforts and states, "I have set my King on Zion, my holy hill" (v. 6). This anointed king is then twice then referred to as God's "Son" ("You are my Son; today I have begotten you," v. 7; "Kiss the Son, lest he be angry, and you perish in the way, for his wrath is quickly kindled. Blessed are all who take refuge in him," v. 12). It was the hope of the people of Israel that one of their kings would be this special king: a king who was adopted as God's son and who reigned in righteousness (cf. Ps. 72:1–4); a king who was feared by all and ruled over all the nations; a king who was worthy to be honored and who protected those who took refuge in him. Israel longed for such a king, but each of the successive kings proved to fall short of this ideal. Miller explains,

> Israel saw in its parade of kings the struggle for power enacted but the final result never accomplished. It did not, however, relinquish the vision of the Lord's rule in history carried out through one who was chosen by God, a righteous and just king, victorious for God, judging the poor with equity, providing blessing for the people, bringing the nations into the worship and service of God.[52]

With the birth and ministry of Jesus, however, the realities of Psalm 2 began to take effect. At his baptism a voice from heaven declared, "You are my beloved Son; with you I am well pleased" (Mark 1:11). Later, when Jesus was transfigured on a mountain in the company of three of his disciples, a voice from the cloud again said, "This is my beloved Son, with whom I am well pleased; listen to him" (Matt. 17:5). At two crucial places in the ministry of Jesus (i.e., at the beginning—his baptism—and toward the end when he begins to speak about his death and resurrection) a voice from heaven confirms Jesus' status as the Son of God. It is not clear at this point if the disciples linked Jesus' sonship with Psalm 2—a Psalm that not only speaks of a son but a son who is also God's chosen and anointed king. And yet, when Jesus began his preaching ministry his message was summarized by Mark as, "The time is fulfilled, and the kingdom of God is at hand; repent and believe in the

---

52. Patrick D. Miller, *Interpreting the Psalms* (Philadelphia: Fortress, 1986), 92; see also Dempster, *Dominion and Dynasty*, 194–95.

gospel" (Mark 1:15). The heart of Jesus' message was that the kingdom had arrived precisely because the King had arrived. A kingdom without a king is nonsense. Thus, when Jesus preached the arrival of the kingdom, he was also preaching the arrival of the king.

Of course, the disciples did not fully comprehend the nature of Jesus' kingdom. Neither did Pilate. Jesus explained to Pilate, "My kingdom is not of this world. If my kingdom were of this world, my servants would have been fighting, that I might not be delivered over to the Jews. But my kingdom is not from the world" (John 18:36). Jesus was the long-awaited king, but not exactly the type of king the Jewish people were expecting. He was supposed to break the nations "with a rod of iron and dash them in pieces like a potter's vessel" (Ps. 2:9). He was supposed to be a king greatly feared "lest he be angry, and you perish in the way, for his wrath is quickly kindled" (Ps. 2:12). Instead, Jesus was handed over to the Romans and was crucified as a criminal. Instead of a crown of gold, he was given a crown of thorns. Instead of a throne, he was given a cross. Instead of manifesting his power over the nations by physically subduing them, he offered up his life to redeem them. Jesus' kingship was not like that of any human king.

It was not until after Jesus' resurrection that the disciples clearly understood the nature of Jesus' kingdom and how he would conquer the nations. Indeed, his cross and resurrection did not prevent the disciples from connecting Jesus with the King-Son of Psalm 2, rather it confirmed it. In his synagogue sermon in Antioch in Pisidia, Paul explained how God's promises to Israel had been realized through Moses, the judges, and King David—and how all of these promises had now been fulfilled in Jesus. He further clarified that those living in Jerusalem did not recognize Jesus for who he really was because they did not "understand the utterances of the prophets" (Acts 13:27). He continued, "And we bring you the good news that what God promised to the fathers, this he has fulfilled to us their children by raising Jesus, as also it is written in the second Psalm, 'You are my Son, today I have begotten you'" (Acts 13:32–33). Paul understood Psalm 2 as containing a promise. He understood that this passage was only fully realized in Jesus. In other words, he viewed the resurrection as the proof that God fulfilled his promise of bringing forth a son who will reign forever. Of course, such an expectation also harkens back to the promise to David in 2 Samuel 7.[53] In the context of Acts 13:33, the "today" of Psalm 2:7 ("You are my Son; today I have begotten you") clearly refers to the day of the resurrection. Polhill writes, "Jesus was indeed the Son of God from all eternity and recognized as such throughout his earthly life (Luke 1:35; 3:22; 9:35). But it was through the resurrection that he was exalted to God's right hand, enthroned as the Son of God, and recog-

---

53. See D. Goldsmith, "Acts 13, 33–37: A Pesher on 2 Samuel 7," *JBL* 87 (1968): 321–24; E. Lövestam, *Son and Saviour: A Study of Acts 13, 32–37* (Lund: Gleerup, 1961), esp. 84–87. Like 2 Samuel 7, Psalm 2 was considered messianic in first-century Judaism.

nized as such by believing humans."[54] Paul also connects the sonship of Jesus to the resurrection in the introduction to his letter to the Romans. He writes, "concerning his Son, who was descended from David according to the flesh and was declared to be the Son of God in power according to the Spirit of holiness by his resurrection from the dead, Jesus Christ our Lord" (Rom. 1:3–4).

Finally, Psalm 2 is quoted twice by the author of Hebrews. The first quotation is in the context of proving that Jesus is superior to the angels (Heb. 1:5). The author is not merely saying that Jesus is the Son and the angels are not, but that Jesus is the anointed Messiah, the King. We know this because in the Old Testament, angels are called "sons of God" (see Job 1:6).[55] The author of Hebrews is declaring that Jesus is a Son unlike the angels, for he is the unique Son of David, the messianic king. The second quotation is in the context demonstrating that Jesus did not exalt himself to be high priest but was appointed by God (Heb. 5:5).[56] Thus, the author again links Jesus' sonship with his special relation to God. He is the son who has unlimited access (as a priest) to his Father.

The kingship of the Messiah and the lineage of David cannot be separated. This was true even when it looked as if the reign of David and his descendants were coming to an end or had been greatly chopped down to size. Based on the sure promises of God, the Old Testament prophets continued to believe that God would someday restore the fortunes of David. That one day God would cause a shoot to sprout forth from the fallen tree. This shoot, or branch, would then fulfill the promises given to Abraham and to King David. Isaiah prophesies:

> There shall come forth a shoot from the stump of Jesse, and a branch from his roots shall bear fruit. And the Spirit of the LORD shall rest upon him, the Spirit of wisdom and understanding, the Spirit of counsel and might, the Spirit of knowledge and the fear of the LORD. And his delight shall be in the fear of the LORD. He shall not judge by what his eyes see, or decide disputes by what his ears hear, but with righteousness he shall judge the poor, and decide with equity for the meek of the earth; and he shall strike the earth with the rod of his mouth, and with the breath of his lips he shall kill the wicked. Righteousness shall be the belt of his waist, and faithfulness the belt of his loins. . . . In that day the root of Jesse, who shall stand as a signal for the peoples—of him shall the nations inquire, and his resting place shall be glorious. (Isa. 11:1–5, 10)

---

54. John B. Polhill, *Acts*, NAC 26 (Nashville: Broadman, 1992), 304. Kaiser maintains that the installment of the son on his throne will ultimately take place at the Second Coming (*Messiah in the Old Testament*, 98–99). The New Testament, however, does not link the enthronement of Jesus at the second coming but with his first coming, especially the resurrection.

55. Cf. the LXX where "sons of God" is replaced with "angels" (*angeloi*).

56. See R. O'Toole, "Christ's Resurrection in Acts 13, 13–52," *Bib* 60 (1979): 361–72.

God does not bring forth the Messiah from a new tree, but from the old stump of Jesse.[57] This "stump" is descriptive of the broken or cut-off Davidic dynasty. Isaiah is indicating that in the future Jesse's (and therefore David's) "family tree" will be cut down because of their unfaithfulness (Isa. 10:33–34). Although the nations that exalt themselves will be brought low, never to rise again, the house of David will rise from the ashes because of God's promises. A shoot will come forth from the tree that was once considered all but dead. This son will grow up "and the government shall be upon his shoulder" and "of the increase of his government and of peace there will be no end, on the throne of David and over his kingdom" (Isa. 9:6–7). The identity of this "shoot" or "branch" has been suggested by some to refer to Hezekiah (or Ahaz or Josiah).[58] It is better, however, to see this as a messianic passage fulfilled in Jesus of Nazareth.

There are a number of reasons why we must see this prophecy as fulfilled in Christ. First, as we have seen, the designation "branch" is messianic in the Old Testament.[59] Second, the whole earth is under the sphere of his domain (Isa. 11:4, 10). This descendant of David is not just the ruler over a small area of land in the Middle East but is ruler of the entire world. Third, the future aspect of the promises also supports a messianic reference by Isaiah. Hezekiah could not be the fulfillment of Isaiah 11:1 since he was already born at the time of the prophecy. Finally, the line of David had not fallen into obscurity during Hezekiah's reign as it had during the first century AD.[60]

Jesus' arrival onto the scene of history fits well with Isaiah's prophecy. He was born of a poor carpenter (Mark 6:3) in a lowly manger (Luke 2:7). Although it was clearly predicted that the coming ruler over Israel was to be born from the clan of Judah in the town of Bethlehem (Mic. 5:2), hardly any of Jesus' contemporaries saw Jesus as fulfilling such a prophecy. After his death and resurrection, however, it soon became abundantly clear that Jesus was indeed the promised Messiah. Repeatedly, the New Testa-

---

57. Many have noted that this "branch" is not referred to as coming forth from the "stump of David" but from the "stump of Jesse." Perhaps the best explanation is that Jesse goes back to a time before the Davidic line had any significance; that is, before it was a royal family. For example, Leupold argues, "Obviously, the reference is to the royal house of David, called in this case, 'stump of Jesse,' because, at the time involved, the glory that inhered in the name of David will have been lost and the family will have sunk to a level at which it stood when Jesse bore the honor of the clan. All of this is another way of saying that a time will come when the illustrious Davidic family will have lost its luster and will have returned to its status of an average undistinguished family" (*Isaiah*, 1:216).

58. Smith comments, "It seems totally inappropriate to identify this new king with Ahaz or Hezekiah" (*Isaiah 1–39*, 268).

59. See Isaiah 4:2; 53:2; Jeremiah 23:5–6; 33:14–17; Ezekiel 17:22; Zechariah 3:8; 6:12.

60. E. W. Hengstenberg comments, "The royal house of David would have entirely declined and sunk into the obscurity of private life, at the time when the Promised One would appear" (*Christology of the Old Testament and a Commentary on the Messianic Predictions* [Grand Rapids: Kregel, 1956], 2:96).

ment emphasizes Jesus as the promised seed of David.[61] He is the one who is perfectly endowed with the Spirit of God (see Matt. 3:16; John 1:32). He is the one who judges with equity and rules with authority. With his Father, he alone knows the secrets of man's heart and, as king, his judgments are faultless.[62] And he is the one who will someday fully establish his kingdom of peace. Christ alone fulfills Isaiah's prophecy concerning a shoot or branch that will have humble beginnings, but will be exalted to judge and rule the nations.

Not only do Isaiah 9:6 and 11:1 refer to a messianic descendant of David, but Isaiah 7:14 is also another possible reference. There we read,

> Therefore the Lord himself will give you a sign. Behold, the virgin shall conceive and bear a son, and shall call his name Immanuel.

The interpretation of this verse is notoriously difficult and no consensus has been attained.[63] There are two main difficulties that arise from this verse. First, the word 'almah can be translated as "young woman" (RSV, NRSV) or "virgin." More technically, the term refers to a young lady who has reached the age of marriage and has an unblemished reputation. Thus, the English term "young woman" is too broad whereas the term "virgin" is too narrow.[64] Most commentators agree that although the focus of the term is not on virginity, it is a secondary (and necessary) part of the meaning of the word. For example, in other uses of the term, it is clear from the context that the person mentioned with the title of 'almah is a virgin (see Gen. 24:43; Exod. 2:8; Ps. 68:25; Song of Sol. 1:3; 6:8). This emphasis is supported by the translation of 'almah in the Septuagint with the Greek parthenos (= virgin).

The second difficulty is that the context of Isaiah 7 demands a somewhat immediate fulfillment. Isaiah 7 records how Kings Rezin of Aram and Pekah of Israel were planning to overthrow Ahaz king of Judah. But God intervenes and declares through his prophet Isaiah that these two kings will not have success (v. 7). The sign given to Ahaz that the Lord will protect Judah is that an 'almah will give birth to a son and before that boy is old enough to refuse evil and choose good, the land of the two kings will be laid

---

61. See Matthew 1:1; 21:9, 15; Mark 10:47; Luke 1:32, 69; 2:4; John 7:42; Acts 2:29–31; Romans 1:3; 15: 12; 2 Timothy 2:8; Revelation 22:16.

62. See John 2:24–25; 4:18–19; 6:64; 21:17; Romans 2:16; 2 Thessalonians 2:8; Revelation 1:16; 2:23.

63. In fact, Leupold comments, "No explanation of v. 14 will ever be *entirely* satisfactory. The best a commentator can hope to achieve at this point is to relieve some of the difficulties that the reader encounters" (H. C. Leupold, *Exposition of Isaiah*, 1:158).

64. Hebrew does have more specific term for "virgin" (*bethulah*), although it is also debated as to whether this term even strictly means "virgin" (see G. J. Wenham, "bĕtûlāh: A Girl of Marriageable Age," *VT* [1972]: 326–47).

to waste (v. 16). Therefore, the age of the boy is given as a time indicator for the predicted fall of King Rezin and King Pekah. It seems to many, if not most, interpreters that the son of King Ahaz, Hezekiah, is the immediate fulfillment of v. 14.

The question before us then is how Matthew 1:22–23 should be understood. Matthew states that the virgin birth of Jesus took place to "fulfill" (*plēroō*) what was recorded in Isaiah 7:14. Was this prophecy only partially fulfilled with the birth of Hezekiah but only truly fulfilled with Jesus? Instead of affirming one option to the exclusion of the other, perhaps a better way to interpret this text is by way of typology. In this case, the Isaiah text was fulfilled with Hezekiah. Matthew then is using Isaiah 7:14 similarly to the way he referenced Hosea 11:1 (Matt. 2:15), Jeremiah 31:15 (Matt. 2:18), and the "Nazarene" statement (Matt. 2:23) as all being "fulfilled" in Jesus. They are fulfilled in Jesus in the sense that they are a type and he is the antitype. That is, a pattern was set in the Old Testament and Jesus, because he is in fact God's Son, is the ultimate fulfillment of that pattern (see chapter 2).

This interpretation affirms the reliability of the New Testament accounts of a virgin birth. Some critical scholars have asserted that the biblical authors created the myth of a virgin birth to claim that Jesus fulfilled this prophecy. One of the problems with such an explanation is that Isaiah 7:14 was not interpreted in the first century as referring to a virgin birth, but was viewed as having been fulfilled with the birth of Hezekiah. Stein explains, "It is difficult to believe that the reading of Isaiah 7:14, apart from an already existing tradition of the virgin birth, would give rise to the biblical accounts in Matthew and Luke.

> *The reality of the virgin birth is what caused the New Testament authors to reexamine the Old Testament rather than the belief that the prophecy was still unfulfilled.*

It was the story that gave rise to the messianic interpretation of the passage, not the reverse."[65] Thus, Matthew indicates Jesus' miraculous virgin conception as a fulfillment of Isaiah 7:14.[66]

---

65. Stein, *Jesus the Messiah*, 66.

66. There are however, a few potential problems with the typological approach. First, some suggest that by definition a "sign" from the Lord must be something miraculous—more than simply the birth of a boy. But while it is true that some signs are miraculous, it is not necessary that all signs are. Some events or actions are signs because they prompt faith in God. Second, the child is to be called *Immanuel* or "God is with us." Does someone other than Jesus, such as Hezekiah, fit that description? Most commentators readily acknowledge the title of the boy's name does not *necessarily* imply that he is divine. It could simply be describing God's commitment not to abandon his people in the midst of the impending crisis. Third, there are some chronological problems with identifying Hezekiah as the fulfillment of the prophecy because he appears to be alive at the time of the prophecy. Finally, the typological approach seems to isolate Isaiah 7:14 from the rest of the book of Isaiah. For example, later in Isaiah 9:6 a son is given who will be called Mighty God and will rule on David's throne. Then in Isaiah 11:1 a descendant from David will come forth from the stump of Jesse who will be full of

We will also consider one text found in the book of Daniel.[67] When interpreting Nebuchadnezzar's dream, Daniel explains that God is not only sovereign over the kingdoms of the world, he will establish his own "kingdom that shall never be destroyed" (Dan. 2:44). Later Daniel himself has a vision:

> I saw in the night visions, and behold, with the clouds of heaven there came one like a son of man, and he came to the Ancient of Days and was presented before him. And to him was given dominion and glory and a kingdom, that all peoples, nations, and languages should serve him; his dominion is an everlasting dominion, which shall not pass away, and his kingdom one that shall not be destroyed. (Dan. 7:13–14)

Although there has been debate about the identity of "one like the son of man," there is no doubt that his status is unique.[68] He is one who comes on the "clouds of heaven" and has access to the presence of the "Ancient of Days." He is given "dominion and glory and a kingdom" with the result that all the nations serve or worship him. Furthermore, he is given an everlasting kingdom that will never pass away (cf. Dan. 2:44). While it is uncertain that Judaism embraced a messianic view of the "Son of Man" in Daniel 7,[69] it is clear that Jesus identifies himself as the fulfillment of the passage.

The title "Son of Man" was Jesus' favorite self-designation. The Gospels record Jesus referring to himself with this title more than eighty times.[70] Consequently, this term is highly significant when seeking to understand Jesus' messianic self-consciousness. What does Jesus mean when he speaks of himself as the "Son of Man"? Because of the repeated allusions to Daniel 7, it is natural to conclude that Jesus sees himself as the one of whom Daniel spoke (Matt. 10:23; 19:28; 25:31; Mark 8:38; 13:26; see also Rev. 14:14). But perhaps the most striking instance is when Jesus testified before the high priest who questioned him as to whether he was the Son of

---

the Spirit of God. Thus, it seems natural to relate the child in 7:14 to the references later mentioned in Isaiah where the texts are clearly messianic. If such is the case, then it is more difficult to merely interpret 7:14 as being fulfilled typologically.

67. See also Daniel 9:25–26 which speaks of "an anointed one" that many interpret as referring to Christ.

68. Some have identified the "son of man" as (1) the archangel Michael (see J. J. Collins, "The Son of Man and the Saints of the Most High in the Book of Daniel," *JBL* 93 [1974]: 50–66), (2) the Jewish nation (see Montgomery, *Daniel*, 218, 317–19), and (3) Jesus the Messiah.

69. The *Similitudes of Enoch* and 2 Esdras 13 have references to a messianic "Son of Man," but there is uncertainty as to the dating and interpretation of the material (13:32, 37, 52). See also Beale, *New Testament Biblical Theology*, 191–99, 393–401.

70. Sixty-eight times in the Synoptic Gospels and thirteen times in John. Luke 24:7 and John 12:34 are the only two occurrences of the term outside of those spoken by Jesus but even these references refer back to a statement made by Jesus.

God. He responded, "I am, and you will see the Son of Man seated at the right hand of Power, and coming with the clouds of heaven" (Mark 14:62). Christopher Wright comments, "Jesus calmly claims to be the Son of Man in full Danielic symbolism, the one whom God will vindicate and entrust with supreme authority. He was claiming to inaugurate the salvation and restoration of the people of God, to be the one who would be presented on their behalf to the Ancient of Days. He was the one who would receive eternal dominion and authority to act in judgment."[71]

Another predictive prophecy concerning the kingly office of the Messiah includes Micah 5:2:

> But you, O Bethlehem Ephrathah, who are too little to be among the clans of Judah, from you shall come forth for me one who is to be ruler in Israel, whose coming forth is from of old, from ancient days.

Micah thus foretells of a future deliverer who is coming to rule Israel and who will be born in Bethlehem. The location of Bethlehem is significant because that was the home of Jesse and the birthplace of his sons, including David. Just as David was the youngest son who lived in the somewhat insignificant town of Bethlehem, so too the Messiah, who will come from David's line, will be from the same small town located a few miles south of Jerusalem.

This passage is quoted in Matthew's Gospel in connection with the wise men searching for the newborn king. It is clear that Matthew highlights the kingly aspect of Jesus' birth. The wise men came to King Herod and asked, "Where is he who has been born king of the Jews? For we saw his star when it rose and have come to worship him" (Matt. 2:2). Herod, of course, was threatened by their acknowledgement of another king and thus inquired of the chief priests and scribes as to where the Messiah was to be born. Interestingly, Matthew records that the wise men were looking for the birth of the *king*, but then Herod inquires about the coming of the *Messiah*—demonstrating the concepts of the Messiah and the coming king were closely linked. Herod, who was Idumean,[72] was only a pretender and therefore threatened by someone who was a real king of the Jews. When the wise men eventually found the newborn king, they worshiped him and offered him gifts that were fitting for a king (Matt. 2:11). Thus, Micah's prophecy was fulfilled with the birth of Christ. The prophet predicted the birth of a ruler and Matthew testifies that Jesus indeed fulfilled this prophecy.

---

71. Christopher Wright, *Knowing Jesus through the Old Testament* (Downers Grove, IL: InterVarsity, 1992), 153.
72. See Josephus, *Antiquities* 15.373; 16.311.

Finally, Zechariah prophesies about the future Messiah-King:

> Rejoice greatly, O daughter of Zion! Shout aloud, O
> daughter of Jerusalem! Behold, your king is coming to you;
> righteous and having salvation is he, humble and mounted
> on a donkey, on a colt, the foal of a donkey. . . . His rule
> shall be from sea to sea, and from the River to the ends of
> the earth (Zech. 9:9–10)

Here, the Messiah is pictured as a righteous, humble king riding a donkey and bringing salvation. Unlike so many of the kings of Israel and Judah, this king is a righteous king who will judge the nations equitably (cf. Isa. 9:7; 11:4–5; 32:1). He is also a humble king who does not mount a horse (a symbol of war) but instead a donkey.[73]

Both Matthew and John cite Zechariah 9:9 in connection with Jesus' entrance into Jerusalem on Palm Sunday. Although there are some minor differences between Matthew's and John's citations of the Old Testament (see Matt. 21:5; John 12:15), the point seems obvious. Jesus is the messianic king who fulfills the prophecy of Zechariah. "He is victorious and yet meek, and his triumph is received rather than won. . . . He rides a donkey rather than a warhorse, and his kingdom will be one of peace rather than of coercion."[74] Although the crowds, as well as the disciples (see John 12:16), did not understand the full significance of Jesus' actions, these were certainly done intentionally by Jesus. He was declaring himself to be the Messiah-King, but not according to the common Jewish understanding. He would also be the Suffering Servant who would lay down his life in order to defeat his enemies. Thus, when he came into Jerusalem as the king, he came as a humble king riding a lowly donkey.

Conclusion

Many of the predictions in the Bible relate to the coming Messiah who was characterized as a prophet, priest, and king. Some of these prophecies are direct predictions that were only fulfilled in the life and ministry of Jesus. Others were viewed as having an immediate partial (or typological) fulfillment, but because

---

73. McComiskey writes, "Since Zion's king establishes peace among the nations (v. 10), it would be anomalous for him to ride an animal that symbolizes war. The donkey, on the other hand, stands out in this text as a deliberate rejection of this symbol of arrogant trust in human might, expressing subservience to the sovereignty of God" ("Zechariah," 1166). So also Grant R. Osborne, *Matthew*, ZECNT (Grand Rapids: Zondervan, 2010), 755; Leon Morris, *The Gospel According to Matthew*, PNTC (Grand Rapids: Eerdmans, 1992), 521; D. A. Carson, *The Gospel According to John*, PNTC (Grand Rapids: Eerdmans), 433; Kaiser, *Messiah in the Old Testament*, 216.
74. R. T. France, *The Gospel of Matthew* (Grand Rapids: Eerdmans, 2007), 777.

the true fulfillment had not yet taken place there was still the anticipation of the prediction to be fulfilled in a greater way. The authors of the New Testament had those same longings and with the coming of Jesus they saw these longings fulfilled. The Old Testament pointed forward to a deliverer and savior who would usher in the kingdom of God. Jesus came preaching the arrival of this kingdom because he saw himself as the messianic king.

Part 3

New Testament Prophecies

Chapter 7

Prophecies Regarding the Coming of the Messiah

After the Old Testament was completed, there was always the belief that God was not finished with his people. He made a promise to redeem them and deliver them from their enemies so that they could dwell in peace and safety forever.

The Gospels are not the start of something new as much as they are the continuation of something that had been predicted. That is to say, the Gospels announce the coming of the long-awaited Messiah who was predicted in the Old Testament. Although the first-century Jewish people found themselves in their own land, they were occupied and oppressed by the Roman government. They longed for deliverance. They longed for freedom. They longed for a Messiah. In this chapter we will discuss the prophetic statements in the Gospels and Acts related to (1) the coming of John the Baptist, (2) the coming of the Messiah, and (3) the coming of the Spirit.

The Forerunner of the Messiah: John the Baptist

Before John the Baptist began preaching in the desert, the prophetic scene had been rather quiet for some time. Although many religious books were written by the Jewish people during the intertestamental period, these writings were not viewed as being inspired by God. Josephus, a first-century Jewish historian, testified,

> From Artaxerxes [464–424 BC] to our own time the complete history has been written, but has not been deemed of equal credit with the earlier records, because of the failure of the exact succession of the prophets. We have given practical proof of our reverence for our own Scriptures. For, although such long ages have now passed, no one has ventured either

> to add, or to remove, or to alter a syllable; and it is an instinct with every Jew, from the day of his birth to regard them as the decrees of God, to abide by them, and, if need be, cheerfully to die for them. (Josephus, *Against Apion* 1.41–42)[1]

Here Josephus readily acknowledges that other writings have been recorded but are not on the same level as those writings deemed Holy Scripture. The reason for this distinction is due to the fact that the "succession of the prophets ceased." Another text reads:

> Further, know that our fathers in former times and former generations had helpers, righteous prophets and holy men. But we were also in our country, and they helped us when we sinned, and they intervened for us with him who has created us since they trusted in their works. And the Mighty One heard them and purged us from our sins. But now, the righteous have been assembled, and the prophets are sleeping. Also we have left our land, and Zion has been taken away from us, and we have nothing new apart from the Mighty One and his Law. (2 Baruch 85:1–3)

The Talmud makes a similar admission: "When the latter prophets died, that is Haggai, Zechariah, and Malachi, then the Holy Spirit came to an end in Israel" (Tosefta Sota 13:3). It was the Holy Spirit who inspired the prophets so when this distinct work of the Spirit ceased, this also meant that God was no longer speaking through the prophets.[2]

Yet, there was the belief that prophecy would resume with the coming of the Messiah (Joel 2:28–32). So, when John the Baptist came on the scene, people were starting to wonder whether God was once again speaking to his people through a prophet. There is no doubt that John was viewed by many as a prophet:

1. *John's birth was surrounded by miraculous circumstances.*

We are told that although his father, Zechariah, and his mother, Elizabeth, were "righteous before God, and walked blamelessly in all the commandments and statutes of the Lord" (Luke 1:7), Elizabeth was very old but still childless (Luke 1:8). Zechariah, who was chosen by lot to enter into the temple to burn incense, saw an angel who told him that God heard his prayers and would grant him a son (Luke 1:8–13).

---

1. Thackeray, *Josephus* 1:179–81 (LCL).
2. See also Sir. 49:10; 1 Macc. 4:46; 9:27; 14:41; *Sib. Or.* 18b (1.385–86).

2. *John was filled with the Holy Spirit even while in his mother's womb* (Luke 1:15).

This is parallel to the prophet Jeremiah: "Before I formed you in the womb I knew you, and before you were born I consecrated you; I appointed you a prophet to the nations" (Jer. 1:15).

3. *John's ministry was the fulfillment of Old Testament prophecies.*

This is attested to by the Gospel writers (Matt. 3:3, quoting Isa. 40:3; Mark 1:2, quoting Mal. 3:1; Isa. 40:3; Luke 3:4–6, quoting Isa. 40:3–5), by Jesus (Matt. 11:10, quoting Mal. 3:1; Luke 7:26, quoting Mal. 3:1), and by John himself (John 1:23, quoting Isa. 40:3). All four Gospels quote Isaiah 40:3 in relation to the ministry of John the Baptist. "In its context the Isaianic passage relates God's promise to bring the exiles home from Babylon on a divinely prepared highway, with the image of all obstacles being moved by God."[3] Thus, John's prophetic task was to prepare the way for the Messiah. Interestingly, the "original context announces God's coming to lead his people in their 'new exodus' through the wilderness from Babylon back to Palestine."[4] It is therefore important that we do not miss the remarkable christological claim that is made in applying Isaiah 40:3 to one who is the forerunner of the *Messiah*. Isaiah 40:3 was also the theme verse for the Qumran community (1QS 8:13–14). Although there are many parallels between John and the Qumran community,[5] there is no firm evidence that John was ever associated with this group. What is clear is that John saw himself as a forerunner of the Messiah who would prepare the way for someone greater than himself.

4. *John functioned like a prophet by calling the people to repentance* (Matt. 3:2, 7–10; Mark 1:4–5; Luke 1:17; 3:3, 7–9; John 1:6).

For example, 2 Kings 17:13 states, "Yet the LORD warned Israel and Judah by every prophet and every seer, saying, 'Turn from your evil ways and keep my commandments and my statutes, in accordance with all the Law that I commanded your fathers, and that I sent to you by my servants the prophets.'"

---

3. Grant R. Osborne, *Matthew*, ZECNT (Grand Rapids: Zondervan, 2010), 111.

4. R. T. France, *The Gospel of Matthew*, NICNT (Grand Rapids: Eerdmans, 2007), 105.

5. Stein explains, "This community of Qumran possessed some striking parallels with John the Baptist and his preaching. Both John and Qumran were priestly in descent, stressed the need for repentance, had a similar though not identical 'baptism,' proclaimed a similar judgment of the Pharisees, were ascetic in their lifestyle and lived in the wilderness. Even more striking, however, was that they both had the same biblical passage as their theme verse" (Isa. 40:3; cf. Mark 1:3 and 1QS 8:12–14) (Robert H. Stein, *Jesus the Messiah: A Survey of the Life of Christ* [Downers Grove, IL: InterVarsity, 1996], 95).

5. *John dressed like a prophet.*

We are told that John wore a garment of camel's hair and a leather belt around his waist (Matt. 3:4; Mark 1:6). This was not a random selection of clothing but is reminiscent of what especially Elijah wore (see 1 Kings 19:19; 2 Kings 1:8; 2:13–14; cf. Zech. 13:4).

6. *John is compared to Elijah the prophet.*

The book of Malachi ends with a prophecy concerning the return of Elijah: "Behold, I will send you Elijah the prophet before the great and awesome day of the LORD comes. And he will turn the hearts of fathers to their children and the hearts of children to their fathers, lest I come and strike the land with a decree of utter destruction" (Mal. 4:5–6). When Zechariah was met by the angel in the temple, the angel announced that his forthcoming son will come "in the spirit and power of Elijah" (Luke 1:17). Jesus not only taught the crowds that John the Baptist was the greatest person born of women but that he also was "Elijah who is to come" (Matt. 11:14). Later Jesus' disciples asked him, "Why do the scribes say that first Elijah must come?" (Matt. 17:10). Jesus then answered them, "Elijah does come, and he will restore all things. But I tell you that Elijah has already come, and they did not recognize him" (Matt. 17:11–12; see also Mark 9:13). It was at this point that "the disciples understood that he was speaking to them of John the Baptist" (Matt. 17:13). When Jesus questioned his disciples about what people say about him, the disciples replied, "Some say John the Baptist, others say Elijah, and others Jeremiah or one of the prophets" (Matt. 16:14; see also Mark 8:28; Luke 9:19). Here, John is linked with two other well-known prophets, Elijah and Jeremiah. Finally, when Herod inquired about the ministry of Jesus, the response given by some was "John the Baptist has been raised from the dead," while others said "He is Elijah" or "He is a prophet, like one of the prophets of old" (Mark 6:14–15; see also Luke 9:7–8). Again, John is linked with the prophets, and especially with Elijah.

7. *John is called a prophet.*

After John's birth, his father Zechariah prophesied saying, "And you, child, will be called the prophet of the Most High; for you will go before the Lord to prepare his ways" (Luke 1:76). Jesus declared to the crowds concerning John the Baptist: "What then did you go out to see? A prophet? Yes, I tell you, and more than a prophet" (Matt. 11:9; see also Luke 7:26). But not only did Jesus consider John a prophet, the Jewish people did as well. We read that Herod wanted to put John to death, but hesitated to do so because the people "held him to be a prophet" (Matt. 14:5). Later, when the chief priests and the elders questioned Jesus about his authority, he responded with a question about the baptism of John—whether it was from heaven or from man. The Jewish leaders refused to answer Jesus because they all held that "John was a prophet" (Matt. 21:26; see also Mark 11:32; Luke 20:6).

When John the Baptist went into the Judean wilderness preaching repentance from sins and baptizing the people, there was a hope and anticipation that God had sent a prophet and perhaps *the* prophet. Luke records, "As the people were in expectation, and all were questioning in their hearts concerning John, whether he might be the Christ" (Luke 3:15). But John was not the Christ. Instead, he was the one who would prepare the way of the Lord. He baptized with water but the Messiah, who was mightier than John, would baptize them with the Holy Spirit (Matt. 3:11; Mark 1:8; Luke 3:16). In fact, when John saw Jesus coming toward him, he declared, "Behold, the Lamb of God, who takes away the sin of the world!" (John 1:29).

The Birth of the Messiah

John the Baptist's ministry in the Judean wilderness caused much speculation and a heightened awareness as to what God was preparing for his people. But even before John went out into the desert calling the people to repentance, Jesus had already been the center of prophetic announcements. Zechariah, Elizabeth, Mary, Simeon, and Anna all bore witness at the birth of Jesus that he was indeed the Messiah.

The father of John, Zechariah, was a priest. When he was chosen to serve in the temple the angel declared to him that he and his wife would have a son in their old age (Luke 1:13). The angel continued prophesying that his son would "turn the hearts of the fathers to the children, and the disobedient to the wisdom of the just, to make ready for the Lord a people prepared" (Luke 1:17). After his son was born and he was again able to speak, he was filled with the Holy Spirit and prophesied about the coming of the Messiah. Only two of the twelve verses relate to the birth of his son John whereas ten verses relate to the coming Messiah. Zechariah realized that the real importance of John was to "go before the Lord to prepare his ways" (Luke 1:76). Once his son was born and his tongue was loosed, Zechariah was filled with the Holy Spirit and prophesied (Luke 1:68–75).

Zechariah blessed God because he had "visited" and "redeemed" his people through the coming of the Messiah which was now a reality both as evidenced by the birth of John and the testimony of Elizabeth (Luke 1:41–45). That Zechariah was referring to the Messiah and not his son John is clarified by the reference to the "horn of salvation" that has been raised up from "the house of David" (Luke 1:69).[6] Zechariah and John were from the house of Levi but the child that Mary was carrying was from the lineage of David. This

---

6. "Horn" is an Old Testament metaphor symbolizing power and strength.

pronouncement of a Messiah was not something that was unexpected but was rather that which God "spoke by the mouth of his holy prophets from of old" (Luke 1:70). But this promise of a Messiah who would deliver the people from their enemies was also based on God's "holy covenant . . . that he swore to our father Abraham" (Luke 1:71–72; cf. Gen. 12:1–3; 22:16–18).

Thus, when Zechariah's son was born, he and Elizabeth were thrilled that the Lord had heard their prayers and had taken away the disgrace of having no children. He could hardly contain his excitement and joy. This would be no ordinary son but one who would be a "prophet of the Most High" who would "go before the Lord to prepare his ways" and "give knowledge of salvation to his people in the forgiveness of their sins" (Luke 1:76). But Zechariah's joy was only possible through the coming of the Messiah that was characterized as the "rising sun" (Luke 1:78). Kaiser relates this phrase to Jesus:

> Indeed, Jesus is the "morning star" who rises in our hearts (2 Pet 1:19). He is "the Root and the Offspring of David, and the bright Morning Star" (Rev. 22:16), "the light of the world" (Jn 8:12). All who trust him will "shine like the sun in the kingdom of their father" (Mt 13:43).[7]

Zechariah's wife, Elizabeth, also testified to the Messiah who was to come. After Mary had conceived her son by the power of the Holy Spirit, she went to visit Elizabeth for three months. As Mary entered the house of her relatives and greeted them, the baby in Elizabeth's womb leaped. Luke then informs his readers that Elizabeth was filled with the Holy Spirit and exclaimed,

> Blessed are you among women, and blessed is the fruit of your womb! And why is this granted to me that the mother of my Lord should come to me? For behold, when the sound of your greeting came to my ears, the baby in my womb leaped for joy. And blessed is she who believed that there would be a fulfillment of what was spoken to her from the Lord. (Luke 1:42–45)

It is clear that Elizabeth's blessing upon Mary is no ordinary blessing or word of congratulations. Astonishingly, Elizabeth refers to Mary as "the mother of my Lord" (Luke 1:43). Morris comments, "The use of the title *my Lord* shows that Elizabeth recognized that Mary's child would be the Messiah" (cf. Ps. 110:1).[8] We do not know precisely how Elizabeth came to this understanding but it was

---

7. Walter C. Kaiser, *The Promise-Plan of God: A Biblical Theology of the Old and New Testaments* (Grand Rapids: Zondervan, 2008), 242.

8. Leon Morris, *Luke*, rev. ed., TNTC (Grand Rapids: Eerdmans, 1988), 83.

in part due to the fact that when Mary announced her greeting, the baby leaped in Elizabeth's womb. Being under the inspiration of the Holy Spirit, Elizabeth interpreted her unborn baby's movement as an expression of joy (Luke 1:44).

Mary also reflected on the goodness of God in relation to the child that she carried. This song of praise is also known as the *Magnificat*, based on the first word of the later Latin translation of this song (Luke 1:46–55).[9] Earlier the angel Gabriel had come to Mary and proclaimed that her son "will be great and will be called the Son of the Most High. And the Lord God will give to him the throne of his father David, and he will reign over the house of Jacob forever, and of his kingdom there will be no end" (Luke 1:32–33). Mary's song highlights some of God's divine attributes, including his power, holiness, and mercy. Her song is "a thanksgiving to God for not only giving to her a son, but a son who would be in the line of David and who would establish his throne and kingdom that would last forever."[10]

All of the previous events occurred before the birth of Jesus. But there were also at least two significant prophetic encounters with the newborn Savior. At the appointed time for purification (see Exod. 13:2; Num. 8:16; 18:15–16), Joseph and Mary took their baby to Jerusalem to present him to the Lord (Luke 2:22). Simeon, who is described as a "righteous" and "devout" man, was waiting in the temple because the Holy Spirit had revealed to him that he would not die before he had seen the Messiah (Luke 2:25–26). When Simeon saw the infant, he took him in his arms and declared:

> Lord, now you are letting your servant depart in peace, according to your word; for my eyes have seen your salvation that you have prepared in the presence of all peoples, a light for revelation to the Gentiles, and for glory to your people Israel. (Luke 2:29–32)

Simeon was waiting for the "consolation of Israel" (Luke 2:25) which is another way of saying he was longing for the coming Messiah, for it was the Messiah who would bring hope and encouragement to the people of God.[11] The Messiah would be the one who would rescue the people from suffering and deliver them from their enemies. The salvation that the Messiah will bring is for "all people"; that is, for "the Gentiles" and for "your people Israel" (Luke 1:31, 32). Finally, Simeon addressed Mary and said, "Behold, this child is appointed for the fall and rising of many in Israel, and for a sign that is opposed (and a sword will pierce through your own soul also), so that thoughts from many hearts may be revealed" (Luke 2:34–35). After holding the Savior

---

9. *Magnificat anima mea Dominum*, "My soul magnifies the Lord" (Luke 1:46).
10. Kaiser, *Promise-Plan of God*, 242.
11. So ibid., 245; Morris, *Luke*, 96–97.

of the world in his arms, Simeon was ready to die. As promised, his eyes had seen the Messiah who would bring comfort to the people and at the same time cause some to follow and others to oppose him. Jesus indeed would bring deliverance for his people, but he also brought heartache to Mary as she saw her son on the cross (John 19:25). But even the cross was a part of God's plan to accomplish what God had earlier revealed to Mary: "You shall call his name Jesus, for he will save his people from their sins" (Matt. 1:21).

The final prophetic witness at Jesus' birth was from Anna the prophetess. Luke records that Anna "did not depart from the temple, worshiping with fasting and prayer night and day. And coming up at that very hour she began to give thanks to God and to speak of him to all who were waiting for the redemption of Jerusalem" (Luke 2:37–38). This text again emphasizes that the people of Israel were waiting for a redeemer to come based on God's promises. Thus, Anna's testimony was that in Jesus, the Son of Mary, these expectations were in the process of being fulfilled. The Messiah was born in fulfillment of God's promises to his people. This Messiah would one day deliver the people of Israel and usher in the kingdom of God.

The Message of the Messiah

Jesus as Prophet

As discussed earlier (see chapter 6), Jesus was not only recognized as a king but also as a prophet. His prophetic office is confirmed by the following evidence:

1. *The crowds and individuals often viewed Jesus as a prophet.* This includes the general perception of the masses (Matt. 21:46; Mark 6:14–15; 8:28; John 7:40) as well as both Jewish (John 9:17) and non-Jewish individuals, such as the Samaritan woman at the well (John 4:19).

2. *The disciples viewed Jesus as a prophet.* This was true both at the beginning (John 1:45) and at the end (Luke 24:19) of his ministry.

3. *Jesus viewed himself as a prophet* (Mark 6:4; Luke 13:33; John 5:45–47). When his hometown rejected him, Jesus declared, "A prophet is not without honor, except in his hometown" (Mark 6:4). He also stated that Moses wrote of him, alluding to Deuteronomy 18:15 (John 5:45–47) and that he had to flee from Herod because "it cannot be that a prophet should perish away from Jerusalem" (Luke 13:33).

4. *Jesus possessed the Spirit like a prophet* (Matt. 12:18; Mark 3:28–30; Luke 4:16–20). After reading Isaiah 61:1–2 ("The Spirit of the Lord is upon me, because he has anointed me to proclaim good news to the

poor. He has sent me to proclaim liberty to the captives and recovering of sight to the blind, to set at liberty those who are oppressed, to proclaim the year of the Lord's favor"), Jesus announced in the synagogue in Nazareth, "Today this Scripture has been fulfilled in your hearing" (Luke 4:21).

5. *Jesus taught authoritatively like a prophet.* There are several ways in which Jesus spoke like a prophet. He pronounced coming judgment (Matt. 11:21–24; 23:13–29; Luke 6:24–26) as well as blessings (Matt. 5:3–11; 13:16–17; Mark 10:29–30). Jesus also often authoritatively proclaimed his sayings as true before he uttered them with the use of the "amen" formula.[12] For example, he proclaimed to Nathaniel, "Truly [*amēn*], truly [*amēn*], I say to you, you will see heaven opened, and the angels of God ascending and descending on the Son of Man" (John 1:51). Furthermore, Jesus taught the law with an authority even greater than Moses' authority. In the Sermon on the Mount, he often announced, "You have heard that it was said. . . . But I say to you. . . ." (Matt. 5:21–22). Jesus even rescinded certain aspects of the law (Mark 7:14–23). The result was that after he taught, "the crowds were astonished at his teaching, because He was teaching them like one who had authority, and not like their scribes" (Matt. 7:28–29).

6. *Jesus performed signs and miracles like a prophet.* This included miracles such as feeding the multitudes (John 6:14), healing a blind man (John 9:17), and raising the dead (Luke 7:16; cf. 1 Kings 17:17–23). In addition, Jesus was able to know someone's thoughts (Mark 2:8; Luke 9:47; John 2:24–25) and even to forgive sins (Mark 2:5).

The Kingdom of God

Jesus' message as prophet, however, relates once again to his status as the Davidic King. That is, the long-awaited King had come and had therefore ushered in the kingdom. When Jesus began his ministry he came preaching the kingdom of God: "The time is fulfilled, and the kingdom of God is at hand; repent and believe the gospel" (Mark 1:15; see also Matt. 4:17, 23; Luke 4:43). There should be no doubt that the message of the kingdom of God was Jesus' central message.[13] The phrases "kingdom of God" and "kingdom of

---

12. This formula is found in all four Gospels and is only used by Jesus. The double "amen" formula occurs twenty-five times in the NT, all in the Gospel of John.
13. Stein comments, "The central theme of the teaching of Jesus is the coming of the kingdom of God" (Robert H. Stein, *The Method and Message of Jesus' Teaching*, rev. ed. [Louisville: Westminster John Knox: 1994], 60). See also Thomas R. Schreiner, *New Testament Theology: Magnifying God in Christ* (Grand Rapids: Baker, 2008), 45, 79.

heaven" are found in sixty-three separate kingdom sayings of Jesus (eighty-five if parallel statements are included).[14] But what exactly is the kingdom of God/heaven? Unfortunately, neither Jesus nor the Gospel writers explain this term but simply assume it. The reason for this assumption is most likely because the concept was not new but was based on the Old Testament. When Jesus began preaching he stated, "The time is fulfilled," which suggests that such a time was anticipated by the Jewish people. Goppelt writes, "When Jesus announced the coming of the kingdom he was not introducing a new term. He proclaimed not that there was a kingdom of God, but that it was now coming."[15] What was the Old Testament expectation of God's kingdom?

While the phrase "kingdom of God/heaven" is not found in the Old Testament, the concept of a kingdom that God rules is common. God is frequently spoken of as the King of both Israel (Exod. 15:18; Num. 23:21; Deut. 33:5; Isa. 43:15) and all the world (2 Kings 19:15; Ps. 29:10; 47:2; 96:10; 97:1; 99:1–4; 145:11; Isa. 6:5; Jer. 46:18). And yet, there is also the expectation that God will one day rule over all his people in an unparalleled fashion (Isa. 24:23; 33:22; 52:7; Zeph. 3:15; Zech. 14:9). Ladd explains, "While God is King over all the earth, he is in a special way the King of his people, Israel. God's rule is therefore something realized in Israel's history. However, it is only partially and imperfectly realized. Therefore, the prophets look forward to a day when God's rule will be fully experienced, not by Israel alone but by all the world."[16]

The Old Testament not only refers to God as king but also states that he has a "kingdom."

> All the ends of the earth will remember and turn to the LORD, and all the families of the nations will worship before You. For the kingdom is the LORD's and He rules over the nations. (Ps. 22:27–28 NASB)

> The LORD has established his throne in the heavens, and his kingdom rules over all. (Ps. 103:19)

Furthermore, there was the hope that the fullness of God's kingdom would one day be established.

---

14. See Stein, *Method and Message*, 60. "Kingdom of God" is found 53 times (5 instances in Matthew, 14 in Mark, 32 in Luke, and 2 in John). "Kingdom of heaven" or more literally "kingdom of the heavens" is found 32 times—all in Matthew. It should be noted that these references do not include statements that only refer to the "kingdom" with no qualifying phrase.
15. Leonhard Goppelt, *Theology of the New Testament*, ed. Jürgen Roloff, trans. John E. Alsup (Grand Rapids: Eerdmans, 1981), 1:45.
16. George Eldon Ladd, *The Presence of the Future: The Eschatology of Biblical Realism* (Grand Rapids: Eerdmans, 1974), 46.

> And in the days of those kings the God of heaven will set up a kingdom that shall never be destroyed, nor shall the kingdom be left to another people. It shall break in pieces all these kingdoms and bring them to an end, and it shall stand forever. (Dan. 2:44)

When Jesus came preaching that the kingdom of God had come, his Jewish audience knew that he was referring to the complete rule of God over Israel and all the nations.

How is the term "kingdom of God" best defined? Most scholars rightly affirm that the kingdom refers not so much to a physical realm as to the reign of God.[17] Jesus himself said, "My kingdom is not of this world. If my kingdom were of this world, my servants would have been fighting, that I might not be delivered over to the Jews. But my kingdom is not from the world" (John 18:36). Therefore, in the Gospels the kingdom refers to the final, decisive exercising of God's sovereign reign. This reign was inaugurated in Jesus' ministry and will be consummated in his return.[18]

Although some maintain that the phrases "kingdom of God" and "kingdom of heaven" represent different realities, most scholars rightly acknowledge that the expressions denote the same reality.[19] There is debate, however, as to why Matthew tends to favor "kingdom of heaven" over "kingdom of God." The majority view is that Matthew, who was writing to a Jewish audience, avoided using the divine name out of reverence and to avoid breaking

---

17. For example, Bavinck states, *"The kingdom of God in the teaching of Jesus is not a political reality but a religious-ethical dominion"* (Herman Bavinck, *The Last Things: Hope for This World and the Next*, ed. John Bolt, trans. John Vriend [Grand Rapids: Baker, 1996], 99). John Bright defines the kingdom of God as "the rule of God over his people, and particularly the vindication of that rule and people at the end of history" (*The Kingdom of God: The Biblical Concept and Its Meaning for the Church* [Nashville: Abingdon-Cokesbury, 1953], 18). See also Ladd, *Presence of the Future*, 122–48. Contra Craig G. Bartholomew, *Where Mortals Dwell: A Christian View of Place for Today* (Grand Rapids: Baker, 2011), 99–101.

18. Ladd comments, "Jesus did not promise his hearers a better future or assure that they would soon enter the Kingdom. Rather he boldly announced that the Kingdom (*Herrschaft*) of God had come to them" (*Presence of the Future*, 111).

19. See Goppelt, *Theology of the New Testament*, 1:44. For example, some classical dispensationalists have taught that the "kingdom of God" refers to a spiritual kingdom of true (gentile) believers, whereas the "kingdom of heaven" refers to a future millennial reign of Christ on earth over Jewish believers. But this distinction cannot be maintained. First, Matthew often uses the phrase "kingdom of heaven" in the parallel accounts in which Mark and/or Luke use "kingdom of God" (cf. Matt. 4:17 with Mark 1:14–15; Matt. 5:3 with Luke 6:20; Matt. 8:11 with Luke 13:28; Matt. 10:7 with Luke 9:2; Matt. 11:11 with Luke 7:28; Matt. 11:12 with Luke 16:16; Matt. 13:33 with Luke 13:20; Matt. 13:11 with Mark 4:11 and Luke 8:10; Matt. 13:31 with Mark 4:30–31 and Luke 13:18–19; Matt. 19:14 with Mark 10:14 and Luke 18:16; Matt. 19:23 with Mark 10:23 with 18:24). Second, Matthew uses the terms interchangeably in the same context: "Truly, I say to you, only with difficulty will a rich person enter the *kingdom of heaven*. Again I tell you, it is easier for a camel to go through the eye of a needle than for a rich person to enter the *kingdom of God*" (Matt. 19:23–24, emphasis added).

the third commandment by using God's name in vain.[20] This type of substitution or referential circumlocution is found elsewhere in the Gospels. The divine name is substituted with "heaven" (Mark 11:30; Luke 15:21), "the angels of God" (Luke 15:10), "the Blessed One" (Mark 14:61–62), "Most High" (Luke 6:35), "great King" (Matt. 5:34–35), and "name" (Matt. 6:9).

Recently, the consensus view that Matthew is using substitution to avoid using the divine name in his use of the "kingdom of heaven" has been challenged. For example, Pennington argues that Matthew uses "heaven" instead of "God" not because of circumlocution but because of Matthew's theological contrast between heaven and earth.[21] Regardless, this view, like the traditional view, maintains that the "kingdom of heaven" and "kingdom of God" refer to the same reality.[22]

Jesus often used parables to teach about the kingdom of God. In fact, this theme is the most common theme of Jesus' parables, with several different features of the kingdom being highlighted.[23] First, Jesus taught that the kingdom of God was a present reality.[24] Through various parables, Jesus taught that the kingdom, although it might seem small and insignificant now (like a mustard seed or a little bit of yeast), will one day become something amazing. Second, Jesus taught that the kingdom of God should be pursued and entered, no matter the cost.[25] He emphasized the sacrifice one should make in order to enter the kingdom, which is compared to a valuable treasure and a pearl of great price. The kingdom is so valuable, it is worth selling everything to obtain it. Elsewhere, Jesus' followers, who are compared to a dishonest manager and unsharing bridesmaids, must do whatever it takes to be ready for the future. Third, Jesus taught that those who have entered the kingdom

20. So John P. Meier, *A Marginal Jew: Rethinking the Historical Jesus* (New York: Doubleday, 1994), 239–40; Stein, *Method and Message*, 63.
21. Jonathan T. Pennington, *Heaven and Earth in the Gospel of Matthew*. NovTSup 126 (Leiden: Brill, 2007), 1–37; idem, "The Kingdom of Heaven in the Gospel of Matthew," *SBJT* 12, no. 1 (2008): 44–51 (esp. 45–46).
22. Pennington argues that the expressions have the same denotation but a different connotation.
23. Blomberg writes, "The central theme uniting all of the lessons of the parables is the kingdom of God. It is both present and future. It includes both a reign and a realm. It involves both personal transformation and social reform. It is not to be equated either with Israel or the church, but is the dynamic power of God's personal revelation of himself in creating a human community of those who serve Jesus in every area of their lives" (Craig L. Blomberg, *Interpreting the Parables* [Downers Grove, IL: InterVarsity, 1990], 326).
24. See, e.g., the parables of the Wedding Feast and Fasting (Mark 2:18–20), the Wineskins (Mark 2:22), the Strong Man (Matt. 12:28–29), the Mustard Seed (Matt. 13:31–32), the Leaven (Matt. 13:33), the Weather Signs (Luke 12:54–56), the Great Supper (Luke 14:16–24), and the Wedding Banquet (Matt. 22:1–4).
25. See, e.g., the parables of the Treasure (Matt. 13:44), the Pearl of Great Price (Matt. 13:45–46), the Tower and War (Luke 14:28–32); the Dishonest Manager (Luke 16:1–9), and the Ten Bridesmaids (Matt. 25:1–13).

by faith will live transformed lives.[26] Someone who is part of the kingdom, who has truly received the Word, will produce the necessary fruit. Fourth, Jesus taught that the God of the kingdom is gracious.[27] Because God is gracious and gives his people more than they deserve, no one should begrudge God his generosity. If God chooses to bless those who have squandered much of their lives, those who have lived "righteously" for most of their lives should rejoice that others have experienced the grace of God. Fifth, Jesus taught that those who fail to enter the God's kingdom will experience God's judgment and wrath.[28]

Finally, we must note that in the teaching of Jesus, as was evidenced in his parables, the kingdom of God/heaven is both a present reality (Matt. 11:11; 12:28; Mark 1:15; 9:1; Luke 11:2; 17:20–21) and a future hope (Matt. 6:9–10; 7:21; 8:11–12; Mark 14:25).[29] That is, when Jesus (the King) came to earth he ushered in the kingdom. This kingdom, however, will not be fully experienced until every knee bows and every tongues confesses Jesus as the King. Again, there are some dispensationalists who claim that Jesus offered the kingdom to the Jews but since they refused the offer, the offer of the kingdom was withdrawn.[30] But this certainly misses the entire point of Jesus' coming and his message. Stein is correct when he comments, "According to the Gospels, Jesus clearly taught that in his coming the long-awaited and long-sought kingdom of God had now arrived. The kingdom of God had come! With Jesus the kingdom of God had not simply drawn close. On the contrary, it had indeed arrived."[31] And yet, the kingdom did not come in its fullness. That would have to wait until the King returned.

The Farewell Discourse

John's Gospel provides us with a fuller perspective of Jesus by offering moments and material from the life and teaching of Christ not found in Matthew, Mark, and Luke. As such, John also contains passages exhibiting both

---

26. See, e.g., the parables of the Sower (Matt. 13:3–8; Mark 4:3–8) and the Rich Fool (Luke 12:16–21).

27. See, e.g., the parables of the Prodigal Son (Luke 15:11–32) and the Workers in the Vineyard (Matt. 20:1–16).

28. See, e.g., the parables of the Great Net (Matt. 13:47–50), the Wheat and the Tares (Matt. 13:24–30), the Sheep and the Goats (Matt. 25:31–46), and the Rich Man and Lazarus (Luke 16:19–31).

29. See G. R. Beasley-Murray, *Jesus and the Kingdom of God* (Grand Rapids: Eerdmans, 1986).

30. For example, see Stanley D. Toussaint and Jay A. Quine, "No, Not Yet: The Contingency of God's Promised Kingdom," *BSac* 164 (April–June 2007): 131–47. They argue that "the kingdom is not present today, because when Israel rejected Jesus, the kingdom was postponed" (131). Ladd is correct when he states, "The very term 'Kingdom of God,' to many Christians means first of all the millennial reign of Christ on earth. This, however, misplaces the emphasis of the Gospels. The distinctive characteristic about Jesus' teaching is that in some real sense, the Kingdom of God has come in his person and mission" (*Presence of the Future*, xi).

31. Stein, *Method and Message*, 73–74.

realized and future eschatology. John 13–17 represents the lengthiest section of eschatological teaching, known as the farewell discourse, and it occurs during Jesus' final Passover meal as he prepares his closest disciples for his death, resurrection, and ascension.[32] The farewell discourse is framed between Jesus washing the disciples' feet (John 13) and Jesus praying for his disciples (John 17), but the actual discourse occurs in John 13:31–16:33.[33] Jesus begins by dropping a bombshell on his disciples: "Little children, yet a little while I am with you. You will seek me, and just as I said to the Jews, so now I also say to you, 'Where I am going you cannot come'" (John 13:33). This statement might refer either to Jesus' death or to his ascension. Both departures are addressed in the chapters that follow.[34] The challenge is sorting out the various senses intended when Jesus speaks of leaving and returning to them.

The farewell discourse refers to the removal and arrival of Jesus' presence in at least three ways:

1. Jesus refers to his removal of impending death and his return to them after his resurrection. Contextually and historically, Jesus' death is only a matter of hours away and the disciples will grapple with the crushing grief of his crucifixion. Jesus assures them that their grief will only be momentary because he will return to them alive after a "little while" (John 14:19; 16:16, 19–22).

2. Jesus refers to his removal by returning to his Father and his return to them at the second coming. Jesus also braces his disciples for his ascension when he will "go to the Father" (John 16:10). This seems to be the focus of John 14:1–3. He comforts his disciples by telling them that he is going to prepare a place for them in his Father's house and that he will come back for them. Although Jesus' *coming back* and *being with* his disciples is often interpreted in a wide variety of ways,[35] it seems best to understand this to be a reference to his second coming.[36]

3. Jesus addresses the removal of his physical presence as he returns to his Father and the inner arrival of his presence through the person of the Holy Spirit. Although the resurrection appearances and second coming are features of how Jesus will be with them again, the indwelling presence of the Holy Spirit in believers represents the pri-

---

32. Craig S. Keener, *The Gospel of John: A Commentary* (Peabody, MA: Hendrickson, 2003), 2:896, 898.
33. Andreas J. Köstenberger, *John*, BECNT (Grand Rapids: Baker, 2004), 419.
34. D. A. Carson, *The Gospel According to John*, PNTC (Grand Rapids: Eerdmans, 1991), 483.
35. Ibid., 488.
36. Köstenberger, *John*, 427. See also Leon Morris, *The Gospel According to John*, rev. ed., NICNT (Grand Rapids: Eerdmans, 1995), 568.

mary focus of the farewell discourse. He promised to send them the Helper, the Spirit of truth, who will dwell in them (John 14:15–17). The Father will send the Spirit in Jesus' name and he will comfort them, guide them, and teach them (John 14:23–31; 15:26–27; 16:1–15). The disciples, therefore, will continue to experience the presence of Christ through the arrival of the Holy Spirit.

In his farewell discourse, Jesus predicted both his return to the Father and his return to his disciple through the presence of the Holy Spirit.

The Spirit of the Messiah

When thinking about predictive prophecy we would be remiss if we did not mention the promised coming of the Holy Spirit. Although the Spirit was active from the very beginning (Gen. 1:2) and throughout God's interaction with the people of Israel, the Old Testament clearly anticipates a new role for the Spirit in the new covenant (Isa. 32:15; 44:13; Joel 2:28–32; Ezek. 11:19–20; 36:25–27; 37:14).

Jeremiah 31:31–34 indicates that the "new covenant" will be different from the old covenant because God will put his law within his people, and he will write it on their hearts. He promises that he will be their God, that they will be his people, and that all will know him. The problem with the Mosaic covenant was not with the covenant itself but with Israel's failure to keep the covenant. Therefore, God promises a new covenant that will not simply impose an outward standard but one that will involve the inward transforming work of the Spirit which will be given to all of God's people and will enable them to keep God's laws. This same Spirit that gave wisdom to the builders of the temple, strengthened the judges and kings, and spoke through the prophets, was now promised to all of God's people. This same Spirit that caused Mary to be with child (Matt. 1:18–32), anointed Jesus at his baptism (Matt. 3:16; Mark 1:10; Luke 3:22), led him into the wilderness (Matt. 4:1; Mark 1:12; Luke 4:1, 14), and anointed him for ministry (Matt. 12:17–21, 28; Luke 4:18), was now to indwell new covenant believers.

The coming of the Holy Spirit was essential for God to fulfill his plan to bless the nations. After his resurrection but before his ascension, Jesus ordered his disciples to wait in Jerusalem until they received "the promise of the Father," which he went on to tell them was the Holy Spirit (Acts 1:4–5). Later, he informed them that after the Holy Spirit came upon them, they would receive power to be his witnesses to the ends of the earth (Acts 1:8). This promise was then fulfilled on the day of Pentecost when the disciples received the Spirit (Acts 2:4). When Peter stood up to proclaim what the signs accompanying the pouring out of the Spirit meant, he quoted Joel 2:28–32: "And in the last days it shall be, God declares, that I will pour out my Spirit on all flesh" (Acts 2:17).[37] But what is the precise significance of the coming of the Spirit at Pentecost?

The traditional Pentecostal interpretation is that the disciples already possessed the Holy Spirit. This point is taken from John 20:22 which states, "And when he had said this, he breathed on them and said to them, 'Receive the Holy Spirit.'" Therefore, if the disciples had already received the Holy Spirit before Pentecost, the significance of the Spirit coming at Pentecost is limited to the empowering work of the Spirit, especially in evangelism (Acts 1:8). Thus, the baptism of the Spirit is a second blessing that is evidenced by the ability to speak in tongues (Acts 2:4). Consequently, Christians today should ask Jesus for a "baptism of the Holy Spirit," following the pattern of the early church. This will result in greater effectiveness or power for missions and evangelism. The proof that a believer has received this blessing is the ability to speak in tongues. Support for this pattern (belief or salvation followed by a later reception of the Spirit) is found not only in Acts 2 but also in Acts 8 (Samaritans), Acts 10 (Cornelius), and Acts 19 (the Ephesian twelve).

Such an interpretation, however, cannot explain all the New Testament data and also tends to minimize the significance of the Spirit's coming at Pentecost. The coming of the Spirit at Pentecost represents a major shift in redemptive history as a sign of the new covenant. Although it is true that the Spirit was active in the Old Testament (Exod. 31:3; Deut. 34:9; Judg. 14:6; 1 Sam. 16:13), all of God's people did not possess the Spirit (Num. 11:29). Furthermore, as we have seen, the distinct feature of the new covenant was the indwelling presence of the Spirit in the hearts of believers (Jer. 31:31–34; Ezek. 36:26–27; Joel 2:28–29).

Although it is true that John 20:22 seems to teach that the Spirit was already received by the disciples before Pentecost, it is difficult to know precisely what John means. As we indicated above, the Pentecostal understanding is that John 20:22 refers to the disciples' regeneration and Acts 2 refers to their empowerment. Another unsatisfactory explanation is that John 20:22 is the Johannine version of Pentecost. That is, some suggest that since John does not record Pentecost elsewhere, he simply inserts it here. The difficulty, however, is that Pentecost occurred fifty days after the resurrection but John records this event on the same day. The best explanation is that the event in John 20 was a symbolic anticipation of what would occur on Pentecost.[38] Earlier in his Gospel, John records Jesus as saying:

---

37. See chapter 4 for how Joel 2:28–32 should be viewed as being fulfilled at Pentecost and therefore does not still await some future, final fulfillment.

38. So D. A. Carson, *The Gospel According to John* (Grand Rapids: Eerdmans, 1991), 649–655; Andreas J. Köstenberger, *A Theology of John's Gospel and Letters* (Grand Rapids: Zondervan, 2009), 399; Schreiner, *New Testament Theology*, 465–66.

> Now this he said about the Spirit, whom those who believed in him were to receive, for as yet the Spirit had not been given, because Jesus was not yet glorified. (John 7:39)

> Nevertheless, I tell you the truth: it is to your advantage that I go away, for if I do not go away, the Helper will not come to you. But if I go, I will send him to you. (John 16:7)

According to this latter text, Jesus plainly declares that the Helper (i.e., the Spirit) will not come until he has ascended to the Father. There is at least one other example of a statement by Jesus that refers to a future fulfillment. In John 17:5 Jesus says, "And now, Father, glorify me in your own presence with the glory that I had with you before the world existed." Here, Jesus speaks of God glorifying him before his death and resurrection but that glorification only came later. And yet, Jesus speaks of it as a present reality.

Therefore, we must acknowledge that the situation for the disciples was unique because they lived in a transition period in redemptive history. The apostles already believed in Jesus (Matt. 16:16–17; John 17:8, 12), and yet they had not yet received the Spirit.[39] The disciples received new power from the Holy Spirit (although they already believed) because they lived in the period of transition between the old and new covenants.[40] But this does not mean that this must or should be the experience for believers today. Such a view flattens out the Bible and ignores unique periods in salvation history.[41] Some might argue that such a transitional period might be true for the

---

39. This is evidenced by the fact that (1) they were still fearful as they met in secrecy with doors locked (John 20:19, 26), (2) Thomas did not believe in Jesus until he saw Jesus (John 20:26–27), and (3) the disciples returned to Galilee to their old employment (John 21:1–3).

40. Grudem comments, "The day of Pentecost was the point of transition between the old covenant work and ministry of the Holy Spirit and the new covenant work and ministry of the Holy Spirit [the newness includes greater power to witness for Christ and overcome sin]. . . . The Day of Pentecost was certainly a remarkable time of transition in the whole history of redemption as recorded in Scripture . . . because on that day the Holy Spirit began to function among God's people with new covenant power. . . . But this fact helps us understand what happened to the disciples at Pentecost. They received this remarkable new empowering from the Holy Spirit *because they were living at the time of the transition between the old covenant work of the Holy Spirit and the new covenant work of the Holy Spirit*. Though it was a 'second experience' of the Holy Spirit, coming as it did long after their conversion, it is not to be taken as a pattern for us, for we are not living at a time of transition in the work of the Holy Spirit" (Wayne Grudem, *Systematic Theology* [Grand Rapids: Zondervan, 1994], 771–72). See also Graeme Goldsworthy, *Preaching the Whole Bible as Christian Scripture* (Grand Rapids: Eerdmans, 2000), 235; idem, *Christ-Centered Biblical Theology: Hermeneutical Foundations and Principles* (Downers Grove, IL: InterVarsity, 2012), 151–52.

41. Goldsworthy rightly notes, "Salvation history . . . highlights the progressive nature of revelation and the fact that texts do not all bear the same relationship to the gospel and to the Christian church today" (Goldsworthy, *Preaching the Whole Bible*, 29). He continues, "Not all texts stand in the same relationship to the contemporary believer as others. . . . The unity of biblical revelation . . . does not mean uniformity of application" (73).

apostles but that this explanation fails to convince in the examples of Acts 8, 10, and 19. In these later "Pentecostal" type experiences, the new converts first believe in Jesus (regeneration) and then only later receive the baptism of the Spirit (second blessing) accompanied with the ability to speak in tongues. In these three accounts, however, the reception of the Spirit is linked with acceptance into the people of God and not related to power in evangelism.[42] Schreiner summarizes,

> The primary purpose for the granting of the Spirit at Pentecost, to the Samaritans, to Cornelius and his friends, and to the Ephesian twelve is to testify that those who receive the Spirit are members of the people of God. The pouring out of the Spirit signifies that the new age has commenced. . . . It seems that the primary purpose was to certify that those who received the Spirit belonged to God's people.[43]

Conclusion

Jesus did not come unannounced. Not only were his conception and birth surrounded by prophetic announcements, but God also raised up a prophet in John the Baptist who prepared his way. As a prophet himself, Jesus proclaimed the kingdom of God and also the coming of the Holy Spirit after his departure. At Pentecost, fifty days after Jesus' ascension, the Spirit of the Messiah descended upon Jesus' disciples, empowering them to preach the gospel to the nations. But just as Jesus' first coming was predicted in the Old Testament, so also his second coming is repeatedly predicted in the New Testament.

---

42. Schreiner states, "The coming of the Spirit in Acts 8; 10; 19 was not primarily to denote empowering for charismatic ministry but rather to signify that those who received the Spirit belonged to the people of God" (*New Testament Theology*, 454).
43. Ibid., 458–59.

Chapter 8

Prophecies Regarding the Return of the Messiah (Part 1: The Gospels and Acts)

One day the Messiah will return to complete what he began when all his enemies will be made a footstool for his feet.

The first coming of Jesus is the pinnacle of redemptive history. His life, death, resurrection, and ascension ushered in the kingdom of God by defeating death and Satan, guaranteeing that those who trust in the Messiah will reign with him forever. And yet, as we discussed earlier, the kingdom did not come in its fullness. This chapter begins our discussion of the return of the Messiah in the New Testament, with subsequent chapters considering material in the epistles and Revelation. In this chapter we will limit our discussion of the second coming primarily to Jesus' statements in the so-called Olivet Discourse (Matt. 24; Mark 13; and Luke 21).[1] Following this discussion we will consider the meaning of the highly popular "Left Behind" texts (Matt. 24:40–41 and Luke 17:34–35).

The Olivet Discourse

The Olivet Discourse is perhaps one of the most challenging portions of Scripture to interpret. Therefore, we must approach the text with humility and a willingness to learn. The central question is whether or not Jesus' predictions were fulfilled with the destruction of the temple or in his second coming. There are at least three major interpretations that must be considered: (1) the preterist interpretation—including the differing interpretations of both full and partial preterists, (2) the already-not yet interpretation, and (3) the futurist interpretation.[2] The way we interpret this passage will determine in part how we understand the second coming.

---

1. For the sake of simplicity, we will normally only give the references from Matthew's version.
2. See *Dictionary of Biblical Prophecy and End Times*, ed. J. Daniel Hays, J. Scott Duvall, and C. Marvin Pate (Grand Rapids: Zondervan, 2007), 318–20.

The Preterist Interpretation

The preterist (from the Latin for "gone by") view can be divided into two camps. Full preterists affirm that all of Jesus' predictions in his eschatological discourse, including references to the coming of the Son of Man (Matt. 24:30, 39, 44), were fulfilled in AD 70 when the temple and Jerusalem were destroyed. The partial preterist view, in continuity with the full preterist view, maintains that the Danielic reference to the coming of the Son of Man in Matthew 24:30 is already fulfilled. Where the two preterist views differ, however, is that partial preterists view Matthew 24:36–44 as referring to the second coming and therefore as yet unfulfilled.

This view has several strengths. First, it stresses the context of the question(s) that Jesus answers which clearly focus on the destruction of the temple and Jerusalem (see esp. Matt. 24:1–2, 15–16). The very reason the dialogue between Jesus and the disciples began was their impression of the grandeur of the temple. Thus, this view provides a clear answer as to why Jesus claims that events in his discourse are so near (see esp. Matt. 24:29, 34). Second, this view accounts for Matthew 24:29 which indicates that the coming of the Son of Man occurs "immediately" after the tribulation. If the coming of the Son of Man refers to the second coming, then Jesus and Matthew were wrong since Jesus did not return immediately after the temple was destroyed.[3] A similar problem is found in Matthew 24:34 which states that "this generation will not pass away until all these things take place." If "all these things" includes the coming of the Son of Man "on the clouds of heaven with power and great glory" (Matt. 24:30), then this verse teaches that the *parousia* would occur before that generation ended. Thus, the only way for that event to have been accomplished during the generation of the disciples is if we interpret the destruction of the temple as involving the coming of Jesus. Third, it allows for metaphorical language. Similar to the Old Testament prophets (Isa. 13:10; 34:4; Ezek. 32:7–8; Joel 2:10, 31; Amos 8:9), Jesus employed metaphorical or cosmic imagery to describe the judgment of God in history ("the sun will be darkened, and the moon will not give its light, and the stars will fall from heaven, and the powers of the heavens will be shaken," Matt. 24:29).[4] These events signify

---

3. France comments, "'But immediately after the distress of those days' constitutes a formidable problem unless one is prepared to argue that Jesus (and Matthew) really did expect the *parousia* to take place in the late first century AD, and that he was mistaken" (R. T. France, *The Gospel of Matthew*, NICNT [Grand Rapids: Eerdmans, 2007], 919).

4. N. T. Wright states, "The 'coming of the son of man' is thus good first-century metaphorical language for two things: the defeat of the enemies of the true people of god [*sic*], and the vindication of the true people themselves. Thus, the *form* that this vindication will take . . . will be precisely the destruction of Jerusalem and the Temple" (*Jesus and the Victory of God* [Minneapolis: Fortress, 1996], 362). France asserts, "Language about cosmic collapse . . . is used by the OT prophets to symbolize God's acts of

that the coming judgment will be from the hand of God who alone controls the sun, moon, and stars (though he will use the Roman army to accomplish his purposes). Thus, when Jesus speaks of the Son of Man "coming on the clouds of heaven" (Matt. 24:30), this is a metaphor of his vindication as the rightful king when the temple is destroyed.[5] Fourth, it takes into account the original context of Daniel's reference to the Son of Man (Dan. 7:13–14) which pictures the Son of Man coming to God in heaven and not coming to man on earth.[6] Therefore, this text refers to the vindication of Jesus before God and not his coming to earth on a cloud. France also notes that the word *parousia* is noticeably missing in Matthew 24:30, although it is found elsewhere in Matthew 24 (vv. 27, 37, 39).

The major problem with the preterist view centers on whether the coming of the Son of Man can be interpreted merely as a reference to the destruction of the temple. There are several reasons why this view fails to convince. First, Jesus states that when the Son of Man "appears" all the tribes of the earth will "see" him coming on the clouds. This passage seems to teach a visible return on the clouds similar to what we find in Acts 1 when Jesus ascended. Luke records that as the disciples were looking on, Jesus "was lifted up, and a cloud took him out of their sight" (v. 9). The angels then instruct the disciples by adding, "This Jesus, who was taken up from you into heaven, will come in the same way as you saw him go into heaven" (v. 11). Similarly, the apostle John writes, "Behold, he is coming with the clouds, and every eye will see him, even those who pierced him, and all tribes of the earth will wail on account of him. Even so. Amen" (Rev. 1:7). France argues that the Son of Man will be seen "by what is happening on earth as the temple is destroyed and the reign of the 'Son-of-Man-in-heaven' begins to take effect in the gathering of his chosen people."[7] This interpretation seems go beyond what the meaning of the

---

judgment within history, with the emphasis on catastrophic political reversals.... If such language was appropriate to describe the end of Babylon or Edom under the judgment of God, why should it not equally describe God's judgment on Jerusalem's temple and the power structure which it symbolized?" (*Matthew*, NICNT, 922).

5. Wright maintains that the disciples heard Jesus' "prophetic announcement of the destruction of the Temple as the announcement, also, of his own vindication; in other words, of his own 'coming'—not floating around on a cloud ... but of his 'coming' *to Jerusalem as the vindicated, rightful king* (*Jesus and the Victory of God*, 342). France summarizes his view: "The time of the temple's destruction will also be the time when it will become clear that the Son of Man, rejected by the leaders of his people, has been vindicated and enthroned at the right hand of God, and that it is he who is now to exercise the universal kingship which is his destiny" (*Matthew*, NICNT, 924).

6. France is so confident that he states, "Jesus' predictive words in [Matt.] 24:29–31 not only allow but, when understood against their OT background, *need* to be interpreted as part of the answer to the first part of the disciples' question about the coming destruction of the temple" (*Matthew*, NICNT, 891).

7. Ibid., 926.

verse can bear.[8] Second, the reference to Daniel 7:13–14 must be interpreted not only in light of the Old Testament, but also in light of how the
New Testament writers understand this text (see Matt. 26:64; Mark 8:38;[9]
14:62; Rev. 1:7).[10]

Third, although metaphorical language may be used that in some contexts refers to local judgments, the context of Matthew's statement suggests a universal application. Also, in Matthew 24:14 the gospel is to be
preached to all the nations before the end will come. In Matthew 24:22
the tribulation is so great that if it had not been cut short "all flesh" (*pasa
sarx*) would not be saved. Fourth, the text mentions how the angels "will
gather the elect from the four winds, from one end of heaven to the other"
(Matt. 24:31). France interprets the ingathering done by the angels as "the
spiritual power underlying human evangelization."[11] Again, such an interpretation seems forced.[12] Elsewhere the angels gather the elect for the final
judgment (Matt. 13:39, 41, 49). In the parable of the weeds, Jesus states
that at the "close of the age" the "Son of Man" will send his "angels" and
throw the unrighteous in a furnace of fire (Matt.13: 39–42). In teaching
about the cost of being his disciple, Jesus warns, "The Son of Man is going
to come with his angels in the glory of his Father, and then he will repay
each person according to what he has done" (Matt. 16:27). In the parable
of the sheep and the goats, Jesus declares, "When the Son of Man comes
in his glory, and all the angels with him, then he will sit on his glorious
throne" (Matt. 25:31). When the high priest places Jesus under oath after his arrest, he responds, "I tell you, from now on you will see the Son
of Man seated at the right hand of Power and coming on the clouds of
heaven" (Matt. 26:64). In these passages there is the consistent theme that
the Son of Man will return to render the final judgment—and not simply a
judgment against Jerusalem in AD 70.[13] Fifth, according to the New Testa-

---

8. So Schreiner, *New Testament Theology*, 807; Robert H. Stein, "N. T. Wright's *Jesus and the Victory of
    God:* A Review Article," *JETS* 44, no. 2 (2001): 213; D. A. Carson, "Matthew," in *The Expositor's Bible
    Commentary*, rev. ed., vol. 9 (Matthew–Mark) (Grand Rapids: Zondervan, 2010), 553–54.
9. Adams states that when Mark 8:38 is interpreted in light of Daniel 7:13 and Zechariah 14:5, "His
    'coming' is no longer a coming to God, but a coming as God's agent, *from heaven to earth*, for the
    purpose of eschatological judgment" (Edward Adams, *The Stars Will Fall from Heaven: "Cosmic Catas-
    trophe" in the New Testament and Its World*, LNTS 347 [London: T&T Clark, 2007], 150).
10. Stein explains, "Far more important for our understanding of what Mark meant by 13:26 is how the
    NT writers understood Dan. 7:13–14, and they understood it not as the Son of Man going to God
    but rather coming from God and going to earth" (Robert H. Stein, *Mark*, BECNT [Grand Rapids:
    Baker, 2008], 613n. 6). See also Adams, *Stars Will Fall from Heaven*, 148.
11. France, *Matthew*, NICNT, 928.
12. Carson maintains, "Only with considerable difficulty can v.31 be interpreted as referring to Christian
    missions" ("Matthew," 568).
13. Carson comments that "the 'coming' (*parousia*) of Christ or of the Son of Man, along with related ex-
    pressions, is so regularly associated with the coming of Jesus at the end of the age in connection with

ment, especially the preaching of the early church, the vindication of Jesus occurred at his resurrection and exaltation and not with the destruction of the temple.[14] Finally, the term *parousia* (Matt. 24:27, 37, 39) elsewhere in the New Testament is used as a technical term for the second coming.[15]

The Futurist Interpretation

The futurist view is just the opposite of the preterist view. Instead of interpreting the prophecy of Jesus as already being fulfilled (in AD 70 when the temple and Jerusalem were destroyed), it views the entire prophecy as still future-oriented. This view claims that the first part of the prophecy (Matt. 24:4–28) refers to the time of the great tribulation before the second coming, whereas the second part (Matt. 24:29–31) refers to the second coming of Christ. A strength of this view is that in Matthew 24:29 Jesus indicates, "Immediately after the tribulation" the Son of Man will return. If the tribulation refers to suffering associated with the destruction of the temple, then Jesus was not altogether accurate since he did not return immediately after the temple's destruction. But if the tribulation refers to the seven years of suffering brought upon the world prior to the second coming, then Jesus' prophecy can be interpreted in a straightforward sense while maintaining Jesus' credibility as a prophet. The main problem with this view is that it seems to ignore the historical context and the question of the disciples. The disciples specifically ask Jesus "when will these things be?" (Matt. 24:3), which can only refer to the destruction of the temple (Matt. 24:1–2).[16] Another weakness is the interpretation of "this generation" in Matthew 24:34. It is maintained by some that this phrase relates to the destruction of the temple and not the second coming. But if the whole of Jesus' discourse relates to the second coming, is it fair to isolate one difficult verse and claim it alone is referring to the destruction of the temple? Even more unlikely is the view that "this generation" refers to human kind in general, to all the Jewish people who reject Jesus, or to the last generation of the end time.[17]

---

the resurrection from the dead . . . that it would take overwhelmingly convincing reasons to overturn this set of associations" (Ibid., 554).

14. See Acts 2:24, 33–36; 4:10–12; 5:30–31; 7:55–56; 13:30–39; Romans 1:4; 8:34; Ephesians 1:20; Philippians 2:8–11; Colossians 3:1; Hebrews 1:3, 13; 8:1; 10:12; 12:2; 1 Peter 3:22.

15. See 1 Corinthians 15:23; 1 Thessalonians 2:19; 3:13; 4:15; 5:23; 2 Thessalonians 2:1, 8; James 5:7–8; 2 Peter 1:16; 3:4; 1 John 2:28; Revelation 1:7.

16. Carson notes, "It is very difficult to imagine that a Christian reader of any of the Synoptics at any period during the first one hundred years of the existence of these documents would fail to see a reference to the destruction of Jerusalem" ("Matthew," 552). He continues, "How could the disciples think Jesus was *not* answering their question but describing a *second* destruction of the city, unless Jesus explicitly disavowed their understanding" (556). See also Adams, *Stars Will Fall from Heaven*, 152.

17. For example, Hoekema maintains, "By 'this generation,' then, Jesus means the rebellious, apostate,

The Already-Not Yet Interpretation

The "already-not yet" view insists that Jesus is prophesying about both the destruction of the temple and about his second coming. Just as the disciples ask a two-pronged question (Matt. 24:3), so Jesus gives them a two-pronged reply.[18] One difficulty in explaining this view is that there are at least four major variations as to where the "already" (i.e., the temple) part stops and the "not yet" (i.e., the second coming) part begins. We will discuss some of the strengths and weaknesses of the variations of this view.

The first option states that the temple section ends at Matthew 24:28 and the second coming section begins at Matthew 24:29. Perhaps the most obvious weakness is when Jesus states that the coming of the Son of Man will occur "immediately" after the great tribulation (Matt. 24:29) and then later adds, "this generation will not pass away until all these things take place" (Matt. 24:34). It appears that Jesus prophesies that his return will occur immediately after the destruction of the temple and will occur within the disciples' lifetime. But this interpretation seems to contradict what Jesus explicitly states in this passage. Whereas Jesus predicts with some specificity about the destruction of the temple, he unequivocally declares that no one knows the "day and hour" of his return (Matt. 24:36). Therefore, if he does not know when he will return, how can we claim that he also teaches that he will return "immediately" after the temple's destruction?[19]

What then does Matthew mean that the second coming will occur "immediately" after the destruction of the temple and associated tribulation?[20] Carson offers a possible explanation: "'Immediately after the distress [*thlipsis*] of those days,' [is] a clear reference back to the *thlipsis* of vv. 9, 22, not to the 'great distress' of vv. 15–21. Thus, the celestial signs and the coming of the Son of Man do not immediately follow 'the abomination that causes desolation' but 'the distress of those days'—i.e., of the

---

unbelieving Jewish people, as they have revealed themselves in the past, are revealing themselves in the present, and will continue to reveal themselves in the future. This unbelieving and evil generation, though they reject Christ now, will continue to exist until the day of his return, and will then receive the judgment which is their due" (Anthony A. Hoekema, *The Bible and the Future* [Grand Rapids: Eerdmans, 1979], 117).

18. The second half of the question is noticeably different in Mark's Gospel. It states, "and what will be the sign when all these things are about to be accomplished?" (Mark 13:4). Matthew's version reads, "and what will be the sign of your coming and of the close of the age?" (Matt. 24:3). Because of this difference, the response given by Jesus in Mark's Gospel pertains to the destruction of Jerusalem (and not the return of Christ) and should be interpreted independently of Matthew's Gospel (see Stein, *Mark*, 591).

19. Leon Morris notes that if Jesus claims he did not know the date of his return, "how could he say confidently that it would occur within a few years?" (*Matthew*, PNTC [Grand Rapids: Eerdmans, 1992], 594).

20. Mark and Luke do not include this word "immediately" in their accounts.

entire interadvent period."[21] In addition, the reference to "these things" being fulfilled during "this generation" seems to indicate that the disciples' generation would be alive when Jesus returns. Yet, it is not necessary to include the coming of the Son of Man as part of "these things" that must first occur.[22] After the disciples marveled at the buildings of the temple, Jesus informed his disciples that "all these things" (*tauta panta*; i.e., the buildings of the temple) will be completely destroyed (Matt. 24:2). The disciples, intrigued by Jesus' declaration, questioned him by asking when "these things" (*tauta*) will happen (Matt. 24:3). In both of these references, "these things" refers to the temple buildings or the events associated with the temple's destruction. So, when Jesus later states that this generation (which always means Jesus' contemporaries[23]) will not pass away until "all these things" (*panta tauta*) take place, the most natural way to understand this phrase is how it was used earlier in the chapter (i.e., as a reference to the destruction of the temple that does not include the second coming and accompanying tribulation).

The second option for dividing the passage, while affirming that the second coming is mentioned in Matthew 24:29–31, also affirms that the reference to the "great tribulation" in Matthew 24:21 probably does not refer to the destruction of the temple but the events preceding the second coming. If this verse describes a tribulation "such as has not been from the beginning of the world until now . . . and never will be," then it cannot describe the suffering experienced during the destruction of Jerusalem. Furthermore, in Matthew 24:22 the tribulation is so great that if it had not been cut short "all flesh" would not be saved. However, prophetic and apocalyptic literature often uses exaggerated language.[24] For example, earlier in this passage Jesus stated that "there will not be left here one stone upon another that will not be thrown down" (Matt. 24:2). And yet, no one accuses Jesus of being a false prophet for using exaggerated language since not every stone was thrown down.[25] In addition, the "for" (*gar*) of verse 21 links the great tribulation to what precedes, making a division between verses 20 and 21 difficult to justify.

---

21. Carson, "Matthew," 567.
22. So Morris, *Matthew*, 612; Stein, *Mark*, 619; Carson, "Matthew," 569; David L. Turner, *Matthew*, BECNT (Grand Rapids: Baker, 2008), 585–86; Adams, *Stars Will Fall from Heaven*, 165. Bavinck comments, "Here the expression *panta tauta* clearly refers to the signs of the coming parousia, not the parousia itself, for else it would make no sense to say that when 'these things' occur, the end is 'near'" (*Last Things*, 124).
23. See Matthew 11:16; 12:41, 42, 45; 23:36; 24:34; Mark 8:12, 38; Luke 7:31; 11:29, 30, 31, 32, 50, 51; 17:25; 21:32.
24. See Robert H. Stein, *A Basic Guide to Interpreting the Bible: Playing by the Rules*, 2nd ed. (Grand Rapids: Baker, 2011), 174–88.
25. Stein explains, "Such use of hyperbolic language is far more expressive and emotive than the use of any scientific or statistical language" (*Mark*, 606).

The third option maintains that the not-yet part of Jesus' eschatological discourse begins in Matthew 24:15 because in this verse Jesus speaks of the "abomination of desolation," which is identified with Paul's reference to the "man of lawlessness" (2 Thess. 2:3–4). Thus, it must refer to an event related to the second coming. But in 1 Maccabees the "abomination of desolation" that is referenced in Daniel 11:31 and 12:11 is referred to as having taken place when Antiochus Epiphanes IV erected a desolating sacrilege on the altar of burnt offering (1:54–59). This indicates that the Jewish people did not regard Daniel's prophecy as requiring an eschatological interpretation.

The fourth option argues that the teachings of Jesus concerning the destruction of the temple and the *parousia* are so intertwined that it is impossible to separate them. The events refer to the coming persecution on Jerusalem but these events also foreshadow the suffering during the great tribulation. This type of "prophetic foreshortening" is common among the prophets where two events are viewed together but unfold in history with a delay between them.[26] Thus, the prophecy of destruction of the temple and accompanying tribulation is both a historical event and a symbol for the tribulation before the *parousia*. Advocates of this view maintain that although Jesus is answering the disciples' second question concerning the end of time, he is also implicitly answering their first question about the temple.[27] The strength of this view is the convenience it has of shifting back and forth between the destruction of the temple and the events preceding the second coming.[28] Yet, this view suffers from a serious challenge in that Jesus gave time references in his discourse ("immediately after the tribulation of those days," Matt. 24:29; "this generation," Matt. 24:34).

Conclusion

The following chart summarizes the various views:[29]

---

26. See, e.g., William W. Klein, Craig L. Blomberg, and Robert L. Hubbard, *Introduction to Biblical Interpretation* (Dallas: Word, 1993), 304.

27. Osborne states, "Jesus begins his answer with the second question of the disciples, the signs that presage the end. As such he is also addressing the implicit assumption that these are connected to the destruction of the temple and Jerusalem" (Grant R. Osborne, *Matthew*, ZECNT [Grand Rapids: Zondervan, 2010], 871).

28. The difficulty in having a clean break somewhere in the text separating references to the temple and references to the second coming is that there are references to the second coming throughout the passage (see Matt. 24:14, 27, 30, 39, and 44).

29. For the full preterist view, see Wright, *Jesus and the Victory of God*, 339–68. For the partial preterist view, see France, *Matthew*, NICNT, 885–943. For the already-not yet view, under category (1) see Carson, "Matthew," 548–72; Stein, *Mark*, 582–626. Under category (2) see Adams, *Stars Will Fall from Heaven*, 133–81. Under category (3) see James R. Edwards, *The Gospel According to Mark*, PNTC (Grand Rapids: Eerdmans; Leicester, England: Apollos, 2002), 383–409. Under category

VIEWS		AD 70 (TEMPLE & JERUSALEM)	SECOND COMING
Preterist	Full	Matt. 24:4–44	-----
	Partial	Matt. 24:4–35	Matt. 24:36–44
Already-Not Yet	1.	Matt. 24:4–28	Matt. 24:29–44
	2.	Matt. 24:4–20	Matt. 24:21–44
	3.	Matt. 24:4–14	Matt. 24:15–44
	4.	Matt. 24:4–44	
Futurist		-----	Matt. 24:4–44

While it is difficult to be dogmatic about any interpretation of the text, the already-not yet view is the most reasonable. Determining precisely where the text is to be divided (if at all) is not easy but between vv. 20 and 21 or vv. 28 and 29 seem to be the best options. Based on this understanding of the text, there are some important details we learn regarding the return of the king:

1. *Christ's return is certain but the time is unknown.*

It is not only impossible to set a date for Christ's return, it is wrong to try to do so.[30] Jesus himself said, "But concerning that day and hour no one knows, not even the angels of heaven, nor the Son, but the Father only" (Matt. 24:36; cf. 25:13; Acts 1:7[31]). Later Jesus states that the Son of Man

---

(4) see Osborne, *Matthew*, 864–906; Turner, *Matthew*, 565–91. It should be noted that most of the "Already-Not Yet" views consider the parable of the fig tree and subsequent teaching (Matt. 24:32–35; Mark 13:28–31; Luke 21:33) as referring to AD 70 and the destruction of Jerusalem. For the futurist view, see Robert H. Gundry, *Mark: A Commentary on His Apology for the Cross* (Grand Rapids: Eerdmans, 1993), 733–50.

30. Grudem insists, "The practical result of this is that anyone who claims to know specifically when Jesus is coming back is automatically to be considered wrong. . . . Anyone who claims to know the date on which Christ will return—from whatever source—should be rejected as incorrect" (Wayne Grudem, *Systematic Theology: An Introduction to Biblical Doctrine* [Grand Rapids: Zondervan, 1994], 1094).

31. In Acts 1:6 the disciples ask, "Lord, will you at this time restore the kingdom to Israel?" Jesus does not answer this question because the question reveals the continued misunderstanding of the disciples. He states, "It is not for you to know times or seasons that the Father has fixed by his own authority" (Acts 1:7). Beale writes that "verse 7 is a response to their wrong assumption that it was proper for them to know the precise time (cf. 1 Thess. 5:1–11) about when the kingdom would be restored to Israel; such knowledge is reserved for the Father alone" (G. K. Beale, *A New Testament Biblical Theology: The Unfolding of the Old Testament in the New* [Grand Rapids: Baker, 2011], 139). See also John B. Polhill, *Acts*, NAC 26 (Nashville: B&H, 1992), 84–85.

is coming "at an hour you do not expect" (Matt. 24:44).[32] Interestingly, Jesus is likened to a thief who comes unexpectedly in the night (Matt. 24:43–44; cf. 1 Thess. 5:1–2; 2 Peter 3:10; Rev. 16:15). And yet, there is also evidence that Jesus believed that there would be a delay before his return. After Jesus was anointed by a woman at the house of Simon the leper, Jesus proclaims, "And truly, I say to you, wherever the gospel is proclaimed in the whole world, what she has done will be told in memory of her" (Mark 14:9). This verse suggests a time when Jesus will not be with the disciples and a time when the gospel will be preached throughout the world. Some of Jesus' parables also suggest a delay of his return. For example, concerning the parable of the ten minas we read, "As they heard these things, he proceeded to tell a parable, because he was near to Jerusalem, and because they supposed that the kingdom of God was to appear immediately. He said therefore, 'A nobleman went into a far country to receive for himself a kingdom and then return'" (Luke 19:11–12). In a parable at the end of Matthew 24, Jesus warns the slave not to say in his heart, "My master is delayed" and therefore take advantage of his master's being absent (v. 48). In the parable of the ten virgins we are told that both the wise and foolish bridesmaids fell asleep "as the bridegroom was delayed" (Matt 25:5). Finally, in the parable of the talents we read, "Now after a long time the master of those servants came and settled accounts with them" (Matt 25:19).

2. *Christ's return should motivate us to readiness.*

Although Jesus taught that his return was near, he did not expect it to be immediate. His point is that since we do not know the exact time of his return, we must always be prepared.[33] Jesus says, "Stay awake, for you do not know on what day your Lord is coming" (Matt. 24:42; cf. Mark 13:32–37). Like a faithful and wise servant, the disciples are to always be prepared for their master's return (Matt. 24:45–51). They are to be like wise bridesmaids who have their lamps ready as they await the coming of the bridegroom (Matt. 25:1–13). They are to use their talents faithfully until the Lord returns so that they hear him say, "Well done, good and faithful servant" (Matt. 25:14–30). They are to offer help to the least of these (Matt. 25:31–46). Therefore, being ready does not mean we seek to calculate the timetable of the Lord's return, but that we are always faithfully serving the Lord by doing his will.

---

32. Hoekema concludes, "If these words mean anything at all, they mean that Christ himself did not know the day or the hour of his return" and therefore "no other statements of his can be interpreted as indicating the exact time of that return" (*Bible and the Future*, 113).

33. Beasley-Murray states, "In general the emphasis of [Jesus' teaching concerning the end] is that the time of the end cannot be known, and thus one should be ready for it at *all* times" (George R. Beasley-Murray, *Jesus and the Kingdom of God* [Grand Rapids: Eerdmans, 1986], 191).

3. *Christ's return will be visible.*

Jesus will come on the clouds and be seen by all the tribes of the earth (Matt. 24:30). Just as in the Old Testament God moved with the clouds,[34] so Christ will return as the Lord of heaven and earth. In addition, the trumpet blast will accompany the arrival of King Jesus (cf. Isa. 27:13; Zech. 9:14; 1 Cor. 15:52; 1 Thess. 4:16).

4. *Christ's return will involve judgment.*

When the Son of Man comes he will return with his angels with power and great glory "and all the tribes of the earth will mourn" (Matt. 24:30–31). When he returns, people will be unaware as in the day when Noah entered the ark and "the flood came and swept them all away" (Matt. 24:37–39). Not everyone will be safe because "one will be taken and one will be left" (Matt. 24:40–41). Those who are unfaithful servants will be punished and thrown into a place where "there will be weeping and gnashing of teeth" (Matt. 24:51; 25:30). Those who are unprepared will seek to enter into his kingdom but Jesus will say to them "I do not know you" (Matt. 25:11). Those who have experienced no inward transformation as demonstrated by their actions to others "will go away into eternal punishment" (Matt. 25:46).

Who Will Be Left Behind?[35]

It is often assumed that the language of being left behind in Matthew 24 and Luke 17 refers to something negative.

> Then two men will be in the field; one will be *taken* and one *left*. Two women will be grinding at the mill; one will be *taken* and one *left*. (Matt. 24:40–41)

> I tell you, in that night there will be two in one bed. One will be *taken* and the other *left*. There will be two women grinding together. One will be *taken* and the other *left*. (Luke 17:34–35)

Many interpret these texts to mean that those taken are raptured to be with the Lord but those left behind will remain on earth to receive God's judgment. A better interpretation, however, is that those who are left behind are

---

34. Exodus 19:9; 34:5; Leviticus 16:2; Numbers 11:25; 12:5; 2 Samuel 22:12; Psalm 18:11–12; 97:2; Isaiah 19:1; Nahum 1:3.

35. For a fuller treatment of this issue, see Benjamin L. Merkle, "Who Will Be Left Behind? Rethinking the Meaning of Matthew 24:40–41 and Luke 17:34–35," *WTJ* 72, no. 1 (2010): 169–79.

the ones who are blessed whereas those who are taken are the ones who are judged by God. This interpretation can be established by investigating the concept of being left behind (1) in the Old Testament, (2) in Jesus' teaching, and (3) in Matthew 24:40–41 and Luke 17:34–35.

Left Behind in the Old Testament

In order to understand the concepts of being *taken* and being *left* behind, it will be helpful to examine these concepts in the Old Testament. The prophets constantly warn Israel and Judah that their enemies will come and destroy their cities as a punishment from God. But God will not utterly destroy them. In his grace God will leave behind a remnant who will cry out for help and salvation. It is those who are *left* behind who are the blessed ones. This pattern is seen many times in the Old Testament prophetic books.

For example, Isaiah prophesies concerning the future of Jerusalem:

> In that day the branch of the LORD shall be beautiful and glorious, and the fruit of the land shall be the pride and honor of the survivors of Israel. And he who is *left* in Zion and remains in Jerusalem will be called holy, everyone who has been recorded for life in Jerusalem, when the Lord shall have washed away the filth of the daughters of Zion and cleansed the bloodstains of Jerusalem from its midst by a spirit of judgment and by a spirit of burning. (Isa. 4:2–4)

This text is a prophecy concerning the destruction of Jerusalem and the consequent exile. Notice that those who are *left* and remain are the holy remnant. In Isaiah 3 the prophet describes how the Lord is "taking away" from Jerusalem and Judah their leaders (vv. 1–3). Because of their unfaithfulness God will wash away the filth of the ungodly people and Zion will be cleansed. But those who are *left* behind are considered the righteous remnant. Later in Isaiah we again read about the coming judgment of God through the Babylonians. Isaiah prophesies to Hezekiah that in the coming days all that the royal house possessed would be carried to Babylon: "Nothing shall be *left*, says the LORD, And some of your own sons, who will come from you, whom you will father, shall be *taken* away, and they shall be eunuchs in the palace of the king of Babylon" (Isa. 39:6–7). The idea of judgment is consistently bound up with the concept of being *taken* away.

Isaiah is not the only prophet to employ such imagery. Jeremiah likewise prophesized concerning the impending disaster that will come upon Jerusalem: "Flee for safety, O people of Benjamin, from the midst of Jerusalem . . . for disaster looms out of the north, and great destruction" (Jer. 6:1). Because the people refused to repent and seek the Lord, they would soon experience the wrath of God. In verses 11–12 the Lord condemns Judah.

> Therefore I am full of the wrath of the LORD; I am weary of holding it in. "Pour it out upon the children in the street, and upon the gatherings of young men, also; both husband and wife shall be *taken*, the elderly and the very aged. Their houses shall be turned over to others, their fields and wives together, for I will stretch out my hand against the inhabitants of the land," declares the LORD.

The imagery here is similar to that found in the Isaiah texts. The Lord is going to punish his people for their sin by bringing judgment on them from other nations. These nations will destroy the city and kill many of its inhabitants. Although in this passage there is no mention of those who are *left* behind, it is clear that those who are *taken* away are the ones judged by God.

Although many other texts might be noted, it will suffice to mention two others from the Minor Prophets. Zephaniah describes God's judgment upon Jerusalem for their open rebellion. Therefore the Lord declares that he will "remove" from their midst those who are proud and arrogant (Zeph. 3:11). He continues, "But I will leave in your midst a people humble and lowly. They shall seek refuge in the name of the LORD, those who are *left* in Israel." (Zeph. 3:12–13). According to this text, the unjust will be *taken* but the righteous will be *left* behind. Finally, the prophet Zechariah speaks the words of the Lord to the rebellious people: "In the whole land, declares the LORD, two thirds shall be cut off and perish, and one third shall be *left* alive" (Zech. 13:8). Again, those who are *taken* (or "cut off") are those who perish whereas those who are *left* behind remain alive.[36]

Like the prophets of the Old Testament, Jesus announces the coming destruction of Jerusalem and he does so using the language of the prophets—language that reminds the hearer or reader of God's judgment upon Jerusalem. Jesus' original audience would have been well aware of such prophetic descriptions. They would have understood that to be *taken* was negative and to be *left* behind referred to something positive.

Left Behind in Jesus' Teaching

The imagery of being *taken* as a sign of God's judgment is found elsewhere in Jesus' teaching. In the parable of the weeds (Matt. 13:24–30, 36–43) Jesus compares the kingdom of heaven to a man who sows good seed in a field. But while he is sleeping, the enemy sows weeds among the wheat. Consequently,

---

36. Those who are *left* alive are not necessarily righteous but in his grace God grants them physical salvation that they may turn to him. Some of these who are *left* may be *taken* into captivity, but in their captivity many will repent and seek the Lord when they see the judgment of God. Consequently, God will bring them back into the land (see Ezek. 6:8–10; 14:21–23; 39:21–29; Dan. 9:4–19).

the wheat and the weeds grow up together only to be separated at the harvest. Jesus interprets this parable by stating that the field is the world and that the wheat represents children of the kingdom whereas the weeds are children of the evil one. The time of the harvest represents the end of the age and the reapers are the angels. He continues, "The Son of Man will send his angels, and they will gather out of his kingdom all causes of sin and law-breakers, and throw them into the fiery furnace" (Matt. 13:41–42). Although we must be cautious of pressing the details of a parable, it is worth noting that in this passage it is the unrighteous who are *taken* away and removed so that those *left* behind can enjoy the kingdom. "Then the righteous will shine like the sun in the kingdom of the Father" (Matt. 13:43).

Similar to the Old Testament prophetic passages depicting God's wrath upon Jerusalem, Matthew 24 is also colored with the theme of judgment. The conversation between Jesus and his disciples begins when Jesus predicts that the temple will be utterly destroyed (v. 2). In answering the disciples' questions about when the temple will be destroyed and the signs of the end of the age, Jesus warns the disciples about false christs, false prophets, and how lawlessness will increase and love will grow cold (vv. 3–14). The judgment language of Jesus is then intensified as he specifically uses judgment imagery from the Old Testament to describe the situation in Jerusalem when it will be decimated.

> Let those who are in Judea flee to the mountains. Let the one who is on the housetop not go down to take what is in his house, and let the one who is in the field not turn back to take his cloak. And alas for women who are pregnant and for those who are nursing infants in those days! (vv. 16–18; cf. Mark 13:14–18; Luke 17:31–32)

The picture here is of a powerful enemy coming to conquer the land and kill its inhabitants. There is no time to gather one's belongings. People will have no time to enter their homes to collect their possessions or turn back from the fields to collect their cloaks. Pregnant women and nursing mothers are to be pitied because of their limitations in attempting to run away from the enemy. This imagery is reminiscent of the destruction of Jerusalem in 586 BC. Just as the Babylonians ransacked the city and slaughtered many of its residents, so too there will be great tribulation when God again judges the city. In order to avoid being "taken away" by the enemy, it is necessary to flee to the hills and run for one's life.

The context of the left behind passages in both Matthew and Luke includes a comparison with Noah and the great flood (Matt. 24:37–39; Luke 17:26–37). As in the days before the flood when people were living life as usual, so it will be when the Son of Man returns. He will come at a time when people are unaware and, like those during the days of Noah, they will be swept away. It is clear from the Genesis account that the flood was brought upon the earth to judge its rebellious inhabitants. Similarly, the Son of Man will return when people least expect. Some will be *taken* away like those in the flood but others will be *left* behind and experience salvation similar to that of Noah and his family.

In the Lukan account there is the additional comparison of Lot and the city of Sodom (Luke 17:28–29). On the day that Lot departed from Sodom "fire and sulfur rained from heaven and destroyed them all" (Luke 17:29). Luke then adds the powerful warning, "Remember Lot's wife" (Luke 17:32). What needs to be emphasized at this point is that this event is a vivid reminder of God's judgment on the ungodly. Those who seek to turn back, like Lot's wife, will fall under condemnation.

Matthew also relates the return of Christ to that of a thief (Matt. 24:42–44). A thief comes to steal at night when the owner of the house is sleeping. Jesus, like the thief, will return at a time when many are not ready and will consequently be judged. Using another analogy, Jesus also warns his audience by informing them that those wicked servants who act unrighteously because their master is delayed will be condemned, cut into pieces, and thrown into a place where there will be weeping and gnashing of teeth (Matt. 24:48–51). A final illustration that emphasizes the judgment element of Jesus' teaching is found in the Lukan narrative. Luke ends the section on the coming judgment with the proverbial statement, "Where the corpse is, there the vultures will gather" (Luke 17:37; cf. Matt. 24:28).

The reason for examining the contexts of the Matthew 24 and Luke 17 passages is to demonstrate that the sayings of Jesus concerning one being *taken* away and one being *left* behind are couched in a prophecy that stresses God's judgment. Similar to the days of Noah, Lot, and the destruction of Jerusalem, so it will be when the Son of Man returns. Many, because they are unprepared, will be *taken* away to destruction, whereas those *left* behind will receive grace and salvation.

Left Behind in Matthew 24:40–41 and Luke 17:34–35

In both the Old and New Testaments the picture of God's judgment involves the ungodly being *taken* away while the righteous are *left* behind. This same pattern is found in Matthew 24:40–41 and Luke 17:34–35. In order to demonstrate that this is indeed the case we will now examine the particular language of these passages, primarily by way of answering several objections.

Most commentators interpret the notion of being *taken* away as something positive and being *left* behind as something negative. For example, Geldenhuys maintains that the text refers to "the faithful being *taken* up to meet him [Jesus] and the unbelievers being *left* to undergo the judgment."[37]

---

37. Norval Geldenhuys, *Commentary on the Gospel of Luke*, NICNT (Grand Rapids: Eerdmans, 1951), 442.

What reasons are offered for this position? France argues that the verb "taken" (*paralambanō*, Matt. 24:40–41; Luke 17:34–35) "implies to take someone to be with you, and therefore here points to the salvation rather than the destruction of the one 'taken'."[38] Although it is true that the verb is normally used in the positive sense (e.g., Jesus "taking along" his disciples), this usage is by no means exclusive. Matthew 27:27 states, "Then the soldiers of the governor took [*paralabontes*] Jesus into the governor's headquarters, and they gathered the whole battalion before him." In this usage of the verb, it is clear that the person being *taken* is not being taken along as a friend or companion. Rather, Jesus is being taken away to be beaten, mocked, and judged by the Roman leaders. Another negative use of the verb is found in John 19:16 where Pilate hands over Jesus to the Jews to be crucified: "So he delivered him over to them to be crucified. So they took [*parelabon*] Jesus." Again, it is evident that the verb is used negatively. Thus, the argument that the verb *paralambanō* inherently communicates a positive notion cannot be sustained.

A stronger argument favoring the interpretation that being left behind is something negative is found in the usage of the verb "left" (*aphiēmi*, Matt. 24:40–41; Luke 17:34–35). It is sometimes noted that this verb is consistently used to refer to something that is abandoned or forsaken (see Matt. 4:20, 22; 19:27, 29; 23:38; 26:56). Although this argument is certainly valid, there may be a reason why Matthew and Luke use the verb *aphiēmi*. In Matthew 24:2 Jesus prophesies, "Truly, I say to you, there will not be *left* (*aphiēmi*) here one stone upon another that will not be thrown down." In this text Jesus is indicating that God's judgment will come against Jerusalem and particularly the temple. Nothing, not even one stone, will escape the coming judgment. But later, regarding his second coming, he states that some people will escape the judgment of God. One will be *taken* but, because of God's mercy, one will be *left*. God's judgment will not visit the one who is *left* but rather it will leave (or abandon) him. Thus, because the visitation of God's judgment is the focus of the passage, it seems fitting to express the escaping of such judgment as being *left* behind (similar to the tenth plague in Egypt where the obedient Israelites were passed over—i.e., they were not *taken* by God's wrath but were *left* behind). They are not ultimately *left* behind or abandoned by God, but are those whom God's wrath passes over and leaves behind. Those who are left behind ultimately experience salvation and the fullness of God's loving presence.

Another argument in favor of the view that those *taken* receive salvation whereas those left behind are judged is based on a comparison with Matthew 24:31. In this text Jesus declares that the Son of Man "will send out his angels

---

38. R. T. France, *Matthew*, TNTC (Grand Rapids: Eerdmans, 1985), 348. France later changed his position, writing, "The verb [*paralambanō*] in itself does not determine the purpose of 'taking,' and it could as well be for judgment (as in Jer 6:11) as for refuge. In light of the preceding verses, when the Flood 'swept away' the unprepared, that is probably the more likely sense here" (*Matthew*, NICNT, 941).

with a loud trumpet call, and they will gather his elect from the four winds, from one end of heaven to the other." It is thought that the concepts of gathering and being *taken* can be equated, although it should be noted that the same verb is not used (Matt. 24:31 = *episunagō* ["gathered"]; Matt. 24:40–41 = *paralambanō* ["taken"]).[39] Just as Matthew 24:31 teaches that God will gather his elect, so also verses 40–41 teach that God's chosen will be *taken* and gathered to be with Christ. But there are at least two factors that cast doubt on such an interpretation. First, the verb "gather" (*episunagō*) used in Matthew 24:31 is a cognate verb to that found in the parable of the weeds where Jesus says, "Gather (*sullegō*) the weeds first and bind them in bundles to be burned, but gather (*sunagō*) the wheat into my barn" (Matt. 13:30). (Interestingly, the verb used to describe the gathering of the children of the devil [*sullegō*] is different from the verb used for the gathering of the children of the kingdom [*sunagō*].) What is important to notice here is that the gathering of the elect takes place after the unbelievers are first gathered (or taken). Thus, when the Son of Man comes, the unbelievers will be gathered first and then he will gather those who remain to enjoy the kingdom with their King. Perhaps this is also what takes place in 1 Thessalonians 4:17. The unbelievers are *taken* and those "who are alive, who are *left*, will be caught up together with them in the clouds to meet the Lord in the air."

Others claim that the imagery of Noah and Lot suggests that those who are left behind are the ones *left* for judgment.[40] Commenting on Luke's version of the passage, Darrell Bock claims, "The most natural reading, based on the previous examples of Noah and Lot, is that one is *taken* for salvation."[41] This reasoning is not difficult to follow. Noah and his family entered the ark whereas everyone else was *left* behind and died in the flood. Lot and his family departed from Sodom and those *left* behind experienced God's fierce wrath. Thus, in both cases it could be argued that those left behind were judged. The problem with Bock's analysis is that it fails to take into account the notion of being *taken*. For, although it might be argued that the people of Noah's day and the people of Sodom were "left behind," it is not convincing to argue that Noah and Lot were "taken away." With the example of Lot, he and his family fled the wrath of God. This imagery is similar to Jesus' teaching that those on the housetops should not enter their houses and those in the fields should not turn back for their cloaks. Instead, they must immediately flee or face the enemy who is coming to carry out the judgment of God. Thus, the analogy fails because the issue is not that some are *taken* for salvation

---

39. For example, Hagner writes, "Presumably those who are 'taken' are among the elect whom the angels of the Son of Man are to gather at his coming (v 31), while those who are *left* await the prospect of judgment" (Donald A. Hagner, *Matthew 14–28*, WBC 33B [Dallas: Word, 1995], 720).
40. For example, John Nolland comments, "In the Lukan (and Matthean setting) the imagery of Noah and Lot encourages us to understand that being taken off is the image of deliverance and being left behind is the image of abandonment to destruction" (*Luke 9:21–18:34*, WBC 35B [Dallas: Word, 1993], 862).
41. Bock, *Luke*, 1437.

while others are left behind for judgment. Rather, the issue is that the enemy is coming and whoever wishes to save his life must flee—and those who do not flee will be *taken* by the wrath of God.

A similar analysis could be made with the example of Noah. There is little doubt that Matthew views those who were killed by the flood as being "taken away":

> For as in those days before the flood they were eating and drinking, marrying and giving in marriage, until the day that Noah entered the ark, and they did not understand until the flood came and *took them all away*; so will the coming of the Son of Man be. (Matt. 24:38–39 NASB, emphasis added).

Verse 39 states that the flood came and "took away" (*ēren*) the people. Although this verb is different than the "taken" (*paralambanetai*) used in verses 40 and 41, the proximity of these phrases strongly suggests that they are parallel. Supporting this view, Gundry notes, "But Matthew's parallelistic insertion of [*ēren*] in v 39, where judgment is in view, makes the 'taking' judgmental in his gospel. Hence, being 'left' means being spared from instead of exposed to judgment."[42] Just as the people of Noah's day were *taken* away, so too, those who are not prepared will be *taken* away for judgment when the Son of Man returns.[43] Regarding the Lukan version of the account Summers comments, "*One will be taken* in judgment. Since judgment is the sole emphasis in the total passage this must be the meaning here. *The other* will be *left* to the happy union with the returning Son of Man."[44]

This analysis is confirmed by the Old Testament reference to Noah and the flood. Genesis 7:23 states, "He blotted out every living thing that was on the face of the ground, man and animals and creeping things and birds of the heavens. They were blotted out from the earth. Only Noah was left, and those who were with him in the ark." In this text the idea of being left behind is contrasted with being killed or judged by God. The people on earth were *taken* by God and thus blotted out. But Noah and his family were left behind and received God's

---

42. Robert H. Gundry, *Matthew: A Commentary on His Handbook for a Mixed Church under Persecution*, 2nd ed. (Grand Rapids: Eerdmans, 1994), 494. This conclusion is also affirmed by Craig L. Blomberg, *Matthew*, NAC 22 [Nashville: Broadman, 1992], 366); Wright, *Jesus and the Victory of God*, 366); Robert H. Mounce, *Matthew*, NIBC (Peabody, MA: Hendrickson, 1991), 229; John MacArthur, *Matthew 24–28* (Chicago: Moody, 1989), 75; France, *Matthew*, NICNT, 941; Ray Summers, *Commentary on Luke* (Waco, TX: Word, 1972), 205.

43. Turner agrees at this point: "During Noah's flood those *taken* were swept away by the water, and those who were *left* were protected by the ark" (*Matthew*, 590). Likewise Summers states, "Noah and Lot are representative of those who are *left*, that is, those who do not fall under God's judgment. The people of Noah's day, the people of Lot's day, and Lot's wife are representatives of those who are *taken*, who perish under God's judgment" (*Luke*, 205).

44. Summers, *Luke*, 205.

mercy. This is a common pattern in the Old Testament. The remnant that is left behind is often contrasted with those who are killed, destroyed, or blotted out.[45] Thus, in echoing the Genesis text, Jesus is teaching us that those who are *taken* are judged whereas those who are left behind receive salvation.

Summary

Although many assume that those *taken* in Matthew 24:40–41 and Luke 17:34–35 are taken to be with Jesus and those left behind are *left* for judgment, this interpretation should be rejected. Throughout the context of these passages Jesus uses judgment language reminiscent of the Babylonian destruction of Jerusalem and the subsequent exile of its inhabitants. Those who were *taken* away were the ones judged by God whereas those left behind were the remnant who received grace. Furthermore, the teaching of Jesus confirms this thesis. In the parable of the weeds the Son of Man sends his angels to gather out the children of the devil and throw them in the fiery furnace whereas the wheat is left behind (Matt. 13:36–43). The context of Matthew 24 and Luke 17 also suggests Jesus is intentionally using judgment and remnant language. Such language naturally brings up images of the former destruction of Jerusalem where the enemy came and "took away" (i.e., killed) those in the city. Finally, the parallel with Noah and the flood in the preceding verses strongly confirms our thesis. Just as in the days of Noah the people were *taken* away by the great flood, so those who are not prepared will be *taken* away when the Son of Man returns.

Conclusion

Jesus' longest and most sustained teaching regarding his return or second coming is found in the Olivet Discourse. Although there is not wide agreement regarding the details of this teaching, the best view affirms that some details in the text refer to the destruction of the temple, while others refer to Christ's second coming (or that they refer to both simultaneously). And, contrary to some popular interpretations of the "left behind" passages, being "left behind" should be viewed as positive, whereas being "taken" is negative (i.e., being taken in judgment). When a prophecy (or any text for that matter) is not read in light of its immediate context and the greater context of the Bible, it is prone to be misunderstood. Jesus, speaking similar to an Old Testament prophet, predicts the destruction of the temple and his subsequent return when he will gather the faithful remnant to himself and judge those who refuse to submit to his Lordship.

---

45. For example, see Genesis 42:38; Exodus 8:9, 11; Numbers 21:35; Deuteronomy 2:34; 3:3; Joshua 8:22; 11:22; Ruth 1:3, 5; 2 Kings 7:13; 10:11, 17; 17:18; 2 Chronicles 30:6; Isaiah 10:20; 24:6; Jeremiah 39:9–10; Ezekiel 17:21; Zechariah 11:9.

Chapter 9

Prophecies Regarding the Return of the Messiah (Part 2: The Epistles)

The Old Testament prophets predicted many events that would come to pass—most of which were fulfilled either in the timeframe of the Old Testament or with the coming of the Messiah.

Jesus himself predicted several future events: the coming of the Holy Spirit, the destruction of the temple, and his return. On the day of Pentecost, fifty days after Jesus was crucified, the Holy Spirit came upon Jesus' disciples in a unique way and in AD 70 the temple was destroyed. But, despite some claims to the contrary, Jesus has not yet returned. In this chapter we will consider the contribution to the topic of predictive prophecy found in the epistles, especially those of the apostle Paul. After we discuss what the New Testament writers mean when they speak of the "last days" or "end times," we will focus our attention on the second coming of Jesus—a prophecy that remains unfulfilled and one in which Paul often references. In particular, we will seek to answer the following questions: (1) What do the epistles teach about Jesus' return? (2) Will there be a secret rapture before Jesus' return? (3) Could Jesus return at any moment? (4) What follows Jesus' return?

The Meaning of the "Last Days"

Christians today often talk about the possibility of being in the "last days" or the "end times" when they consider the depravity of man displayed in the news or hear of near cataclysmic natural disasters. But the answer to whether we are now in the last days has already been given to us in the Bible. Unequivocally, the apostle Paul (as well as the other New Testament authors) was convinced that he was living in the last days. The Old Testament prophets used the expression "last days" to refer to time when God would fulfill his promises to Israel by sending them a Messiah from David's lineage who would usher in the fullness of the kingdom (Isa. 9:6–7; 11:1–9; Jer. 30:9; 33:14–16), defeating their enemies (Jer. 23:20; Joel 2:11, 30–31; Amos 5:18–20; Mic. 4:1) and bringing upon them God's blessings (Isa. 2:2–4; 65:20–25; Hos. 3:5; Joel 3:1). With the coming of Jesus—especially in his death, resurrection, ascension and the subsequent coming of the Holy Spirit—the last days had begun. The first coming of Jesus constitutes the initial fulfillment of God's promises to his people which will only be finally realized when he comes again.

Already in Acts, Luke records Peter claiming that the coming of the Holy Spirit is a sign that we are in the last days. On the day of Pentecost, Peter stood up and quoted Joel 2:28–32: "And in the last days [*eschatias hēmerais*] it shall be, God declares, that I will pour out my Spirit on all flesh...."(Acts 2:17).[1] This understanding of a shift in the progress in God's plan of redemption was also affirmed by Paul. In Romans 13:11–12, Paul urges the Christians at Rome to comprehend "the time" because "the hour has come for you to wake from sleep. For salvation is nearer to us now than when we first believed. The night is far gone; the day is at hand. So then let us cast off the works of darkness and put on the armor of light." Notice the time-related words that Paul uses: "time," "hour," "nearer," "night," "day," and "at hand." Paul saw himself living at the dawning of a new day which would bring in the fullness of our salvation. This day that is drawing near refers to the imminence of Jesus' return which serves as a motivating factor for Christians to live godly lives. Thus, Paul believed that he lived in the last days and that the next major event in God's plan of redemption was the return of Christ.

In the Pastoral Epistles Paul twice specifically indicates that we are living in the last days. In 1 Timothy 4:1 he writes, "Now the Spirit expressly says that in later times [*husterios kairois*] some will depart from the faith by devoting themselves to deceitful spirits and teachings of demons." In this verse Paul is not making a prediction about what people will do in the future but what they were doing in the context of Timothy's ministry in the church at Ephesus. Paul's purpose for writing to Timothy was to address the situation in the church and to give Timothy the encouragement he needed in the midst of a crisis. When did the Spirit expressly say that false teachers and false believers would infiltrate the church? This statement most likely refers either to Jesus' warning in the Olivet Discourse

---

1. The original text of Joel 2:28 reads, "And it shall come to pass *afterward* [*meta tauta*], that I will pour out my Spirit on all flesh" (emphasis added). Thus, in light of the new eschatological situation based on the events of Pentecost, Peter (or Luke) changed the text from "afterward" to "last days."

(Matt. 24:10–11)[2] or to Paul's own warning to the Ephesian elders (Acts 20:29–30).[3] Knight aptly summarizes,

> The NT community is conscious of being 'in the last days'. . . . The phrase with the verb in the future tense . . . might at first incline one to think that Paul is warning about something *yet* to come. But the NT community used futuristic sounding language to describe the present age. . . . Therefore, Paul is speaking about a present phenomenon using emphatic future language characteristic of prophecy. That he goes on to an argument addressed to a present situation (vv. 3–5) and that he urges Timothy to instruct the church members in this regard here and now (v. 6) substantiate this understanding.[4]

Paul makes a similar statement in 2 Timothy 3:1 where he again warns Timothy, "But understand this, that in the last days [*eschatais hēmerais*] there will come times of difficulty." Just as in the "latter times" some would fall away from the faith and devote themselves to demonic teaching, in the "last days" difficult times will come. In the context Paul specifies that the difficult times will be the result of people who dishonor Christ by their lifestyle. In verses 2–4, he lists nineteen different vices that will characterize people in these last times. Again, it is perhaps tempting to think that Paul is prophesying about some distant time in the future but the context will simply not allow such an interpretation. For, directly after listing the sinful behavior of people in the last time, Paul urges Timothy: "Avoid such people" (2 Tim. 3:5). Thus, it is evident that Paul includes this description about the end times precisely because it affected Timothy's current ministry. Towner comments, "Used in this way, the phrase was understood to imply that with Jesus' appearance, the End, marked by divine intervention, had been inaugurated and would culminate in God's final intervention (in the parousia of Christ) to complete salvation and execute judgment."[5] Without a doubt, Paul taught that we are now in the last days.[6] But

---

2. So George W. Knight, *The Pastoral Epistles*, NIGTC (Grand Rapids: Eerdmans, 1994), 188–89. Matthew 24:10–11: "And then many will fall away and betray one another and hate one another. And many false prophets will arise and lead many astray."

3. So William B. Mounce, *Pastoral Epistles*, WBC 46 (Nashville: Thomas Nelson, 2000), 234; Philip H. Towner, *The Letters to Timothy and Titus*, NICNT (Grand Rapids: Eerdmans, 2006), 288. Acts 20:29–30: "I know that after my departure fierce wolves will come in among you, not sparing the flock; and from among your own selves will arise men speaking twisted things, to draw away the disciples after them."

4. Knight, *Pastoral Epistles*, 188–89. See also Mounce, *Pastoral Epistles*, 234.

5. Towner, *Letter to Timothy and Titus*, 553.

6. Knight maintains that the phrase "last days" refers "to the time of the Messiah, that last period of days before the final messianic action takes place. . . . Paul is reminding Timothy that the Christian

this is not only the position of Paul, it is also the confirmed belief of the other New Testament writers.

While not a book of prophecy proper, the epistle to the Hebrews shares many affinities with the apocalyptic genre and is thoroughly eschatological in its orientation. For this reason, Hebrews provides us with a thoroughly eschatological perspective based on the finished work of Christ. The incarnation, death, resurrection, and ascension of Christ represent the culmination of biblical prophecy in that he has inaugurated the dawn of the age to come. The fact that Christ has come means that we are living in the last days, enjoying the benefits of the age to come, and we are "already" experiencing the reality of God's kingdom. Thus, in Hebrews 1:1–2 we read, "Long ago, at many times and in many ways, God spoke to our fathers by the prophets, but in these last days [*eschatou tōn hēmerōn*] he has spoken to us by his Son." The author later uses a different phrase when he links the death of Christ to the shift in redemptive history: "for then he would have had to suffer repeatedly since the foundation of the world. But as it is, he has appeared once for all at the end of the ages [*sunteleia tōn aiōnōn*] to put away sin by the sacrifice of himself" (Heb. 9:26). James likewise indicates that his readers were already living in the "last days." He writes, "Your gold and silver have corroded, and their corrosion will be evidence against you and will eat your flesh like fire. You have laid up treasure in the last days [*eschatais hēmerais*]" (James 5:3).

Peter indicates the same reality as Paul, the author of Hebrews, and James by linking the death of the Messiah to the transition in God's enfolding plan in history. He explains that the death of Jesus "was foreknown before the foundation of the world but was made manifest in the last times [*eschatou tōn chronōn*] for the sake of you" (1 Peter 1:20). In his second epistle, Peter ironically identifies his opponents as a fulfillment of prophecy by virtue of the fact that they mock the idea of the fulfillment of prophecy. He writes, "knowing this first of all, that scoffers will come in the last days [*eschatōn tōn hēmerōn*] with scoffing, following their own sinful desires" (2 Pet. 3:3). The indication that the last days have commenced is reminiscent of the expectations about false teachers voiced by Christ (Matt. 24:3–4, 11) and Paul (1 Tim. 4:1–5; 2 Tim. 3:1–9), and is very similar to Jude 18 ("They said to you, 'In the last time [*eschatou tou chronou*] there will be scoffers, following their own ungodly passions'"). Second Peter, like the rest of the New Testament, affirms the inauguration of the last days through the resurrection of Christ and the outpouring the Holy Spirit (Acts 2:17; Heb. 1:2).

Finally, John's first epistle discusses this theme when he refers to "antichrists." That is, the presence of "antichrists" currently in the world is evidence

---

community is living in the 'last days,' and, because that is true, he must come to grips with what characterizes those 'days'" (*Pastoral Epistles*, 428–39). Likewise Mounce states, "Context requires that the vices of vv 2–5 and hence the 'last days' of v 1 be in the present time for Timothy. . . . 'last days,' refers to the time period between Christ's first and second coming" (*Pastoral Epistles*, 543–44).

that we are currently living in the eschatological "last hour" (*eschatē hōra*). He says this is "how we know it is the last hour" (1 John 2:18) and that the spirit of the antichrist is now already in the world (1 John 4:3). The phrase "last hour" is more of a theological assertion than it is a chronological indicator.[7] When viewed as a technical term, it denotes a period of time, whether long or short, that will usher in the culmination of the ages resulting in the consummation of the final judgment and salvation promised by God. The concept of the last days is rooted in Old Testament expectations of a time when God would manifestly intervene to accomplish his purposes for the world and his people (cf. Isa. 2:2; Dan. 11:40–12:13).[8]

> *The New Testament writers firmly believed that the arrival, death, and resurrection of Jesus the Messiah inaugurated an eschatological shift indicating that the last days have now commenced and will be brought to the proper conclusion at the return of Christ.*

What Do the Epistles Teach about Jesus' Return?

Just as there is confusion regarding the second coming of Jesus in our day, so also there was confusion in Paul's day. There was confusion as to (1) the fate of those who had already died before Jesus returned (1 Thess. 4:13–18), (2) whether Jesus had already returned (2 Thess. 2:1–3), and (3) whether it was necessary to continue to work in light of the second coming (2 Thess. 3:6–13). The heart of Paul's teaching concerning the second coming is found in 1–2 Thessalonians, although there are references found throughout Paul's writings. Because Paul's letters were situational (i.e., the issues he addressed in his letters were based on the particular situation of the church[es]), he does not focus on the second coming equally in all of his letters. Paul addresses the second coming more in the Thessalonian correspondence than in his other letters because the church at Thessalonica was confused about this teaching and needed corrective instruction.

Paul employs three different words to refer to the return of Jesus: coming (*parousia*), appearance (*epiphaneia*), and revelation (*apokalypsis*). "Coming" denotes the arrival or presence of someone. Although the word technically does not mean "return," it has come to refer to the coming of Jesus that is distinct from his first coming (i.e., the incarnation). Thus, the word came to stand for the future coming of Jesus that will involve a personal, bodily appearance (see 1 Cor. 15:23; 1 Thess. 2:19; 3:13; 4:15; 5:23; 2 Thess. 2:1, 8).[9] The term "appearance" is found especially in the Pastoral Epistles and refers to the full revelation of Jesus as the one who will judge the living and the dead

---

7. Gary M. Burge, *Letters of John*, NIVAC (Grand Rapids: Zondervan, 1996), 126.

8. Judith M. Lieu, *I, II, & III John*, NTL (Louisville: Westminster John Knox, 2008), 98.

9. Cf. 1 Corinthians 16:17; 2 Corinthians 7:6–7; 10:10; Philippians 1:26; 2:12; James 5:8.

(2 Thess. 2:8; 1 Tim. 6:14; 2 Tim. 4:1, 8; Titus 2:13). Finally, the term "revelation" suggests that what is now hidden will one day be unveiled (1 Cor. 1:7; 2 Thess. 1:7). The Old Testament prophets often spoke of "the day of the Lord" (e.g., Isa. 13:6, 9; Joel 1:15; 2:1; Amos 5:18; Obad. 15; Zeph. 1:7, 14), when God would judge Israel's enemies and deliver his people. So also Paul speaks of "the day of the Lord" as the great and final act of God when Jesus returns as the King of kings to judge his enemies and deliver his people.[10]

Although the faith of the church was grounded on the first coming of Jesus (his life, ministry, death, resurrection, and ascension), the fullness of the kingdom had not yet arrived. Christians have to fight against the presence of sin in their lives, endure persecution, and bear up under the wearing down of their bodies. The kingdom will only be fully consummated when Jesus returns with his holy angels to defeat sin, Satan, and death once and for all. Thus, the church longs for Christ to return so that he might finish what he began. The prayers "Maranatha" (meaning "our Lord come," 1 Cor. 16:22) and "Come, Lord Jesus" (Rev. 22:20) demonstrate that the return of Christ was part of the hope of the early church. Paul specifically refers to the appearing of Jesus as "our blessed hope" (Titus 2:13). Believers await the return of Jesus because it represents the consummation of our salvation when we will be delivered from God's wrath (1 Thess. 1:10). In addition, believers long for that day because the body that is now corrupted by sin will be transformed to be like Christ's glorious body (Phil. 3:20–21). This hope of Christ's return and living in God's presence does not quash our desire for holiness but is a motivating factor to serve God faithfully and keep his commands (1 Thess. 3:13; 5:23; 1 Tim. 6:14).

But the second coming of Jesus will not be a joyful day for all people. Those who have rejected the gospel will face the wrath of God (1 Thess. 1:10). Paul declares that "when Jesus is revealed from heaven with his mighty angels" God will "repay with affliction" those who persecuted his people (2 Thess. 1:6–7). He adds that God will inflict "vengeance" on them and they will "suffer the punishment of eternal destruction" (2 Thess. 1:8–9). The references to the angels accompanying Christ, along with the sound of the trumpet, paint the picture of a mighty army coming to defeat its enemy (1 Cor. 15:52; 1 Thess. 4:16; 2 Thess. 1:7; 2:8; cf. Matt. 16:27; 24:30–31; 25:31; Jude 14).

In 1 Thessalonians 4:13–18 we learn that the Thessalonian Christians were confused over the fate of believers who died before the second coming. For some reason they assumed that those who died would suffer some disadvantage when Jesus returned. As a result, they were grieving over loved ones who died in the Lord. Therefore, Paul assures them that the dead in Christ will not miss out. In fact, he declares that they will be resurrected when Christ

---

10. See Romans 2:5, 16; 1 Corinthians 1:8; 3:13; 5:5; 2 Corinthians 1:14; 1 Thessalonians 5:2; 2 Thessalonians 1:10; 2:2; 2 Timothy 1:18; 4:8. Instead of "the day of the Lord," sometimes Paul will speak of "the day," "the day of the Lord Jesus Christ," or "that day."

returns and they will meet him in the air. The purpose of Paul's instruction was to comfort those who were grieving by offering them the hope of the resurrection at the time of Jesus' return (1 Thess. 4:13, 18).

In 1 Thessalonians 5:1–11, Paul transitions from mainly instruction to admonition. Similar to Jesus' statement that the Son of Man will come as a thief (Matt. 24:43), Paul affirms that Jesus' return "will come like a thief in the night" (1 Thess. 5:2). Therefore, since it is not possible to calculate the timing of his coming, we must always be ready. Indeed, Jesus will come when least expected, when the world is touting "peace and security," unaware of the coming judgment (v. 3). On the other hand, the "children of the light" must not walk in darkness but must be constantly prepared (vv. 4–5). Consequently, Paul exhorts the believers not to sleep but to keep awake and be sober (v. 6). In the midst of persecution, Paul reminds them that God will repay their oppressors and grant the Thessalonian believers final salvation whether they are alive at the time of Christ's return or whether they have died.

Paul probably wrote 2 Thessalonians shortly after his first letter.[11] Apparently, the Thessalonians were still confused about the second coming. In fact, some claimed they had received a letter written by Paul affirming that the apostle himself believed that Christ had already returned (spiritually) or that, in light of the intense persecution (2 Thess. 1:4–7), his coming would occur momentarily (2 Thess. 2:1–2).[12] Paul's response is that these claims are false because (1) he never said or wrote any such teaching (2 Thess. 2:1–2), and (2) the apostasy has not taken place nor has "the man of lawlessness" been revealed (2 Thess. 2:3–12). Because Paul is convinced that neither of these events has occurred, he insists that Jesus has not yet come back (and will not come back momentarily). The identity of the man of lawlessness is not abundantly clear. Apparently, he will lead many in the church astray (the great apostasy), will exalt himself above "every so-called god or object of worship," and will take "his seat in the temple of God" (v. 4). Paul continues by indicating that the appearing of the lawless one will not occur until the "restrainer" is removed. Because the Thessalonians were previously taught by Paul, they were privy to information that we do not possess (2 Thess. 2:5). Paul could therefore assume certain details that he does not make clear in this letter, presenting us with a number of interpretive challenges. We will seek to address the following questions: (1)

---

11. So Leon Morris, *The First and Second Epistles to the Thessalonians*, rev. ed., NICNT (Grand Rapids: Eerdmans, 1991), 14.

12. Wanamaker explains, "If the Thessalonians did in fact believe that the day of the Lord had come, they most likely understood it not as a literal twenty-four hour period but as the final period of the present order culminating in the coming of the Lord Jesus. They may have believed in something similar to the Jewish idea of the 'messianic woes,' a period of severe distress before the appearance of the messiah, who would usher in the period of salvation. From this perspective they may have considered their own suffering as part of the final phase before the coming of the Lord" (Charles A. Wanamaker, *The Epistles to the Thessalonians*, NIGTC [Grand Rapids: Eerdmans; Carlisle: Paternoster, 1990], 240).

Who is the "man of lawlessness"? (2) What is the apostasy or rebellion? (3) What is meant by the "temple of God"? (4) What/who is the "restrainer"?

The "man of lawlessness" is the focus of Paul's treatment regarding the second coming in 2 Thessalonians 2:1–12.[13] He is also called "the son of destruction" since "he will live under the threat of God's coming judgment."[14] Jesus warned his followers not to be deceived by the numerous false christs who would come and lead many astray (Matt. 24:5, 23–24). The exact identity of "the man of lawlessness" is not known. Some in the early church identified Roman emperors. A popular Protestant interpretation since the Reformation related this reference to the papacy. It seems likely that the man of lawlessness is the same person that the apostle John identifies as the "antichrist" (1 John 2:18, 22; 4:3; 2 John 7) and who is pictured as a beast in Revelation 13.[15] Beyond these possible parallels, it is impossible to provide more detail as to the identity of this person. Morris warns, "All attempts to equate the Man of Lawlessness with historical personages break down on the fact that Paul was writing of someone who would appear only at the end of the age."[16]

The second question that 2 Thessalonians 2:1–12 raises relates to the meaning of the "apostasy" (*apostasia*) or rebellion that precedes the coming of the man of lawlessness. There are three main interpretations: (1) a general rebellion against God,[17] (2) a rebellion of the Jewish people against God,[18] or (3) apostasy in the church.[19] Probably the best interpretation is that Paul is referring to apostasy in the church which signifies that a large number of church members will fall away. Perhaps this coincides with the increase of persecution that Jesus earlier prophesied (see Matt. 24:21–22).

There is also debate as to what is meant when Paul declares that the man of lawlessness "takes his seat in the temple of God." In particular, what does

---

13. Paul mentions "lawlessness" four times in this passage (vv. 3, 7, 8, 9). In v. 9, however, only the relative pronoun is used (the ESV supplies the antecedent).
14. Gary S. Shogren, *1 & 2 Thessalonians*, ZECNT (Grand Rapids: Zondervan, 2012), 280.
15. So F. F. Bruce, *1 & 2 Thessalonians*, WBC 45 (Waco, TX: Word, 1982), 179–81; Daniel L. Akin, *1, 2, 3 John*, NAC 38 (Nashville: B&H, 2001), 269–70. This parallel is strengthened by the similar teaching that the spirit of the antichrist "is now in the world already" (1 John 4:3) and that the "mystery of lawlessness is already at work" (2 Thess. 2:7).
16. Morris, *Thessalonians*, 221.
17. So ibid., 218–19; Bruce, *1 & 2 Thessalonians*, 167.
18. So Wanamaker, *Thessalonians*, 244; Keith A. Mathison, *From Age to Age: The Unfolding of Biblical Eschatology* (Phillipsburg: P&R, 2009), 525–27. Wanamaker states that the apocalyptic tradition in which Paul was working maintained that "the people of God, that is the Jews, would rebel against God and the Law at the time of the end" (244).
19. So G. K. Beale, *The Temple and the Church's Mission: A Biblical Theology of the Dwelling Place of God*, NSBT (Downers Grove, IL: InterVarsity, 2004), 274–75; Thomas R. Schreiner, *New Testament Theology: Magnifying God in Christ* (Grand Rapids: Baker, 2008), 820; Shogren, *1 & 2 Thessalonians*, 279. Beale argues for a large-scale falling away from the faith by professing Christians "because of the immediate context of false teaching (2:1–2, 9–12) and the clear illusion to Daniel's prediction of an end-time opponent who will bring about a large-scale compromise of faith among God's people" (203–4).

Paul mean by "temple" (*naos*)? There are three main views: (1) the literal view, (2) the literal-metaphorical view, and (3) the metaphorical view. The literal view interprets this text in a straightforward manner identifying the temple as the Jewish temple in Jerusalem.[20] For example, Morris writes that this text refers to "the inmost shrine. . . . He will actually take his seat in a formal way in a sanctuary."[21] Many have noted that in AD 40 Emperor Gaius (Caligula) attempted to erect a statue of himself in the temple as a sign of his deity.[22] It is possible, then, that Paul and his readers have this historical reference in mind. The literal-metaphorical view claims that Paul's reference to the temple is the actual temple in Jerusalem but that he is using this reference metaphorically.[23] In other words, this is a "graphic way of saying that he plans to usurp the authority of God."[24] The third interpretation claims that Paul is speaking metaphorically of the church as the temple of God.[25] That is, "the lawless one engenders apostasy in the church and identifies himself as God."[26] Elsewhere in Paul the temple of God/the Lord refers to the church (1 Cor. 3:16–17; 2 Cor. 6:16; Eph. 2:21). In addition, if the "apostasy" mentioned in v. 3 refers to many in the church being led astray, how likely is it that Christians would be tempted to apostatize if the man of lawlessness proclaimed his authority in a temple that Christians no longer consider important to their faith?[27]

Finally, we will briefly discuss the meaning of "the restrainer." Paul states that Jesus has not yet returned since the man of lawlessness has not been revealed, and that the man of lawlessness cannot yet be manifested because something (v. 6) or someone (v. 7) is now restraining him.[28] The difficulty we are presented with stems from Paul's previous relationship with the Thessalonians. He had visited them and taught them. He even proclaims in v. 5, "Do you not remember that when I was still with you I told you these things?" Morris admits,

---

20. So Morris, *Thessalonians*, 223; Wanamaker, *Thessalonians*, 246.
21. Morris, *Thessalonians*, 223.
22. See Josephus, *Antiquities* 18.261–309.
23. So Bruce, *1 & 2 Thessalonians*, 168–69; I. H. Marshall, *1 and 2 Thessalonians: Based on the Revised Standard Version* (Grand Rapids: Eerdmans, 1983), 190–92; Shogren, *1 & 2 Thessalonians*, 283–84; Anthony A. Hoekema, *The Bible and the Future* (Grand Rapids: Eerdmans, 1979), 160; Herman Ridderbos, *Paul: An Outline of His Theology*, trans. John R. de Witt (Grand Rapids: Eerdmans, 1975), 520–21; Geerhardus Vos, "Eschatology of the New Testament," in *Redemptive History and Biblical Interpretation: The Shorter Writings of Geerhardus Vos*, ed. Richard B. Gaffin (Phillipsburg, NJ: P&R, 1980), 37.
24. Bruce, *1 & 2 Thessalonians*, 169.
25. So Beale, *Temple*, 269–92; idem, *New Testament Biblical Theology*, 614–48; Schreiner, *New Testament Theology*, 820.
26. Schreiner, *New Testament Theology*, 820. Thielman maintains that this phrase is "an action that Paul means probably in a symbolic sense of this man's opposition to God" (Frank Thielman, *Theology of the New Testament: A Canonical and Synthetic Approach* [Grand Rapids: Zondervan, 2005], 255).
27. So Beale, *Temple*, 279. See also idem, *1–2 Thessalonians*, IVPNTC (Downers Grove, IL: InterVarsity, 2003), 220.
28. Part of the difficulty in interpreting what Paul means is that he uses both a neuter form ("what is restraining," *to katexon*) as well as a masculine form ("he who restrains," *ho katexōn*).

"The plain fact is that Paul and his readers knew what he was talking about, and we do not. . . . It is best that we frankly acknowledge our ignorance."[29] And yet, throughout the history of the church, interpreters have identified "the restrainer" as (1) the Roman Empire and/or the emperor (cf. Rom. 13:1–7),[30] (2) the system of law and order provided by the government,[31] (3) the Jewish state and/or James,[32] (4) Paul and/or his gospel mission,[33] (5) an angel,[34] (6) the Holy Spirit,[35] (7) God,[36] or (8) Satan or some other demonic being.[37] But simply because we cannot identify with certainty who the restrainer is in this passage, does not mean we cannot be certain regarding Paul's overarching meaning in the text. Jesus had not yet returned because the restrainer was still active and thus the man of lawlessness had not yet been revealed. Morris writes, "The important thing is that some power was in operation, and that the Man of Lawlessness could not possibly put in his appearance until this power was removed."[38] God

29. Morris, *Thessalonians*, 228. Bruce likewise acknowledges that "guesses at its meaning are all that the exegete can manage" (*1 & 2 Thessalonians*, 175).

30. Tertullian comments, "What is this but the Roman state, whose removal when it has been divided among ten kings will bring on Antichrist?" (*On the Resurrection of the Flesh*, 24). Chrysostom notes that while some interpret the restrainer as a reference to the Spirit, he prefers the view that it refers to the Roman Empire. He argues that "if he meant to say the Spirit, he would not have spoken obscurely, but plainly. . . . But because he said this of the Roman empire, he naturally . . . speaks covertly and darkly. . . . [Therefore] when the Roman empire is taken out of the way, then [the Antichrist] shall come" (*Homily 4 on 2 Thessalonians*).

31. So Morris, *Thessalonians*, 227; Bruce, *1 & 2 Thessalonians*, 177, 188.

32. Warfield notes, "The restraining power . . . appears to be the Jewish state. For the continued existence of the Jewish state was both graciously and naturally a protection to Christianity, and hence a restraint on the revelation of the persecuting power." More specifically, he thought that the masculine form of the "restrainer" referred to James of Jerusalem (B. B. Warfield, *Biblical and Theological Studies* [Philadelphia: P&R, 1968], 473).

33. So Oscar Cullmann, *Christ and Time: The Primitive Christian Conception of Time and History*, rev. ed., trans. Floyd V. Filson (Philadelphia: Westminster, 1964), 164–66. But why would Paul speak of himself and his mission in these terms? Why would he need to be removed? He saw himself potentially living until Christ returned (1 Thess. 4:13–18).

34. Marshall comments, "It is ultimately God who will allow the rebel to be manifested only when the present opportunity of preaching and hearing the gospel is brought to an end by the removal of the angelic figure who is now in charge" (*1 and 2 Thessalonians*, 199). See also Beale, *1–2 Thessalonians*, 213–21; Shogren, *1 & 2 Thessalonians*, 287–88.

35. *The Scofield Reference Bible* explains, "The restrainer is a person—'he,' and since a 'mystery' always implies a supernatural element . . . , this Person can be no other than the Holy Spirit in the church, to be 'taken out of the way'" (C. I. Scofield, ed. [New York: Oxford University Press, 1917], 1272). So also J. Dwight Pentecost, *Things to Come: A Study in Biblical Eschatology* (Grand Rapids: Zondervan, 1958), 262–63, 296; Mathison, *From Age to Age*, 528.

36. So Roger D. Aus, "God's Plan and God's Power: Isaiah 66 and the Restraining Factors of 2 Thess 2:6–7," *JBL* 96, no. 4 (1977): 537–53.

37. So James E. Frame, *A Critical and Exegetical Commentary on the Epistles of St. Paul to the Thessalonians*, ICC (New York: Charles Scribner's Sons, 1912), 259–62; Ernest Best, *A Commentary on the First and Second Epistles to the Thessalonians*, BNTC (London: Black, 1977), 295–301.

38. Morris, *Thessalonians*, 288.

is sovereign over all things and will accomplish his purpose in his timing. Then, and only then, will the man of lawlessness be revealed, later to be defeated by Christ himself.

Another problem that surfaced among some of the Christians in Thessalonica was the refusal to work for a living (2 Thess. 3:6–13). Perhaps they reasoned that since Christ had already returned (spiritually?) and the fullness of the kingdom was imminent, menial employment was unnecessary.[39] Paul, therefore, informs them to "keep away from any brother who is walking in idleness" and is not following the example of Paul and his co-workers who toiled and labored night and day in order that they not be a burden to anyone in the church (vv. 6–9). Therefore, Paul instructs them saying, "If anyone is not willing to work, let him not eat" (v. 10). So Paul exhorts such people who "walk in idleness" to "do their work quietly and to earn their own living" (vv. 11–12). The imminence of the second coming is never an excuse to ignore our daily responsibilities in life.

Will There Be a Secret Rapture Before Jesus' Return?

Some pastors, teachers, and scholars are convinced that 1 Thessalonians 4:16–17 teaches that before Jesus returns in judgment (i.e., the second coming), he will come secretly and "rapture" the church from earth to be with Christ in heaven.[40] A seven-year period will follow, the last half of which includes the great tribulation and the appearance of the antichrist. This pretribulational view of the rapture cannot be sustained from the New Testament based on the following reasons.[41] First, the term "rapture" is absent from this passage—it comes from the Latin translation of the Greek word *harpadzō* translated as "caught up."[42] While this catching up to meet the Lord in the air may

---

39. For example, Marshall theorizes that their "heightened sense of belief that the day of the Lord had come . . . was leading to this continuing attitude of indiscipline and laziness. . . . This unwillingness to work could have been encouraged by the belief that the parousia was at hand, so that there was no need to provide for the future" (*1 and 2 Thessalonians*, 218–19). Thielman likewise notes, "This unwillingness 'to settle down and earn the bread they eat' (3:12) has probably resulted from the false eschatological convictions that Paul attacks in chapter 2" (*Theology of the New Testament*, 253).

40. For example, see John F. Walvoord, *The Prophecy Knowledge Handbook* (Wheaton, IL: Victor, 1990), 481–84; Pentecost, *Things to Come*, 193. Pentecost states that the basis of the pretribulational rapture position is (1) "the literal method of interpretation of the Scriptures"; (2) "The church and Israel are two distinct groups with whom God has a divine plan"; (3) "The church is a mystery, unrevealed in the Old Testament"; and (4) "This mystery program with the Church must be completed before God can resume his program with Israel and bring it to completion" (193).

41. For a sustained refutation of a secret rapture, see George Eldon Ladd, *The Blessed Hope* (Grand Rapids: Eerdmans, 1965).

42. The Greek term is *harpazō* and means to "snatch" or "seize." The Latin translation is *rapere*, which is where we get the English term "rapture." The word is mostly used to physically grasp or seize someone or something but is also used of Philip when the Spirit of God carried him away to another location (Acts 8:39) and of Paul when he was "caught up" to the third heaven (2 Cor. 12:2, 4). Cf. Genesis 5:24 LXX where the same term is used to describe Enoch being taken up into heaven.

suggest a rapture of sorts, it is important to remember that Paul is addressing the topic of the resurrection of the saints not the removal of the church. Paul explains that believers who have died will be resurrected at the return of Christ and those who are alive at that time will receive their glorified bodies automatically (cf. 1 Cor. 15:51–53).

Second, in verse 15 the term *parousia* is presumably used for the rapture but earlier in 1 Thessalonians 3:13 the same term was used to describe the "coming of our Lord Jesus with all his saints," which clearly refers to the second coming. In addition, *parousia* is used in 2 Thessalonians 2:8 which declares that the Lord Jesus will defeat the man of lawlessness by "the breath of his mouth and bring [him] to nothing by the appearance of his coming." If both of these examples refer to the second coming, what evidence is there in the context to suggest that 1 Thessalonians 4:16–17 should be taken any differently?[43]

Third, other texts seem to indicate that the church will go through the period known as the great tribulation. For example, in Matthew 24:21–22 Jesus states that there will be a "great tribulation" and that it will be cut short "for the sake of the elect." A few verses later Jesus describes the coming of the Son of Man in similar terminology to that found in 1 Thessalonians 4:16–17 (both texts have reference to a "trumpet" and "clouds"). This *parousia* occurs after the great tribulation (see Matt. 24:29, "immediately after the tribulation of those days"). Furthermore, in 2 Thessalonians 2, Paul indicates that the appearance of the man of lawlessness and his persecution of God's people will occur *before* Jesus' return.[44] In addition, if the secret rapture precedes the second coming, Paul could have that fact as an argument for why the day of the Lord could not yet have taken place.[45]

Fourth, the text seems to indicate that much noise will be associated with the Lord's return. Paul writes that there will be a (1) a cry of command, (2) the voice of an archangel, and (3) the sound of the trumpet of God. These are not the

---

43. The same could be said of the terms "revelation" (*apokalypsis*) and "appearance." Some claim that "revelation" in 1 Corinthians 1:7 ("as you wait for the revealing [*apokalypsis*] of our Lord Jesus Christ") refers to the rapture but the same term is used in 2 Thessalonians 1:7 ("*This will take place* at the revelation [*apokalypsei*] of the Lord Jesus from heaven with His powerful angels," HCSB) to describe the second coming. Likewise it is sometimes claimed that "appearance" (*epiphaneia*) in 1 Timothy 6:13–14 ("I charge you in the presence of God . . . to keep the commandment unstained and free from reproach until the appearing [*epiphaneias*] of our Lord Jesus Christ") refers to the rapture but the same term is used in 2 Thessalonians 2:8 ("The Lord Jesus will kill [the man of lawlessness] with the breath of his mouth and bring [him] to nothing by the appearance [*epiphaneia*] of his coming") to describe the *parousia*. Ladd summarizes, "Certainly if one can make anything of language at all, no distinction can be made between the parousia, the apocalypse, and the epiphany of our Lord" (George Eldon Ladd, *The Last Things: An Eschatology for Laymen* [Grand Rapids: Eerdmans, 1978], 56).

44. Concerning 2 Thessalonians 2:5–10 Schreiner notes, "Since the believers' relief and the unbelievers' punishment occur at the same time, there is no reason to think the 'rapture' precedes the second coming by seven years" (*Paul*, 461).

45. So Schreiner, *Paul*, 461; Ladd, *Blessed Hope*, 75.

descriptions one would use to describe a covert operation. Morris maintains that "it is very hard to fit this passage into a secret rapture. . . . It is difficult to understand how he could more plainly describe something that is open and public."[46]

Fifth, it is often assumed that those saints who were either alive or resurrected will return to heaven with Jesus. Yet, the view that the saints return with Jesus to earth garners more New Testament evidence. First Thessalonians 4:17 says that believers will "meet" (*apantēsis*) the Lord in the air. Bruce explains the significance of this word: "When a dignitary paid an official visit (*parousia*) to a city in Hellenistic times, the action of the leading citizens in going out to meet him and escort him back on the final stage of his journey was called the [*apantēsis*]."[47] Perhaps this concept relates to Matthew 25:6 where the bridal party is summoned to "come out to meet" (*apantēsis*) the bridegroom so with their lamps they might escort him to the banquet hall. Or, what is found in Acts 28:15 when the Christians from Rome "came as far as the Forum of Appius and Three Taverns to meet (*apantēsis*)" Paul and his companions to escort them on their journey to Rome. Bruce summarizes, "These analogies . . . suggest the possibility that the Lord is pictured here as escorted on the remainder of his journey to earth by his people."[48] Thus, instead of a secret rapture to heaven, 1 Thessalonians 4:13–18 suggests a visible return of the Son of Man to earth with great fanfare and glory.[49] The church will suffer through the persecution (as it has done all throughout history) but God's elect will remain faithful and will meet the Lord in the air in order to usher him back to earth as the great King.[50]

Could Jesus Return at Any Moment?[51]

Today there is often a hesitancy to affirm the imminence of the Lord's second coming—the teaching that Jesus could come at any moment. Perhaps the main reason is because Scripture clearly states that certain events must take place before Jesus comes again. Therefore, there is a fear to claim that Jesus could come

---

46. Morris, *Thessalonians*, 145. Likewise, Schreiner notes, "It is clear from this text that Jesus will return with fanfare, rendering improbable the popular notion that 'a secret rapture' precedes the coming of Jesus by seven years" (*New Testament Theology*, 819).

47. Bruce, *1 & 2 Thessalonians*, 102; see also E. Peterson, "ἀπάντησις" in *TDNT*, 1:380–81; Wanamaker, *Thessalonians*, 175; Marshall, *1 and 2 Thessalonians*, 131.

48. Bruce, *1 & 2 Thessalonians*, 103; see also Hoekema, *Bible and the Future*, 168; contra Wanamaker, *Thessalonians*, 175–76.

49. So Ridderbos, *Paul*, 535–36.

50. Hoekema explains, "What these words (in 1 Thess. 4:16–17) do not teach is that after this meeting in the air the Lord will reverse his direction and go back to heaven, taking the raised and transformed members of the church with him" (*Bible and the Future*, 168).

51. For a fuller discussion of this topic, see Benjamin L. Merkle, "Could Jesus Return at Any Moment? Rethinking the Imminence of the Second Coming," *TrinJ* 26 (2005): 279–92.

at any moment since certain events have yet to take place.[52] Yet, should such fear keep the Church from affirming that the return of Jesus is imminent? How can we do justice to the verses which exhort Christians to be constantly ready for Jesus' return in light of the fact that we do not know when it will be? For example, Jesus states, "Therefore, stay awake, for you do not know on what day your Lord is coming. . . . Watch therefore, for you know neither the day nor the hour" (Matt. 24:42; 25:13). If certain events have yet to be fulfilled, might the Church become lackadaisical knowing that Jesus' return is not imminent?[53] In light of the New Testament admonitions for constant preparedness, we believe it is necessary to affirm the imminence of the second coming.

And yet, there are at least four events that are mentioned as taking place before the second coming: (1) the gospel preached to all the nations; (2) the conversion of "all Israel"; (3) the great tribulation and the great apostasy; and (4) the coming of the Antichrist. In this section, we will consider how we may maintain that these four events must take place before Jesus returns and, at the same time, insist that his return is imminent.

First, we will consider the preaching of the gospel to all the nations. Jesus states, "And this gospel of the kingdom will be proclaimed throughout the whole world as a testimony to all nations, and then the end will come" (Matt. 24:14). What does it mean for the gospel to be "preached" to the entire world? Does it include the conversion of those who hear the preaching of the Word? If so, how many must be converted? What if previous generations believed but the current generation rejects the gospel? And how are we to understand the meaning of "nations"? Does it refer to every individual "people group" as defined by modern missiologists? If so, whose definition of "people group" are we to use?[54] And how do we know our definition is correct?[55] The problem is that

---

52. For example, Berkhof maintains, "According to Scripture several important events must occur before the return of the Lord, and therefore it cannot be called imminent" (L. Berkhof, *Systematic Theology*, 4th rev. and enl. ed. [Grand Rapids: Eerdmans, 1941], 696).

53. Hoekema writes, "Does not a consideration of these signs carry with it the danger of pushing off the return of Christ into the far-distant future, so that we no longer need to be concerned about being always ready? Is not the lack of a lively expectation of the Parousia among many Christians today due to an excessive emphasis on the doctrine of the signs of the times?" (*Bible and the Future*, 130).

54. Ralph Winter maintains there are about 24,000 people groups in the world (Ralph D. Winter, "Unreached Peoples: What, Where, and Why?" in Patrick Sookhdeo, ed., *New Frontiers in Mission* [Grand Rapids: Baker, 1987], 153). The first edition of the *World Christian Encyclopedia* edited by David Barrett mentions 8,990 people groups (David B Barrett, ed., *World Christian Encyclopedia* [Nairobi: Oxford University Press, 1981], 110), but the second edition refers to 12,600 (David B. Barrett, George T. Kurian, Todd M. Johnson, ed., *World Christian Encyclopedia* [New York: Oxford University Press, 2001], 2:16). In specifying the number of unreached people groups, C. Peter Wagner writes, "For years many of us used the figure 16,750. . . . Some say the number may turn out to be 100,000 or more" ("On the Cutting Edge of Mission Strategy," in *Perspectives on the World Christian Movement*, 3rd ed., ed. Ralph D. Winter and Steven C. Hawthorne [Pasadena: William Carey Library, 1999], 535).

55. Hoekema comments, "Into how many languages and dialects must the Bible, or parts of the Bible, be translated before that goal will have been reached? How many members of a nation must be evan-

it is impossible for us to know exactly how this verse will be fulfilled in history. In Romans 15:19 Paul writes, "From Jerusalem and all the way around to Illyricum I have fulfilled the ministry of the gospel of Christ." Surely Paul did not reach each and every people group according to our modern definitions. Our point here is not that it is wrong to focus on preaching the gospel to unreached people groups, but simply that our understanding of people groups is probably different than what is mentioned in Matthew 24:14. Could Jesus come back now? Or must the gospel first be preached to more unreached people groups? Our contention is that based on this verse alone Jesus could come back at any time since we cannot know for certain how this verse will be fulfilled. We believe this ambiguity is intentional since we have also been told that no one knows when Jesus will return. If we knew precisely what was meant by this verse, we could then calculate when the end would come.

A second event that will precede the second coming is the conversion of "all Israel" (Rom. 11:26). Since many interpret this verse to mean future mass conversion of ethnic Jews, they maintain that the return of Christ cannot be imminent since this has not yet happened. Yet, such an interpretation of Romans 11:26 is open to debate. The three main interpretations of the phrase "all Israel will be saved" are as follows: (1) all the elect, both Jew and Gentile; (2) the ethnic nation of Israel as a whole; (3) all the elect of ethnic Israel throughout history. The main issue here is whether any of these views insist that Jesus could not return at any moment because Israel has not yet been saved.

The first view, that "all Israel" refers to both Jewish and Gentile Christians saved throughout history, does not require a mass conversion of the nation of Israel before Christ's return (though it does not necessarily deny it).[56] Therefore, it is possible to maintain the imminence of Christ's return while holding this view. The main problem with this interpretation, however, is that the previous ten occurrences of the term "Israel" in Romans 9–11 clearly refer to those who are a part of ethnic (not spiritual) Israel.

The second view is the modern majority view and holds that in the future God will remove the "partial hardening" that ethnic Israel is now experiencing

---

gelized before one can say that the gospel is a testimony to that nation? What, in fact, constitutes 'a nation'?" (*Bible and the Future*, 139).

56. For example, Calvin states, "I extend the word *Israel* to all the people of God, according to this meaning: when the Gentiles shall come in, the Jews also shall return from their defection to the obedience of faith, and thus shall be completed the salvation of the whole Israel of God, which must be gathered from both" (John Calvin, *Commentary on the Epistle to the Romans*, trans. John King [reprint, Grand Rapids: Baker, 1993], 19:437). Likewise Wright comments, "What Paul is saying is this. God's method of saving 'all Israel' is to harden ethnic Israel (cp. 9.14 ff.), i.e., not to judge her at once, so as to create a period of time during which the gentile mission could be undertaken, *during the course of which* it remains God's will that the present 'remnant' of believing Jews might be enlarged by the process of 'jealousy', and consequent faith. . . . This whole process is God's way of saving his whole people: that is the meaning of καὶ οὕτως πᾶς Ἰσραὴλ σωθήσεται [and so all Israel will be saved]" (N. T. Wright, *The Climax of the Covenant* [Minneapolis: Fortress, 1991], 250).

which will bring a majority of Jews to faith in Christ. That is, "all Israel" refers to the mass of Jewish people living on the earth at the end of time, who, after the full number of elect Gentiles are gathered in, will be a part of a large-scale mass conversion. This event will take place just previous to (or at the moment of) Christ's return. Support for this view comes from the Old Testament and rabbinical literature where the term "all Israel" does not necessarily include every single Israelite. Cranfield explains the salvation of "all Israel" in three distinct stages: "first the unbelief of the greater part of Israel . . . then completion of the coming in of the Gentiles, and finally the salvation of 'all Israel.'"[57] Those who hold to this view come from a range of eschatological positions. Dispensationalists maintain that Jesus' return (in the secret rapture) is imminent since the conversion of "all Israel" takes place after the rapture during the seven year tribulation period.[58] Virtually all premillennialists, postmillennialists, and some amillennialists hold to this view as well.[59] Regardless of whatever millennial view is held, we believe that the fulfillment of this prophecy must be held in such a way that still affirms the imminence of the second coming.

The final view maintains that Paul is not referring to a mass conversion of ethnic Israel (nor is he referring to elect Jews and Gentiles), but rather that there will always be a remnant of believing Jews until the end of time.[60] That is, God will always save a remnant of Jews throughout history. Israel will experience *only* a partial hardening until the end of time (i.e., until the fullness of the Gentiles come in). Based on this interpretation we are not so much awaiting a future event, but the completion of an ongoing reality. Thus, this view is easily compatible with the imminence of Jesus' return (see Appendix 1 for more discussion on this topic).

But what about the great tribulation and the great apostasy? Surely those are future events that have yet to occur? Again, the texts that teach these events

---

57. C. E. B. Cranfield, *Romans*, ICC (Edinburgh: T&T Clark, 1979), 2:572.

58. So Pentecost, *Things to Come*, 504–7; John F. Walvoord, *The Millennial Kingdom* (Grand Rapids: Zondervan, 1959), 167–93.

59. Postmillennialists include Charles Hodge, *Romans* (reprint; Edinburgh: Banner of Truth, 1972), 374; John Murray, *The Epistles to the Romans*, NICNT (Grand Rapids: Eerdmans, 1968), 2:96–98. Amillennialists include Geerhardus Vos, *Pauline Eschatology*, 87–91; Kim Riddlebarger, *A Case for Amillennialism: Understand the End Times* (Grand Rapids: Baker, 2003), 180–94; Sam Storms, *Kingdom Come: The Amillennial Alternative* (Ross-shire, Scotland: Mentor, 2013).

60. Bavinck states, "All Israel (*pas Israël*) in 11:26 is not, therefore, the people of Israel that at the end of time will be converted in mass. Nor is it the church of the Jews and the Gentiles together. But it is the pleroma that in the course of centuries will be brought in from Israel" (Herman Bavinck, *The Last Things*, trans. John Vriend [Grand Rapids: Baker, 1996], 106). Berkhof writes, "'All Israel' is to be understood as a designation not of the whole nation but of the whole number of the elect out of the ancient covenant people" (Berkhof, *Systematic Theology*, 699). Ridderbos states: "That he [Paul] would thereby have in mind a conversion of Israel at one point in the eschatological end time does not appear from Romans 11" (Ridderbos, *Paul*, 358). Hughes writes, "'All Israel' or 'the fulness of Israel,' then, is the full number of those Jews . . . who by God's grace hear and by faith receive the message of the Gospel" (Philip Edgcumbe Hughes, *Interpreting Prophecy* [Grand Rapids: Eerdmans, 1976], 96).

are variously interpreted. Matthew 24:21–22 reads, "For then there will be great tribulation, such as has not been from the beginning of the world until now, no, and never will be. And if those days had not been cut short, no human being would be saved. But for the sake of the elect those days will be cut short." As we discussed in the previous chapter, some interpret these verses as referring to the destruction of Jerusalem in AD 70 and thus as already fulfilled. But it is also possible to interpret these verses as describing a future period of unprecedented difficulties. Although there are indications that there will be a "great tribulation" that immediately precedes Jesus' second coming, the "sign of tribulation" does not occur only at the end of time.[61] Therefore, the tribulation that occurs immediately before the end is only an intensification of an already present tribulation. But again we ask the question, what exactly will this great tribulation look like? Where will it occur? How long will it last? Will everybody know about it? Since we cannot be certain as to the nature of the fulfillment of Jesus' prophecy, we must be open to the fact that such signs might be missed by us. Is it not possible that the great tribulation is already taking place in some places where Christians are being killed for their faith? It is commonly stated that there were more Christian martyrs in the twentieth century than the previous nineteen centuries combined. Therefore, when we see such persecution, we should be ready and on our guard. Such suffering is a sign of the approaching return of Jesus.

Another sign that will precede the second coming is the great apostasy. Jesus warns us, "And then many will fall away and betray one another and hate one another. And many false prophets will arise and lead many astray. And because lawlessness will be increased, the love of many will grow cold .... For false christs and false prophets will arise and perform great signs and wonders, so as to lead astray, if possible, even the elect" (Matt. 24:10–12, 24). Is Jesus referring to the time of the Temple's (and Jerusalem's) destruction or is he referring to the time just prior to Jesus' return? It is entirely possible that he is referring to both. Thus, apostasy will not simply take place at the end of time but, like the tribulation, was occurring at the time of the New Testament (1 Tim. 4:1; 3:1–5; Heb. 6:6; 10:29; 1 John 2:19), and will occur throughout time. Nevertheless, Paul does speak about an apostasy that will take place right before the *parousia*. He writes, "Now concerning the coming of our Lord Jesus Christ" that the day of the Lord "will not come, unless the rebellion comes first, and the man of lawlessness is revealed" (1 Thess. 2:1–3). Paul indicates that before Jesus returns, the great apostasy would occur and the "man of lawlessness" would be revealed. Therefore, before Jesus returns, apostasy will intensify and will be strengthened by the appearance of the "man of lawlessness" who will come with signs and wonders and will deceive those who do not believe the truth (2 Thess. 2:9–10).

---

61. In Matthew 24:9 Jesus states, "Then they will deliver you up to tribulation and put you to death, and you will be hated by all nations for my name's sake."

The final sign that we will discuss is the sign of the Antichrist. We have already quoted 2 Thessalonians 2:1–3 where Paul instructs his readers that the "man of lawlessness" will be revealed before the second coming. In the Olivet Discourse, Jesus warns of "false Christs and false prophets" who will deceive many (Matt. 24:24). Out of the entire New Testament, the infamous word "antichrist" (*antikristos*) is only found in John's epistles (1 John 2:18, 22; 4:3; 2 John 7). For example, he comments, "Who is the liar but he who denies that Jesus is the Christ? This is the antichrist, he who denies the Father and the Son" (1 John 2:22). Even in John's day there were those who could be considered "antichrists." Again we read, "For many deceivers have gone out into the world, those who do not confess the coming of Jesus Christ in the flesh. Such a one is the deceiver and the antichrist" (2 John 7). John distinguishes between antichrists (plural) and the antichrist (singular). The plural term, antichrists, then, is virtually synonymous with the "false prophets" and "false messiahs/christs" foretold in the Olivet Discourse (Matt. 24:11, 24; Mark 13:22).

But John also speaks of an antichrist who is yet to come: "Children, it is the last hour, and as you have heard that antichrist is coming, so now many antichrists have come. Therefore we know that it is the last hour" (1 John 2:18). It seems likely that the coming antichrist in John should most likely be associated with the "abomination of desolation" (Mark 13:14), the "man of lawlessness" (2 Thess. 2:3–4) and "the beast" (Rev. 13:1–9, 11–18; 11:7). By referring to the "spirit of the antichrist" (1 John 4:3), however, John must have conceived of it is a supernatural being. What is more, he is likely seen as a human representative and incarnation of the evil one spoken of by Jesus himself (Matt. 6:13; John 17:15; cf. John 8:44).). Thus, like the other signs, the sign of the antichrist is present throughout history but will come to a culmination at the end of time.

According to Paul, the "man of lawlessness" will arise out of the great apostasy and will seek to exalt himself over God by demanding worship of no one else but himself (2 Thess. 2:4). He will severely persecute those who refuse to worship him. He will use signs and wonders to deceive the people and will give them false teachings (vv. 9, 11). Thus, in imitating the miracles and teaching ability of Jesus, he will appear to be the new Messiah. But this false messiah will be defeated at Jesus' second coming (v. 8). Throughout history some believed Nero, the Pope, Stalin, Hitler, and others to be the eschatological antichrist. While they were indeed wrong, we must understand that every generation has those who are opposed to Christ and could rightly be called antichrists. Again, simply because "the man of lawlessness" is yet to be revealed, does not mean that we should avoid being alert and watchful for Christ's return. We simply do not know where or how *the* antichrist will emerge onto the scene of history. But we do know that when Christ appears this eschatological antichrist will be defeated and that God's people will reign victoriously.

Thus, although certain "signs" have been present throughout history, such signs will intensify before Christ returns again. That is, these signs will become clearer before they reach their climax. Apostasy will become more prevalent, persecution and suffering will increase, and the "man of lawlessness" will be revealed. Yet, it is going too far to say that the second coming must still be a long way off since we do not know precisely how these signs will intensify in actual history. We must always be prepared. Certain things must happen before Christ returns but exactly how and where these signs are fulfilled is difficult to say. Consequently, we must always be open to the possibility that Christ could return at any time.

Therefore, we believe it is possible to affirm the imminent return of Christ while still maintaining that certain events must take place before he returns. The difficulty is trying to understand how prophecy will be fulfilled in history. Even John the Baptist, who believed Jesus to be the Messiah, began to have doubts about Jesus since Jesus was not fulfilling certain prophecies as he understood them. While in prison John sent his disciples to Jesus in order to ask him, "Are You the Expected One, or shall we look for someone else?" (Matt. 11:3 NASB). If John the Baptist was unsure about the fulfillment of prophecies, what assurance do we have regarding predictions related to Christ's second coming? That unfulfilled prophecies will be fulfilled is certain, but precisely how they will be fulfilled is uncertain.[62]

Some may object by stating that this view only gives rise to doubt and uncertainty. But we maintain that the seemingly contradictory emphasis on the imminence and the delay of the second coming was designed to make it impossible for us to know the exact time of his return. Ladd explains, "This is where the Gospels leave us: anticipating an imminent event and yet unable to date its coming. Logically this may appear contradictory, but it is a tension with an ethical purpose—to make date-setting impossible and therefore to demand constant readiness."[63] Thus, according to the New Testament we do not know when Jesus will return. To say that he cannot return now is, in our opinion, presumptuous. We must be open and prepared for that possibility. Yes, we strive to understand the signs of the times, but we must also admit that the precise fulfillment of many verses of Scripture is ambiguous to us. This ambiguity, we believe, is God's design.

What Follows Jesus' Return?

We have established that the next major event in God's plan in redemptive history is the return of King Jesus. This return will be preceded by certain events

---

62. Hoekema writes, "If believers like John the Baptist could have problems of this sort with predictions about Christ's first coming, what guarantee do we have that believers will not have similar difficulties with predictions about Christ's second coming? We are confident that all predictions about Christ's return and the end of the world will be fulfilled, but we do not know exactly how they will be fulfilled" (*Bible and the Future*, 133).

63. George Eldon Ladd, *The Presence of the Future* (Grand Rapids: Eerdmans, 1974), 328.

but due to the purposeful vagueness of prophecies, some aspects of these events may be fulfilled in a manner we do not expect. As a result, we must always be ready for Christ's return. But what will take place after Christ's return? In this section we will seek to answer this question focusing mainly on Paul's writings but we will also look to the rest of the New Testament to gain insight.

There appears to be at least three events that will occur at or after the Lord's return: (1) the dead are raised; (2) believers will receive transformed bodies; (3) believers will be rewarded and unbelievers will be judged. First, as we discussed earlier in this chapter, the New Testament teaches that the dead will be raised when Christ returns. Paul states in 1 Thessalonians 4:16 that when the Lord descends from heaven, "the dead in Christ will rise first." Earlier Jesus declared, "Do not marvel at this, for an hour is coming when all who are in the tombs will hear his voice and come out, those who have done good to the resurrection of life, and those who have done evil to the resurrection of judgment" (John 5:28–29). Jesus announced that those in the tombs "will hear his voice" and be resurrected to new life. Perhaps this voice they will hear is what Paul alluded to when he said that Christ will descend from heaven "with a cry of command" (1 Thess. 4:16). In this case, when Christ returns, he utters a command and all the dead will hear his voice and be resurrected to life. In 1 Corinthians 15, Paul also connects the return of Christ to the resurrection of believers. He writes, "For as in Adam all die, so also in Christ shall all be made alive. But each in his own order: Christ the firstfruits, then at his coming those who belong to Christ" (vv. 22–23). Just as Christ was resurrected and has become the firstfruits (i.e., a guarantee of more to come), those who are "in Christ" or "who belong to Christ" will be made alive (= resurrected) at his *parousia*. Later Paul adds when the last trumpet sounds (cf. 1 Thess. 4:16), "the dead will be raised imperishable" (1 Cor. 15:52).

A second event that will follow the return of Christ is that believers will receive a transformed body. This was already mentioned in the last passage where Paul indicates that believers will be raised "imperishable." He explains that "this mortal body must put on immortality" (1 Cor. 15:53). Though there is continuity between the believer's current body and the one to come, there is also an amazing transformation that will occur so that the new body will be imperishable and immortal. In Philippians 3:20–21, Paul reminds his readers of their future. He states, "Our citizenship is in heaven, and from it we await a Savior, the Lord Jesus Christ, who will transform our lowly body to be like his glorious body, by the power that enables him even to subject all things to himself." Believers await their Savior who will come and transform their bodies to be like his own glorious body. Elsewhere the apostle John writes, "We know that when [Jesus] appears we shall be like him" (1 John 3:2).

The third event that will take place is that believers will be rewarded and unbelievers will be judged. Before this judging will occur, believers and unbelievers will be separated. In Matthew 24 and Luke 17, Jesus indicated that at the coming of the Son of Man a great division will occur in that one will be taken (in judgment), whereas one will be left behind to receive the blessings of God (Matt. 24:40–41; Luke 17:34–35).[64] Later, Jesus explains that "when the Son of Man comes in his glory, and all the angels with him, then he will sit on his glorious throne" (Matt. 25:31). As all the nations are gathered before him, Jesus will "separate people one from another as a shepherd separates the sheep from the goats" (Matt. 25:32). Just as a farmer separates the wheat from the tares, so also Jesus will separate the righteous from the unrighteous (see Matt. 13:40–43). The concept of unbelievers being judged is found in many other passages including 1 Peter 4:5–6, 17–18; 2 Peter 2:4–10; 3:7, and Jude 4, 15.

We are told that the righteous will be rewarded by the King. This does not mean that salvation is granted on the basis of works but that God will reward the faithfulness of his children. In his eschatological discourse Jesus states, "Blessed is that servant whom his master will find so doing when he comes. Truly, I say to you, he will set him over all his possessions" (Matt. 24:46–47). Matthew earlier records Jesus' teaching: "For the Son of Man is going to come with his angels in the glory of his Father, and then he will repay each person according to what he has done" (Matt. 16:27; cf. Rev. 22:12). Similarly, Paul indicates that God "will render to each one according to his works: to those who by patience in well-doing seek for glory and honor and immortality, he will give eternal life" (Rom. 2:6–7). And yet, the focus of the reward seems to be our union with God based on the righteousness we receive by being in Christ. Paul states, "There is laid up for me the crown of righteousness, which the Lord, the righteous judge, will award to me on that Day, and not only to me but also to all who have loved his appearing" (2 Tim. 4:8). Here Paul refers to a "crown of righteousness" which probably means "a crown, that is, righteousness."[65] The crown that Paul envisions is not a literal crown but the righteous status that he has through Christ. Similarly, Peter exclaims, "When the chief Shepherd appears, you will receive the unfading crown of glory" (1 Peter 5:4). Again, the joy of the believer's reward is not found in some external crown, but in the glory of being with their Lord forever. Jesus declared that those whom God has declared righteous and are blessed by his Father will inherit eternal life and the kingdom that God prepared for them from the foundation of the world (Matt. 25:34, 46).

On the other hand, we are clearly taught in Scripture that unbelievers will be judged by God. They will be sent to a place where there is "weeping and gnashing of teeth" (Matt. 24:51). Paul informs the Christians in Rome that the unrighteous will experience God's judgment "on the day of wrath when God's righteous judgment will be revealed" (Rom. 2:5). On those who are self-seeking and do not obey the truth "there will be wrath and fury" (Rom. 2:8). In 2 Thessalonians, Paul states that "when the Lord Jesus is revealed from heaven with his mighty angels in flaming fire," he will inflict

---

64. See the previous chapter for a discussion of what it means to be "left behind."
65. So Knight, *Pastoral Epistles*, 461.

"vengeance on those who do not know God and on those who do not obey the gospel of our Lord Jesus" (2:7–8). He continues by stating, "They will suffer the punishment of eternal destruction" (2:9). Thus, at the time of Jesus' return, there will be a separation of the righteous who will be blessed by God and the unrighteous who will receive the wrath of God.

Various millennial views, of course, interpret the details of the end in a different manner. Premillennialists insist that there are at least two separate resurrections: one for believers at the return of Jesus before the millennium and one for unbelievers after the millennium. The basis for this view is the two resurrections found in Revelation 20. On the other hand, amillennialists maintain that at the return of Christ believers and unbelievers will be resurrected and judged at the same time (see Appendix 2 for more discussion on the millennium).

Regardless of which view is held regarding the details of the events that will follow Christ's return, Paul clearly teaches that believers will be resurrected at the return of Christ and will be with him forever. On the other hand, unbelievers will be judged by Christ for the rejection of him as the Messiah.

Conclusion

In this chapter we have been focusing on the teaching of the New Testament epistles (especially Paul) regarding predictive prophecy. We saw a consistent message which affirmed the belief that, since the resurrection of Jesus, we have been living in the end times or last days. The life, death, resurrection, and ascension of Jesus are the climax of redemptive history and therefore the next major event in God's plan was the coming of Christ. Newman explains, "[The course of things] has . . . altered its direction, as regards his second coming, and runs, not towards the end, but along it, and on the brink of it; and is at all times equally near that great event, which, did it run towards, it would at once run into. Christ, then, is ever at our doors."[66] Most of Paul's New Testament teaching about the second coming was given to correct misunderstanding and offer encouragement. Although some of the details are difficult, if not impossible, to grasp (e.g., who is the "man of lawlessness" or "the restrainer"?), his general teaching is clear. Jesus will return visibly with his angels at an unexpected time which means that we should always be prepared for his return. There is no evidence of a secret rapture but that does not mean that Jesus could not return at any moment. As Jesus and Paul predicted, certain signs must be fulfilled before the *parousia* but precisely how and when those events are fulfilled is, by God's design, difficult to say. At his return Christ, believers (and unbelievers?) will be resurrected and judged. Believers will be granted eternal life in God's kingdom and unbelievers will suffer God's wrath.

---

66. J. H. Newman, "Waiting for Christ," in *The Preaching of John Henry Newman*, ed. W. D. White (Philadelphia: Fortress, 1969), 178.

Chapter 10

Prophecies Regarding the Return of the Messiah (Part 3: Revelation)

No other biblical book captures the imagination, invites speculation, and thoroughly mystifies readers more than the Revelation to John.

As a brand new believer in the early 1990s, I (Alan) remember attending a Bible study on the book of Revelation where the teacher attempted to show how current events were a direct fulfillment of prophecy. It was as if a treasure trove of prophetic fulfillment erupted and undeniable proofs abounded with every newscast. This began a love affair with the book of Revelation that carried me all the way to a PhD dissertation. While my fascination with this mysterious book has never changed, my interpretation of it has traversed the gamut of views to arrive at an understanding different from that of my earlier years. Initially, my fascination grew from a desire to know God's blueprint for the future as a means to understand the present. The problem is that I became increasingly disenchanted with the inconsistency of interpretations that changed with each newspaper report, geopolitical development, and technological advancement. I began to focus more on the biblical text instead of the text of popular prophecy books. As I continued to study, read, take classes, teach, and dig deeply into the text, my fascination developed into a desire to interpret the biblical text in a way that is historically informed, hermeneutically aware, contextually driven, and theologically focused.

John's Apocalypse is a *prophecy* originally addressed to believers living in Asia Minor at the end of the first century. As a book of prophecy, it certainly *forecasts future expectations* of the final consummation associated with the return of Christ, the Day of Judgment, and the renewal of creation. Yet, prophecy is also like a *barometer* gauging the *present situations* of its original audience coupled with exhortations to behave a certain way in response. The challenge is balancing the historical and future aspects

213

of the message in this highly symbolic book. On one hand, John provides us with a divinely revealed vision of future events. The visible and glorious return of Christ, the general resurrection, and the final judgment still loom on the future horizon of human experience. The Apocalypse is the climax of the biblical revelation as it weaves all the threads of prophecy together with the narrative of God's purposeful plan for his creation. If we dismiss the futuristic orientation of the Apocalypse, we strip the canon of Scripture of the proper conclusion anticipated throughout the biblical text. On the other hand, Revelation is also a message that would have been meaningful to its ancient audience in a way that communicated directly to them. To neglect the historically conditioned nature of the Apocalypse is to rip it from the pages of its historical context and release it to the subjective dispositions of the modern interpreter. Balancing the historical and future aspects of the Apocalypse requires that we give careful attention to the theology of the text in order to better understand this powerful and complex book of prophecy.

In this chapter, we will explore a number of issues and passages in the book of Revelation to help understand this magnificent book of prophecy. This chapter will specifically focus on issues related to interpreting the book of Revelation as both a literary work and as an apocalyptic and visionary prophecy.

Understanding Revelation's Prophetic Genre

How we classify the genre of the book of Revelation bears significantly upon our reading of the text because it establishes an appropriate grid of expectation for understanding its meaning. Genre is not only important for understanding literary works, but the same principle holds true for understanding other media of communication like music and movies. If a movie begins with a spaceship flying above an alien planet, then the audience knows it is a movie in the science fiction genre. As a science fiction film, the audience expects to see alien creatures, advanced technology, and the creation of unknown worlds. Things that are ordinarily outside the realm of reality and human experience are accepted and understood as essential components of the unfolding story. What makes sense in the genre of science fiction, however, would be horribly out of place in a film adaptation of *Pride and Prejudice*. If an alien suddenly and violently burst out of Mr. Darcy's chest, the audience would have no category or frame of reference to understand what is happening in the story. In the same way, if one attempts to read Revelation descriptively as a historical narrative of actual events or didactically as a series of doctrinal instructions, the meaning will be obscured by the highly symbolic imagery deriving from its visionary nature. Sensitivity to Revelation's genre may not solve all the challenges of interpreting this book, but it provides the reader with the necessary framework to understand this book of prophecy.

Revelation exhibits a variety of genre features related to epistles, Jewish apocalypses, and prophecy. Because the book begins with the word *apokalypsis* (1:1), some have maintained an immediate genre classification of apocalypse, especially given the use of apocalyptic language and imagery. A more accurate genre designation, however, occurs in Revelation 1:3 and 22:7, 10, 18–19 (cf. 11:16; 19:10) where John clearly identifies the book as a *prophētia* ("prophecy"). It also contains many epistolary features in the prologue (1:5–8) and epilogue (22:6–21), in addition to the "seven letters" to the churches (2:1–3:22), but Revelation's genre is a prophecy with apocalyptic aspects. Therefore, Revelation constitutes a mixed genre. The book falls into the overall genre of prophecy, but it clearly corresponds with apocalyptic writings in many respects so that it is best regarded as "prophetic-apocalyptic."[1] Revelation is a prophecy using an apocalyptic medium and preserved as a letter addressed to first-century churches.

Understanding Revelation's Symbolism[2]

The apocalyptic visions are indeed mysterious and enigmatic, but they are intended to reveal meaning rather than conceal it. The interpreter's task is to determine how the symbol functions in its context and what it signifies. To grasp the meaning of a symbol one must recognize both the mental or conceptual idea—*connotation*—and the image that it represents—*denotation*. Visionary accounts represent a genre of biblical literature employing the full arsenal of figurative language (similes, metaphors, and symbols) to communicate through the imagery engorged with meaning. Symbols represent a type of metaphor in which a visual or linguistic sign of a known object or concept is used to express an unknown object or concept.[3] A symbol may be defined as "a relatively stable and repeatable element of perceptual experience, standing for some larger meaning or set of meanings which cannot be given, or not fully given, in perceptual experience itself."[4]

The symbols in the prophetic-apocalyptic texts derive from a prophet's visual experience as a means to express *in* words what cannot be necessarily expressed *with* words. Edith M. Humphrey accurately remarks, "Visions are, after all, visions, and to 'decode' them into a proposition or method is to change not only the form but also the meaning."[5] This is quite unlike a historical narrative where the primary theological meaning corresponds rather straightforwardly

---

1. George E. Ladd, "Why Not Prophetic-Apocalyptic?" *JBL* 76 (1957): 192–200.
2. This section is a revision of Alan S. Bandy, "The Hermeneutics of Symbolism: How to Interpret the Symbols of John's Apocalypse," *SBJT* 14, no. 1 (2010): 46–58.
3. Ian Paul, "The Book of Revelation: Image, Symbol and Metaphor," in *Studies in the Book of Revelation*, ed. Steve Moyise (Edinburgh: T&T Clark, 2001), 135.
4. Philip Wheelwright, *Metaphor and Reality* (Bloomington: Indiana University Press, 1962), 92.
5. Edith M. Humphrey, *And I Turned to See the Voice: The Rhetoric of Vision in the New Testament* (Grand Rapids: Baker, 2007), 21.

to the events narrated. The symbolism in prophetic-apocalyptic texts expresses the theological meaning directly and only indirectly points to the underlying event.[6] The prophet communicates through symbolic imagery so as to recreate the details of the vision, but the symbols point beyond the text to spiritual, theological, and also physical realities. Symbols function in such a way as to ring a bell of recognition, but they may set off a variety of bells beyond what is intended in the text. While some symbols potentially trigger a plethora of connotations, we recommend the judicious use of interpretive steps to arrive at the most probable intended meaning for a given symbol.

1. *Recognize the symbolic imagery associated with the description of people or beings, colors, numbers, institutions, places, and events.*

The first step is to recognize the presence of symbolic imagery in the text. This should seem simple enough, but all too often interpreters fail to recognize that almost everything in the book of Revelation resonates with symbolic connotations. Think of the book of Revelation as an impressionistic painting of heavenly things instead of a video recording of the future world. John paints verbal pictures depicting the contents of his vision with symbolic hues and shades. His descriptions are intended to evoke a sense of wonder, awe, and worship as well as to communicate prophetic eschatological expectations. Therefore, almost all the descriptions of people or beings, colors, numbers, institutions, places, and events carry a metaphorical or symbolic connotation.

This is especially true if a person, number, color, or anything else recurs throughout the book. For example, the number seven not only occurs explicitly, but it also occurs implicitly with the sevenfold repetition of certain words or phrases. The symbolic weight of the number seven as representative of completion or perfection can hardly be overstated. Much of the imagery in the Apocalypse, however, is not symbolism, but more descriptive to heighten the coloring of the picture adding vividness and movement to its scenes so a careful reading of the text will avoid making everything a symbol for something else.

2. *Look for interpretations of those symbols within the context of the entire book.*

The second step is to look for an interpretation of symbols within the entire context of the vision narrative. Often symbols are interpreted either by John or some other heavenly being. These are fairly easy to identify because of

---

6. Vern S. Poythress, "Genre and Hermeneutics in Rev 20:1–6," *JETS* 36 (1993): 42. Poythress also suggests that proper interpretation of the symbols in Revelation must take account the distinction of at least four levels of communication: (1) the *linguistic* level, consisting of the textual record itself; (2) the *visionary* level, consisting of the visual experience that John had; (3) the *referential* level, consisting of the historical reference; and (4) a *symbolic* level, consisting of the interpretation of what the symbolic imagery actually connotes about its historical referent.

the formula: *symbol* + *"they are"/"these are"/"which are" (relative or demonstrative pronouns/verb of being) = identification.* The following chart briefly demonstrates some of the occurrences of the self-interpreted symbols in Revelation:[7]

SELF-INTERPRETING SYMBOLS			
Reference	Symbol	Interpretative Signal	Symbol Identified
Rev. 1:20	Seven stars	"they are"	The seven angels of the churches
Rev. 1:20	Seven lampstands	"they are"	The seven churches
Rev. 4:5	Seven lamps before God's throne	"which are"	The seven spirits of God
Rev. 5:6	The seven horns and seven eyes of the Lamb	"which are"	The seven spirits of God sent into all the earth
Rev. 5:8	Gold bowls full of incense	"which are"	The prayers of the saints
Rev. 7:14	The multitude in white robes	"these are"	The saints coming out of the tribulation
Rev. 11:4	The two witnesses	"these are"	The two olive trees and two lampstands standing before the Lord
Rev. 14:4	The 144,000	"these are"	Those who did not defile themselves and they followed the Lamb
Rev. 17:9	The seven heads of the beast	"they are"	They are seven hills (Rome) and also seven kings (emperors?)
Rev. 19:8	The pure white robes of fine linen	"for … is"	The righteous deeds of the saints

7. For examples of the interpretation of other symbols in the text, see Henry Barclay Swete, *Commentary on Revelation* (Grand Rapids: Kregel, 1977), cxxxiv; John F. Walvoord, *The Revelation of Jesus Christ* (Chicago: Moody, 1989), 29–30.

While these self-interpreted symbols do help to narrow the range of referents for a given symbol, they may also create a whole new set of questions. They sometimes interpret the symbol with another symbol. The seven lamps represent the seven spirits of God and the seven spirits of God figuratively represent the Holy Spirit. The two witnesses are identified as the two olive trees and two lampstands. The olive trees and lampstands are symbolic representations borrowed from Zechariah 4 to denote the Spirit-empowered people of God. Although potential confusion exists when a symbol is interpreted with a symbol, but even when this occurs the intended meaning of the symbol is still more limited within the immediate context. Once the referent is identified within the text, it typically becomes the fixed meaning for that particular symbol in the book of Revelation.

3. *Determine if the symbol is drawn from an allusion to another canonical text.*

A third step for adjudicating the meaning of a symbol relates to the use of the Old Testament. The text of John's vision is saturated with allusions to the Old Testament. John frequently employs the language and imagery of the Old Testament to provide his readers with a framework for understanding the significance of what he saw. This does not imply that John was performing an exegesis of the Old Testament, but rather he borrows the wording, images, themes, and eschatological expectations from the Old Testament. These allusions are pressed into the service of the textual imagery. The interpreter must first determine if the text alludes to an Old Testament subtext. After the allusion is verified, the interpreter seeks to understand the meaning of the Old Testament passage in its context. Next, one needs to compare carefully the similarities and differences between the Old Testament and its allusion in Revelation. Once the texts are compared one may see how John ascribes a particular meaning to the Old Testament language and imagery by using and reworking it into the account of his vision.

4. *Compare the symbol with other apocalyptic writings to determine if it is a common symbol with a relatively standard meaning.*

John primarily uses Old Testament imagery, but he may occasionally employ imagery belonging to the common stock of apocalyptic writings. Some images have no parallels in the text of the biblical canon. A comparative reading of other apocalyptic texts and Jewish writings may shed light on the book of Revelation. Keep in mind that any existing parallels between Revelation and these writings do not necessitate, demand, or imply any form of literary dependence on the part of the author of the book of Revelation.[8] What we would affirm is that

---

8. Richard Bauckham, *The Climax of Prophecy: Studies on the Book of Revelation* (London: T&T Clark, 1993), 88–91.

these writings shared similar eschatological and apocalyptic traditions.[9] Also we stress that these are not exact parallels in that they rarely share identical wording. When examining a potential apocalyptic parallel, it is very important to observe the distinctions and understand how the variations affect the meaning of the symbol when used in the book of Revelation. These parallels only provide a glimpse into the tradition history of the imagery by seeing how other writings employed similar imagery. An awareness of these traditional apocalyptic images helps to clarify some of the symbolic imagery in the book of Revelation.[10]

5. *Look for any possible connections between the symbol and the cultural-historical context.*

The fifth step looks beyond the text in an attempt to set the imagery within the cultural and historical context of first-century Asia Minor. Two thousand years of history separates modern readers of the book of Revelation from the social, cultural, and political environment of the original recipients. Some of the confusion regarding the imagery of the Apocalypse derives directly from the fact that John wrote to people that all shared a common understanding of their surrounding culture within the Roman Empire. Images of beasts, kings, and cities wielding enormous military and political power over its citizens may seem strange and foreign to the modern reader living in North America. To the readers of John's vision, however, they would have picked up on the cultural connotations associated with these images. This would be equivalent to someone writing in the twenty-first century in the United States referring to "smoke ascending from the twin towers." People would instantly recall the dreadful events of September 11, 2001 and the World Trade Center. Fast-forward two thousand years into the future, someone in China reads the reference to "twin towers" and he or she may completely miss the allusion to those events. A historically informed reading of the text will often clear up the haze of certain symbols.

6. *Consult scholarly treatments of the symbol in commentaries and other works.*

The sixth step is to see how scholars have interpreted the symbols. This step may occur in tandem with steps one through five. The complex nature of symbolism requires the mature insights of seasoned experts who have devoted serious time and study to the text of Revelation. Keep in mind, however, that serious time and study does not guarantee that their interpretation is plausible or probable. Avoid depending on any one commentator. Each scholar brings his

---

9. Ibid., 88.
10. Ibid., 38–83. Bauckham demonstrates the exegetical and hermeneutical value of this comparative analysis by examining four images in the book of Revelation. These are the blood up to the horses' bridles; the completion of the number of martyrs; the giving up of the dead; and the silence in heaven.

or her own set of presuppositions to the text that may produce radically differing interpretations. One commentator may say that a symbol has a range of meanings and another may posit a very particular referent with astounding confidence. While scholars may not have all the answers, they have certainly thought through the issues and their years of reading the text will, more often than not, provide a very helpful understanding for the meaning of Revelation's imagery.

7. *Remain humble in your conclusions.*

Interpreting the book of Revelation requires a massive amount of humility and an openness to return to the text again and again. Once you have completely studied the text avoid thinking that you have now unlocked all the mysteries of the Apocalypse. Continue to research. Repeat steps one through six on a regular basis. This process will prevent you from falling into the temptation of thinking that you alone have the right interpretation of this mysterious and complex book. No one except Jesus has the final answer on the meaning of the book of Revelation. While this may seem a bit discouraging, it is actually intended to encourage a lifetime of Bible study.

Understanding Revelation's Structure[11]

John's apocalyptic prophecy is not a patchwork of disorganized, unconnected, dreamlike vignettes lacking any rhyme or reason as to its literary structure. Neither is it a series of cryptic aphorisms, like the writings of Nostradamus, predicting future events in random verse. The book of Revelation is an intricately interwoven literary masterpiece intended to convey a unified message. When approaching Revelation, it is important to understand that the material is arranged and structured in a specific manner that best conveys the intended message. John intends to present the message of his vision so that the churches will understand and act accordingly. This unity is evident with the repeated command "to hear" (2:7, 11, 17, 29; 3:6, 13, 22; 13:9) followed by promised blessings (1:3; 14:13; 16:15; 19:9; 20:6; 22:7, 14) for obedience. The original recipients of the Apocalypse would have been able to detect its structure because of the presence of structural markers. These markers include, but are not limited to, the repetition of words, the use of certain conjunctions and prepositional phrases, spatial and temporal indicators, as well as shifts in tense or person.

Revelation has a prologue (1:1–8) and an epilogue (22:6–21). The Apocalypse is most likely divided into four visions marked by the phrase "in the Spirit" (1:9; 4:2; 17:3; 21:10). A pronounced series of sevens feature prominently in the vision (2:1–3:22; 6:1–8:1; 8:2–11:19; 15:1–16:21), but debate

---

11. This section is a revision of Alan S. Bandy, "The Layers of the Apocalypse: An Integrative Approach to Revelation's Macrostructure," *JSNT* 31, no. 4 (2009): 469–99.

exists over the extent of the entire structure based on seven series of seven. There are narrative interludes that appear to interrupt the series of sevens.[12] Another structural feature is the intended contrast between the harlot city of Babylon (Rev. 17–18) and the bride city of the New Jerusalem (ch. 21–22). If our purpose is to sketch out one structural arrangement, however, it does not preclude other proposed arrangements or some combination of others.[13]

Revelation contains four separate, but interrelated, visions introduced by the phrase "in the Spirit" (*en pneumati*). One of the main reasons to view this as a major sectional division is because every occurrence of this phrase locates the seer in a different place. The phrase indicates a shift of setting from Patmos (1:9); to the heavenly throne room (4:1–2); into a desert (17:3); and finally to a great high mountain (21:10). Another reason to suggest this fourfold structure is that the phrase "I will show you" (*deixō soi*) occurs three times (4:1; 17:1; 21:9) and each occurrence coincides with "in the Spirit" (4:2; 17:3; 21:10). Therefore, the four major visions of Revelation are as follows:

VISION	DESCRIPTION	LOCATION	TEXT
1	The inaugural vision of the glorified Christ who investigates his seven churches	On Patmos	1:10–3:22
2	The divine court proceedings and the trial of the nations with seven seals, trumpets, and bowls	In the Heavenly Throne Room	4:1–16:21
3	The judgment of Babylon, the return of Christ, and the final judgment of humanity	In a desert	17:1–21:8
4	The vindication and eternal reward of the saints comprised of the New Jerusalem and the renewal of creation	On a high mountain	21:9–22:4

---

12. These interruptions have been called intercalations (R. J. Loenertz, *The Apocalypse of Saint John*, trans. Hilary Carpenter [New York: Sheed & Ward, 1948], xiv–xix; Elisabeth Schüssler Fiorenza, "Composition and Structure of the Book of Revelation," *CBQ* 39 [1977]: 360–61); interlocking (Adela Yarbro Collins, *The Combat Myth in the Book of Revelation* [Eugene, OR: Wipf and Stock, 2001; repr., Missoula: Scholars Press, 1976], 16–19; Mark Seaborn Hall, "The Hook Interlocking Structure of Revelation: The Most Important Verses in the Book and How They May Unify Its Structure," *NovT* 44 [2002]: 278–96); and interweaving (Bauckham, *Climax of Prophecy*, 9).

13. As Beale helpfully observed, "there are structures within structures or perhaps different 'levels' of structure that are not mutually incompatible" (G. K. Beale, *The Book of Revelation*, NIGTC [Grand Rapids: Eerdmans, 1999], 108).

These four major vision segments contain numerous smaller visionary subsections. The minor visionary transitions are often signaled by verbs of seeing and hearing.[14] The phrase "and I saw"[15] is one of the primary transition markers used to demonstrate progression in the narrative without necessarily introducing a totally new vision episode. These smaller subsections not only represent essential components of the overall vision but also provide a sense of movement by constantly introducing new images and scenes. This kaleido-scopic style of narration creates the feeling of entering into John's vision as he recounts the dazzling sights unfolding before him. The flow of the vision is emphasized through these first person statements similar to something like "I saw this and then I saw that, and then I saw and heard such and such."

One of these subsections contains a clearly delineated pattern of a series of sevens or septets. Although John demonstrates a proclivity for explicitly arranging his material into groups of sevens, only three or four septets are explicitly numbered. There are seven churches (2:1–3:22), seven seals (6:1–8:1), seven trumpets (8:2–11:19), and seven bowls (15:1–16:21). Notice that the explicitly numbered sevens primarily comprise the bulk of material in the second vision (seals, trumpets, and bowls). The reasons for the series of sevens in the second vision will be explored below in more detail, but for now it is important to maintain John's preference for the number seven because it is a highly symbolic number indicating the notion of perfection or completion.

Other subsections of visionary material are interspersed throughout the seals, trumpets, and bowls. These subsections interrupt the flow of the sevens as narrative interludes. The first two interludes emerge between the breaking of the sixth and seventh seals (7:1–17) and also between the sounding of the sixth and seventh trumpets (10:1–11:14). These interludes appear in the narrative for theological reasons. They are bound to the preceding sections and provide answers for questions that the audience might be asking. The first interlude begins after the breaking of the sixth seal. The sixth seal (6:12–17) unleashes devastating catastrophes sending the earth's inhabitants fleeing into caves while praying to die rather than face God's wrath. In their fear of the wrath of God and the Lamb, they ask, "Who can stand?" The succeeding narrative interlude (7:1–17) answers this question by depicting the protective sealing and salvation of God's people who are standing before the throne.[16]

---

14. The aorist verb *ēkousa* ("I heard") occurs frequently (1:10; 4:1; 5:11, 13; 6:1, 3, 5, 6, 7; 7:4; 8:13; 9:13, 16; 10:4, 8; 12:10; 14:2, 13; 16:1, 5, 7; 18:4; 19:1, 6; 21:3; 22:8) but does not seem to function like a structural marker.

15. A total of thirty-two occurrences of just *kai eidon* ("and I saw") not separated by additional words (5:1, 2, 6, 11; 6:1, 2, 5, 8, 12; 7:2; 8:2, 13; 9:1; 10:1; 13:1, 11; 14:1, 6, 14; 15:1, 2; 16:13; 17:3, 6; 19:11, 17, 19; 20:1, 4, 11, 12; 21:1).

16. Beale offers the best treatment of the relationship between the question in 6:17 and chapter 7. He first lists the positive arguments favoring a direct relationship: (1) 6:17 and 7:9 are close to each other and both use *histēmi* ("stand"); (2) both refer to people standing before the throne and the Lamb; (3)

The second interlude occurs when the fifth and sixth trumpets unleash devastating plagues upon the earth's inhabitants (9:1–21). The people fail to respond appropriately by refusing to repent from their sins.[17] The following narrative interlude (10:1–11:14) not only provides justification for the plagues, but also depicts the people of God in their roles as prophetic witnesses before the nations. These interludes enable the audience to identify its role within the narrative, first as protected and then as prophetic witnesses.[18] The purpose of the interludes, then, is to challenge the churches to remain faithful and endure through opposition because God was protecting them as his witnesses in the world.

A third interlude exists, but it differs from the first two in that it occurs at the end of the seventh trumpet and precedes the introduction of the seven bowls. Revelation 12 represents a dramatic shift in the flow of John's vision narrative by depicting a number of "signs" unfolding in the heavens: "And a great sign [sēmeion] appeared in heaven" (12:1); "and another sign [sēmeion] appeared in heaven" (12:3); and again with "And I saw another great and marvelous sign [sēmeion] in heaven" (15:1). This third interlude, the "signs" narrative, occurs prior to the final outpouring of God's punitive bowl judgments. As with other interludes, the signs narrative focuses on the role of the people of God.[19] This third interlude (12:1–15:4) portrays the saints engaged in a holy war against Satan. It falls into three divisions, depicting a holy war in heaven (ch. 12), a holy war on earth (ch. 13), and the vindication of the saints followed by the judgment of the wicked (ch. 14). Amid the scenes of this cosmic warfare, John makes the purpose of this interlude explicit by interjecting calls for encouragement (12:10–12), patient endurance (13:9–10), and the ultimate vindication of the saints (14:6–13).

A final observation about the structure of Revelation is that vision three (17:1–21:8) and vision four (21:9–22:5) represent a contrast between the prostitute city—Babylon the Great—and the holy bride city—New Jerusalem.[20] In the third vision (17:1–21:8), John sees a prostitute named Babylon (17:15) who represents Rome (17:9). The rest of the vision depicts all the events associated with her judgment (18:1–24), the return of Christ (19:1–21), his

---

the picture of the Lamb "standing" before the throne in 5:6 is closely associated with his resurrection existence, suggesting that those "standing" before the throne in 7:9 are resurrected saints; and (4) the saints are said to stand "on the sea of glass" close to the later mention of the "Lamb" (15:2–3; Beale, *Book of Revelation*, 405).

17. This is reminiscent of Amos 4 where God sent a series of plagues upon Israel but they did not repent.
18. Cf. Robert Dalrymple, "These Are the Ones," *Bib* 86 (2005): 396–406; G. R. Beasley-Murray, *The Book of Revelation* (London: Oliphants, 1974), 31.
19. Osborne states, "Thus, this is the final of the three interludes and like them details the church's involvement in these end-time events" (Grant Osborne, *Revelation*, BECNT [Grand Rapids: Baker, 2002], 452).
20. Charles H. Giblin, "Structural and Thematic Correlations in the Theology of Revelation 16–22," *Bib* 55 (1974): 488–89.

millennial reign (20:1–10); and the resurrection of all who ever lived for the purpose of the final judgment (20:11–15). The fourth vision (21:9–22:5) portrays the beauty and brilliance of the bride city of the New Jerusalem coming down to earth from heaven. This vision falls into two divisions: the first description presents the Holy City as an eternal Holy of Holies (21:9–27) and the second presents it as a new Eden (22:1–5).[21] These two final visions serve to contrast the fate of those who worship the beast with the glory awaiting the followers of the Lamb.[22] When viewed together, these two visions form the climax of the prophecy in that it provides the culmination of everything anticipated in John's vision.

Understanding Revelation's Content

Revelation has proven to be one of the most difficult books of the Bible to interpret. For centuries, interpreters have wrestled with this text only to produce widely divergent explanations. The result is we now have an array of hermeneutical approaches and competing theological systems that all have their own take on the meaning of the text. How one reads Revelation largely depends on a particular understanding of history, symbolism, and eschatology. Interpreters differ in their view of the relationship between John's vision and history. Does the book of Revelation reflect past events, present events, purely future events, or some combination of all three? The way one answers these questions significantly influences how one interprets the book. Interpreters disagree on the meaning of John's symbols. Some interpreters seek literal referents to explain the symbols, but others look for more literary or metaphorical meanings. What is more, eschatology often becomes a major theological locus for how one may view the relationship between history, the future, and Revelation as a prophecy. The history of interpretation reveals various trends, theological perspectives, and hermeneutical commitments associated with how readers have answered these questions.

These so-called "approaches" to Revelation, when applied consistently, produce very distinctive interpretations. The *preterist approach* views the relationship of history and the Apocalypse from the vantage point that the events prophesied only related to the past. One school of preterism interprets the Revelation as a message of judgment against apostate Israel for rejecting Christ by prophesying the destruction of Jerusalem (AD 70).[23] Other preterist interpreters see the Roman Empire and the situation of Christians as the

---

21. Osborne, *Revelation*, 604.
22. Barbara R. Rossing, *The Choice Between Two Cities: Whore, Bride, and Empire in the Apocalypse*, HTS 48 (Harrisburg: Trinity, 1999), 14–15.
23. See Kenneth L. Gentry, "A Preterist View of Revelation," in *Four Views on the Book of Revelation*, ed. C. Marvin Pate (Grand Rapids: Zondervan, 1998), 37–92.

focus of John's vision prophesying the fall of Rome.[24] The *historicist approach* reads John's vision as a forecast of the course of history in Western Europe with particular emphasis on popes, kings, and wars. The *idealist, timeless,* or *symbolic approach* ignores the historical question altogether by positing that the book of Revelation is not about events in the space-time continuum, but rather it symbolically portrays the spiritual and timeless nature of the battle between good and evil.[25] The *futurist approach* contends that Revelation 4–22 refers to future events. Futurism may be further divided into *dispensational* futurism and *modified* or *moderate* futurism.[26]

We will examine several passages and topics in Revelation that are notoriously difficult to interpret. It seems some passages and topics, more than others, clearly bring out the differences of interpretation represented by the various approaches. While we will maintain an awareness of these approaches, our treatment of the text of Revelation will not follow any one of them exclusively. Rather, we will seek to present an interpretation that makes sense of the text with regard to Revelation's genre, structure, and theology. The following discussion will focus on examining (1) the relationship between the septets, (2) the meaning of the 144,000, (3) the identity of the two witnesses, and (4) the nature of the millennium.

The Seven Seals, Trumpets, and Bowls

The relationship between the seals, trumpets, and bowls has long plagued interpreters. These septets of judgments are characterized by an increased severity with each successive set. They appear to exhibit both repetition and progression in the unfolding sevenfold series of judgments. All the septets culminate with announcements or statements regarding the consummation of God's judgment and the establishment of his kingdom on earth. One purpose for the sevenfold series of judgments is to provoke the earth's inhabitants to repentance (6:15–16; 9:20–21; 16:9, 11). The judgments are an implementation of divine judgment on wickedness in incremental installments. Therefore, these septets represent some type of successive judgments to dem-

---

24. On the types of preterist interpretation see Beale, *Book of Revelation*, 44–45; and Osborne, *Revelation*, 19–20.
25. The famous dictum of William Milligan epitomizes this approach: "we are not to look in the Apocalypse for special events, but for an exhibition of the principles which govern the history both of the world and the Church" (*The Revelation of St. John*, 2nd ed. [London: Macmillan, 1887], 154–55). Advocates of this approach include Raymond Calkins, William Hendrickson, A. A. Hoekema, Phillip E. Hughes, and Sam Hamstra, Jr. For an idealist view of Revelation see Sam Hamstra Jr., "An Idealist View of Revelation," in *Four Views on the Book of Revelation*, ed. C. Marvin Pate (Grand Rapids: Zondervan, 1998), 95–131.
26. For the title of "modified futurism," see Beale, *Book of Revelation*, 47, but for the title of "moderate futurism," see George Eldon Ladd, *A Theology of the New Testament*, rev. ed. (Grand Rapids: Eerdmans, 1993), 673.

onstrate the guilt of humanity and at the same time to provoke repentance.[27] The problem is that opinions are vastly divided regarding how the septets are related to one another. There are three primary theories for viewing the relationship of the septets: (1) chronological succession; (2) recapitulation; and (3) telescopic progression.

Chronological Succession

Chronological or sequential succession, mostly associated with the futurist position, maintains the series of septets occur in a chronologically sequential order.[28] The sequence of the seals occurs prior to the introduction of the trumpets, which are completed before the pouring out of the bowls. Despite how interpreters arrange the breaks, divisions, and overlaps of the septets, they all share the common view that there is a clear progression from one set to the other.[29] The basic flow may be depicted as a series moving in a sequential order, but each septet is distinct from the other. The strength of this view is its simplicity as a straightforward reading of the text, but it does not always adequately account for any possible repetitious overlap between the septets.

Recapitulation

Recapitulation argues that the each septet represents an intensification and closer look at the same judgments.[30] The judgments signaled by the trumpets, then, correspond to and parallel what happens with the breaking of the seals and the bowls cover the same period as the seals and trumpets. One of the strengths of recapitulation is that it best explains the repetitive patterns and themes evident throughout the septets and the entire book. Interspersed throughout and at the conclusion of each septet are statements announcing judgment and salvation. For example, with the breaking of the sixth seal in 6:12–17 there are cosmic shakings and the people cry out due to the arrival of God's wrath. This language is extremely similar to the announcement of judgment and salvation followed by cosmic shakings at the sounding of the seventh trumpet in 11:14–19 and at the outpouring of the

---

27. For an example of the remedial nature of the judgments as a means of provoking repentance, see Amos 4:6–11. Although this passage specifically pertains to Israel, the principle remains true for the judgment of the nations in the three series of septets.
28. R. H. Charles, *The Revelation of St. John*, ICC (New York: Scribner's, 1920), 1:xxv; Dwight Pentecost, *Things to Come* (Grand Rapids: Zondervan, 1958), 187–88.
29. See the helpful analysis of Beale, *Book of Revelation*, 116–19.
30. Charles H. Giblin, "Recapitulation and the Literary Coherence of John's Apocalypse," *CBQ* 56 (Jan 1994): 81–95; David E. Aune, *Revelation 1–5*, WBC, 52A (Nashville: Thomas Nelson, 1997), xci–xciii; Beale, *Book of Revelation*, 121–26.

seventh bowl in 16:17–18. The idea, then, is that the septets are parallel to each other, but each successive series offers a more intensive perspective. The apparent overlap between the bowls, trumpets, and seals would suggest that they recapitulate each other. Recapitulation offers a cogent way to view the septets as a unified whole covering the same period of time. The problem is that this view does not adequately account for the dissimilarities between each series of septets. While a number of similarities exist, a comparative analysis reveals even greater dissimilarities between the seals, trumpets, and bowls. The dissimilarities among the septets cannot all be explained as just a different perspective.

Telescopic Theory

The telescopic or dovetailing theory maintains that the seventh seal contains the seven trumpets and the seventh trumpet comprises the seven bowls.[31] It is a close relative to chronological succession and also has a strong futurist tendency. Richard Bauckham argues:

> The judgment of the seventh seal-opening, the climax of the first series, described by this formula in 8:5, encompasses the whole course of the judgments of the seven trumpets, and similarly the judgment of the seventh trumpet, described by this formula in 11:19b, encompasses the whole series of bowl judgments, climaxing in the final, fullest elaboration of the formula in 16:18–21. Thus the formula indicates that it is the same final judgment which is reached in the seventh of each of the three series.[32]

A progressive telescopic theory appears to offer the most satisfying explanation for the literary relationship between the septets.[33]

Although some repetitive overlap seems to occur, the septets are best viewed as a sequence of related but chronologically successive judgments. Christ initiates the first sequence when he cracks open the first seal (6:1). The breaking of the seventh seal introduces the seven trumpets (8:1). Subsequent-

---

31. Robert L. Thomas, "The Structure of the Apocalypse: Recapitulation or Progression?" *MSJ* 4, no. 1 (Spring 1993): 45–66; Isbon T. Beckwith, *The Apocalypse of John* (Grand Rapids: Baker, 1919), 606–11; John F. Walvoord, *Revelation*, rev. ed. (Philip E. Rawley & Mark Hitchcock, eds.; Chicago: Moody, 2011), 149; George Eldon Ladd, *A Commentary on the Revelation of John* (Grand Rapids: Eerdmans, 1972), 122; J. Ramsey Michaels, *Revelation*, IVPNTC 20 (Downers Grove, IL: InterVarsity, 1997), 27–29.

32. Bauckham, *Climax of Prophecy*, 8.

33. On this view as opposed to recapitulation, see the helpful article and charts by Thomas, "The Structure of the Apocalypse: Recapitulation or Progression?" 45–66; D. R. Davis, "The Relationship between the Seals, Trumpets, and Bowls in the Book of Revelation," *JETS* 16 (1973): 158–59.

ly, the blowing of the seventh trumpet introduces the seven bowls containing God's wrath in full strength (15:7). The number seven symbolically conveys the idea that each series of judgments represents a complete set, which culminates in the declaration that "it is done" when the last angel pours out the contents of the seventh bowl (16:17).

We suggest the seals correspond to the inauguration of the *eschaton* initiated shortly after Christ's ascension to his throne as he is handed the scroll with seven seals (5:1). Since the contents of the scroll cannot be read until all the seals are broken, it is best to understand the seals as some sort of preliminary judgments. They are preliminary in that they occur prior to the time of the seven trumpets. Before the plagues of the trumpets are allowed to harm the earth, God's servants must first be protected with his seal (7:1–3). The increased intensity of those judgments along with the need to protect God's servants indicates that trumpets introduce a new and more serious phase of God's judgment. This suggests that the seals present an earlier stage in the sequence of judgment. The trials introduced by the seals may correspond to the "birth pains" (Mark 13:8) occurring prior to coming days of tribulation that

> *The seals introduce the coming wrath of God and the Lamb while the trumpets announce this impending wrath, but the bowls actually constitute the execution of his wrathful judgment.*

will precede the return of Christ (Mark 13:19). The seals represent the continuous nature of the "already/not yet" tensions characteristic of the intervening time between "this age" and the consummation of the "age to come."

The trumpets may correspond to the period known as the Great Tribulation. Hence, prior to the first trumpet an interlude occurs pertaining to the "sealing" of God's people to protect them from the judgments inflicted on the earth's inhabitants during this period (cf. 7:1–3). The seventh trumpet, comprising the third woe, signals the final consummation of God's judgment (11:15–19) by introducing the angels with the seven bowls filled with his wrath (15:5–8). The declarations accompanying the blowing of the seventh trumpet in 11:15–19 suggests it announces the completion of God's wrath. Because the seventh trumpet contains the seven bowls, they represent the culmination of God's judgment. The bowls, then, represent the outpouring of God's wrath upon the nations in full judgment.

144,000 and the Unnumbered Multitude

When it comes to difficult questions in the book of Revelation, few others rival the identity and interpretation of the 144,000 (7:4–8). What makes this passage so contentious is ultimately a matter of hermeneutics and how interpreters answer several questions about the text. Does this number refer to a literal group of ethnic Israelites from the twelve tribes or is it a symbolic reference to the church as spiritual Israel? Why is this enumerated group, whoever they are, singled out from the larger whole? Why are they sealed and what does that mean? What is the numerological significance of 144,000? What is the relationship between the 144,000 and the unnumbered multitude in the second half of this passage? Are Revelation 7:4–8 and 7:9–17 depicting two entirely separate groups or do they portray the same group from two different perspectives? How one answers these questions not only determines the interpretation, but also has significant theological and eschatological implications.

Propositions for the identity of the 144,000 primarily diverge at the point of literal and figurative interpretation.[34] On one hand, literal interpretations read the text in a straightforward manner as referring to 12,000 Jewish people from each of the twelve tribes of Israel.[35] While they allow for a symbolic conation for the specific enumeration, the language of the "tribes of Israel" would denote Jews or Jewish Christians and exclude the Gentile church. They would say "there is a clear distinction in the mind of the author between these 144,000 . . . and the great multitude who come from every nation, tribe, people and language who stand before the throne in vv. 9–11."[36] On the other hand, figurative interpretations argue that the 144,000 symbolically denote the Christian church as spiritual Israel or Christian martyrs or some other collective reference to Jew and Gentile Christians.[37] They contend the entire interlude offers two perspectives regarding the same group of people (i.e., the 144,000 and the multitude). The 144,000 represent the church sealed with God's protective seal from the ensuing judgments (e.g., the Tribulation), whereas the international multitude standing before the throne represents the entire congregation of the redeemed coming out of the Tribulation (7:14). John essentially provides a before and after snapshot of the church as an assurance that God capably protects and saves his people during those days of distress.

Although the 144,000 are composed of 12,000 from each of the twelve tribes of Israel, this group most likely represents the church rather than ethnic Israelites. The fact that the most natural way of reading the text would suggest

---

34. This passage constitutes a notoriously knotty maze of interpretative possibilities. For a summary of interpretive views on the 144,000, see Beale, *Book of Revelation*, 416–23; David E. Aune, *Revelation 6–16*, WBC, 52B (Nashville: Thomas Nelson, 1998), 440–45; Stephen S. Smalley, *The Revelation to John: A Commentary on the Greek Text of the Apocalypse* (Downers Grove, IL: InterVarsity, 2005), 184–88.

35. For those who contend that the 144,000 strictly refers to ethnic Israelites or a group of Jewish Christians, see Robert L. Thomas, *Revelation 1–7: An Exegetical Commentary* (Chicago: Moody, 1995), 475–83; Walvoord, *Revelation*, 140–41; A. Geyser, "The Twelve Tribes in Revelation: Judean and Judeo-Christian Apocalypticism," *NTS* 28 (1982): 388–99; Paige Patterson, *Revelation*, NAC 39 (Nashville: B&H, 2012), 193–99.

36. Patterson, *Revelation*, 194.

37. For the view that the 144,000 refers (1) to Christian martyrs, see Caird and Bauckham; (2) to all Christians of every age, see Beale (*Book of Revelation*, 416–23), Aune (*Revelation 6–16*, 440–45), Osborne (*Revelation*, 303), and Mounce (*Revelation*, 158); and to (3) only Christians in the very last days, see Beasley-Murray (*Revelation*, 139–40).

an exclusively Jewish group is one of the strongest arguments in favor of a literal view.[38] John Walvoord once remarked, "It would be ridiculous to carry the typology of Israel representing the church to the extent of dividing them into twelve tribes as was done here."[39] Walvoord's argument makes sense if one maintains a strong distinction between the terms "Israel" and "Church." If Israel always refers to ethnic or national Israel, then it becomes confusing if Israel suddenly refers to the church in a spiritual or typological way. However, there are several reasons why a figurative interpretation is more preferable.

First, in Revelation 7:3, the 144,000 are explicitly called "servants of God," which everywhere else in the Apocalypse refers to Christians (both Jewish and Gentile). The term "servants" (*doulos*) occurs a total of fourteen times (1:1 [x2]; 2:20; 6:15; 7:3; 10:7; 11:18; 13:16; 15:3; 19:2, 5, 18; 22:3, 6). The majority of uses specifically refer to prophets, but the term does also denote Christians in general.[40] John draws a distinction between Jews and Christians, but only in terms of those who believe in Christ versus unbelieving Jews in opposition (2:9; 3:9). One popular argument for a separation between Church and Israel stems from an absence of the word "church" in Revelation 4:1–19:10. The problem is that the word "church" is also not mentioned in Mark, Luke, John, 2 Timothy, Titus, 1 and 2 Peter, 1 John, 2 John, Jude and not until chapter 16 in Romans.[41] The absence of the term "church" does not mandate that the *concept* of the church be excluded. Other terms, words, phrases, or concepts exist in Revelation that refer to the church in many ways so that the reference to 144,000 could very well refer to something other than a literal group composed of Jewish members from each tribe.

Second, the list of tribes provided (7:5–8) is unlike any other known list of tribes in the Old Testament. Tribal lists were arranged geographically based on the inheritance distributed to each tribe (Num. 34:19; Josh. 21:4; Judg. 1:2; 1 Chron. 12:24), but tribal lists in the Old Testament were not uniform and often varied (Cf. Gen. 35:22–26; 46:8–27; 49:2–28; Exod. 1:2–4; Num. 1:5–15; 13:4–14; Deut. 33:1–26). The tribal list in Revelation 7 is unique in the following features: (1) Judah heads the list, rather than Reuben; (2) the combination of Joseph with Manasseh, rather than Ephraim; (3) the omission of Dan; and (4) the inclusion of Levi is unusual because the Levites did not receive a land inheritance.[42] We suggest the unusual presentation of the

---

38. In other words, the detailed enumeration of tribes does not normally lend itself as a way of talking about the Christian church (see Patterson, *Revelation*, 194–95).
39. Walvoord, *Revelation*, 141.
40. We also see the term "saints," which commonly refers to Christians in the church, occurring throughout Revelation (5:8; 8:3–4; 11:18; 13:7; 10; 14:12; 16:6; 17:6; 18:20; 24; 19:8). While the term "church" may not occur in Revelation 4–21, the concept of church as God's people is evident throughout the book.
41. Robert H. Gundry, *The Church and the Tribulation* (Grand Rapids: Zondervan, 1973), 78–79.
42. See Bauckham, *Climax of Prophecy*, 220–23; Bauckham, "The List of the Tribes in Revelation 7 Again," *JSNT* 42 (1991): 99–115; Mounce, *Revelation*, 169–68; Christopher R. Smith, "The Portrayal

list of the twelve tribes of Israel is because John did not intend it to be understood as the literal twelve tribes.

Thirdly, there is an interpretive connection between *hearing* the number (7:4) and *seeing* an innumerable multitude (7:9). On the surface it would appear that the two images of the 144,000 and the multitude must refer to different groups. But Revelation often depicts one thing in multiple ways and various images. This dual imagery for a single referent is most clearly evident in 5:5–6 where John *hears* about the Lion of Judah, but he *sees* the slain Lamb standing. The epithets and descriptions of Christ significantly combine the concepts of military conquest together with his sacrificial death and resurrection. The contrast between hearing and seeing is exactly what occurs with the 144,000 and the multitude. To hear about one thing and see another thing indicates a pattern whereby something is heard followed by a vision that refers to the same thing by using different images. Twice one of the elders assists John in understanding the vision by alerting him to two significant characters. The first time the elder functions as an interpretive guide pertains to the Lion of the Tribe of Judah (5:5). The second time is when he tells John that the international multitude of the redeemed are the ones who have come out of the Great Tribulation (7:13–14). The theology implied in these comparisons between the Lion/Lamb and the 144,000/multitude of redeemed is that the way to overcome victoriously is not in political or military power, but the way of the sacrificial lamb.

Finally, the symbolic nature of 144,000 as indicative of completeness strongly favors not taking it too literally (cf. 14:1–5; 21:16–17). Revelation is a highly symbolic book that embeds symbolic meaning with its use of numbers. Commentators virtually agree unanimously that numbers like 3, 4, 7, 10, and 12 all have symbolic connotations. What is true of smaller numbers is equally true of unusually large numbers like 144,000. It is the sum of 12 x 12 x 10 x 10 x10 or 12^2 x 1000. The use of the square numbers of twelve denotes the idea of completeness or perfection.[43] More specifically, it expresses completion in the salvific sense. This association with salvation is reinforced by the reappearance of 12,000 and 144 as part of the given dimensions of the New Jerusalem (21:16–17). If the symbolic significance of the number 144,000 is best understood as salvific completion, it suggests that the primary meaning of the 144,000 in 7:4–8 represents a complete group of God's redeemed people. The sealing of the 144,000 occurs chronologically prior to the sounding of the trumpets to protect them from those judgments. The 144,000 appear a second time in 14:1–5 at the conclusion of the trumpets just prior to the introduction of the bowls (15:1). This represents a before-and-after refer-

---

of the Church as the New Israel in the Names and Order of the Tribes in Revelation 7.5–8," *JSNT* 39 (1990): 111–18; Christopher R. Smith, "The Tribes of Revelation 7 and the Literary Competence of John the Seer," *JETS* 38 (1995): 213–18.

43. Bauckham, *Climax of Prophecy*, 218; Osborne, *Revelation*, 310–11; Beale, *Book of Revelation*, 416.

ence to the 144,000 to assure the believers that God will faithfully save all his sealed servants.[44] This group of redeemed saints appears again in 15:3–4 as those who overcame the beast, his image, and his number.

The Two Witnesses

Revelation 11:1–13 contains two separate but interrelated visionary accounts of measuring the temple (11:1–2) followed the ministry of the two witnesses (11:3–13). These two accounts represent one of the most challenging passages to interpret in Revelation. All the different interpretations boil down to whether or not the referents in the vision are *literal*—a literal temple in Jerusalem and two literal prophets witnessing in Jerusalem—or *symbolic*—the temple represents the people of God/church in the midst of worship and persecution and the two witnesses represent the church in a prophetic role.

Commentators usually affirm one of four possible explanations for the reference to the temple (11:1–2). First, preterist interpreters assert that this clearly presupposes that the temple in Jerusalem is still standing.[45] Second, some suggest Revelation 11:1–2 was written prior to AD 70 but was later added during the reign of Domitian.[46] A third option regards it as a future third temple that will be built in Jerusalem during the tribulation.[47] The fourth option views the temple as a symbolic reference rather than a literal stone and mortar building.[48] The first and third options represent the simplest and most natural explanations of the text, but the text itself may not support a literal referent for the temple.

Revelation frequently employs figurative and symbolic language and there are no immediate reasons to suppose that 11:1–2 should be interpreted any differently from the rest of the vision. In a prophetic fashion, John is given a reed to measure the temple. Measuring in the Old Testament often conveyed a symbolic way to connote either destruction (2 Sam. 8:2; Isa. 28:16–

---

44. David E. Aune, "Following the Lamb: The Apocalypse," in *Patterns of Discipleship in the New Testament,* ed. Richard N. Longenecker (Grand Rapids: Eerdmans, 1996), 278–79.

45. John A. T. Robinson, *Redating the New Testament* (Philadelphia: Westminster, 1976), 224: Kenneth L. Gentry, Jr., *Before Jerusalem Fell: Dating the Book of Revelation*, rev. ed. (Powder Springs, GA: American Vision, 1998), 104–5; J. Christian Wilson, "The Problem of the Domitianic Date of Revelation," *NTS* 39 (1993): 597–98.

46. Aune, *Revelation 1–5*, lx–lxi; idem, *Revelation 6–16*, 585–86.

47. The expectation of a future third to be built in the future is a very popular view within the majority of popular literature on prophecy and end times, especially those who affirm Dispensationalism (Walvoord, Pentecost, Lahaye, Hagee, et. al.).

48. Swete, *Commentary on Revelation,* 132–33; George B. Caird, *The Revelation of Saint John*, BNTC (Peabody, MA: Hendrickson, 1966/1999), 131–32; Mounce, *The Book of Revelation,* 218–20; Bauckham, *Climax of Prophecy,* 272; Beale, *Book of Revelation,* 557–71; Craig S. Keener, *Revelation,* NIVAC (Grand Rapids: Zondervan, 2000), 287–89; Marko Jauhiainen, "The Measuring of the Sanctuary Reconsidered (Rev 11,1–2)," *Bib* 83, no. 4 (2002): 507n. 2; Osborne, *Revelation,* 408–15.

17; 34:11; Lam. 2:8; Amos 7:7–9) or divine protection (Jer. 31:38–40; Ezek. 40:1–6; 42:20; Zech. 1:16; 2:1–2). We find that Ezekiel 40–48, Zechariah 2:1–2, and Daniel 8:11–14 loom in the background of this particular passage.

The terms used for the temple imply a non-literal usage. The language regarding the temple could just as easily denote a heavenly or symbolic temple as it could a literal temple. The word used for temple (*naos*) refers specifically to the temple sanctuary rather than the entire temple complex (*hieros*). John uses *naos* throughout Revelation to refer to the heavenly temple (3:12; 7:15; 11:19; 14:15, 17; 15:5, 6, 8; 16:1, 17).[49] Likewise, the term translated as "altar" frequently occurs denoting the heavenly altar of incense (6:9; 8:3, 5; 9:13; 14:18; 16:7). Since the typical usage of temple language refers to heavenly rather than earthly institutions, it seems likely that the temple in 11:1–2 may symbolically represent the people of God. The association of the church with the temple is corroborated in the New Testament where the church is described as the temple of the Holy Spirit (1 Cor. 3:16–17; 6:19; 2 Cor. 5:15; Eph. 2:21–22; 1 Peter 2:5; Rev. 3:12).

The two "witnesses" (*martusin*) function as prophets (cf. 11:10). That there are two witnesses fulfills the judicial requirement of two witnesses to establish something as true (Num. 35:30; Deut. 17:6; 19:15). The phrase "they will prophesy" emphasizes their prophetic mission. The witnesses are commissioned to proclaim a message of impending judgment against many peoples, nations, languages, and kings. Even their attire of sackcloth highlights their prophetic message of judgment by evoking familiar Old Testament images related to times of individual and national mourning and repentance.[50] Supernatural displays of power reminiscent of Moses and Elijah accompany their prophetic message. During the days appointed for them to prophesy they are divinely protected from any physical harm. If someone attempts to harm them, fire issues forth from the mouth of the witnesses and consumes their enemies. This fire is reminiscent of Elijah calling down fire upon his opponents in 2 Kings 1:9–16. Their commission to prophesy grants them the authority to prevent rain like Elijah and to turn water into to blood like Moses. They also have the ability to inflict any kind of additional plagues on the earth. Both witnesses apparently share these abilities equally since no distinction is made regarding which witness can perform which miracle. These supernatural displays of power validate their testimony and verify them as true prophets speaking on Christ's behalf.

Identifying these two witnesses largely depends on whether or not they are representative of two individuals or a group of people. The most natural explanation is to identify them as the eschatological return of Moses and Elijah or

---

49. On the view that it refers to the heavenly temple, see Charles H. Giblin, "Revelation 11:1–13: Its Form, Function, and Contextual Integration," *NTS* 30 (1984): 433–59.

50. 1 Kings 20:31–32; 21:27; 1 Chronicles 21:16; Nehemiah 9:1; Isaiah 22:12; 32:11; 58:5; Jeremiah 4:8; 6:26; 48:37; Jonah 3:5–8; Matthew 11:21; Luke 10:13.

at least two future individuals like them.[51] The clear allusion to the ministries of Elijah and Moses coupled with the Jewish expectation of their return lends credibility to this view (Deut. 18:18; Mal. 4:5–6; cf. Sir. 48:10). Jewish tradition expected the eschatological return of figures like Moses, Elijah, and Enoch.[52]

However, John offers a clue to their identification in 11:4 by identifying the two witnesses as the two olive trees and two lampstands that stand before the Lord of the Earth. This verse constitutes a direct allusion to Zechariah 4:1–14 regarding Joshua (the post-exilic high priest) and Zerubbabel (the postexilic Davidic descendant). Zechariah sees *one lampstand* with seven lamps sitting upon it and seven oil channels keeping the lamps supplied with olive oil. He also sees two olive trees flanking the left and right side of the lampstand. Despite the obvious lexical parallels between Zechariah 4:1–14 and Revelation 11:4, John sees *two lampstands* instead of one. John also equates the trees with the lampstands, but in Zechariah they are kept distinct. This suggests John modified the imagery so as not to equate his vision as simply a rehashing of Zechariah's. The reason for this shift is probably because the symbol of lampstands in the Apocalypse is already identified as the churches (1:20). If John intended to use "lampstand" to denote any other entity or individual he fails to make this usage explicit.

Despite the combined challenges of interpreting this passage, along with the abundance of competing interpretations, it is possible to arrive at an understanding of the text that does justice to the symbolic nature of the visionary images, the abundant use of Old Testament allusions, and the overall message of the book. John writes to encourage weary and persecuted Christians to remain faithful to Christ by depicting them as the protected but persecuted holy people of God who are commissioned as prophetic witnesses to pagan nations.

The Millennium

No other topic in the book of Revelation has generated as much debate throughout church history as the meaning of the millennium in Revelation 20:1–10. The exact meaning of the phrase "a thousand years" (*chilia etē*) and its theological significance during the end times continues to divide interpreters into various eschatological camps. Interpreters generally affirm one of the three major views regarding the nature and timing of the millennium: (1) *premillennialism* holds that after Christ returns to earth he will establish an earthly millennial kingdom; (2) *postmillennialism* maintains that the success of the gospel will produce a millennial kingdom which will culminate with Christ's climactic return at the end of that period; and (3) *amillennial-*

---

51. Daniel K. K. Wong, "The Two Witnesses in Revelation 11," *BSac* 154 (July 1997): 344–54.
52. See Aune, *Revelation 6–16*, 600; Keener, *Revelation*, 290–91.

ism believes that the millennium started at Christ's resurrection and will be concluded at his final coming. The question of the millennium has a rich history of interpretation, but, for simplicity sake, the debate ultimately revolves around those who identify it either as *a future earthly kingdom* extending for a thousand years or *a heavenly and spiritual kingdom* symbolically representing the time between the advents of Christ.

During the first few centuries of church history, the earliest church fathers took a particular interest in the nature of the future kingdom of Christ when he would/will come to inaugurate a thousand-year reign with the resurrected saints (20:1–6). The ancient belief in a literal thousand-year earthly reign of Christ to be realized at some point in the future is called *chiliasm*, which derives its name from the Greek work for a thousand (*chilioi*), and is associated with modern forms of millennialism.[53] Most interpreters during the second and third centuries were chiliasts, including Papias of Hierapolis, Justin Martyr, and Irenaeus.

Aurelius Augustine (354–430), bishop of Hippo, articulated an eschatological perspective called *amillennialism* because he rejected a literal interpretation of the millennium in Revelation 20. The term *amillennial,* however, is a bit of a misnomer and the term *spiritual* may more accurately reflect the hermeneutical methodology underlying Augustine's eschatology. Augustine viewed the millennium as the rule of the saints with Christ in "his present kingdom, the church" (*Civ.* 20.9). He interprets the binding of Satan as within the "abyss" of the hearts of the wicked.[54] This binding marks the beginning of the millennium and the spread of the church because Jesus said the strong man must first be bound before plundering his house (Matt. 12:29). Satan, according to Augustine, is the strong man and he is bound whenever men and women are converted to the Christian faith (*Civ.* 20.8). The "first resurrection" and the "second resurrection" represent two kinds of life, that of the soul and that of the body. The first resurrection occurs when the soul, though dead, is brought to life through conversion and baptism, and the second resurrection is the coming to life of the body at the final and general resurrection.[55]

---

53. This definition of chiliasm comes from Charles E. Hill, *Regnum Caelorum: Patterns of Millennial Thought in Early Christianity*, 2nd ed. (Grand Rapids: Eerdmans, 2001), 5.

54. Augustine clarifies that "the binding of the devil means that he is not permitted to exert his whole power to draw men off to his party by forcibly compelling or guilefully deluding them" (*Civ.* 20.9 [LCL, Greene]).

55. Commenting on John 5:25–26, Augustine remarks: "He is not yet speaking of the second resurrection, that is, of the body, which is to be in the end, but of the first, which now is. In fact, it is in order to make this distinction that he says: 'The hour is coming and now is.' Moreover, this resurrection is not that of the body, but of the soul. For souls, too, have their own death, in irreligion and sin, and it is with this death that those are dead of whom the same Lord says: 'let the dead bury their dead'; that is, let those who are dead in soul bury those who are dead in body" (*Civ.* 20.6 [LCL, Greene]). He continues to describe the first resurrection as a spiritual rebirth of the soul from the death of sin, but the second resurrection of the body as occurring at the end of the age.

The question of the millennium is not a matter of orthodoxy. Faithful Christians who believe in the authority and truthfulness of Scripture may genuinely disagree with one another without it devolving into labeling each other a heretic, liberal, fundamentalist, or some other epithet resounding with negative connotations. The question of the millennium, in our opinion, is really a matter of hermeneutics and biblical theology. Opposing readings of Revelation 20 exist because interpreters have employed different hermeneutical keys in an attempt to understand the meaning and theology of the text. Our purpose is not to offer a definitive interpretation of Revelation 20:1–10; rather, we primarily want to suggest some features of the text to take into consideration when approaching this passage.

The literary context of this passage is that it occurs as part of the third vision, encompassing Revelation 17:1–21:8. The third vision most likely represents a different perspective on the final events briefly described during the trumpets and bowls. This vision exhibits five distinct movements: (1) Babylon introduced (17:3–18); (2) Babylon judged with the eschatological judgment of the nations (18:1–19:10); (3) the return of Christ as a divine warrior (19:11–21); (4) the first and second resurrections as the eschatological judgment of individuals (20:1–15); (5) the saints introduced to their eternal reward after the final judgment (21:1–8). Contextually, then, this passage comes after the depiction of Christ's return to earth to establish his kingdom through a military victory over the beast and his army (19:11–21). Immediately after this victory, he orders the dragon bound and imprisoned for the duration of a thousand years (20:1–3; cf. Isa. 24:21–22).

The meaning of the binding of Satan for a thousand years is another issue that significantly shapes the way one views the entire passage. At the end of the battle in Revelation 19:20 the beast and his prophet are thrown into the lake of fire, but the dragon is "bound" in the abyss (20:3). At the end of the thousand years, the dragon is thrown into the lake of fire after the final battle (20:7–10). This passage challenges readers by forcing them to ask specific questions. What is the abyss? What is the meaning of Satan's binding? When and where does this occur? Is the duration of a thousand years a literal or figurative timeframe? The answers to these questions determine just about everything else regarding how one understands the millennium.

An angel descends from heaven holding a massive chain and a key to unlock the abyss (20:3).[56] This abyss is opened to imprison and restrict Satan from deceiving the nations for a thousand years. The concept of "keys" locking and unlocking is used to depict God's sovereign control and authority over Satan and the demonic spirits. The idea of imprisonment is conveyed though

---

56. The mention of a descending angel with a key to the abyss parallels Revelation 9:1–2, which describes an angel unlocking the abyss to release the strange demonic locust creatures to torment humanity at the sounding of the fifth trumpet.

the verbs describing how the angel "seized," "bound," and "threw" Satan into the abyss and then he "shut" and "sealed" the door closed. The point is that Satan is bound in the abyss, he cannot escape, and therefore he can no longer deceive the nations. While it is clear that Satan is securely bound, the question debated among interpreters is whether this binding occurred at the death and resurrection of Christ or whether it is a future eschatological event after the return of Christ.

Premillennial interpreters look to the passages highlighting the current ongoing work of Satan in the world as evidence that the binding of Revelation 20:3 is still future (Luke 22:3, 31; Acts 5:3; 2 Cor. 4:3–4; 11:14; Eph. 2:2; 1 Thess. 2:18; 2 Tim. 2:26). Conversely, amillennial interpreters point to passages highlighting the fall and binding of Satan accomplished by the ministry of Christ (Matt. 12:29; Mark 3:27; Luke 10:17–19; John 12:31; Col. 2:15; Heb. 2:14; 1 John 3:8). Beale argues that the binding of Satan in Revelation 20:3 does not "restrict all his activities but highlights the fact that Jesus is sovereign over him and his demonic forces."[57] If the binding of Satan only represents a limitation of his activities, then why use such strong language of imprisonment that implies a full restriction? Beale further argues that the ascent of the beast from the abyss in Revelation 11:7 "should probably be equated with Satan's ascent from the abyss in 20:3b, 7."[58] The problem is that Satan is portrayed as the dragon, which is distinct from the beast in the narrative. Revelation 13 presents an unholy trinity of the dragon, the beast from the sea, and the false prophet (a beast from the land). Revelation 19 depicts the return of Christ and the defeat of the beast and the false prophet who are subsequently thrown into the lake of fire. Revelation 20, then, discusses the fate of the dragon as temporarily imprisoned in the abyss during a millennial reign of Christ and later is thrown into the lake of fire subsequent to a final rebellion. It is not clear how the narrative would allow for viewing the dragon as synonymous with the beast when they are kept distinct elsewhere in Revelation. Whether Satan is presently bound or will be bound in the future, he will be released at the end of the thousand years only to face eternal torment in the lake of fire.

The meaning of the thousand years or millennium is another foundational issue for interpreting this passage. The numerical reference to a thousand years recurs throughout Revelation 20 all in conjunction with the binding of Satan and the reign of Christ with the resurrected saints (20:2, 3, 4, 5, 6, 7). Should we understand the thousand years as a literal chronological designation or a figurative reference to some symbolic period of time? Answers to this question fall into one of three categories: (1) literally, as one thousand earthly years; (2) figuratively, as one thousand years being a way of saying a really long time; and

---

57. Beale, *Book of Revelation*, 985.
58. Ibid., 987.

(3) symbolically, the one thousand years conveys the idea of a complete or perfect time. Interpreters who favor the literal view contend, among other reasons, that the number is repeated six times in the passages so that it should primarily be understood as a literal time period.[59] However, all the numbers in Revelation consistently have a symbolic significance and therefore the reference to one thousand most likely is primarily intended to convey a symbolic connotation.[60]

The meaning of the first resurrection as prior to the millennium has been another major point of divergence among interpreters. G. B. Caird once asked, "Why, once Satan had been securely sealed in the abyss, must he be let loose to wreak further havoc? . . . Why the millennium? And what blessings does it confer on the martyrs that make it worth their while to wait a thousand years for the greater bliss of heaven?"[61] In light of these questions, amillennial interpretations may have the higher ground by interpreting Revelation 20:4–6 as a symbolic reference to the church age. The first resurrection, then, refers to the death of the saints who then are "resurrected" to live with Christ in heaven thus constituting the millennial reign. The amillennial interpretation, however, is not without its share of difficulties. The first resurrection in Revelation is located within an eschatological context that anticipates a future fulfillment rather than a presently realized reality. The interpretation of a spiritual resurrection does not adequately explain the first resurrection as connected to the beheaded souls (6:9–11; 20:4). If they are martyrs who have already died physically, then the resurrection envisioned appears to be physical rather than spiritual.

The second resurrection, in Revelation 20:11–15, pertains to the individual judgment of all humanity (i.e., "the rest of the dead"). This resurrection constitutes the final judicial act of God before the complete renewal of the created order (i.e., the eschatological "age to come"). The descent of the Great White Throne from heaven is more than the earth can handle as it dissolves in the presence of the awesome purity of its creator (v. 11; cf. 6:14; 20). As with the judgment associated with the first resurrection, John incorporates imagery from Daniel 7:9–10 where the Ancient of Days holds court and books are opened (cf. Dan. 12:2–3). These books are opened as the primary evidence consulted during the investigative trial of every individual human being. The multiple books are the written records of each person's conduct (20:12).[62] The only hope for salva-

---

59. Walvoord, *Revelation*, 300; Patterson, *Revelation*, 352–53; Thomas, *Revelation 8–22*, 407–9; Harold W. Hoehner, "Evidence from Revelation 20," in *A Case for Premillennialism*, ed. Donald K. Campbell and Jeffry L. Townsend (Chicago: Moody, 1992), 249.

60. Osborne observes, "Multiples of tens were commonly used in Jewish writings symbolically. . . this refers to an indefinite but perfect period of time, obviously much longer than the period the Antichrist 'reigns' (forty-two months) but still a symbolic period" (*Revelation*, 701).

61. Caird, *Revelation of St. John*, 249.

62. Judgment according to the written record of a person's life was a common theme in Jewish writings (cf. *4 Ezra* 6:20; *Ascen. Isa.* 9:22–23; *Test. Abr.* 12:4–18).

tion depends solely on whether or not his or her name is written in the Lamb's book of life (20:14). Therefore, all those suffering eternally in the lake of fire are there because of what they have done, while all those enjoying the eternal bliss of the New Jerusalem are there because of what the Lamb has done (1:5–6).

Conclusion

We have come to the end of our journey through the book of Revelation. It is very likely that reading this chapter may produce more questions than answers, but it is our hope that the reader is more hermeneutically and theologically equipped to return to the study of the text. Although Revelation presents numerous challenges, John's vision is at home in the world of first-century Asia Minor. It was a message to believers facing pressures to conform to the idolatrous structures of their surrounding culture. Revelation colorfully and impressively portrays the triumph of Christ and his kingdom over the fallen and corrupt world as it is today. The book itself exhibits a structure and narrative flow that offers the reader a guide to recognize how to follow its kaleidoscopic visions. Difficult passages may remain debated by interpreters of different theological and hermeneutical persuasions, but readers may successfully locate where the passages belong in the context of the entire vision. What is more, interpreters may begin to see patterns and trends when it comes to determining the meaning of symbols, numbers, words, and phrases. Our goal is not that the reader walks away with a definitive interpretation of Revelation, but rather that the reader would have a great sense of the meaning, beauty, complexity, and theology of this book as it applies to faith and practice.

Conclusion

Why Prophecy Matters

Prophecy is an essential part of the entire biblical revelation.

Prophecy plays a more vital role in Scripture than many people might realize. God has revealed himself, his ways, his will, his plan and purpose in the Holy Scriptures. This revelation was often communicated by a prophet and written as prophecy. We have argued that prophecy may very well contain predictions of the future, but it always addresses a specific audience within a given historical context. As such, when we read prophecy we must recognize prophecy accomplishes a number of functions within the community of God's people. Prophecy addresses sin, injustice, wickedness, and covenantal unfaithfulness. Prophecy warns of judgment and consequences of such transgressions. Prophecy calls for repentance and responsive action. Prophecy comforts the oppressed and weary. Prophecy declares the promises and decrees of God. Prophecy describes God's salvation in the present and the future. Prophecy points to the person and work of the Messiah—Jesus of Nazareth.

We have argued for a robust understanding of prophecy from a biblical-theological and gospel-centered perspective. Understanding prophecy from a biblical-theological perspective means that prophecy is fully integrated into the theology, themes, and storyline of the Bible. Prophecy is not an isolated series of utterances, but rather prophecy resonates throughout Genesis to Revelation with a chorus of themes, exhortations, and promises. Prophecy also finds its object and fulfillment in the Gospel as revealed in the life, ministry, death, resurrection, and future return of Jesus Christ. The gospel is about what God has accomplished in the person and work of Jesus not just for the redemption of humanity, but for all of creation. The consummation of God's plan and purpose, as revealed through prophecy, will become a reality when Christ returns to earth and renews creation.

What to Expect for Future Fulfillment

When it comes to the future fulfillment of predictions in biblical prophecy, we would avoid any attempt to find one-to-one correspondences with each and every specific detail in a prophetic text. To collect and collate snippets of prophecies into one comprehensive detailed map of the future can be exciting, but to do so often requires taking Scripture out of context (both literarily and historically). Many of these attempts at constructing some sort of prophetic map of the future derive from a belief that prophecy vividly depicts modern day events and if someone has the right key to unlock the code it will reveal the future with crystal clarity.[1] To be sure, prophecy does offer us a glimpse of things yet to come, but we would suggest

> We must resist becoming obsessed with knowing the details of the future because it takes us beyond Scripture into the realm of speculation.

looking for the broad contours of future events as affirmed in multiple texts. For example, Augustine, known for advancing amillennialism, succinctly laid out a series of events that he believed would literally occur in the future:

> And so in that judgment, or in connection with it, we have learned that the following events are to occur: Elijah the Tishbite will come; the Jews will believe; Antichrist will persecute; Christ will judge; the dead will rise again; the good and the wicked will be sorted out; the world will be burned in flames and will be renewed. Now all these events, we must believe, will come to pass; but how, or in what order, the experience of the future will teach us with a completeness that our human understanding cannot attain. Yet I think that they will occur in the order in which I have just listed.[2]

Augustine lists the broad contours of what he believes will happen but does not elaborate on the details of how or when these things will unfold. What one chooses to include in a list of prophetic future events will depend on what he or she believes is clearly taught in Scripture. Interpreters may disagree about what and what not to include in their list of definite eschatological expectations and how they might be fulfilled.

We believe that Christians may expect a continuation or increase of global unrest (eg., wars, economic troubles, natural disasters); an increase of persecution and hostility toward the gospel message; the continued spread

---

1. There are many popular books that follow this approach to prophecy, but the best example is Hal Lindsey, *Apocalypse Code* (Little Rock, AR: Western Front, 1997).
2. *Civ.* 20.30 (LCL; Greene).

of the gospel through missions and evangelism; an increase of false prophets and messiahs; a period of intense tribulation (whatever that may entail); the ascension of a satanically inspired Antichrist; the visible, physical, and victorious Return of Christ to earth; the resurrection of the dead; the final judgment; and the renewal of creation. We, however, agree with Augustine who wisely remarked, "the experience of the future will teach us with a completeness that our human understanding cannot attain."

How to Apply Prophecy

Prophecy Reveals the Will and Ways of God to Us

Nothing is more important for a believer than to know God intimately. Prophecy, as God's Word to us, shows us what God has said and done for his people through history. We witness his mighty acts, learn of his laws and decrees, and hear what he wanted his people to know through the prophets. We can grasp the plan of God revealed in the pages of the Bible. While the words spoken through the prophets are given within a historical context, the God who spoke is timeless and unchanging. What was true of God in the past is still true in the present. As individuals and as the community of God's people, prophecy is relevant for us in our daily lives because it helps us understand who God is and how he works. We can hold tightly to his promises because he is faithful. We can discover the unchanging truth about God's character, will, and ways. The God who spoke to the prophets still speaks to us through the prophets. As we learn about him through Scripture, we draw more closely to him into a living relationship that conforms us to his likeness.

Prophecy Confronts Sins and Calls for Repentance

The prophets exposed the sin of God's people. Through their words, the searchlight of the Holy Spirit penetrates through the darkness of our souls to expose our own guilt and need for repentance. We all like sheep are prone to wander from our good shepherd. We sometimes harden our hearts, plug our ears, and refuse to see with our eyes just like the ancient people of Israel. The prophets spoke clearly and boldly as they decried sin and unsettled those who hid behind religious ritual or excuses. We must read prophecy introspectively and recognize that what God called sin in the past is still sin in the present. As individuals and as the community of God's people, prophecy is relevant for us in our daily lives because it forces us to deal with sin, complacency, and injustice so that we may conform ourselves to God's will. The preponderance of shameful scandals within the church is perhaps symptomatic of our need for a healthy dose of biblical prophecy.

Prophecy Comforts and Encourages God's Oppressed and Faithful Followers

The message of the prophets was not all negative and confrontational. Numerous passages of prophecy are filled with promises of salvation and words of comfort in the midst of great difficulty. Prophecy reveals the tremendous love, compassion, and care that God has for his people. The Old Testament prophecies point toward the coming Messiah who will deliver his people from sin and restore them. The Gospel of Jesus Christ is climax and center of prophecy. Christ was born, died, and rose again so that we, who are God's children, are more than conquerors through him who loved us. No matter what we may experience through trials, oppression, suffering, sickness, persecution, and poverty, Christ is with us. What is more, he will fully redeem us from sin, vindicate us, and let us reign with him in the new creation. If the flickering flame of hope is almost extinguished by the storms of tribulations, read prophecy. Prophecy reminds us of God's love, care, and sovereignty. Prophecy nourishes the withered soul parched from famine. Prophecy ignites a flaming torch of hope as a beacon of truth to all. As individuals and as the community of God's people, prophecy is relevant for us in our daily lives because it comforts us through the crises of this life. Prophecy gives us hope that he will accomplish his purpose for everything he has created.

Prophecy Directs Us to Jesus Christ

We have argued repeated and passionately for a gospel-centered perspective of prophecy because it is all about Jesus. He is the promised Messiah. He is the risen Lord and firstborn from the dead. He is the coming King who will set everything to rights and liberate all of creation from the curse of sin. Prophecy occupies a vast amount of the biblical revelation. While not every prophecy is messianic, prophecy as a whole should be read in light of Jesus. As individuals and as the community of God's people, prophecy is relevant for us in our daily lives because it reveals Jesus in all his glory.

Prophecy Reminds Us That God Is Sovereign over History, People, and Events

When we read the history of God's dealings with Israel and the nations, it is apparent that at every point God is in complete control. He raises up and destroys leaders and nations at particular times in history for a particular reason. He has a plan and he works all things together in order to accomplish it. In the same way that God was in complete control in the past, he is in complete control in the present. No matter what may happen in politics, economics, culture, society, and the environment, God is seated securely on his throne as the sovereign ruler over all the cosmos. Because he is the almighty sovereign creator God, he will bring all things to their proper conclusion. As individuals and as the community of God's people, prophecy is relevant for us in our daily lives because it reminds us that he's got the whole world in his hands. When we look at the world around us and think about all the bad things that happen, we might be tempted to despair. We may be tempted to worry and want to take matters into our own hands, rather than entrust all things to him who judges justly. Prophecy gives us a God's-eye view on the affairs of the world and his ultimate plan for creation. While we may not understand why things are the way they are, we can confidently place our faith in the God of prophecy.

In short, prophecy is for God's people to hear, study, practice, and proclaim. God chose to communicate his Word and revelation through the genre of prophecy for a reason. Prophecy is a powerful and effective means of divine communication. We remember the words, images, and messages. Prophecy is rooted and connected to the human experience. It is not some obscure or cryptic portion of Scripture only intended for experts, but rather prophecy is intended for all of God's people. We wrote this book because we are convinced that prophecy matters for the church, but all too often prophecy becomes the object of fanciful and flawed interpretations. While this book does not deal with prophecy in an exhaustive manner, we hope that it will enable pastors, teachers, and congregations to approach and engage prophecy in light of biblical theology and the gospel. Prophecy, like Scripture as a whole, is an inexhaustible treasure trove of spiritual gems and nuggets of divine truth that continually draw us back to dig deeper. May this book be a helpful guide in your quest to understand prophecy.

Appendixes

Appendix 1

The Meaning of "All Israel" in Romans 11:26

Bandy: "All Israel" Refers to a
Future Mass Conversion of Ethnic Jews

In Romans 9–11, Paul offers a comprehensive discussion concerning the complex relationship between ethnic Israel and the Gentile church. I use the adjectives "ethnic" and "Gentile" very intentionally because Paul consistently goes to great lengths to argue for the inclusion of Gentiles equally with ethnic Israelites into the people of God and as heirs of the promises to Abraham (Rom. 4:16–17; Gal. 3:28–29; Eph. 2:11–22; Col. 3:10–11). To make a hard and absolute distinction between Israel and the Church as two separate peoples of God goes against the grain of Paul's theology. Paul contends that since both Jews and Gentiles are both equally sinners, they are equally justified by faith in Christ because God does not show favoritism (Rom. 2:11; 3:21–26). Inclusion into the new covenant people of God as heirs of the promises to Abraham is not based on race or ethnicity, but comes through faith in Christ (Rom. 4:16–17). Naturally, one may be prompted to ask about God's promises to the physical descendants of Abraham—ethnic Israel—and their status as God's people. Paul, therefore, addresses the questions about the status, choice, and future of ethnic Israel beginning in Romans 9.

Paul expresses the perspective that God established the promises, covenants, law, prophets, and the Messiah through the people of Israel (Rom. 9:4–5). The specific concern Paul addresses is whether or not God's Word and promises to Israel have failed since the majority of Jewish people have rejected Jesus as the Messiah (Rom. 9:6). He answers this concern with a remnant theology and a robust theology of God's prerogatives and purposes of election. To begin, Paul avers that not all Israelites are considered Israel and not all physical descendants of Abraham are his children. The true people of God—Israel—includes some, but not all, of the Jewish people. The succeeding passage (Rom. 9:7–29) clarifies that inclusion into Israel and Abraham's family is not automatically granted based on genetics, but rather is based on God's election. Those who are "in Christ" comprise the Israel of God (Gal. 6:16), the "true circumcision" (Rom.

2:28–29; Phil. 3:3), and the family of Abraham (Rom. 4:9–25; Gal. 3:7, 14, 29), and are grafted into the true olive tree of Israel (Rom. 11:17–24). Paul's point is that God has the right to have "mercy" on the Gentiles by incorporating them into the new covenant people, he also has the right to "harden" the Jewish people for a time (Rom. 9:18; 11:7). Paul's purpose is to explain why the Gentiles are included and why the majority of ethnic Israelites are excluded. They are excluded because they have not pursued righteousness by faith in Christ (Rom. 9:32), but God has preserved a remnant of Jewish people who do indeed believe (Rom. 9:27; 11:4–5).

The crucial question is whether the "church" completely replaces "Israel" or whether there is some distinction maintained between Israel and the church in the argument of Romans 9–11. I tend to agree with Schreiner when he remarks, "Nowhere in Rom. 9–11 is the term 'Israel' transferred to the church, and the issue that Paul confronts here is whether the promises made to ethnic Israel will be fulfilled. . . . Paul argues that a winnowing process has always occurred in the midst of ethnic Israel."[1] While Paul may argue at length for the inclusion of the Gentiles into the people of God and that only a remnant of ethnic Jews are chosen by grace (Rom. 11:5), he does not completely subsume his use of Israel in the sense of "spiritual Israel." He maintains a distinction between Israel in the spiritual sense and Israel in the ethnic sense.[2] After positing that only a remnant was chosen by grace and the rest were "hardened" (Rom. 11:7–9), Paul then asks if Israel has stumbled so as to have fallen beyond recovery? Israel's "stumble" refers to the rejection of Christ and the righteousness by faith.[3] The word "fall" (*piptō*) relates to an irretrievable and complete spiritual ruin.[4] So what he is asking is if ethnic Israel has stumbled irretrievably and if they are beyond recovery.[5] Paul refutes even the possibility of that thought with "by no means" or "absolutely not" (*mē genoito*). What is more, he explicitly states that their "trespass" opened the door for the inclusion of the Gentiles as a means to provoke Israel to jealousy (Rom. 11:11). This suggests, then, that their "fall" or "hardening" is temporary and that a future restoration is in view.

Paul anticipates a future mass conversion of ethnic Jews because he contrasts the benefits of their exclusion for the Gentiles with the fullness of their inclusion for the world. Paul makes two statements that suggest the temporary nature of Israel's hardening. First he asks "if their trespass means riches for the world, and if their failure means riches for the Gentiles, how much more will

---

1. Thomas R. Schreiner, *Romans*, BECNT (Grand Rapids: Baker, 2003), 494.
2. See Douglas J. Moo, *The Epistle to the Romans*, NICNT (Grand Rapids: Eerdmans, 1996), 686. Moo argues that Paul is addressing the question of whether Israel as a whole, in contrast to the Gentiles, can be saved. Paul is not just referring to the "hardened," but Israel as a corporate body.
3. Ibid., 687.
4. BDAG, 815.
5. Robert H. Mounce, *Romans*, NAC 27 (Nashville: B&H, 1995), 217–18.

their full inclusion mean!" (Rom. 11:12).[6] In the second statement he contends, "if their [ethnic Israel's] rejection means the reconciliation of the world, what will their acceptance mean but life from the dead?" (Rom. 11:15). Paul frames his entire discussion in salvation-historical terms in which God's dealing with ethnic Israel is part of a much larger process. Israel's rejection results in a blessing for the Gentiles, but will in turn lead back to salvation for Israel in that they will be prompted by jealousy to want the blessing originally promised to them.[7] Paul intimates that the inclusion and resurrection will result in life from the dead (Rom. 11:15). The phrase "life from the dead" has been interpreted in a variety of ways, but it either refers to resurrection in a spiritual sense of salvation or it refers to resurrection in a physical sense of eschatological salvation.[8] Moo argues that the phrase "from the dead" is found forty-seven times in the New Testament and all but one refers to the resurrection.[9] If Paul has the eschatological resurrection at the end of the age in view, it follows then that the salvation of "all Israel" (Rom. 11:26) will be the climax of this age.[10]

The major theme of chapters 9–11 is not so much to stress the fate of Israel, but to give a warning to the Gentiles not to presume on their fortunate position as a wild branch that had been grafted into Israel, which is a cultivated olive tree.[11] His point is that God removed the natural branches of the cultivated olive tree—ethnic Jews—because of unbelief and consequently grafted in branches from a wild olive tree—Gentiles—by faith in Christ. The Gentiles, therefore, should take heed lest they be removed from the olive tree by their unbelief. Yet, the natural branches will be grafted back into the olive tree if they do not persist in unbelief (Rom. 11:23). This engrafting of ethnic Israel is not only theoretically possible, but Paul explicitly states that the current "partial hardening" of Israel will come to an end after "the fullness of the time of the Gentiles" (Rom. 11:25). Paul expects the inclusion of ethnic Israel back into "true Israel" (i.e., the olive tree, children of Abraham) at a future time associated with the end of the age. Paul does not argue that all ethnic Israelites throughout history will

---

6. It is important to note that the ESV and the NIV perhaps over-translate Rom. 11:12 as "their full inclusion" when the Greek is a bit more ambiguous as simply "their fullness." While I think that "their fullness" could allow for other interpretations for the meaning of "all Israel" (Rom. 11:26), it appears to me that contextually "their fullness" is in contrast to "their failure" so that the idea of "their full inclusion" is justified.

7. Moo, *Epistle to the Romans*, 687–88.

8. The majority of commentators interpret "life from the dead" as a reference to physical resurrection at the end of the age, but for those who interpret it as a metaphorical reference to salvation from spiritual death to spiritual life, see Mounce, *Romans*, 219; J. A. Fitzmyer, *Romans*, AB 33 (New York: Doubleday, 1993), 613; John Stott, *Romans: God's Good News for the World* (Downers Grove, IL: InterVarsity, 1994), 298–99.

9. Moo, *Epistle to the Romans*, 695. See also the arguments in Schreiner, *Romans*, 599.

10. Schreiner, *Romans*, 599.

11. Mounce, *Romans*, 218–19.

be saved, but God will have mercy on ethnic Israel after a period of time of showing his mercy on all nations.[12]

The reference to "all Israel" in Romans 11:26 is best understood as an eschatological mass conversion of ethnic Jews at the end of the age. Throughout Romans 11, Paul has consistently used the term Israel in the sense of "ethnic" Israel rather than "spiritual" Israel. There is nothing, then, in this context to suggest that "all Israel" is not a reference to "ethnic Israel." Second, Paul uses a number of temporal designations to locate the salvation of all Israel in the eschatological future. If the salvation of "all Israel" is eschatological, then it must be limited to only include ethnic Jews at that time in history as instead of all Jews throughout history. Third, Paul seems to suggest that this salvation will occur at the return of Christ. Paul conflates Isaiah 59:20–21a and Isaiah 27:9 in a messianic and eschatological manner in direct association with the salvation of all Israel. Finally, the future salvation of ethnic Israel is explicitly expected because of election. Romans 11:28–31 is perhaps Paul's strongest affirmation of God's plan and purpose for ethnic Israel as rooted in his covenant-keeping faithfulness:

> As regards the gospel, they are enemies for your sake. But as regards election, they are beloved for the sake of their forefathers. For the gifts and the calling of God are irrevocable. For just as you were at one time disobedient to God but now have received mercy because of their disobedience, so they too have now been disobedient in order that by the mercy shown to you they also may now receive mercy.

Although currently the majority of ethnic Israel is cut out of the new covenant people of God because of their unbelief in Christ, Paul expects a future mass conversion of the Jewish people who will put their faith in Christ at the end of the age. This conversion means that ethnic Jews who currently do not believe in Christ will be grafted back into the people of God along with all the believing Gentiles.

Merkle: "All Israel" Refers to All the Elect Remnant of Ethnic Israel Throughout History[13]

This interpretation maintains that God will always save a remnant of Jews throughout history. That is, Israel will experience *only* a partial hardening until the end of time (i.e., until the fullness of the Gentiles come in). There are several reasons why this interpretation is to be preferred.

12. Schreiner, *Romans*, 622.
13. For a full-length article on this topic, see Benjamin L. Merkle, "Romans 11 and the Future of Ethnic Israel," *JETS* 43 (2000): 709–21.

The first reason relates to the context of Romans 9–11. All acknowledge that Romans 9–11 forms a unit in Paul's thought. Therefore, any interpretation of Romans 11 must also be consistent with Romans 9 and 10. In chapter 9, Paul demonstrates how God is indeed faithful to his promises although most of Israel has rejected the Messiah. Paul states in 9:6, "For not all who are descended from Israel belong to Israel." God never promised Abraham that his descendants would be saved based on their ethnic identity. True Israel consists of those who are the children of promise, rather than children of the flesh. God never promised that every individual Jew would be saved but only those whom he unconditionally elected within Israel. Paul then presents two examples of God's sovereign discrimination within Israel. In Isaac, not in Ishmael, Abraham's descendants were named (9:7); and it was Jacob, not Esau, who was chosen to perpetuate the covenant lineage and in whom the covenant promises were to be fulfilled (9:9–10). Therefore, Paul refutes the notion that God's Word has failed by pointing out that God's promises apply to the spiritual offspring within ethnic Israel.[14] Nowhere in chapters 9 or 10 do we anticipate Paul speaking of a mass end-time conversion of Jews. Charles Horne states the dilemma for those claiming a special future for Israel.

> If Paul is speaking in 11:26 of a future mass conversion of the nation of Israel, then he is destroying the entire development of his argument in chaps. 9–11. For the one important point that he is trying to establish constantly is exactly this: that God's promises attain fulfillment not in the nation as such (that is, all of ethnic Israel) but rather in the remnant according to the election of grace.[15]

The second reason relates to the nature of the question that Paul is asking (11:1, 11). In 11:1 Paul asks the question, "Has God rejected his people?" The question is *not*, "Has God cast off ethnic Israel with respect to his special plan for their future?" It seems, however, that this question is often subconsciously read that way. To ask the question in that manner misses Paul's real concern and prejudices one towards interpreting the rest of the chapter as advocating a special future for Israel. The nature of the question, however, does not anticipate

---

14. Bavinck rightly concludes: "It is a priori very unlikely that Paul later reconsidered this reasoning, supplementing and improving it in the sense that the promises of God are not fully realized in the salvation of spiritual Israel but will be fully realized only when in the last days a national conversion of Israel takes place" (Herman Bavinck, *The Last Things*, trans. John Vriend [Grand Rapids: Baker, 1996], 105).

15. Charles Horne, "The Meaning of the Phrase 'And Thus All Israel Will Be Saved' (Romans 11:26)," *JETS* 21 (1978): 333. Wright addresses the same dilemma: "The problem about the content of Romans 9–11 then becomes one of *integration*. Put simply, the issue is this: if Paul rejects the possibility of a status of special privilege for Jews in chs. 9 and 10, how does he manage, apparently, to reinstate such a position in ch. 11?" (N. T. Wright, *The Climax of the Covenant* [Minneapolis: Fortress, 1991], 236).

a future mass conversion. The question Paul asks is, "Has God cut off ethnic Israel *altogether*?" or, "Is there any hope for the continuation of a saving activity of God among Israelites?"[16] The same could be said of the question in verse 11 where Paul asks, "Have they stumbled so as to fall?" (HCSB). Again, Paul is not asking if there is going to be a future mass conversion of Israel. Rather, he is asking if Israel has completely forfeited their past privilege. James Dunn uses a running metaphor to describe Israel's predicament: "their stumble is not so serious as it at first sounds. It is not a complete fall, as, for example, the sprawling on one's face which puts a runner completely out of the race."[17]

The third reason is that Paul's emphasis is not on the future but on the present situation of ethnic Israel (vv. 1, 5, 13–14, 30–31). In answer to the question raised in verse 1, Paul offers himself as proof that God has not cast off his people. He argues, "For I myself am an Israelite, a descendant of Abraham, a member of the tribe of Benjamin."[18] Paul's immediate answer to the question he raised in verse 1 involves the present, not the future. Furthermore, in verse 5 Paul states, "So too at the present time there is a remnant, chosen by grace." Paul specifically emphasizes the present situation of Israel by using the phrase "at this present time" (*en tō nun kairō*). In the preceding verses Paul illustrates his point with the example of Elijah. Just as in Elijah's day there was a remnant, so now there is a remnant within Israel. God did not reject his people during the days of Elijah and has not done so now. Verses 13 and 14 also support our conclusion. Paul writes, "Now I am speaking to you Gentiles. Inasmuch then as I am an apostle to the Gentiles, I magnify my ministry in order somehow to make my fellow Jews jealous, and thus save some of them." Notice that Paul's own ministry was involved in the salvation of some. The principle that a "remnant" will remain throughout every age is the basis for Paul's hope that "some" would be saved during his ministry. Finally, verses 30 and 31 support our thesis that Paul is concerned with the present more than with the future. He writes, "For just as you [Gentiles] were at one time disobedient to God but now have received mercy because of their disobedience, so they [Jews] too have now been disobedient in order that by the mercy

---

16. Robertson explains: "Ethnic Israel had rejected their Messiah. They had crucified the Christ. Would it not therefore be quite logical to conclude that God would reject ethnic Israel? If a Gentile rejects Christ, he is lost. Israel rejected the Christ nationally. Should they not be lost nationally? Why should God continue to act savingly within Israel? They received all the special favor of the Lord (9:4, 5), and yet rejected the Lord's Christ. Why should they not be cast off completely?" (O. Palmer Robertson, "Is There a Distinctive Future for Ethnic Israel in Romans 11?" in *Perspectives on Evangelical Theology: Papers from the Thirtieth Annual Meeting of the Evangelical Theological Society*, ed. Kenneth Kantzer and Stanley Gundry [Grand Rapids: Baker, 1979], 213). A revised version of this article can now be found in Robertson's *The Israel of God: Yesterday, Today, and Tomorrow* (Phillipsburg, NJ: P&R, 2000), 167–92.
17. James G. D. Dunn, *The Theology of Paul the Apostle* (Grand Rapids: Eerdmans, 1998), 522–23.
18. Hendriksen paraphrases Paul's question and answer: "Does anyone need proof that God fulfills his promise and has not rejected Israel? Well, then look at me. God did not reject me, and I am an Israelite" (William Hendriksen, *Exposition of Paul's Letter to the Romans* [Grand Rapids: Baker, 1981], 361).

shown to you they also may now receive mercy." The threefold "now" (*nun*) of these two verses indicates Paul's emphasis on the present situation of Israel. Paul states that even now Israel is receiving mercy.

The fourth reason relates to the nature of the "mystery" in verse 25. Paul writes, "I want you to understand this mystery, brothers: a partial hardening has come upon Israel, until the fullness of the Gentiles has come in. And in this way all Israel will be saved" (11:25–26). The "mystery" includes a three-fold schema: (1) the hardening of part of Israel, (2) the coming in of the full-ness of the Gentiles and (3) the salvation of all Israel. The hardening of Israel should be understood quantitatively ("in part") and not temporally ("for a while"). The verse should not be understood as meaning "for a while harden-ing has happened to Israel" but "a partial hardening (or 'a hardening in part') has happened to Israel." Also, by a "partial hardening" Paul does not mean that all of Israel is only partially hardened, but that some are fully hardened while the elect remnant are being saved. In no way does the phrase suggest that God intends to initiate a special salvation era for Israel in the future.

This hardening, Paul says, will last "until the fullness of the Gentiles has come in." But the meaning is not that the hardening will last until a certain time and then will be reversed. Rather, the idea is that the hardening will be partial, and only partial, up until the end of time (i.e., until the fullness of the Gentiles are saved). Therefore, Paul is not suggesting a time when the harden-ing will be reversed but a time when the hardening is eschatologically fulfilled.

There is also misunderstanding related to the nature of the phrase, "And so [*houtōs*] all Israel will be saved." Notice that Paul does not say "And *then* all Israel will be saved." Paul is not thinking temporally ("and then"), but modally ("and in this manner"). His meaning, then, is this: although the promises of salvation were originally given to Israel, most of them rejected the bringer of that salvation, the Messiah. Consequently, the Messiah was announced and received by the Gentiles. This caused Israel to be moved to jealousy and as a result many from Israel believed and thereby received God's promises. This process will continue until the full number of Gentiles are brought in and "in this manner" all the elect of ethnic Israel will be saved.

Some may object to this interpretation by stating that Paul does not say "all the elect" will be saved but that "all" of Israel will be saved. But we need to remember that Paul had already taught that "not all Israel is of Israel." Furthermore, if "all" meant a great number of Jews at the end of time, does that interpretation do justice to the meaning of "all"? It would, in fact, only include a small fraction of Jews which is not as climactic as it might first ap-pear. Based on this interpretation we are not so much awaiting a future event, but the completion of an ongoing reality.

Appendix 2

The Meaning of the Millennium

Bandy: A Historic Premillennial Perspective

In the earliest period after the apostles, most of the discussions on the end times focused on the nature of the future kingdom of Christ when he comes to inaugurate a thousand years of ruling with the resurrected saints on earth based on Revelation 20:1–6. The belief in a literal thousand-year earthly reign of Christ to be realized at some point in the future is called chiliasm—from the Greek word for a thousand. The vast majority of interpreters during the second and third centuries were chiliasts. Their interpretation of Revelation 20:1–6, however, was eclipsed by more allegorical and spiritual approaches emphasizing the timeless and successive fulfillment of these prophecies throughout church history.

Premillennialism, as a whole, affirms a futurist approach for interpreting the book of Revelation that views chapters 4–22 as referring to future events. Not all premillennialists, however, agree as to how Revelation portrays the unfolding of these future events. Therefore they usually take one of two basic positions: (1) historic premillennialism, deriving from the chiliasm of the early church; and (2) dispensational premillennialism, which developed during the nineteenth century in Great Britain and was popularized in America with the Scofield Study Bible.

Historic premillennialism has been increasingly adopted or adapted by a number of conservative evangelical scholars over the last forty years.[1] For a more exhaustive study, I recommend the helpful book titled *A Case for Historic Premillennialism: An Alternative to "Left Behind" Eschatology*, edited by Craig Blomberg and Sung Wook Chung.[2]

---

1. Evangelical Christian leaders and scholars who have been associated with, labeled, or have claimed historic premillennialism include George Eldon Ladd, Francis Schaeffer, Walter Martin, J. Barton Payne, John Warwick Montgomery, Robert Gundry, James Montgomery Boice, John Piper, Wayne Grudem, Douglas Moo, Craig Blomberg, Richard Hess, Timothy Weber, and Russell Moore, to name a few.
2. Craig L. Blomberg and Sung Wook Chung, eds., *A Case for Historical Premillennialism: An Alternative to "Left Behind" Eschatology* (Grand Rapids: Baker, 2009).

Historic premillennialism basically affirms some variation of the future fulfillment of prophecy, especially a literal, visible, glorious, and victorious return of Christ to earth at the end of the age. This position typically affirms that when Jesus returns, he will bind Satan, the saints will be raised (first resurrection), and they will reign with Christ in a millennium of peace and prosperity. Yet, not all historical premillennialists insist on a literal interpretation of the thousand years.[3] At the end of this millennium, Satan will be released and allowed one last attempt to rally the nations in battle against Christ—a futile effort doomed to failure and the lake of fire. The great white throne will descend, followed by a general resurrection (second resurrection) and judgment of all people who have ever lived. After the final judgment, God will create a new heaven and new earth (i.e., the New Jerusalem), where he will dwell with his people for eternity.

Historic premillennialists affirm only one return of Christ and typically believe that the church will persevere through the tribulation. This position differs from that of dispensationalists, who maintain that the second coming of Christ will involve a secret return for the church prior to the tribulation, followed by his visible return after seven years. One reason historic premillennialists do not necessarily affirm the need for the pretribulation rapture is due to the reality of the new covenant that makes all believers in Jesus the spiritual descendants of Abraham and, therefore, covenant members of the people of God—true Israel (Rom. 11:1–24; Gal. 3:28–29; Eph. 2:11–22).

However, this does not mean that they deny a future hope for ethnic Israel (Rom. 11:25–32); they would say instead that God's promises include, rather than exclude, the church in his plan for Israel. What is more, they believe that the kingdom of God has already been inaugurated with the resurrection and ascension of Christ, but is not yet fully realized on earth. We now live between "this age" and the "age to come" in that the kingdom is already a reality, but not yet fully consummated on earth.

Many view historic premillennialism as superior to both dispensationalism and amillennialism because it avoids what some see as the extreme literalism of the former and the excessive spiritualization of the latter. It accords better with the literary context by affirming a chronological relationship between the return of Christ in Revelation 19 and the first resurrection and millennium of chapter 20. While amillennial interpreters read the relationship as one of recapitulation, the flow of the narrative suggests that the events of chapter 20 are chronologically successive is an exegetically and theologically stronger position.

Historic premillennialism maintains an eschatological framework for interpreting the binding of Satan. If Satan is currently bound so as not

---

3. I believe that all numbers in Revelation have symbolic meaning and therefore should not be taken literally in every instance. As such, I am not convinced that the millennium is actually comprised of a thousand literal years.

to deceive the nations during this period (Rev. 20:3; cf. Rev. 12:7–12; Matt. 12:28–29), how does this correspond with current activity of Satan as described in Revelation 12? For example, Revelation 12:9 states that Satan was cast to the *earth* not the *abyss* (Rev. 20:1–2) and that he is the one who currently deceives the whole world, but in Revelation 20:3 he is prevented from deceiving the nations. The differences between the current activity of Satan in Revelation 12 and 20 are not mutually compatible. Consequently, it makes better sense to view the binding of Satan as eschatologically future.

Historic premillennialism offers a more consistent interpretation of the first resurrection as a literal bodily resurrection rather than as a reference to initial salvation when one becomes a believer or as a reference to a believer arising to life in heaven after death. Without question, salvation involves the regeneration of one who is spiritually dead so as to say one has been made alive (Eph. 2:1–10). The question is, however, whether that is how regeneration is referenced in John's Apocalypse. In this context, salvation usually has an eschatological focus in the sense of final salvation. For example, the messages to the seven churches all end with a promise of future salvation (Rev. 2:7; 2:11, 17, 26–28; 3:5, 12, 21)—a salvation depicted visually in Revelation 20–22. Salvation in Revelation may often be metaphorically described, theologically complex, and artistically beautiful, but it is often tied to concrete realities.

In the case of Revelation 20:4–6, there is nothing in the context to suggest the language of resurrection means anything other than physical resurrection from the dead. In Revelation 20:4, the reference to "the souls" (*tas psychas*) coupled with the verbs "came to life" (*ezēsan*) and "reigned" (*ebasileusan*) strongly suggests a literal resurrection instead of a spiritual one.[4] The entire scene in 20:4–6 corresponds to Daniel 7:9–10 where the Ancient of Days holds court in judgment and Daniel 7:22–27 where he renders a favorable verdict for the saints by giving them the kingdom.[5] The qualifying phrase "those who had been beheaded for the testimony of Jesus and for the word of God" appears to limit the first resurrection primarily to the martyrs.[6] The language clearly connects these souls with the other slaughtered faithful witnesses (6:9). In other words, the souls from underneath the altar received a favorable verdict that placed them on thrones. The judicial verdict awarded to these saints includes the right to reign with

---

4. G. K. Beale, *The Book of Revelation*, NIGTC (Grand Rapids: Eerdmans, 1999), 998; contra Charles H. Giblin, "The Millennium (Rev. 20.4–6) as Heaven," *NTS* 45 (1999): 553–70.

5. Robert H. Mounce, *The Book of Revelation*, NICNT (Grand Rapids: Eerdmans, 1977), 354; Beale, *Book of Revelation*, 997; Stephen S. Smalley, *The Revelation to John: A Commentary on the Greek Text of the Apocalypse* (Downers Grove, IL: InterVarsity, 2005), 506; Ian Boxall, *The Revelation of Saint John*, BNTC (Peabody, MA: Hendrickson, 2006), 283.

6. See also George B. Caird, *The Revelation of Saint John*, BNTC (Peabody, MA: Hendrickson, 1966/1999), 252.

Christ, which would include judicial authority (cf. 2:26–27; 3:21; 5:10; 20:6).[7] The ones who are raised to life are explicitly stated as the ones who have died for their Christian testimony. Therefore, it seems reasonable to interpret the first resurrection as a reference to resurrection promised specifically for believers in the future.

Thus, historic premillennialism is appealing because it enables interpreters to maintain the future orientation of John's vision while affirming a historically-sensitive approach that utilizes the best interpretive methods used today by evangelical scholars. They recognize that Revelation was originally written to churches in Asia Minor at the end of the first century and must have had meaning for the original audience. That meaning, then, is something that would be true and applicable for all Christians as they seek to remain faithful to Christ in the midst of a satanically influenced society. The primary strength of historic premillennialism, in my opinion, is that it treats the book of Revelation as a prophecy to be obeyed with a message that has always been relevant for the church throughout church history—both past and present.

Merkle: An Amillennial Perspective

The amillennial view of Revelation 20 affirms that the thousand-year binding of Satan refers to the period between the two advents of Christ. Two items should be noted about this interpretation. First, it recognizes that Revelation contains figurative or symbolic imagery typical of prophetic or apocalyptic literature. The images are not to be taken literally, although they point to literal events and realities (e.g., the dragon John sees is not to be taken literally, but the dragon represents Satan who is real). So, although the angel coming down from heaven in Revelation 20 is pictured as having a literal chain to bind Satan and a literal key to lock him up, these symbols relate to us God's intention to limit Satan's influence on the world. This binding is said to last a thousand years. If the chain, key, and prison are symbolic pictures, then it is likely that the thousand years is also symbolic and represents a certain period of time, but not necessarily a literal one thousand years. Second, John tells us that Satan is bound "so that he might not deceive the nations any longer" (Rev. 20:3). Thus, Satan's influence is not completely removed but is specifically tied to his ability to deceive the nations. In contrast to the Old Testament era when nations were living

---

7. Reddish comments, "The saints' vindication represents a great reversal of roles from judged to judges." He further avers, "This is a scene of role reversals. The martyrs have had to stand before the imperial throne (at least figuratively) and receive the sentence of death. Now they are the ones who are seated on thrones and deliver judgment. . . . The millennium is John's way of offering encouragement to the martyrs. Those who have paid the greatest price receive the greatest reward" (Mitchell G. Reddish, *Revelation* [Macon, GA: Smyth and Helwys, 2001], 394–95).

in darkness oblivious to God's special revelation, now the gospel is being taken to all the nations. This spreading of the gospel will result in people from every tribe, language, people, and nation being represented before the throne of God (Rev. 5:9).

One of the strengths of the amillennial approach is that it is gospel-centered. That is, it views the life, death, resurrection, and ascension of Christ as the center of redemptive history. Because of his work on the cross and subsequent resurrection, Jesus has conquered death, defeated Satan, and now reigns in heaven waiting until all his enemies will be put under his feet. Thus, at his first coming Jesus defeated Satan by binding "the strong man" in order to "plunder his house" (Matt. 12:29). During his ministry Jesus said he "saw Satan fall like lightning from heaven," which was symbolic of his fall from power (Luke 10:18). The author of Hebrews informs us that the incarnation of the Son was necessary so that "through death he might destroy the one who has the power of death, that is, the devil" (Heb. 2:14). Similarly, the apostle John states, "The reason the Son of God appeared was to destroy the works of the devil" (1 John 3:8). Jesus was able to commission his disciples by stating that "all authority in heaven and on earth" had been given to him (Matt. 28:18). Thus, the decisive battle took place at the cross and resurrection where Satan's ultimate defeat was sealed. Indeed, he is still a roaring lion (1 Peter 5:8), but he is a lion on a leash (2 Peter 2:4; Jude 6).

Finally, the traditional premillennial view of Revelation 20 has implications that are contradictory to the most straightforward interpretation of clearer passages in the New Testament.[8] These implications include: (1) the present earth will endure far beyond the return of Christ; (2) the unrighteous will not be judged when Christ returns; (3) natural bodies will be present during the millennium; and (4) people will have the opportunity to receive salvation during the millennium.

First, the New Testament clearly teaches that the present earth will not endure past the return of Christ. For example, 2 Peter 3:10–13 states that the earth will be renewed on "the day of the Lord" (v. 10) when the "heavens will pass away with a roar" (v. 10) and "the heavenly bodies will be burned up and dissolved" (v. 10). Furthermore, we are to wait for and hasten "the coming of the day of God" (v. 12) because on that day "the heavens will be set on fire and dissolved, and the heavenly bodies will melt as they burn!" (v. 12). Additionally, in Romans 8:18–23 Paul personifies the earth's present condition and desire for restoration. He indicates that the present decaying earth is longing and waiting for a particular event; namely, "the revealing of the sons of God" (v. 19). Apparently, the revealing of the sons of God will bring about the end of the earth's groaning and set it free "from its bondage to corruption" (v. 21) which refers to

---

8. For a more detailed treatment of this issue, see Benjamin L. Merkle and W. Tyler Krug, "Hermeneutical Challenges for a Premillennial Interpretation of Revelation 20," *EvQ* 86, no. 3 (2014): 210–26.

the day when believers will receive glorified resurrection bodies. If the revealing of the sons of God, which will occur at the return of Christ, is temporally contiguous with the liberation of the earth from its bondage to decay, then it follows that the present earth will *not* endure beyond the return of Christ.

Second, the New Testament clearly teaches that unbelievers will be judged when Christ returns. In 2 Thessalonians 1:6–10 (NIV) Paul says that the wicked will be judged "when the Lord Jesus is revealed from heaven in blazing fire" (v. 7), "on the day he comes" (v. 10), when he comes "to be glorified in his holy people" (v. 10), and when he is "marveled at among all those who have believed" (v. 10). Notice that Paul links the judgment of the wicked not to Christ's presence on earth, but to his coming when he is revealed from heaven. Therefore, it follows from this that unbelievers will *not* endure beyond the return of Christ without judgment (see also Rev. 19:17–21).

Third, the New Testament clearly teaches that natural, perishable bodies do not endure beyond the return of Christ. In other words, the resurrection of believers and unbelievers occurs when Christ returns. In 1 Corinthians 15:50–52 Paul reminds his readers that "flesh and blood cannot inherit the kingdom of God" (v. 50). Those in natural, corruptible bodies cannot enter into the eternal kingdom that Christ will inaugurate when he returns. Paul indicates that the perishable, mortal body "must" be clothed with an imperishable, immortal body (v. 53). But this would not be necessary if believers were merely entering a millennial period in which they remained on the present earth along with unbelievers who had natural bodies. Furthermore, in John 5:28–29 Jesus states that the "hour" is coming when both "those who have done good" and "those who have done evil" will be resurrected. In this text there is no hint of a delay between the resurrection and judgment of believers and that of unbelievers. Indeed, Jesus indicates that it will all occur at the same "hour" or at the same time. Consequently, natural bodies do not endure beyond the return of Christ.

Fourth, the New Testament clearly teaches that there will be no opportunity for individuals to repent and receive salvation after the return of Christ. In discussing the scoffers who will come in the last days doubting the reality of Christ's promised return, Peter presents the following hope: "The Lord is not slow in keeping his promise, as some understand slowness. Instead he is patient with you, not wanting anyone to perish, but everyone to come to repentance" (2 Peter 3:9 NIV). If the reason for the delay of Christ's return is his desire to further extend the opportunity of the gospel, then it follows that when he comes that opportunity will be terminated. In addition, the parable of the ten virgins in Matthew 25 offers us insight regarding just how long the opportunity to repent and believe will extend. Verse 5 tells us that the bridegroom was a long time in coming but that eventually, at midnight, the cry rang out: "Here is the bridegroom! Come out to meet him" (v. 6). While five of the virgins were wise and brought oil for their lamps, the five foolish virgins did not and were forced to go off and buy more oil. Verse 10 then reports that the bridegroom came while the foolish virgins were away. Upon his return, the wise virgins went with him into the wedding banquet and the door was shut. When the foolish virgins finally arrived and requested to be allowed into the wedding banquet, the bridegroom solemnly replies, "Truly, I say to you, I do not know you" (v. 12). When the bridegroom returns, those who are prepared will enter with him into the wedding banquet, after which the door will be shut and no one else allowed to enter. Thus, after Christ returns, the offer to repent and believe the gospel comes to an end.

We must be careful not to let one text in Revelation trump other teachings of the Bible. This is especially true when we consider that Revelation is a vision given to John that includes highly symbolic or figurative language and is a book that is highly debated. Regarding the third implication mentioned above, George L. Murray warns,

> We have to state that there is not one passage in the Old or the New Testament that clearly and plainly teaches two resurrections, separated by an interval of one thousand years, with the possible exception of one verse in the twentieth chapter of Revelation. . . . The anomaly confronting us here is that one can read the whole Bible without discovering an inkling of this doctrine until he arrives at its third from the last chapter. If, on coming to that chapter, he shall give a literal interpretation to one sentence of a highly symbolical passage, he will then find it necessary to retrace his steps and interpret all the eschatological teachings of the Bible in a manner agreeable to this one sentence. The recognized rule of exegesis is to interpret an obscure passage of Scripture in the light of a clear statement. In this case, clear statements are being interpreted to agree with the literal interpretation of one sentence from a context replete with symbolism, the true meaning of which is highly debatable.[9]

We are on hermeneutically safer ground when we let the clearer and less-debated texts help interpret the more enigmatic ones. The most straightfor-

---

9. George L. Murray, *Millennial Studies: A Search for Truth* (Grand Rapids: Baker, 1948), 153–54. Similarly Strimple cautions, "Is it not a valid principle of biblical interpretation that less clear, more difficult portions of the Bible are to be interpreted in the light of the more clear portions, . . . the figurative in light of the literal? . . . [We question] whether we should be willing to set aside the entire New Testament, or force it into artificial interpretations, on the basis of one brief passage in an apocalypse that is admittedly highly figurative, rich in symbols, and therefore somewhat difficult" (Robert B. Strimple, "Amillennialism," in *The Millennium and Beyond*, ed. Paul E. Engle and Steve B. Cowan [Grand Rapids: Zondervan, 1999], 119–20).

ward interpretation of the rest of the New Testament argues against a premillennial interpretation of the millennium. I agree with G. E. Ladd, a historical
premillennialist, that Revelation 20 "is the only passage in the entire Bible
which teaches a temporal *millennial* kingdom."[10] But to interpret the rest of
the New Testament through Revelation 20 is to violate two basic principles of
hermeneutics: (1) the more obscure passages should be interpreted in light of
clearer passages and (2) the interpretation that is consistent with the greater
amount of biblical support should be favored. Thus, when Revelation 20 is
interpreted, we must make sure that our interpretation does not contradict
the more obvious interpretations of the rest of the New Testament.

---

10. George E. Ladd, *A Commentary on the Revelation of John* (Grand Rapids: Eerdmans, 1972), 267.
    Blomberg writes that Ladd "liked to say in class that he could have been an amillennialist if it were
    not for Revelation 20" (Craig L. Blomberg, "Posttribulationism of the New Testament: Leaving 'Left
    Behind' Behind," in *A Case for Historical Premillennialism: An Alternative to "Left Behind" Eschatology*,
    ed. Craig L. Blomberg and Sung Wook Chung [Grand Rapids: Baker, 2009], 67).